# Penny fo

## Roy Pugh

*With Best wishes*
*RJmPugh*

HARLAW HERITAGE

For my brother Ken, lest he forget
and
In memory of those who have gone

First published in 2006 by
Harlaw Heritage
21 Marchbank Gardens
Balerno, Midlothian
EH14 7ET
Scotland

ISBN 0 9540465 3 6

Origination by Harlaw Heritage
Printed and bound in Scotland
by
Scotprint, Haddington

# CONTENTS

Acknowledgements

Illustrations

Introduction

Postscript

**Front Cover Photograph**
Two pals, Common Close, Castle Place, which ran between the High St and
Castle St.

## Acknowledgements

I wish to thank the Royal Commission on the Ancient and Historic Monuments of Scotland and Dunbar and District History Society for permission to use certain illustrations. Special thanks to Liz Tear (Stephenson) for permission to use the photograph on the front cover.

I am also indebted to David Lunam for allowing me to use photographs of his sisters May and Norah and his relatives Jenny and James Herkes; Mark Beattie for the rare photograph of the area which became Summerfield Road and Lammermuir Crescent. And as always, thanks go to Hope Mason and Robin Murdoch for permission to use their images. I am also grateful to Betty Jeffrey and Robin Mellors for providing me with information about neighbours in Lammermuir Crescent. Thanks again to Robin Murdoch for editing and preparing the text, restoring many of my badly damaged family photographs and for publishing this book.

But, most of all, I am indebted to my late mother who, until her death in 2002, reminded me of family anecdotes etc. Much of what I have written must be seen through her eyes. Sadly, she did not live to see this book published.

In writing this account of my childhood and adolescence, which portrays people as they appeared to me in those far-off days, I may have done injustice to the occasional individual. I hope they will forgive me and remember that after all, I was only young.

> *The spring is past and yet it has not sprung;*
> *The fruit is dead and yet the leaves be green;*
> *My youth is gone and yet I am but young;*
> *I saw the world and yet I was not seen;*
> *My thread is cut and yet it was not spun;*
> *And now I live and now my life is done.*

Lines written by C Tichborne awaiting execution in the Tower of London in 1586 for his part in the Babington Plot to free Mary, Queen of Scots from Fotheringhay Castle, where she was held prisoner by Elizabeth I.

> *Sweet Thames, run softly till I end my son,*
> *Sweet Thames, run softly, for I speak not loud or long.*

Lines from *The Fire Sermon* by T S Eliot

## Illustrations

The illustrations in this book appear in a block of pages, near the centre. All are accompanied by informative captions and therefore a separate list has not been included in this introductory section.

Many of the original photographs derive from poor quality or small images, typical of the cheap type of camera, if any, possessed by working class families in the 1940s and 50s. It has been possible to digitally enhance and repair many of the defects, however, many are still poorer quality than we would have liked. The captions for some of the collective photographs are incomplete due to an inability to remember who the individuals were. The author would be pleased to receive any informaion which would help to fill in the blanks. We apologise unresevedly for any limitations in the quality and accuracy of the illustrations and captions.

## Introduction

Lest I be accused of melodrama, let me hasten to explain the reason why I have quoted these lines from Tichborne's poem. They aren't included for any morbid reason; they are simply a fine piece of Elizabethan poetry, poignant and emotional. I chose the lines because they sum up my feelings about a part of my life that has passed. The quote from T S Eliot is also appropriate since my years grow fewer and time hurries on apace, leaving less and less hours to record what mattered to me over half a century ago. This book is about the past. Someone once famously wrote that the past is another country. Very apt. But is the past ever over? It 's always incomplete because occasionally, life surprises us and we meet people from that faraway time who stir up memories, wanting to remember it themselves.

Tichborne's haunting poem suggests to me something of my early life in Dunbar, a life I thought was consigned to photographs, diaries and the inner self. It was comfortably tucked away in a drawer - or so I thought. But the contents of that drawer keep spilling out every now and then, often when I least expect them to surface. Nowadays, I find myself increasingly rummaging through the drawer when something vital from my past, something I grope to remember niggles me and denies me sleep.

This is the story of my life until the age of seventeen. It isn't a remarkable story, nor is it even moderately good literature. What makes it interesting is that there are still some from that time who remember a Dunbar that is a closed book to the current generation. It was a truly unique time and place. Or does that hold true of all childhoods? Were I religious, I would say it was created deliberately, to imbue its inhabitants with a sense of pride in having lived here in that magical time, that beautiful place. It certainly formed and informed my character. To a great extent, identity is forged on the anvil of memories. I absorbed Dunbar's customs, rituals and seasons along with the very air I breathed. I know that Dunbar made me what I am, that it taught me to appreciate the simple, lovely things it offered.

Writing a book about your childhood inevitably lays you open to accusations of self-absorption, which are entirely justified. But no personal memoir is worth the candle unless it has the courage of its convictions. If it isn't self-absorbed, it can't be true. I was raised on the Shakespearean maxim in *Hamlet*; my Uncle Jimmy Cockburn wasn't a literary man but he might have been. What he said to me wasn't a quote from *Hamlet* which I am sure he never read but he used the first line of that famous quotation:

> *To thine own self be true*
> *and it must follow, as the night the day,*
> *thou canst not then be false to any man.*

Jimmy Cockburn recognised integrity of spirit even if he never read any works of great literature. But he could read people, detecting the false and the true through natural instinct. He was rarely wrong in his judgements. In many ways, this book is as much a tribute to him, as it is to other people who, like him are sadly no longer with us.

With memory, a difficulty is always present. While one's childhood owes much to the imagination - and any writer who neglects the imagination suffers the consequences - it has to be acknowledged that in everyone's memories of the past, the sun always shone in summer, snow always fell on Christmas Eve, autumn was a veritable *cornucopia* and every spring brought hope for another good year. So it seemed and possibly was. Well, some of the time. Memory unconfirmed by personal memoirs such as diaries is the enemy of historical truth. In this book, I have struggled to avoid the trap of implying that everything was perfect; I know that it wasn't. And I also know only too well that memory can only ever offer an approximation of the past. It is indicative but it can never be exhaustive. Nor is it wholly reliable which makes all autobiography suspect. I know that the essence of good autobiography isn't simply recollecting events - hopefully, with accuracy - but explaining or understanding their significance in the context of the time in which they occurred. This requires hindsight, arguably the only exact science in human behaviour; it also requires that what is being recalled will be reported without undue embellishment. I hope in the course of writing this account, I have met these requirements.

Trying to evoke a world of more than sixty years ago is a risky business. Among the several lessons life has taught me is that it is fragile and transient; it is there in the footprints we leave behind us in the sand, knowing they will be erased by the next tide. Having watched this ritual more times than I care to remember and knowing how quickly the footprints disappeared, I had the foresight to scribble lines in diaries and notebooks, anecdotal evidence of what I felt then. I wrote down some personal experiences, the important ones which shaped my life, things that happened to me rather than those which I caused to happen. I didn't realise then that what I was doing was outlining the format of a book. It has taken nearly fifty years to put it all down, so here it is, warts and all. As I said earlier, it isn't great literature; it is nothing more than an attempt to record a small part of a world that is gone.

It never ceases to amaze me that some people wish to forget their childhood, or are embarrassed by it. After all, memories are what we are. If we choose to ignore these memories - even the sad ones - we run the risk of losing our intrinsic identity. Human beings possess the ability to communicate or store information; but we are creatures who live a good deal of our lives locked within ourselves. In my opinion, those who dismiss or suppress their inner selves become empty shells, a fact disturbingly proved by amnesiacs and those who are unfortunate to suffer from the distressing effects of *Alzheimer's Disease* - I nearly forgot the name of it just now....

Dunbar taught me many invaluable lessons. I learnt to value the importance of friendship, love and sincerity. It gave me a rich inner life, a landscape that has sustained me over many difficult years when I was unhappy and felt useless and ineffective. We are shaped by our early environment and what happens to us in that environment. Dismissing the important signposts in our adolescence is to my mind a sure way to get lost. I was never lost in Dunbar. I am not ashamed of my roots. I see no reason to be.

Attempting to give shape and form to the things you felt so acutely many years ago is difficult but not impossible. I have tried to recreate my feelings and experiences as honestly as I am able. This book is a journey back to a place that no longer exists. Fortunately for me, a large part of me never left Dunbar though I was away for thirty years. I wish to remember my time here and the parts that others played in my progression from childhood to something approaching manhood. I say approaching, for the boy in me is still strong....

And now the apologies, inevitable in, what hopefully, is an honest and truthful book. Autobiography is bound to highlight information about many people who were characters in the play. If in these pages I have misrepresented or misjudged any of my contemporaries of that time, I ask their forgiveness and forbearance and it certainly wasn't my intention to settle old scores or harm reputations. If certain parts of this book offend some sensibilities and sensitivities, I apologise now, unreservedly so.

I believe that childhood is the most important period in our lives. I agree with the poet William Wordsworth that *The child is father of the man (Poems referring to Childhood, I)* By the time childhood ends, everything about us that matters, which makes us individuals and who we are, has already happened. As adults, we simply repeat the lessons we learnt as children, just as does history. More than usually imaginative children tend to be lonely in later life; almost certainly, they are destined to become avid devourers of books. A few become writers.

I hope those who take the trouble to read this account will enjoy its main purpose - the celebration of an era of innocence, even if it is unashamedly nostalgic. I believe we cannot ignore nor abandon the memories of the small things in early life. If we do, they may knock on our doors when we least expect them, demanding that we let them in. After all, in the end, memories are what we become.

Colinton,   March 1999
Dunbar,     March 2006

# 1

## Beginnings

According to my birth certificate, I came into this world at 8.05pm on 17th February 1941. Born under the sign of Aquarius, the Water-Carrier, confusingly an air sign, this may account in part for my paradoxical nature. I opened my eyes for the first time in the small back bedroom of my mother's three bedroom council house at No 75 Lammermuir Crescent, Dunbar. The fact that I arrived at night may also have predisposed me to a preference for the wee, small hours.

I have never understood why they say childbirth is painful. I never felt a thing. For my mother, the trauma of my arrival was increased by the fact that there had been a heavy snowfall and the doctor was in the Lammermuir Hills attending to another patient, so he was unable to be present at the event. My mother delivered me herself, lying helpless in bed with me still attached to her as she was unable to sever the umbilical cord. So the first hours of my life were spent in an ignominious position at the foot of her bed, which may be symbolic. My mother had expelled me but couldn't let me go. Like Samson, eyeless in Gaza, I stumbled into life from the start, colliding with real and psychological obstacles. Perhaps as I lay there, I was already predisposed to living the life of a lone wolf, that my survival would depend on my aptitude for coping with being along. Most newborn babies are immediately thrust into their mothers' arms, so the bonding begins at once; perhaps the delay affected me for life. In such cases, the individual is predisposed to creating a rich and independent inner self that is vital to survival; that self is formed by surroundings, the various influences of family and friends. And of course, in my case, books and literature. Perhaps for this reason, I believe in the adage that poets are born, not made.

Eventually, the doctor and the district nurse arrived that cold snowy February night. Dr Anderson fussed about, humouring my mother and mildly scolding her for not holding on a bit longer. Years later, my mother told me that the doctor, who had a lovely bedside manner but was less than skilled in other respects, instructed the nurse to cut the umbilical cord while he filled in the usual forms.

'All I need to know is the time of his birth, Jean. Can you remem
ber?'
My mother said she'd never forget it. Then the doctor spoke to the nurse:
'Jean's fussy. She doesn't like men at her births.'
My birth certificate records that my father, Robert William Pugh was a bom-

bardier [private] in the Royal Artillery, my mother Georgina Pugh's M[aiden] S[urname] being Cockburn. They were married on 31st March 1939, my mother's 25th birthday. My birth was registered on 28th February 1941 by M K Grahame, Assistant Registrar. On the reverse of the certificate, a manuscript note in a different hand informs me that I was baptised on Sunday, May 25th 1941 by the Rev J C Ritchie, minister of Belhaven Church. On that day exactly a year before, the evacuation of 337,000 British, French and Belgian troops from Dunkirk had begun.

I believe I was the first person to be born in No 75 Lammermuir Crescent. My elder brother Norman was the last to be born in the family home at Castle Place, in the *Common Close* (now no more) situated on the right of Castle Wynd. He was born on 30th March 1933, just before my grandmother, my mother and her two brothers moved to Lammermuir Crescent, newly built that year. An early photograph shows the area before the development, taken probably in 1929 or 1930. You can see the few bungalows at the beginning of what became Lammermuir Crescent, the houses at the foot of Boroughdales, then to the far left, Knockenhair and Gala Green, with the spire of Belhaven Kirk visible

Thus I entered the world in 1941; the war with Germany had entered its third calendar year, a fact of which I was blissfully unaware. The housing estate where I was born was part of a major expansion aimed at re-housing a large part of the townspeople who'd lived in sub-standard accommodation in the High Street and the slums around the harbour area. Our house was semi-detached with a broad, sloping roof of black roof tiles (pantile) and gardens on three sides. The front garden was a joy to my grandmother Cockburn who had lived on Amisfield Estate at Haddington - now Haddington Golf Course – as she had green fingers and sorely missed being able to cultivate flowers in Castle Place, the rear of which was given over to a drying green and wash house used by the several families in the tenement.

My grandmother Margaret Dingwall was born in Bolton, a small village near Haddington. Her trade was market gardening and she propagated the most beautiful roses I have ever seen. Somehow she contrived to meet and marry my grandfather George, or Dod Cockburn. Grandfather was a van man employed by A T Smith, a local grocer at No 71 High Street. Van man was something of a misnomer, as grandfather Cockburn drove a horse and cart, selling groceries in and around Dunbar. In his cups on a Saturday night, he swore that our family was related to Sir George Home, the last to hold the title Earl of Dunbar. Baron Home of Berwick was elevated to an earl by a grateful James VI and I in 1605 for his part in bringing justice to the Borders, for implementing his religious policies in Scotland and seeking out those connected with the Gunpowder Plot. I can find no basis for my grandfather's contention other than a tenuous and distant connection between the family of Sir George Home of Manderston and Spott and grandfather's family, which contained several

# Beginnings

Mandersons, one of whom became Provost of Dunbar in 1947 and served in that capacity until 1957. Provost Alexander Manderson was my mother's cousin and a joiner to trade, residing at Woodbush, where the town's wood store was once kept. His house was adjacent to the old Grammar School, a site now occupied by a modern housing estate; the entrance to *Woodbush House* had two stone pillars topped by what were said to have been cannonballs from the battle with Cromwell in 1650. Like other local historical artefacts, they have long since disappeared.

Grandfather Cockburn was fond of two pursuits - whisky and swimming, in that order. His prowess in both were apparently prodigious and impressive. A typical Saturday night found him on his rural rounds - he rarely got home before midnight - which took him to several outlying villages like Stenton, Oldhamstocks, Innerwick and finally Spott. He had a drink in every pub along the way. Apparently, he was something of a salesman and could sell groceries even after other van men had preceded him. Perhaps it was connected with the drink and his ability to entertain people with his stories. On Sunday morning, his way of sobering up was to swim from the *Doo Rock* where the local swimming pool used to be, to a rock - possibly the one known locally as *Wallace's Head* which bears an iron pole on which lamps were once hung to guide in shipping. For added penance, he usually carried my mother - his youngest daughter - on his back. The local fishermen christened him *Cork* and he lived up to his nickname. Sadly he developed cancer of the jaw in 1921 after he fell drunk between the shafts of his cart and lay in the frosty night near the Latch Park until his faithful old horse woke him by licking his face. Grandfather loved the horse and it repaid him with loyalty. He used to steal extra oats and hay for the poor beast as he said it was never properly fed. After his accident, grandfather began to complain of toothache and had all his molars pulled from the affected side of his mouth; by then however, the cancer had taken hold. He died on 8th April 1923 at the age of forty-three, leaving a widow, two sons, five daughters and a Persian cat called Pearl White. His employer took several shillings a week from my grandmother to pay for the damage done to the cart. The fact that grandfather had been one of the best salesmen in Dunbar didn't enter into it.

In those days, the *Common Close* was a safe place for children playing, usually in the communal drying green and wash-house; I can't be certain but I am sure the families in the tenements had outside toilets in those days, so when the new estates were built in 1933, it must have been a luxury to have inside toilets and your own drying green and garden. By the time Granny Cockburn moved to Lammermuir Crescent in 1933, four of her five daughters had married. In the house were her two sons George (Doddie), Jimmy, my mother Georgina (Jean) and her first grandchild, Norman who was only a few months old that year. I don't know what happened to Pearl White, the cat.

Norman's father was a soldier who seemed to come from good stock and he certainly wanted to do the honourable thing by my mother. Norman Hall applied for a special licence to marry her but driving to Haddington on his motorbike, the intending bridal pair were drenched in a sudden downpour and had to take shelter in the disused church at the Barney Mains road end. Proud as she always was of her appearance, my mother flatly refused to continue to Haddington Registry Office because she was *drookit* [soaked]. Despite Gunner Hall's impassioned pleas, she adamantly refused to go any further; nor was she swayed by his protest that he was likely to posted abroad any day. They never did tie the knot; Gunner Hall's regiment left Castle Park barracks a few days later, en route for India. They never saw each other again. The only communication my mother ever received from Norman Hall was unsigned but she was sure it was from him. It was a Second World War POW Christmas postcard, the standard card issued by the Germans for British prisoners to send to their families. I recall it featured men in the uniform of the three services linking arms. It came from Stalag VIIB or some such place identified only by Roman numerals, presumably for security reasons; it contained standard phrases assuring the recipient that the sender was well/not well/wounded; those that didn't apply were deleted. I recall seeing the card in the 1970s but somehow it was lost over the intervening years, to my regret. Perhaps my mother discarded it in one of her periodic spring cleanings.

Granny Cockburn doted on Norman; his Aunt Margaret or Maggie as she was known, wanted to adopt him as she couldn't have children. My mother wouldn't hear of it. Norman was hers, always would be. It didn't stop Maggie lavishing gifts on him; beret, velvet coat with moleskin collar, small walking stick. Norman was introduced to fashionable clothes at an early age and he never lost his love for them, something he inherited from my mother, who also dressed him well. One day, a large limousine drew up outside No 75 Lammermuir Crescent and the chauffeur in peaked cap and breeches stepped out; he knocked on the door to inquire if the sweet little boy was my mother's child. She said he was. He said that his mistress wanted to adopt him. He received the same answer as Aunt Maggie. Then the lady got out of the car and tried again. She said she was titled and couldn't provide her husband with the heir he so desperately wanted to carry on the line. She got short shrift. Years later, when Norman heard of the incident, he was ungracious enough to say to my mother she'd denied him the chance to be Lord Norman!

True to her maternal instinct or her inherent stubbornness, mother brought Norman up despite her financial difficulties, especially after Granny Cockburn died on 10th November 1937. When my mother married my father in 1939, he adopted Norman legally as his son. My mother never lost her special regard for her firstborn, although she confused and perplexed him throughout his life until his untimely death from viral influenza in 1989.

Norman was fortunate to have known our maternal grandmother, even if only briefly. If there is a heaven, she is the lady I most want to have dinner with there, to share her memories. She was by all accounts a shy old lady whom my mother maintained was only ever in two shops in Dunbar in her time here. She wasn't standoffish; she was also something of a nurse and midwife and helped many of her neighbours when they were ill. She thought nothing of unblocking drains and toilets, exhorting the offending householders to refrain from flushing soup bones down the loo! Three centuries before, she would have been known as a *guid-wife* or *wise-wife* - and burnt at the stake for witchcraft. One of her remedies for a cut finger was to wrap it in spiders' webs; medical science has since discovered that spider gossamer contains a coagulating agent.

When she moved to Lammermuir Crescent in 1933, Granny Cockburn transformed the usual builders' mess into a garden, beautifying it with her lovely tea and hybrid roses that leaned against our front window in high summer. When they were in bloom, I always thought of her. Her roses are the most enduring memory I have in my early years. They came in all colours - clotted cream, deep gold, pale yellow, orange, scarlet, red - and with their pervading scent which lingered on warm summer nights. When she died in 1937 - the day before Armistice Day - my mother festooned her photograph with Haig poppies, a tradition she kept up until her own death in 2002.

Just before the Second World War broke, my mother was living alone with Norman. My Uncle George married Margaret Hay, a Kirkcaldy woman and they had a son called Jim, named I believe after my Uncle Jimmy, the latter spending as many weekends as he could with my mother. Jimmy had entered what was then known as gentlemen's service - a butler - in Hoylake after a spell as a 'boots' in a private school there. He fell in love with one of the maids, then he contracted rheumatic fever in about 1937. The care of rheumatoid patient was rudimentary then; Jimmy was bed-ridden in hospital and the doctors insisted that he sit upright in bed during his stay there. His spine bones locked, so he emerged from the voluntary hospital bent almost double. When he saw himself in a mirror, he couldn't face his Mary again. I don't know the full story but he left Hoylake and came back to Dunbar to lodge with my mother until he found a job. He was fortunate enough to obtain the post of timekeeper with *George Wimpey* and just as the war started, he was moved to Dyce, Aberdeen, then Buckie. Years later, Uncle Jimmy told me that when he was in Aberdeen, he met Professor Barnes Wallis who was then testing his 'bouncing bomb' at Dyce, the device which destroyed two of the three dams in the predominantly industrial Ruhr Valley in the famous Dambusters' Raid in 1942. *Wimpey's* had made models of the dams so that Wallis could test his theory. Another wartime memory he recounted was having breakfast at his 'digs' in Aberdeen one Saturday morning, watching a dogfight between British and German pilots over the North Sea. He said it was nearly as good as the films!

Jimmy never married. Lizzie, the eldest sister married George Henderson, the father of my cousin Margaret, a lovely woman who died too soon at the age of 42 in 1959. George Henderson MC himself died young; at age 22, serving on the Western Front in the Royal Field Artillery; he was killed on 25th October 1918, only seventeen days before the Armistice was signed. Lizzie's second husband was a man called Wood to whom she had two daughters, Emily and Norma. I don't know what happened to Mr Wood but Aunt Lizzie had a son Dennis to a man I think was called 'Pony' Moore. We always knew Dennis as Wood but on the War Memorial in Dunbar, his name is recorded as Dennis Moore. Lizzie died aged 53 in 1949, a few months before her beloved son and my friend Dennis was killed in Malaya on National Service in September 1949.

Bella, a brilliant scholar and gold medallist at Dunbar Grammar School married a soldier called Oates and they went to India for a time; to Mr Oates, she had daughters Mary, Pat, Winifred, Jacqueline, Marilyn and son George. Like Aunt Lizzie, Maggie married twice, her first husband a soldier she met in London during the Blitz, the second a Rosyth Dockyard clerk called Marshall who re-christened her Peggy. Jessie or Jet as she was known also took a military husband called Hiscock and moved to Wales, where she died; she had one daughter Betty whom I believe is also dead now. So my mother and my aunts all married military men; perhaps they were impressed by the uniforms.

My aunts and cousins were fairly remote figures in my early emotional landscape. Uncle George seemed to want to keep to himself, although I was friendly with my Aunt Margaret Cockburn (Hay) and their son Jimmy. Uncle Jimmy, the bachelor, became a surrogate father to my brothers Norman, Ken and to a certain extent, me. I am sad to say that ours wasn't a particularly close-knit family, which is not unusual in Scotland.

So I was born at the time of aconites and snowdrops, significant little flowers in my personal odyssey, for they herald the onset of spring. Even today, I am gladdened by the appearance of the snowdrops pushing through the cold earth at Lochend, one of my favourite walks whatever the season.

I was a difficult child through no fault of my own. In the first three months of my life, my mother was hospitalised, suffering from what she called a mastoid breast, an infection brought about by breast-feeding I suppose. There were no antibiotics in those days so the complaint meant a stay in hospital. During that time, I was looked after by the Harkess family next door. The family consisted of Marion or 'Mairn' the mother whom I knew as Gramma, daughter Ann and sons John and Tommy, none of them married until John broke the mould later in his life. So I had an honorary granny, an aunt and two uncles to see to my needs. They did that to a fault. Each time I as much as squeaked, I was picked up and petted, pampered and patted. John and Ann were particularly attentive; to them, I was always known as *Oor Bairn*. I came to expect instant attention - and got it. By the time my mother came home, I was spoiled rotten. I screamed the place down the minute no one came to attend me. My mother was driven frantic with my incessant wailing. Desperate, she finally contacted Dr Anderson who advised her to let me scream my head off as it was just temper.  His diagnostic skills and remedies often left much to be desired, but on this occasion, he was right.  Maybe he had read the latest baby manual by Truby King – a World War Two Doctor Spock.  Her book advised mothers to crack down on their offspring.  Strict four-hourly feeds, leave the baby to cry itself to sleep, no picking-up or coddling during tantrums.  My mother took his advice.  I was no longer cuddled or cosseted by my wartime neighbours when my mother came back from the hospital.  Dr Anderson was specific about the cause and the cure

> 'Temper caused by excessive petting.  That's all it is.  If he's fed
> and clean, there's  nothing wrong with him, Jean.  Put him in his
> pram in the back bedroom.  Open the window and let him scream
> the place down.  He'll soon get the message when nobody comes.'

Crude but effective psychology.  I yelled my head off a few afternoons to the consternation of my adopted relatives next door.  My mother was adamant.

> 'I'm only following Dr Anderson's orders' was all she said.

It worked.  Years later, my mother told me she used to take me out in my pram late on summer evenings, walking as far away as Spott village to make sure I'd sleep at night.  She did it as much for herself as for me.  I was a normal child who needed a lot of sleep.  My mother made sure it was on her terms.  The neighbours said she was wrong to walk me so late, keep me awake for so long, but she wouldn't listen.  Maybe the result is that I am still a night owl and even now, I think nothing of going for walks late at night.

I have very few recollections of the first five years of my life although I do remember sitting beside my mother and Norman in our front garden on summer evenings.  I certainly recall Norman playing with me there.  For some time, I couldn't pronounce his name, so he rejoiced in the name I gave him - *Gaga*.  Where on earth did that come from?  The name suggests someone who's misplaced his marbles.  Maybe it was my way of connecting him with the garden where we played.  Maybe he said the word 'garden' so often that I thought it was his name.  Such oddities present a challenge to even the most experienced child psychologists.

The garden was my whole world at that time.  It wasn't large by any standards but it was well kept.  Apart from my grandmother's famous roses, I remember a holly tree someone had misguidedly planted beside the front door.  It got out of control and eventually had to be chopped down and dug out, an extremely difficult task.  I was sorry to see it go because I loved its beautiful red berries in winter.  When I see a holly tree today, I always think of our house in Lammermuir Crescent.

My earliest recollections are difficult to date.  I can see the small cot in which I slept in my mother's small bedroom.  Obviously I was unaware of ours being a working class family and even if I'd known, it would have meant nothing to me.  We were better off than some families as my father was a professional soldier who would never be unemployed.  The street we lived in was quiet and I thought it was rather fine. I often used to watch the older kids playing in the street through the slats in our garden gate. I wanted to join them under the gas lamps but I was too small for their rough and tumble games. In daytime, I was allowed to play in the front garden but I longed to go further a-field. In those days, the countryside began at the end of our street where it intersected with Summerfield Road. Beyond that intersection were fields of wheat and barley. Summerfield Road ran uphill to the main Edinburgh Road which was out of bounds to small children since it was used by lorries, tractors and the few cars on the road then. At the junction with Edinburgh Road was Blair's Dairy, where I had my first Adventure. Kate Blair, the dairymaid would become a great friend in later years; then, she was a stranger. I shall describe how that came to pass later on.

One of my greatest regrets was that I never knew my Scottish grandparents; I met my English grandfather once. I think it was in 1943 when my mother took me to Wolverhampton; by then, Fanny Pugh, my paternal grandmother was dead. I can't remember the train journey; perhaps we went by night because of the war restrictions and the blackout.

I have no memory of Robert William, my paternal grandfather, not even what he looked like. He was a butcher to trade and all I remember my mother saying about our visit was that there was never anything but meat - despite the wartime rationing - on the dinner table:

'Not a cookie or fancy cake in sight. Nothing but sides of beef and pork and ham. That's the English for you.' (My mother had a sweet tooth).

Wolverhampton is a blurred memory of tall chimneys belching smoke and steam. Or did I learn of the fact years later, at one of our geography lessons at school? The city then was a major industrial centre manufacturing cars, iron and steel products, implements and tools. It was in this Dante's *Inferno* that I was to take my first faltering steps on two feet, for at that time I was, in modern parlance, vertically challenged.

At the outset of the holiday, everyone seemed content to allow me to scuttle across the linoleum-covered floors, exploring the rooms on horizontal terms. The house always seemed to be crammed with people coming and going all day long - probably my father's relatives wanting to meet his Scottish bride and son. All I could see were different pairs of (to me) gigantic feet, mostly I recollect, women in high-heeled shoes. Occasionally, a tall man would come and lift me into the air. I thought he was going to eat me, as every time he lifted me ceiling-wards, the man would open his mouth wide. He laughed a lot on these occasions but that didn't lessen my anxiety. I was always relieved to get back to familiar, horizontal territory, where I could scuttle away on all fours into some dark corner. Then one day, a lady I subsequently learnt was my English Aunt Dorothy decided it was high time I stood on my own two feet. Literally.

8

# Beginnings

First she made me stand up straight - well, nearly so - and waddled me about the room for a bit, then took me to my mother who was seated in a large armchair. Dorothy planted me between my mother's knees, whereupon I tried to sit down on the floor. Up I was hauled. Dorothy sat in the armchair opposite and tried to coax me to come over to her. Try as she might, I refused to budge an inch, clinging to my mother's knees for dear life. Then Dorothy hit on the idea of a bribe, or inducement to attract me over to her. She went into the scullery and returned with a large pair of black boot brushes she held out to me tantalisingly. I was interested, so much so that I made a staggering, stumbling attempt in her direction only to fall flat on my face. Howls of fright rather than pain gave way to indignant sniffling. Then she tried again. Same result. By this time, I was losing interest in these brushes but Dorothy persevered. By the time the holiday was over, I was staggering about on none too steady feet, swaying like a punch-drunk boxer, or perhaps just a plain drunk. As Dr Johnson once famously remarked, I was like a dog walking on its hind legs - it wasn't done well but surprising that it could be done at all. I began to enjoy the game but I didn't get to keep the boot brushes. More howls from me left the family unimpressed, especially the man who lifted me to the ceiling and who turned out to be my father. My Aunt Dorothy wasn't terribly imaginative; she might have tried a more glittering prize, like sweets. Anyway, it didn't matter as I probably wouldn't have been given the sweets. I was conned in England the same way the English have been conning other races for centuries; after the soldiers of the British Army defeated them in unequal battles, the administrators and the Christian clergy coaxed them off their knees and civilised them. Generations of clerks and churchmen made their reputations in the far-flung corners of the world; they hired the defeated indigenous populations – notably in India - to work for their Empire, offering the English Bible and the English way of life by way of consolation prizes. The ancient world's *Pax Romana* rose like the phoenix from the ashes, reincarnated as *Pax Britannica*

After my English holiday, I recall little of my life until I was about three, when I made my Great Escape. My mother forbade me to go out of the garden gate but like all children and some adults, I had a thirst for exploration. What was beyond the forbidden gate? I had to know. One day, the postman banged the garden gate too hard behind him and it didn't shut. Excitedly, I watched it swing open from left to right. This was my chance. I toddled off into the great beyond with my trusty companion, a little yellow wooden duck on wheels which I towed behind me with a piece of string. I remember seeing fields ahead of me but I couldn't climb the fence, so I walked up Summerfield Road to Kate Blair's Dairy at *Summerfield Mains*. Somehow, I managed to crawl through the five-barred gate into the cow field opposite the *Mains*, now the site of the modern Grammar School. I was free!

Meanwhile, my mother realised I was gone. Frantic with worry, she ran into the street. Had anybody seen a small, curly fair-haired boy with a duck on wheels? No. Then finally, as she got to the end of Lammermuir Crescent and the open fields ahead (they would later be developed as the Tree Scheme, a Council estate built in the early 1950s; it derived its name from the fact that every street is named after a tree – Ash, Cedar, Pine, Poplar, Rowan etc.)- which no doubt worried her even more as the corn was high. However, a neighbour living at the end of Lammermuir Crescent remembered seeing a wee blond haired lad trailing a toy duck on wheels walking up Summerfield Road towards Belhaven Church. Panic set in. That was worse than the prospect of a child stumbling about in the cornfields. Belhaven Church was sited on the main Edinburgh Road, where most of the traffic was in those days. Fear mounting, my mother set off, asking everyone she met if they'd seen me. Yes. He went thataway. Thataway was Kate Blair's field. Running now, my mother found Kate in the dairy. She asked her if she'd seen me.

'Aye, Ah did that, a wee while ago. He's among the beasts. I was jist aboot tae get him. Noo dinnae worry yesel, hen'. The coo's willnae herm him. They hae calves. They're mithers theirselves. Ah'll chum ye efter Ah've mucked oot the byre.'

It was small comfort to a distraught mother who was not familiar with the world of animals and their needs. Despite her fear of anything bigger than a cat, she went into the field, braving the cows and thus proving that the female of any species will sacrifice her own safety to save her own offspring.

She found me in a circle of cows, most facing outwards, possibly to protect me. They were swishing their muddy tails back and forth, occasionally slapping me across the face or chest, daubing me with wet earth. My mother caught me up in her armpit gathered my duck under the other and strode out of that field. She was so relieved that she hugged and kissed me. That I remember. I also remember she clobbered me when we got home, probably to deter me from future expeditions. At home, I was stripped and dumped into a bath and washed from head to foot. It was some time before I ventured out of the garden gate again.

My next memory is of illness. I may have been deficient of some essential vitamin in the war-time diet imposed on the population but I recall I had nasty boils on my shins. I lay in the small cot in my mother's bedroom, awaiting the doctor. Being the family of a regular soldier, we got free or subsidised medical treatment in those pre-NHS days, so my mother was never afraid to call out Dr Anderson unlike other families who couldn't afford the basic fee of five shillings [25p]. Dr Anderson was as I have said earlier a kindly old bachelor who had served on whaling ships. He had a marvellous and reassuring bedside manner; years later, working in St Andrew's House in Edinburgh, I came into contact with a doctor-administrator who'd known old Anderson. He said that while Dr Anderson was good at reassuring people, having a 'good bedside manner', he had questionable medical skills; at the inception of the NHS, Dr Anderson decided to return to the whalers. He said it was because his spinster sister and receptionist had died. Maybe he knew his days on land were numbered as he would have had to meet the stringent demands of the embryonic NHS and his qualifications might not have passed scrutiny.

At any rate, my mother had great faith in him. The benevolent Dr Anderson came into the bedroom, smiling as usual. He asked how his little man was. I said my feet were sore. He said he would make them better again. He examined the pustules, then left the room, forgetting to close the door. I heard him say this to my mother.

'They're nasty boils, Jean. If they're not ripe, I'll have to lance them. It'll be quick. The wee laddie'll not feel much pain, though there may be scars.'

Lance the boils? With a *lance*? So he was going to use that long spear-thing that knights in armour used to deadly effect, as I had seen in my picture books. Would the doctor come into the room on a horse, bearing a long pole with an iron tip? I was terrified.

Dr Anderson appeared round the door again, smiling. Instantly relieved to see he didn't have a spear in his hand, I looked up at him and smiled. He said if I were a good boy and didn't cry, he would give me a present. I was interested. What would the present be, I asked. Like the music hall magician he vaguely resembled, he beamed at me and extracted the promised present from his black bag. I looked at it in disappointment. Between thumb and forefinger, he held what to me looked like a small white stone. I wasn't in the least bit impressed.

'It's a fresh egg, laddie. For your tea. It'll make you well again. It's a treat.'

He clearly expected me to be grateful. In those wartime years of rationing, eggs came in the form of a yellow powder in a cardboard box. I'd never seen a real egg before. He handed it to me as my mother made appreciative noises behind him. Clutching it firmly in my tiny fist, I broke it. I was amazed when I saw the slimy contents, a mixture of yellow and clear liquid. My mother shouted that I was a silly boy and scurried away to fetch a saucer to retrieve the goo that was running through my fingers. The doctor smiled benevolently.

'Never mind, laddie. I've got another one here.'

Dr Anderson must have been attending to somebody on a farm who'd paid for his services in eggs. In those days, rural doctors were often paid in kind rather than cash. In wartime Britain, fresh eggs were a luxury enjoyed only by a few.

As it turned out, Dr Anderson didn't have to use his 'lance' (scalpel) as the boils were ripe. He simply burst them by applying pressure with his thumbs. After cleaning the wounds, he applied something purple; I later found out it was gentian violet, a popular medicinal remedy of the day, reputedly efficacious in skin complaints. Some years later, he used the same remedy to cure boils on my chin; he simply poured gentian violet on a wad of cotton wool and fixed it to my chin, making me look like an undernourished Santa Claus.

# Beginnings

My mother took away the second egg and put it in the scullery pantry. In those days, eggs were scrambled or made into omelettes; what else could you do with egg powder? But that teatime, I was given my egg in its shell. When my mother cracked it open, I looked at its contents with disgust. The yoke was a bright yellow but it was embedded in a thick, white substance I thought was fat. I hated fat. There was no way I would eat that rubbery fat. I ate the yellow and refused the rest. I think the first egg I had smashed was mixed with the utility egg powder with which I was familiar; to me, it was edible and preferable to the horrible real thing.

Then I took what I suppose was the 'flu. I had hallucinations. I recall reading *The Dandy* comic the night I became feverish. I saw Desperate Dan's huge fist coming out of the bedroom wall. He was snarling at me, which was out of character. He was strangling Korky the Cat and promising me I would be next. I woke up screaming and bathed in sweat. I didn't know where I was and couldn't understand why the usually benevolent Desperate Dan was trying to attack me. When I got well again, I returned to that blissfully happy and ignorant time called childhood.

I have only two memories of my father at that time. One must have been in June or July 1945 and pleasant; the other wasn't. I know that my father was in France on D-Day plus four and that he was with General Montgomery, liberating northern Holland. His return home on leave after that was the second time I saw him. A tall man - he was six feet three inches and had to stoop to get into our house - I can still see his lean figure, sleek white hair and the thin, long line of his determined jaw. He looked stern and forbidding until he smiled. The pleasant memory was when he opened his kitbag in the living room of 75 Lammermuir Crescent. I recall the peculiar smell of it, a smell I now know was a mixture of soap, hair-oil and unwashed laundry. But out of the depths of its olive-green interior, he drew out a box the size of a biscuit tin. When he removed the lid, I saw the largest number of sweets I'd ever seen outside a sweetie shop window. There were bars of *Cadbury's* chocolate, *Fry's* cream bars, packets of *Rowntree's* pastilles and fruit gums, *Mars* bars, toffees and caramels. It was a veritable cornucopia of sugar. Norman and I were given a couple of bars of chocolate, then the tin disappeared into my mother's bedroom. Sweets being on the ration, she was determined they would last as long as she could make them.

The unpleasant memory occurred a few days later, when my father said he would wash me. In those days, the kitchen sink was a favourite wash place despite the fact that we had a perfectly good bathroom with all the necessaries; possibly a preference for the kitchen was a throwback to the days in Castle Place. At any rate, my father stood me in a basin on the floor, stripping me and washing me all over with a face flannel. As he was drying me off, he dropped the towel into the basin. He put his fingers to his lips and said I wasn't to tell Mum. It was my first big mistake.

# Beginnings

As soon I was dressed in my pyjamas, I scuttled into the living room, where I promptly giggled and told my mother of the towel incident. The next minute, my father was towering over me and he clipped me round the ear. As I recollect, he lifted me clean off my feet with one swipe of his large hand and I fell against a chair.

My mother called him a bully, a rotten big Englishman. He stood over me, lying sobbing on the carpet.

'When I tell him to do or not do something, he'll obey me.'

Oh, I did. Ever after. I never crossed him again but for many years, I resented him. After all, he was only a visitor, whereas we lived in the house all the time. Many children of the immediate post-war years must have harboured similar feelings for Dads they didn't know and probably saw for the first time a few years after their birth. Dads who were regular British Army soldiers like mine came home occasionally, disrupting the routine of the household. For a while, I regarded my father as a guest, not someone who belonged in the house.

As I grew older, my brother Norman began to take a malicious delight in informing me that one day, I would have to go to school. For the moment though, life was sweet and rolled along without many mishaps. Our house was about 300 yards from the main Edinburgh-London railway line, so I grew up with the sound of trains. They never bothered me, especially not at night. There were few passenger trains after midnight when the London sleeper would rattle past slowly, for in those days, it stopped at Dunbar. The traffic consisted mainly of goods trains; the shuffling chain reaction of jolting noises made by the wagon couplings as they were shunted were actually sleep-inducing.

At that time, I shared the front bedroom with Norman and often when I lay awake, I would get up and look out of the window at Doon Hill which was partly visible through a gap in the houses in Lammermuir Crescent. Over the years, I watched the seasons change in the face of that hill. It was brown and bare in winter, sometimes covered with a light dusting of snow or frost; lush and green at first in spring, it seemed to catch fire in summer when the gorse came into flower, great swathes of yellow flames spreading over the entire surface. In autumn, there always seemed to be a blue haze of smoke drifting over the brow of the hill when the farmers burned off the bracken or the stubble corn in the valley. For me, then and now, Doon Hill always seems more attractive in late afternoon or early evening. The hill has a peculiar light all of its own; I used to think the sun lived inside it. But perhaps my favourite view of it was at night, especially when it was drenched in the eerie silver light of the moon.

My two brothers and I were born at home as was the case in those days. As I said earlier, Norman came into the world in the old tenement at Castle Place, safe, solid Granny Cockburn acting as midwife. Ken and I were born in the back bedroom at 75 Lammermuir Crescent, in our mother's bed, both births unattended by doctor or midwife, although Ken was luckier than me in that he

# Beginnings

was born on 20th May 1946 in fine weather. However, the nurse who would have attended the birth was enjoying her day off at the cinema. By the time she received word of the birth, Ken was literally in the same position as I had been in February 1941, languishing at the foot of my mother's bed, still attached to her by the umbilical cord. (My mother couldn't let go of us; I often think that in some respects that was symbolic, because she kept us at home for as long as she could). In Ken's case, it had been agreed that if he were a girl, he would be named after the nurse who delivered him. Nurse Burns said she would be happy if my mother gave Ken her surname as his second name, so he was christened Kenneth Burns Pugh. Ken and I were informed that we had been brought to the house by a stork from the Bass Rock. We believed it at the time, like many other kids.

Having a baby brother was inconvenient for me. Apart from disrupting the household routine, I wasn't allowed to touch him in case I gave him 'something'. Also, I was now the middle child and that can mean trouble from older and younger siblings, as I would discover. Like all babies, Ken squeaked and squawked a lot, so silence was banished. However, he settled down and quickly established the reputation of being a 'good' - meaning a quiet - baby. The demure photographs of him are proof of his quiet nature during his early years.

Meanwhile, the advent of a baby brother in that year of 1946 coincided with my starting school in August, a distressing event which is described in greater detail in Chapter 10.

The winter of 1946-47 was one of the severest on record. I can remember the great drifts of snow piling up in the roads; I also can visualise Norman digging out our garden path, making snow walls on either side. It was particularly bad in February, my sixth birthday. We thought the snow would never stop falling. Outlying villages were cut off for weeks on end. At Garvald, the Cistercian monks of Sancta Maria Abbey were building their new monastery at Nunraw; they sledged downhill to the village bringing the villagers milk they'd got from their own cows and bread they'd baked themselves. I think the infants were kept home from school on the worst days of blizzards because I recall sitting at my bedroom window, looking out on a white world. On these days, Doon Hill simply disappeared. Perhaps that winter gave me my enduring love of snow, although it is best seen from inside a warm house; rural snowfalls are pretty, city ones are inconvenient, for they snarl up the traffic and quickly turn to dirty slush.

I am sure I inherited my love of all kinds of weather from my mother. She had an uncanny knack of being able to forecast rain or snow. Her little rhyme about impending snow went something like this:

*The folk in the east*
*are plucking their geese*
*so what will robin do then, poor thing?*

She also knew when it was going to rain, all the kinds and directions of the wind and their individual features and the weather they brought. The soft winds of summer were predictable and welcomed because they allowed her to get the laundry done. With unfailing accuracy, she could predict the arrival of the cold east winds of spring and she made us wrap up well on such days, even before the wind began to blow. These were often snow-bearing winds; my mother used to say to me when I scanned the skies for snow in January that I would have it in plenty in February.

'That's your birthday month. It's always white on your day. It
snowed the day you were born. And it always will.'
She was rarely wrong, not even in the year of 2002, when she died. If it wasn't actual snow, it was usually frost. I remember birthdays ushered in with a white gruel of frost, a smirr of sleet or drift of snow, although my last three birthdays have been free from frost and snow, perhaps another sign of global warming.

One other memory persists of that time. We had a built-in wardrobe in the front bedroom. It had a peculiar, musty smell because in there, we stored our gas masks from the war – the rubber smell persisted until the cupboard was demolished - old clothes and what my father claimed was a regimental dress sword, a crocodile skin horse-whip and army *jodhpurs*, the last two being relics of the days he soldiered in India. I inherited the breeches and wore them when I worked on the farms in summer; the leather patches on the insides protected my inner thighs from tall thistles. To get into that cupboard, you had to step up as it was raised above the floor; I walked into it rarely without fear and trepidation, thinking that Norman would creep up and lock me inside. But I was drawn to it because that was where all my Christmas annuals and toys were stored. My worst fears were realised one rainy Saturday afternoon; while rummaging inside for a book or a toy, Norman sneaked up and shut me in, locking the door and ignoring my muffled shouts that dwindled to pleading, then silence. I was in that dusty, musty darkness for two hours, an interminable time for a small boy. I guess I was fortunate not to develop claustrophobia, or fear of confined spaces, although I still get slightly nervous in telephone kiosks and lifts.

A year is a long time in the life of a child. I counted the weeks between August and November (Hallowe'en and Guy Fawkes' Night), then Christmas, then my birthday, followed by Easter, then the intervening months until the school holidays at the end of June. These were red letter times; those that intervened only whetted your appetite for them. The intervening gaps were of course endless although the important anniversaries eventually came round. The best way to cope with the gaps was to ignore them and get on with the day-to-day business of ordinary life.

Winter seemed to go on forever. On wet days, one of my favourite pastimes was to rake through drawers and wardrobes. We didn't have a great deal of furniture but my mother was a great hoarder, a habit like queuing, both of which most housewives acquired during the war years. One drawer held a particular passion for me. It was part of a small vanity piece consisting of a couple of narrow drawers surmounted by a small adjustable mirror. It usually stood on my mother's dressing table. It contained things like ration books, birth certificates, christening cards, glass jewellery, vicious sprung hair combs with fearsome conger-eel teeth that she used to make waves in her (and our) hair. There were safety pins, small bottles with strange smells - what I later learnt was *sal volatile* or smelling salt ammonium crystals which ladies used to inhale when they were feeling faint. Once I took a deeper than usual snort of that bottle; it almost blew my head off. There was also nail varnish remover which I sniffed avidly because it made me think of pears; such behaviour would be frowned upon today but then, it was innocent. There were little white chips of what I thought were bits of pottery or broken cups. They lay in the dust. I asked Norman what they were and he told me they were baby teeth. Possibly some were hers, some were his and soon, my own and Ken's would be added. I was hurt that these teeth lay there. I'd been told that the fairies came to take away your teeth and left you sixpence. Norman once extracted one of my baby teeth using the old trick of a piece of string tied to a loose tooth, the other end fixed to a door handle. The door was then slammed violently.

'Now you'll get a tanner!' he laughed.

A tanner was slang for a sixpence [2.5p]. It suddenly dawned on me that I could make a bit of money out of the old baby teeth stored in my mother's drawer. I was duly caught pinching one and forced to admit I was going to put it under my pillow 'for the fairies'. I was given a right royal rollicking and told that the fairies would never leave me money ever again. They didn't....

My mother spoke to herself a lot, probably because she was starved of adult company, with only children to talk to. In those days, children were expected to be 'seen and not heard', which is something modern parents would do well to emulate; for so many of their little darlings have too much to say - or shout, especially in some supermarket, demanding some treat. But my mother spoke most when she was in trouble or vexed or confused; she was particularly vocal when she was knitting, especially when turning the heel of a sock, a very difficult operation as I am told. And we always knew she was troubled in mind or spirit when she stared into the fire, mumbling to herself. I used to sit at her feet, reading my weekly copy of *Sunny Stories*. I loved these tales by Enid Blyton, for they gave my imagination a boost and made me feel warm inside. (Blyton is no longer considered politically correct as she wrote about a coloured boy called little Black Sambo). Norman would come in and snatch the comic from me, tormenting me by holding above his head; I'd chase after him feebly, shouting that he was 'menting [tormenting] me until my mother's short fuse went and she would yell at us both to be quiet. She didn't have a great deal of patience at that time, probably because of money worries after my father left her with only the basic money the army allowed wives and dependents - what they called compulsory allotment. The voluntary allotment by a soldier to his family could be reduced or withheld at his request. My mother's common threat when we were unruly was that we would be put in a Home. This brought instant silence. Being put into a home was my greatest fear in childhood. I used to sit before the fire, clasp and suck my kneecaps, staring at my face distortedly reflected in the brass fender, struggling to keep back the tears.....

Such, then, was my beginning. I lived with a basically caring, harassed and hard-working mother who suffered badly from a nervous complaint in those days. My other companions were a bear, a golliwog and a doll called Greta – my mother believed in sexual equality - and an older brother who tormented the life out of me, a younger one who frustrated my attempts to play my own games until he grew up a little and made me his hero. I hardly noticed my father's increasingly longer absences.

Stories of my childhood are scattered through the following pages. A book like this could never have been written in sequential style for the simple reason that, while writing it, other memories came to the surface, memories I'd forgotten. In any case, time doesn't arrange itself tidily to suit our purposes. I found it more convenient to write to chapter headings; I hope these will prove self-explanatory and give a clear indication of what they are about.

I still possess a diary for 1958 that has helped to supplement my memories of that year. I have also kept a few mementoes such as my school report cards for years 1956 to 1958; I also managed to rescue one of my Christmas annuals - *Film Fun* for 1953 – before my mother gave it and so many others away to local kids. Other items include a few score of chipped and broken lead soldiers; like icons to a medieval monk, I occasionally take them down from the loft to look at them, remembering where I bought this Cowboy, that Indian. They offer random glimpses of the past but the *aide memoirs* are scant.

The main character in the book is of course Dunbar, which I learnt to love so much. A few years ago when I was studying the old castle at Dunbar for material for my book *Swords, Loaves and Fishes,* someone approached me. At the time, I was still living outside Edinburgh, visiting my mother that weekend. I was standing on the summit of the Castle Rock, peering down into the harbour entrance and I could sense this man hovering at my back. I felt he wanted to ask me something but at the same time, he clearly didn't wish to intrude on my privacy. Finally, he came over to me. He said he was a visitor to Dunbar and that he'd been following me for a few minutes. Then he asked me if I belonged to Dunbar.

I said yes I did - or used to. He smiled a little at that.

'You never stop belonging to a place' was all he said before he turned away.

# 2

## War Memoirs

I have a few hazy recollections of the Second World War, a conflict that literally passed over Dunbar, with one or two incidents from the air. Being a war baby, I was too young to know what was going on, although at the age of four, I had a vague sense that Something Was Not Quite Right. Apart from the one visit from my father already mentioned in Chapter 1 - I think I must have been about three and he may have been on embarkation leave prior to taking part in the D-Day landings in June 1944 - not much has registered in my memory.

As I have said in chapter 1, I was conceived at the time of the lowest ebb in Britain's fortunes in the war, when the British Expeditionary Force was expelled at Dunkirk. I was also born around the time when the Luftwaffe switched from the Blitz of London to provincial cities like Coventry, Birmingham and Clydebank - the *Baedeker* Raids, so-named from the popular guidebook of the day. Thus, the period of my gestation to birth was - like that of many others - one of acute depression. I wonder what modern child psychologists would make of that? Did it pre-dispose my generation to bouts of depression? I think not. We didn't have a clue what was going on.

I certainly recall seeing our soldiers in the Dunbar streets; I also remember prisoners-of-war in a field now occupied by Floors housing estate, below *Knockenhair House*. The former were very much in evidence at the Castle Park Barracks at *Lauderdale House*, where sentries were on guard round-the-clock at what is today a public convenience, formerly *The Captain's Cabin*, a rock emporium-cum-holiday junk shop. When Norman took me out in my pram, he always stopped at the guardroom/sentry box to chat to the men on duty. I seem to remember them patting me on the head, like a wee dog. They were probably thinking of their own children. I have this vague recollection of one leaning over me, wearing a funny hat and shouldering what I later learnt was a rifle. He wore a strange, rough olive-coloured uniform and gave me a bar of chocolate. When I was a bit older, I was allowed to visit the *NAAFI* (Navy, Army and Air Force Institute) shop adjacent to the Catholic Church Hall in the Westgate. There I would buy tupenny packets of salted peanuts, a treat I have enjoyed ever since.

The Castle Park barracks dated from 1855, when the War Office purchased the property for training artillery militia; then it became a cavalry depot at the outbreak of the Boer War and again in 1914. Dunbar had already faced the threat of invasion by Napoleon in 1803-04, when the town and the beaches at Belhaven and West Barns became vast armed camps of wooden huts occupied by the militia cavalry and infantry.  So in 1939, history repeated itself, these areas again being fortified.  This time the threat would be from the air, so the long, flat beach at Belhaven Bay and beyond was sown with large wooden poles embedded in concrete bases to prevent the landing of glider-borne troops from occupied Norway.  And to counter a likely assault by tanks in a sea-borne landing, the whole area was protected by double and sometimes treble rows of tank-traps - massive concrete blocks arranged in a zigzag pattern to accommodate riflemen and - in theory at any rate - to prevent the Panzers moving inland.  Much good they would have been, as similar defences were in place in Normandy and were quickly overrun by our troops on the first of the D-Day landings on 6th June 1944.  But in war, anything visibly done to combat an enemy threatening the homeland is aimed more at morale boosting among the civilian population.  I believe that in Dunbar, the morale was high.  The townspeople in general - and the Home Guard in particular - were ready for anything Herr Hitler could throw at them - provided it didn't explode.  How could Hitler possibly expect to win the war confronted by such determined people?

I was only a few weeks old when the Luftwaffe dropped two bombs near the railway line at Countess Road.  Both missed the railway, one detonated, the other didn't.  (It wasn't until the 1960s that the unexploded bomb was removed.  Everyone of that generation knew the bomb was there because there was a slight depression in the cornfield near Lochend Wood, a patch of ground where nothing grew).  It is unlikely that the attack was deliberate; more than likely, the pilots simply jettisoned their bombs at an opportune target to lighten their load in their return flight to France or Norway.

The second raid was much closer to our house.  Sturdy and secure as it was, it couldn't possibly have withstood a direct hit and there was only one brick-built air-raid shelter a few yards away at *Paylors' Corner*, named for a family who lived there for many years. Anyway, one night, a bomb was dropped near the Municipal Gasworks. According to the *Haddingtonshire Courier* of the day, a piece of shrapnel landed about 25 feet from the main gasometer.  As it happened, there was only minor damage sustained by the nearby houses.  My mother's back bedroom window was slightly cracked in the upper left-hand corner as I recall, a fact she pointed-out to the Burgh Surveyor in 1965.  He had asked whether the crack was the result of some boy playing golf in the school playing fields over the garden wall.  My mother left him in no doubt of the facts:

    'No, it was that bloody Hitler in 1942. I reported it twenty-three

    years ago.  You took your time coming tae fix it.'

Such is a typical local war memory....

I remember our across-the-road neighbour Chrissie MacPherson who joined up and came home proudly wearing her ATS (Auxiliary Territorial Service) uniform, her kepi pulled down severely over her eyes, which I think was intended to give her a menacing look.  Chrissie was as gentle as they come.

But perhaps my most vivid and poignant war memory is being taken to see the prisoners-of-war in the Floors housing estate field opposite Gala Green. I think it was Norman who took me there. I can recall being lifted up to peer over the low boundary wall, seeing these men wearing strange clothes and funny hats. Somehow, they made me think of animals in my zoo book.

'Gaga, why men there?'

As I mentioned earlier, *Gaga* was my name for Norman which I couldn't pronounce. Norman didn't hesitate to reply.

'They're bloody Germans, that's why.'

That didn't really help. Then one of the men left the group hoeing turnips or cabbages; he came over to us and spoke in English. He explained that he wasn't a German but an Austrian. It made no difference to Norman. They were the same as Germans, enemies of Britain. The POWs working in that field were housed in a camp near Innerwick and were driven to and from the fields in soft-skinned vehicles. There were certainly Germans among 'our' prisoners, as I later learnt from Alec or Eck Lough, one of the men set to watch over them. I was fascinated by these men and wasn't in the least frightened of them.

I begged my mother for some bread to feed to the men. It would be like the zoo, I thought. So back I went clutching the remains of a half loaf which Norman broke into pieces for me to hand to the grateful men. One or two lingered after the bread was gone and somehow managed to convey to Norman that they'd like to give me a present. We were asked to come back and so we did, with more bread. That day, one of the soldiers stood with his hands behind his back, then showed us what he was holding - a beautiful little wooden horse on wheels. It was flat, painted brown and the wheels were pea-green on a red base. It had a string to pull it along, in the same fashion as the little yellow duck which went everywhere with me in those days. He handed the toy to me and I was thrilled. It was a work of art and I treasured it for many years until my mother gave it away to some child in the street. Another soldier produced a small ring with a blue glass inset; I wore that for a long time. I later learnt that the horse had been made from bits of packing case, the ring from a tea-spoon. The German soldiers loved children and many were clever at making toys. I went home that afternoon, wearing my ring and pulling the little horse behind me. I thought the world was a nice place, full of nice men.

During one of her many clear-outs, my mother gave the horse and the ring to a neighbour's kid, something I mourn today as they were tangible war memories. A child has no enemies in war. There are only soldiers. Everywhere in the world, soldiers have usually been kind to children whose lives have been disrupted or destroyed by war. One of the several exceptions was the fate of Jewish children during the Second World War, when Nazi Germany gassed thousands of them without a hint of conscience.

Other memorable wartime gifts came from our own men - well, a Dunbar man who lived near us and who served in the RAF. When he came home on leave, he presented Norman with a beautifully made bomber with camouflage painting, thread for the wireless aerial and a perspex-covered cockpit. Its guns were nails with their heads sawn off. It was large and heavy but very well made. I was given a Spitfire painted dark green and brown. I could just about manage to hold it above my head, playing with its tiny propeller which I could spin with my forefinger. These toys were lovingly kept and played with through the 1940s and 1950s until again, they disappeared during a bout of spring - cleaning.

There were of course casualties in the district, although most occurred in foreign fields. Years after the conflict, I discovered that the railway station at Innerwick was attacked by German bombers, one bomb going under the railway bridge and another landing in a potato field. One railwayman was killed and three wounded by machine gun fire. The raiders sped off to buzz Dunbar, then headed out to the North Sea, no doubt chased off by Spitfires from 602 (City of Glasgow) Squadron stationed at Drem aerodrome.

Then a momentous occasion occurred on 6th February 1945. The Great Fire at 75 Lammermuir Crescent. How do I know the precise date? I am not blessed with the greatest memory in the world, but I know it was a Friday night as my brother Norman always attended the Boys' Brigade on Friday nights. Besides, years later, when researching *Swords, Loaves and Fishes,* I found a reference to the fire in the Burgh Council minutes of 13th February 1945; the rubric to the minutes simply states 'Fire at 75 Lammermuir Crescent; the entry reads as follows:

'A fire having occurred at the house, 75 Lammermuir Crescent, a claim was intimated to the Insurance Company, and a sum of £8:10/ - [£8.50] in name of damage was admitted.' (Source: National Ar chive of Scotland SRO ref B18/13/21)

Maybe that's all it was to the gentlemen who served on the Council – Provost Phipps Oswald Turnbull, Councillors Chapman, Hannan etc, the Town Clerk, J W Brooke and others. It nearly meant my premature demise.

All her life, my mother was terrified of two things – fire and water. Water leaking, water flooding and water freezing in pipes are bad enough but such calamities rarely result in loss of life or permanent injury. Fire is something entirely different. In February 1945, I was nearly lost – well, at least I was in potential danger – because of a fire in my mother's bedroom. Given the relatively primitive method of lighting houses in those days, it's a wonder there weren't more fires like that in our house.

Our fire must have happened at about 9.30pm on the night of the 6th February. My mother never went to the cinema of a Friday for the simple reason that my brother Norman, who normally 'minded', me went to the Parish Kirk Hall to drill with the Boys Brigade (BBs). Friday night was her night for catching up on household chores – darning socks mainly. Her normal routine on Friday nights was to slip me into her bed in the bedroom off the living room until I fell asleep, then I was transferred into a small cot or bed in the room. She always lit a candle in the bedroom in case I woke or was frightened; in those days, we had no electric light and gas wasn't installed in the bedrooms. Sometimes she would doze off in front of the fire in an armchair near her bedroom door.

It would have been well after 9pm when Norman came home. Hearing his step in the hall, she got up to take her sewing basket into her bedroom. Norman followed her, complaining bitterly about the punishment he'd received that night for some infringement of BB rules. (It was later that I found out he'd been thrashed over the knuckles by a particularly strict disciplinarian 'officer' – could he have been Captain Charles Gray whom I think was then in charge of the Boys' Brigade? The officer had used a cane on his knuckles. That night, he showed my mother his swollen fingers and vowed he would leave the BBs. He was more upset by his humiliation than his physical pain. My mother apparently went into the scullery to make some tea and he followed her, throwing the bedroom door violently open behind him as he followed her. They were so engrossed in conversation, my mother threatening to get the police to the BB officer for assault, both she and Norman failed to notice that the bedroom was unusually bright. My mother remarked on the fact, then she smelt the smoke and ran into the bedroom to find the back of the door enveloped in flames that reached the ceiling. Her silk kimono which hung on a hook on the back of the door had wafted over the candle when Norman had flung the door open behind him. Highly inflammable, the silk dressing gown had gone up in seconds.

Panic set in. My mother screamed and told Norman to 'run next door for the Harkess lads'-John and Tommy, while she ran into the scullery to fill a pail of water. She was about to throw it on the door when John Harkess appeared and calmly asked her for a small rug or towel for him to dip into the bucket. He told her that throwing water on the door would make things worse, so he dipped a small rug into the pail and beat out the flames. (I often wonder if my Uncle John – as I called him for many years – had some training as a Fire Precautions Volunteer during the war).

During this small drama, I slept blissfully ignorant of it all. Even my mother had forgotten I was sleeping in her bed, when Uncle John told my mother to let me sleep on. He was a bit of an amateur psychologist was my Uncle John. I never knew about the fire or the danger I had been in until the next day, when I recall asking my mother why the door was black and charred and its gilt hooks discoloured and twisted. She was calm by then and said there had been a 'wee accident' but that I wasn't to worry about it, as Uncle John had sorted it.

For my generation, the most vivid memories of the war occurred after it ended. First of all, strategically important places like Belhaven Bay and West Barns Links which were under army control and had been out of bounds for six years became play areas. There were trench systems at Winterfield Golf Course – notably at the fifteenth tee - which we used in our war games. Another favourite haunt were the tank-traps along the Belhaven and West Barns beaches, great places for playing war or hide-and-seek. West Barns Links remained a rifle range for many years after the war and nearby Hedderwick Sands were used for tank manoeuvres. The rifle range ended at the high sand dunes, where the targets were placed. We used to go there to gather the hundreds of spent bullets scattered in the sand, once or twice even during target practice I shudder to admit. Some of the more fearless - and foolish - boys like my late friend Jock Gardner used to lie and watch the spent bullets kick up little puffs of sand; a great feat was to run out and retrieve them, still hot from the rifle.

By the time we were allowed to play at Belhaven, the beach had been cleared of mines and most of the wooden poles embedded in the sand had been sawn down to stumps. At low tide, water was trapped in the depressions at the bases of these poles and we used to catch small crabs and fishes stranded in these pools by the receding tide. The concrete bases remained until well into the 1960s, by which time they'd become part of the seascape, crusted with barnacles and limpets and festooned with green seaweed. Finally, they were removed to allow sand yachting, once a popular sport at Belhaven. The odd survivor of these poles can still be found in the salt marsh leading to Hedderwick and Spike Island.

For many years, trenches remained unfilled at Winterfield, fronted by rusting barbed wire held in place by iron screw supports; my favourite place was the coastline where now exists the fifteenth tee, where we played at invasions. Few traces of the trenches survive today, although near the tee is the remains of an Observation Post beside the anti-tank blocks that are scattered along the beach there. Another favoured play area I mentioned earlier was the tank obstacles at West Barns Links, many of which were subsequently moved to shore up the banking near the fourteenth green at Winterfield facing Seafield Bridge. Several specimens are still in their original positions in the woods at Tyninghame Bay, north west of the river Tyne; they lie in the woods covered in moss and look like giant furry dice.

There were a few air raid shelters in the vicinity. One at Seafield, beside the *Divy Dyke*, was used as an unofficial loo for those caught short on afternoon walks; it was probably dismantled for that reason. Others can be found in what is now the *John Muir Country Park* where there is evidence of use by those responding to an unexpected call of nature or some who have found themselves suddenly gripped by a romantic impulse....

Another relic of that time lay for many years at the edge of the rocky shore near the first tee at Dunbar Golf Course. Boys walking there on Sunday afternoons knew it well, for it provided them with an excellent target in the course of developing their stone-throwing skills. A rusted mine with its teat-like detonators provided endless hours for target practice; the trick was to hit one of the teats which entitled the missile-thrower to imitate the sound of a mine exploding. The relic was finally removed a few years ago, being an eyesore the club officials felt they could do without.

Fortunately, I was too young to know the privations - if indeed they were such - that were visited on the dinner tables of the war years. It was a case of what you never had, you never missed. Our table stood at the window of the living room in the summer months, then it was moved to the centre of the room before the fire in winter. I recall pricking the black-out blinds with a fork to alleviate the boredom of waiting for food; making peepholes of course defeated the purpose of these blinds which were there to shut out the light, thus confounding any night flying enemy planes. My mother caught me engaged in this interesting game one winter night in 1944.

'Ye'll get me shot! Leave the bloody blinds alone!'
I thought it funny at the time.
The inconvenience of rationing went on far longer than most people believe today. The rationing of sweets was the worst privation for the young and the women. Next to the ever present fears of the consequences of out-of-control fire and water, my mother had the added - if temporary - fear of any of us losing our identity cards and ration books. She kept both in a safe place throughout the war and afterwards, until the administrative all-clear sounded in about 1953. I was fascinated by my identity card, which I still possess. You had to produce this card when anyone -usually the police - asked for it. When I examined my identity card more closely years later, I marvelled at the ingenuity of the authorities during the war. My card bears the serial number S706g; it warns the holder never to lose it or allow it to be stolen. The reason for the card was bluntly if mysteriously stated: you possessed it 'under conditions of national emergency for important purposes.' What *were* these 'important purposes'? The words suggest a whiff of *Big Brother* in George Orwell's *1984*. The card bears my full name; what intrigued me was that it is dated three days before I was born! I used to marvel at how far seeing and accurate the bureaucrats were in those days. To think that these faceless men not only knew what my name would be before I was born, they'd known I'd be a boy! The answer to this amazing ability to foretell the future accurately is of course obvious. The card had been issued *after* my birth and was dated on the day my mother applied for it, then it was back-dated.

Ration books were equally sacred documents; like those of so many others, ours were stained by the greasy fingers of butchers and grocers. Without a ration book, you starved. Well, in theory. Ration books came in various different colours so that you knew which was a food or meat ration book, a clothing book or for luxury goods like tinned fruit (plums and peaches) and sweets. The British are exceptionally adept at bureaucracy and everything had its *raison d'etre* in wartime. Each person was allotted a certain number of 'points' which entitled the ration book holder to so many ounces of tea, sugar, butter, meat, clothing and other 'utility' commodities like socks. For example, a tin of plums or rhubarb in syrup might attract 9 points, a new suit would mean 26 points (men and women were allowed 60 coupons a year in 1941, later reduced to 48) and a pair of silk stockings cost 2 points. When you bought your bread or whatever, you handed over money and your ration book; the shop assistant would then cut out the relevant coupons. Rationing taught housewives to be careful and thrifty.

I know from programmes like *Dad's Army* that the Black Market was alive and thrived during the war; this human activity is a by-product of the conflicts between governments and peoples all over the world and at different times in human history. There was probably a robust Black Market in Dunbar, though I was too young to be aware of it. The alternative was barter. A housewife would exchange rationed commodities she didn't need or want for ones she did. My mother had a mutually beneficial arrangement with a relative. My mother didn't like butter and we were programmed not to either; so she exchanged her butter ration for her relative's sugar ration. This arrangement worked very well until one occasion, the woman called to collect her half pound of butter but said she hadn't been able to obtain her sugar ration as there was a shortage - possibly because it was autumn, the height of the jam-making season. My mother accepted her excuse and duly handed over the half pound of butter. When she was putting the butter in her relative's bag, she saw there was a pound of sugar in it. She later learnt that the woman had played the same trick on another neighbour. She was disgusted that a blood relative would deceive her. That incident ended their barter system - and their friendship. My mother later told me that the woman was deceitful and that she'd stolen from us, which was of course true. Recalling the incident today, I think my mother should have confronted the woman; there may have been a reason for the deception. However, at the time she could only think of the insult to her intelligence and her family's welfare. You didn't cheat on your neighbours and friends in those austere years of rationing. Those who did were literally taking food from others' mouths.

One of our family astonished us by marrying a prisoner-of-war. Uncle Josef was an Austrian who decided to remain in Scotland after the war ended. He married one of my mother's nieces and took a job on East Barns farm, employed by Bobby Hope, one of two brothers who farmed there and at Oxwellmains. But farming wasn't for *Jofish,* as I called him; he took his wife and first child to Doncaster, where he found employment as a miner. A gentle man, he died recently, sadly missed by his family and is still remembered lovingly by the former East Barns villagers who survive today.

The rationing of sweets was sorest to bear in a population with little else by way of comfort, especially among the women and children. Men still could have a (rationed) whisky allocation and a few pints each week but the women and children were deprived by a shortage of sugar. Gradually, a Labour government elected in 1946 - that was how a grateful country rewarded its wartime leader Churchill, one of the finest and ablest men Britain ever produced - relaxed the control over many foodstuffs but it kept the brake on sweets, one of the last items to come off ration eight years after the war ended. When in 1953 that day came, there were huge queues outside every sweetshop in Dunbar. I recall the best sweet shop was that of Miss MacDonald, who kept an upmarket place in the West Port, later owned by my life-long friend, Laura Togneri. An orderly crowd of kids were served with their hearts' delight although money was still a rationing factor. No matter, in 1953, the Coronation year of queen Elizabeth the First - oh yes, for on 2nd June that year - Coronation Day - that is what she became as far as Scotland is concerned - most kids were given extra pocket money to indulge themselves.

The war lingered on in less dramatic, niggling ways. I recall posters with little cartoon characters called *Dr Carrot* and *Potato Pete*. Others exhorted us to eat *National Wholemeal Bread*; another urged us *Not to Waste Food*. Posters like these were to be seen in the window of the local Food Office in the West Port, dog-eared propaganda leaflets that survived long after the war ended. The Food Office was adjacent to the modern pet shop; it had blanked-out windows painted grey and dispensed *National Dried Milk Powder* - excellent for making ersatz sweets - and orange juice to expectant and nursing mothers as well as those with young children. It was a daily occurrence to see mothers arguing at the door of this mysterious building. I think now that the Food Office windows were painted opaque to dissuade the gossips wanting to know who in Dunbar were officially regarded as 'needy and poor' folk.

In those days, we were advised to drink lots of *Bovril* and *Oxo*. The medical profession urged us to eat more carrots, as they were essential for your eyesight.; after all, hadn't our airmen eaten tons of them to enable them to see in the dark. Oh really? Surely this was a myth or propaganda. Shouldn't we have been eating what cats ate because they are most adept at seeing what is out there in the darkness?

It has recently been acknowledged that the wartime diet was in fact the healthiest before and during the war. I have also discovered from Government statistics for 1941 - the year I was born - that the number of births per thousand of the population dropped to their lowest in recorded birth and mortality rates - something like 13.9 per thousand. This was surely not connected in any way with dietary restrictions; it was simply due to the fact that men were away at the war. By 1946, the birth rate had recovered, reaching 20.6 per thousand of the population.

Some of the wartime jingles on posters have survived in memory as have the visual images. Famous at one time were slogans like *Billy Brown from London Town* and *Coughs and Sneezes Spread Diseases*. There were also little characters like *Mr Therm* advertising the benefits to be had from gas.

# War Memoirs

Another famous slogan the Ministry of Supply used was *Make Do and Mend*, an exhortation aimed chiefly at women to save cloth by wearing 'utility clothes' and to 'make do and mend' old clothes. But of all those which remain uppermost in my mind was the famous poster urging us to *Dig for Victory*; it showed a headless one-legged man - so it seemed - with one foot on a garden spade.

Although we won the war - well, the Allies did - rationing went on far longer than expected; it even got more stringent. Meat was severely rationed, along with petrol and fresh eggs. Recently, I found some old newspaper cuttings my mother had kept in a box containing important documents like birth and marriage certificates. These papers show prices of various commodities at the time:

| | |
|---|---|
| *Robertson's* Jam | : 1/7 (7p) |
| *Daily Express* | : one penny (old) |
| Toothpaste | : 1/3 (6p) |
| Twenty cigarettes | : 3/6 (17p) |
| Cinema ticket (child) | : threepence (just over 1p) |
| Four ounces of sweets | : threepence |

Thus a child who received sixpence pocket money a week could afford a trip to the Saturday matinee and a quarter pound bag of sweets.

For the children of the war and immediate post-war years, privation was not quite so bad as it was for the adult population. A bankrupt Britain didn't end rationing entirely until I reached my thirteenth birthday. I recall my mother cheerfully burning the last of our ration books on the fire when rationing finally ended on 2nd July 1954. Meat was the last commodity to come off ration; to celebrate, we had a roast joint the first Sunday afterwards.

There is at least one apocryphal story about rationing in Dunbar. It concerned the local chimney sweep, Matthew Boyle, or *Mattie Bile* as he was colloquially known. *Mattie* wasn't fussy about the colour of his socks as long as they were black, probably on account of his profession. Anyway, my mother told me that during the rationing, he was in need of two pairs of black socks, so he went to the local *Co-op* drapery in the High Street. He was handing over the money along with his ration book when the assistant noticed that the coupons weren't clothing coupons. The young lady broke the sad news as gently as she could:

'I'm sorry Mattie. I can't let you have the socks. These aren't clothing coupons, they're sweetie coupons.'

Quick as a flash, *Mattie* riposted:

'Weel lassie, that's fine. The socks are for sweetie [meaning sweaty] feet.'

The wireless was to the war generation what television is to today's audiences. Life would have been intolerable without it. One of the programmes we tuned into regularly was the *Radio Doctor* whom I believe continued to broadcast until 1950, by which time we had the NHS. Newscasters like Alvar Liddell [the emphasis being on the second half of his surname] and Frank Phillips were household names. They were better known to us than some adults in the community. Who of that time can forget the legendary 'This is the Nine o' Clock News and this is Alvar Li-ddell speaking'? The news was invariably delivered in his flat, unemotional voice as he reported both good and bad news. On the lighter side, there was *Workers' Playtime* with Wilfrid Pickles exhorting Joe to ''ave a go.' There was also *Music While You Work.* These programmes were delivered from the factory floor, a morale-boosting exercise designed to convince the rest of us that the workers worked while they were being entertained. Whenever someone won a prize, Pickles would cheerfully instruct his wife to 'Give ' im the mooney, Ma-bel.' The famous show was piped into other factories; Wilfrid Pickles and Ma-bel lasted until the 1950s, as did the ever-popular *ITMA (It's That Man Again-* reputedly Hitler*)* with Tommy Hanley and his chums. Hanley's surreal anarchy was loved by all and anticipated that of the equally famous *Goon Show* in 1951.

Hanley introduced a range of characters which became household names loved throughout the war years and after it. Among these characters who took on a life of their own were His Washout, the Mayor of Much-Foaming-at-the-Mouth; Squire of Much Fiddling; Signor So-So; Funf the German Spy; Ali Oop the pedlar whose catchphrase was 'I go, I come back'. Famous of all perhaps was the immortal Mrs Mopp, her catchphrase laden with sexual innuendo:

'Can I do you now, Sir?'

Other memorable characters were the Diver ('I'm going down now, Sir. Don't forget the Diver.'), Mona Lott, Claude and Cecil ('After you, Claude. No, after you, Cecil'), Frisby Dyke, a Liverpudlian and Vodkin the Russian, a character whose name was a particular stroke of genius. I think one of the regular features in the show were jungle drums beating and the drummer mouthing silly verses in time to the bongos; a typical example was

'Down in the jungle, livin' in a tent,

better than a pre-fab, NO RENT!'

There was also Jack Train and his dipsomaniac Colonel Chinstrap whose rhetorical question 'Why must the Chancellor always tax necessities?' [meaning booze] was echoed by many. His other line was 'I don't mind if I do' which became the universal response from anyone offered a drink. Then there was Vic Oliver, Bebe Daniels and Ben Lyon in *Life with the Lyons, The Archers, Mrs Dale's Diary* and Arthur Askey with his catchphrase 'Eye thenk yew.'

Vera Lynn, the Forces' Sweetheart remained a popular singer long after the war with her *White Cliffs of Dover, We'll Meet Again, I'll Be Seeing You.* My father was a heretic where she was concerned; he considered her contemporary Anne Shelton a better singer.

Programmes specifically aimed at children were the evergreen *Childrens' Hour* with Uncle Mac; the *Ovalteenies,* a propaganda programme which urged children to drink *Ovaltine* and invited them to join *The League of Ovalteenies,* wear the special badge and decipher messages in code by reading their code book, usually extolling the virtues of the bedtime drink.

In those days, the wireless needed time to 'warm up' as it was fuelled by something called an accumulator, a kind of electric battery for storing electrical energy and rendering it portable - invaluable in the days before domestic electricity was introduced to homes in Dunbar in the early 1950s. The accumulator had to be re-charged every week at *Stark's* Garage, which was situated in the area now known as Old Kirk Close in the High Street; this was my job when my mother decided I was responsible enough to undertake it. When the display panel lit up, it showed the usual national stations like the BBC Home Service; in addition were stations with exotic-sounding names - Hilversum, Frankfurt, Luxembourg and AFN (American Forces Network) which after 1945 was broadcast from occupied Germany.

As I mentioned in the previous chapter, when my father came home on his first post-war leave from BAOR (British Army of Occupation of the Rhine), he showered us with sweets. He arrived with bulging kitbag and the army-issue green cardboard suitcase. After greeting us all, he undid the drawstring of the kitbag and invited Norman and I to rummage through it, promising there would be something that would interest us. I mentioned earlier how I recalled the smell of soap, stale laundry and sweaty socks as we burrowed to find the tin box stuffed to the brim with all kinds of confectionery. I had never held so many sweets in my hands.

The equanimity of the household was always disrupted when Dad came home. I lost my pride of place on the hearthrug before the coal fire because he had to stretch his long legs out from his armchair. But I didn't mind that too much because I was consoled by an assortment of goodies retailed by the famous confectionary manufacturers *Fry, Rowntree* and *Cadbury.* When Dad was home he wanted to redecorate the place so that was yet another upheaval; his leave over, he returned to Germany and normal service was resumed.

Between the two world wars, the Church and the State drew closer. In Scotland as elsewhere in Britain, the Church became militant and reinforced its mission. In wartime, it was hysterically patriotic, urging Christian Soldiers Onward, a hymn which figured in practically every wartime church service in Belhaven Church, the church my family joined as it was closer to home than the Parish, or as it was known to families in our vicinity, the 'high' kirk in Dunbar. The irony of both world wars was that every belligerent country, be it the Germans or the democracies, believed God was on its side. (Although I am a devout and committed atheist, I sometimes ask myself if God knows who is on his side). The German army belt buckle of World War One bore the legend *Gott Mit Uns* [God with us]; the British Army didn't seem to need such reassurance, believing itself to be on a Christian mission to free the world and was therefore automatically divinely favoured. It was more straightforward in the

First World War. In the Second World War, the Nazis were clearly evil incarnate and the Church had a field day. I personally have never been able to reconcile the fact that the combatants in both conflicts professed themselves Christian and fought in the name of God. There is scarcely a village, town or city in Britain which does not have a memorial to those who fell in the two world wars. I was always proud of my countrymen on 11th November, especially when the entire school (including the infants) assembled in the quadrangle at 11am on the day to commemorate the war dead of the burgh and parish. The water trough brimmed with poppies and we observed two minutes' silence to mark the silencing of the guns on 11th November 1918. No pupil ever mocked the occasion, or misbehaved during the brief, solemn, impressive ceremony, when the headmaster, Robert Macauley, recited the poem *For the Fallen* by Laurence Binyon; I was moved to tears when he quoted the famous and indescribably sad but noble lines:

> *They shall not grow, as we that are left to grow old:*
> *Age shall not weary them, nor the years condemn.*
> *At the going down of the sun and in the morning*
> *We will remember them.*

These simple but moving lines affect me still....

It was many years later that I discovered that the Second World War didn't end officially until 1949 so that technically, those who died as a result of war wounds between 1945 and that date are considered casualties of war. The end of the State of Emergency - a euphemism if ever there was one - was ratified by Order in Council of His Majesty's parliament on 31st March 1949. In that same year, I first heard the word 'bandit' used to describe the Communist-inspired insurgents in Malaya who rebelled against British rule there. I imagined those 'bandits' wore spotted red handkerchiefs over their faces like in the 'B' westerns I saw at the Saturday matinees. Later that year, the word would have a bitter meaning for my family.

As I wrote in the previous chapter, my cousin Dennis Moore was a fine young man whose half-sisters Norma, Emily and Margaret loved to distraction. Dennis was tall, handsome, gentle and he visited our house most Sunday mornings to play cards with my Uncle Jimmy and my brother Norman. He was training to be a gardener with Sir Reginald Wingate at *Knockenhair House*; Wingate was a relic of the Sudan and Egyptian wars, a Victorian and Grand Old Man who'd served under Kitchener, knew Gordon of Khartoum, Lawrence of Arabia and many other famous military people. Dennis loved his work and because in those days, gardening was a skilled job, he could have deferred his National Service until he completed his apprenticeship. Wingate advised Dennis to get it over with and promised to keep his job open until he returned home. So off he went to join the Scots Guards.

I still remember that dreary, wet Sunday - why does it always seem to rain on Sundays? - when he came to say goodbye to us. He had this to say to my mother, to whom he'd grown closer after his own mother died earlier in the year:

'It won't be for long Auntie Jean. I'll be back before you know it.'

The next we heard of him was that he'd been posted to Malaya, a place which meant nothing to me, although I looked it up in my school atlas.

I didn't know it then but a State of Emergency had been declared in 1948 to combat the Communist terrorists. Among the several British regiments sent out to protect British interests were the 2nd Battalion Coldstream Guards, the 3rd Grenadier Guards and Dennis' regiment, the 2nd Battalion Scots Guards, collectively known as the 2nd Guards Brigade.

Some 5,000 terrorists were occupying jungle camps from where they sallied to murder rubber planters, tin miners and intimidate the native workers. The Communists intended to bankrupt the country and thus discredit the British imperialists as they called them, not without some justification. During 1949, the British Army, mainly consisting of National Servicemen, had a measure of success, killing or capturing many of the insurgents.

Three years after Dennis was killed in Malaya, I saw the film *The Planter's Wife* with Jack Hawkins and Claudette Colbert; ostensibly about marital discord, it brought home the dangers of living on remote rubber plantations in post-Second World War Malaya. I shan't go into the causes that led to the so-called 'police action' in Malaya other than to summarise the events; the Malayan communists had assisted the British against the Japanese during the war and after it ended, saw a window of opportunity to gain their independence. It was one of many nationalist movements aimed at dismantling the anachronistic British Empire.

Malaya eventually became a republic. Before it achieved independence, many British soldiers lost their lives. The senior staff quickly realised that the only effective answer to the incursions by the bandits was to locate and destroy their armed camps. On one of these deep penetration jungle patrols, Dennis Moore was killed on 25th September 1949.

Not unexpectedly, the national newspapers were full of patriotic indignation. Dennis Moore died in that far off country simply because he was in the wrong place at the wrong time. In those days, our household paper was the *Daily Express* and my mother would anxiously scan it to see if there was any mention of action and casualties. We grew increasingly worried as we'd not heard from Dennis for some weeks - he wrote home regularly - especially when we knew that his regiment was on jungle patrol. It must have been his half-sister Norma or Emily who received the War Office telegram reporting Dennis killed on active service. The *Express* published a full account of the incident.

According to family memory, Dennis had accompanied a young officer and a sergeant as part of a detail to retrieve the bodies of soldiers caught in an ambush. One of the bodies had been booby-trapped with hand grenades; when

Dennis and his sergeant lifted the corpse, the grenades detonated, killing both and the officer. That was the account told by my mother but I have since traced a different account in a contemporary issue of the local newspaper, the *Haddingtonshire Courier.* It states that Dennis, a sergeant and an officer had tracked three guerrillas down and ambushed them in the jungle. As they were collecting the bodies, a fourth member of the gang whom they'd not known about lobbed a hand grenade among them, killing all three instantly.

That morning I went to school full of rage and sadness - rage at the atrocity, sadness because I would never see my favourite cousin again. It was heart-breaking and final. Death had touched me for the first time and it hurt. I was proud to have been related to Dennis Moore but that didn't in any way compensate for the loss of a fine young man. For a long time, I hated the Malayans and decided that Communism was a dirty word. I haven't changed much in my opinion over the intervening years.

The next conflict came the following year, in Korea. Of that war, I have little recollection although as before, my mother read accounts from the news-paper. After the Japanese capitulated in 1945, the country was occupied by Russian and American troops, the former in the north, the latter in the south. In 1950, the communist-backed North launched an unprovoked and surprise attack on South Korea across the 38th parallel, the military demarcation line agreed by the armies of occupation. Then the Chinese entered on the side of the North Koreans. A British Brigade was sent to join the United Nations forces in the South and two of its regiments were severely cut-up at the Imjin River, when the UN forces were attacked by over 200,000 troops from the North. The conflict made famous the *Glorious Gloucesters*, a regiment that refused to abandon its position and fought almost to the last man. There were only 30 survivors out of the 600-strong outfit. For me, the sacrifice of these brave men somehow compensated for the tragic death of my cousin Dennis.

After that came the farcical debacle of Suez in 1956, when President Nasser of Egypt nationalised the Suez Canal. Britain was assisted by French and Israeli troops but apart from the brilliant campaign fought by the Israelis in the Sinai Desert, the two world powers capitulated. Suez finally brought it home to Britain that she was no longer a major world power.

My only real recollection of this brief war in the summer of 1956 was when the tannoy at the local swimming pool announced that all Class A Re-servists in the forces who were on holiday were to report to Dunbar Police Station to register their addresses. I remember a few men getting up, leaving their wives and children with worried, frightened looks on their faces. Thank-fully, my brother Norman, who served for three years in the RAF, was classed at a lower category of reservist

In this part of Scotland, we were fortunate insofar as in modern times, we never knew the tramp of alien feet, nor were our lives threatened to any significant extent by hostile bombs. Now, over fifty years on, I cannot say that

# War Memoirs

I remember the sound of the fighting planes going over Dunbar, although after the war, sometimes at night when I lay awake, I thought about that time. I had a vivid imagination even then. Even now, when I heard the drone of an aeroplane passing over the house at night, it brings back stories told about the war by the fireside.

So these are my war memoirs - or lack of them. Like most of my generation, I came out of the Second World War and its immediate aftermath relatively unscarred. Paradoxically, for one who is a pacifist, the military has always interested me. Perhaps some of my father rubbed off on me. To me there is justification for war. Sometimes.

Now sleepy Dunbar turns in her bed at night and breathes easily. My generation and those that followed have much to be thankful for; hopefully, those to come will never have war memoirs, even minor ones like my own.

# 3

## Altered States

My childhood progressed much in the same way as that of my contemporaries. However, change was on the domestic horizon but did I know of it? When it came in 1948, Ken was aged two; at fifteen, Norman had been away from school for a year, earning a few shillings a week as a telegram boy in the local Post Office. That job didn't last long as Norman had left school without a Leaving Certificate and he refused to sit an exam the Postmaster of the day said was necessary in absence of the certificate. He left the GPO to work with *Hurry's Bakery* but the heat of the ovens made him ill, so he took another job with the *Lammermuir Laundry* in Spott Road, working as a van boy with Jimmy Wilson, collecting and delivering laundry in Dunbar and the Borders area. Jimmy Wilson is a fine man who years later was employed by *George Wimpey* as a bus driver, taking workmen to and from Edinburgh and working on the building site himself, jobs my uncle Jimmy got for him.

That we were a working class family never crossed my mind, nor if I'd known it, would it have troubled me in the least, although when our so-called 'betters' visited the house, my mother reminded us that we had to 'keep our place'. I knew vaguely what she meant when confronted by strangers who spoke 'proper' English, not the local *patois* that is as harsh - if colourful - today as it was then. In those days I was seven, spindly legged, spotty, anaemic and painfully shy with strangers and 'betters'. I was particularly nervous in the company of women; they'd run their households to suit themselves during the war and many saw their returning husband/heroes at worst as intruders, at best as a nuisance, having enjoyed a taste of independence and a spell of wage-earning. I am no male chauvinist but some of these women were fearsome creatures, afraid of nothing and no one. I don't know why but I judged women in those days by the size of their noses, a trait I haven't entirely lost; those with long noses and flared nostrils have always been bad news. Perhaps subconsciously, I compared them with horses which when excited or aggressive, flare their nostrils. Short noses were preferable, less menacing. Again, perhaps the comics I read reinforced my prejudices; the short-nosed characters were usually kind and gentle, the long-nosed ones were aggressive, bossy, stuck-up or just plain nosey.

Noses may have brought me to realise that not all was well between my mother and father - she had a short nose, he a long one, with flared nostrils. At any rate, my mother seemed to grow more and more agitated when his letters arrived from Germany. At last, she broke the news to Norman and myself, Ken being too young to understand. My father was insisting - demanding - that we move to married quarters in Germany. She said she would refuse to go because Dunbar was our home and we needed proper schooling; she also told us that married quarters were nothing like our own home.

> 'Just you go to the barracks and look at the scruffy places where these poor lassies live. Washing on the line and never a hint of sun to whiten them. Their washing's grey. My boys deserve better than that.'

She was right in many respects; married quarters in those days were nothing like they are today. From the *Pathe News* broadcasts at the cinema, we knew that in Germany, soldiers' wives and families lived in prefabricated houses with corrugated roofs or *Nissen* huts separated by muddy paths. Besides, they had no gardens. No way would she live in such conditions, which she rightly considered were primitive.

I was out of my depth and worried. Before the Break came, life was comfortable. In retrospect, I believe I had a happy childhood despite the privations of the war and my father's subsequent abandoning of us. There was a stigma however. The conventions of Scottish society were still fairly inflexible; a household without a man was unnatural, although allowances were made for women who'd lost their husbands in the war. People wondered whether a woman could bring up a family alone without resorting to petty crime - or worse - if there was no work to be had. The answer was yes in my mother's case, for she worked at anything and everything in her day.

I seem to have adjusted fairly quickly to my father's desertion; after all, I hardly knew him and his visits home had amounted to something like less than six weeks in my seven years. For me, the worst pain was caused by the Break itself rather than the consequences of it. The first cracks in my parents' relationship weren't obvious; I'm also unconvinced that my father ever completely fell out of love with my mother although he acted as though he did. He sent very bitter, nasty and threatening letters home, probably out of frustration or exasperation. In those days, women were expected to obey their husbands; perhaps this was more so in England than in Scotland, although many Scottish women were equally conventional in this respect. There were a few free spirits in Dunbar who boasted they'd never see a man in their road; that breed existed then and exists even more so today.

I think the real reason my mother refused to go to Germany was that she was terrified of being uprooted from her familiar surroundings - she loved Dunbar until the day she died - and separated from her friends. I am sure she felt the council house in Lammermuir Crescent was her own - which it was, as my father's name wasn't on the rent book - and that if she left it, she'd never get it back. I also think she felt that if she left Dunbar, she'd become more vulnerable and dependent on a man whom she, in fairness, hardly knew. All her life, she told people in Dunbar that she'd spent only six weeks with my father in eight years; for once, she wasn't exaggerating. She was afraid that he would curtail her freedom. Also, she feared the family would become wanderers since after the war, many British dependencies were seeking independence and the army was invariably sent to trouble spots to keep the peace by force of arms when diplomacy failed. I think she saw us being constantly on the move like gypsies, rootless and with nowhere decent to call our own.

I can pinpoint almost precisely when the Break came - not because I have a retentive memory but because to this day, I possess a letter from my father to my mother dated 8th February 1947. In it, he professes his love for her. It is a typical soldier's letter, replete with slightly purple passages repeated throughout. There is no hint of impending crisis but reading between the lines, it was the last act of a desperate man. By the summer of 1947, my parents had effectively separated.

The bitter letters they exchanged in the following six months no longer exist; I know that, for I watched my mother throw my father's letters on the fire so many times. Finally, he wrote to say that he'd not be coming back to Dunbar and that we would have to shift for ourselves. My father denied her all of his voluntary allotment of pay, leaving only the compulsory minimum the army deducted from soldiers to support their wives and children. When my mother learned of the news from the War Office, she sat before the fire. I recall her weeping bitterly. She was informed that she would have to make do with £4:12:6 [£4.62] a week to support herself and two of her three children.

In the same letter my father wrote warning of her reduced income, he asked my mother for a divorce as he'd met a German woman whom he loved and who was carrying his child. That was the last straw.

'Imagine him going with a dirty FRAWLEEN! After what the Germans
did to our men. I'll never, never take him back, not even if he comes
down the garden path on his bloody knees.'

(When I took German at school in 1957, I learnt that a FRAWLEEN wasn't a prostitute which was what my mother implied in her bitterness; *fraulein* is German for Miss, a young unmarried woman).

My mother adamantly refused to give Dad a divorce. It wasn't so easy to get a divorce in those days and my mother was terrified at the prospect of losing even what little money she was receiving from my father. So she remained married and lived at 75 Lammermuir Crescent, her home for the past fifteen years. It was to be more than ten years before I saw my father again. When he returned in 1958, he was a stranger and I think he knew he would never really belong there again - if he ever had. In the intervening years, most of our immediate neighbours were sympathetic - the Harkess family next door, old Gramma Herkes or Craw two doors down, Alice Gillon, Mrs McPherson and Annie Lough. Annie was particularly supportive. She lived on the corner opposite our house, never used her front door as it faced the front and you had to go to it via the back door and front garden. Annie shouted a lot, smoked like a chimney so her voice sounded like gravel or coke being thrown down a tin chute. Annie had a heart of gold. She never married and brought up three sons and a daughter on her own as well as looking after her elderly father. There are many stories told of her. My favourite is about the time she gave bureaucracy a bloody nose. A Social Security officer visiting to assess her claim for benefit was confused by the fact that there was no path to her front door from the street. Then he spotted Annie, puffing away as usual, on this occasion, in her front garden.

'Hello there, Mrs Lough! How do I get in?'
Back came the proudly defiant reply.

'Ye get in by the tradesman's entrance, son. And it's MISS Lough.'
She had us in stitches. Nothing and no one could intimidate our Annie. She was a proud and independent lady. When she died, Dunbar lost one of her most colourful and lovable characters and her family mourned her premature death deeply. I wasn't able to attend the funeral but I wrote to her son Sandy; I wanted him to know that our family had loved her too.

After the first few months of living on a good deal less than she'd been accustomed to, my mother's face became strained and lined. She grew more crotchety every day and started clobbering us more than usually when we got on her nerves. Again, she threatened to put Ken and I in a Home.

'Aye. A Home. But it won't be like this one. There'll not be anybody to tuck you in at night.'
Sometimes I attempted to comfort her. I'd put my arms round her waist and depending on the state of her mind, she'd either tousle my hair or push me away. When she was troubled, she would tell me to stop hugging her.

'Och, will you leave me be? You're making my corsets dig into me. Away and play.'
One day, I asked her for money for sweets. Without answering, she got her purse and opened it for me to see the contents. All it contained was a couple of shillings [10p].

'That's all I've got till Allotment Day. There's nae money for meat let alone sweeties.'
Allotment Day was that magical day when a postal order arrived from the Paymaster General's Office in England. It was cashed at once, the money being put into small piles to pay the rent, the gas, the food, the insurance and the hire purchase payments to Edinburgh firms from which my mother bought furniture, the only way she could.

However, despite our parlous state, we were in the same boat as other children who had to do without a father for one reason or another. We were resilient and proud that we were surviving without a father, no matter how precariously. It was loss of money rather than loss of a man about the house that affected us most. Norman dutifully handed over his pittance from his laundry job each Friday and received a few shillings as pocket money. My mother took a job. Or to be precise, jobs. In summer, she worked in boarding houses, making beds, cleaning rooms, preparing vegetables for lunch, coming home at three pm for her own lunch, then returning for the evening meals she had to serve up. In spring, she worked in the fields weeding and thinning young carrots, beetroot and turnips; in autumn, she went to the *tattie howkin'* [potato lifting], lifting and docking turnips, pulling leeks and cabbages. Then it would be quiet in winter, when she might take a job in a shop for a few weeks up to Christmas. January and February were always poor months - poor in the sense of no earnings.

I desperately wanted to contribute my bit but the employment of children laws forbade young people from taking employment until they were aged thirteen. The laws were a great victory for the liberal-minded Victorians who deprecated sweated child and female labour but I could have cheerfully taken up light work such as delivering milk or newspapers before I was thirteen. My chance came after the passage of time.

I became more withdrawn and lonely when away from home, even for a few hours each day at school. I felt awkward in the company of boys my own age. They seemed to be able to do as they pleased, whereas I had household chores to do - raking and removing the ashes from the fireplace, chopping kindling whether we needed it or not. Also, many of the lads had bicycles and went on cycle runs. It would be another eight years before I acquired a nearly new second-hand bike - a *Rudge Raleigh* - when my Uncle Jimmy had a modest win on the football pools. He won just over £300 in 1956, quite a tidy sum. He later lamented that he'd put a farthing instead of a halfpenny on his coupon.

'I'd have won £700 if I'd put on my usual stake.'
No matter, he shared it with us. That was the calibre of the man.

I never learned how to ride a bike. My first attempt was on a neighbour's son's tricycle, then Norman decided I should try a two-wheeler at the age of seven. I lasted all of five minutes on it. After a few short, trial runs in Lammermuir Crescent, with Norman clinging onto the saddle and steadying me, he said I should try a long run from our house to Summerfield Road. As we neared the corner, he let me go but pretended he was still holding on to me. I managed to turn the corner, where there was a small decline. Wobbling along, I stared in horror at a car coming straight towards me. Oblivious to Norman shouting at me to turn left and use the brakes, I was petrified and confused. Try to do two things at once? My co-ordination then left much to be desired. I was terrified. I shot into the hedge of No 77 Summerfield Road, ending up in a tangle. I got up, dazed and frightened, kicked the bike and stormed off in high dudgeon. I never sat on a bike again until I was thirteen, when I discovered that I'd found the balance I'd so miserably lacked six years earlier.

As already mentioned in Chapter 1, the best of our neighbours were the Harkess family next door. They continued to be my extended family - Aunt Ann, Uncle John and Uncle Tommy and of course old Gramma Marion or Mairn. In those days, they had a shorthaired black and white mongrel called

# Altered States

Bonzo who was my greatest pal. He was a little ragamuffin dog with a fantastic personality. He used to watch at the window for me coming home from school at lunchtime and in the afternoon. Auntie Ann would hear his bark and let him out. He bounded crazily towards me, his front legs splayed, his silky black ears flying in the wind. He jumped up, licking my face and hands until I could stand it no more, then I'd order him to walk beside me. He couldn't stop his joyful jumping at my side. He was the classic clowning mongrel with black patches all over his otherwise white body. He had a black eye and two black ears. He was so full of energy and Auntie Ann said he was more my dog than hers.

On Saturdays and Sundays, Ken and I took Bonzo for long walks; sometimes along the golf course, he'd chase a rabbit and once got stuck down a hole that gave us both no end of anxiety. He was mad about *Rowntree's* fruit gums and once gnawed a hole in the pocket of my only Sunday (short-trousered) suit jacket pocket to get at my tube of gums. One day, he ate something poisonous - I think it might have been a rabbit that had died of myxomatosis in the Sailors' Park field behind our house. He sickened for three days. I hoped that he'd come bounding towards me again on each of these days. Then Ann met me coming home from school one dinnertime. All she said was this:

'Sorry, laddie. Bonzo's gone.'

She was heartbroken too but wouldn't show it for fear of setting me off. I didn't need any prompting. I bawled my head off for several nights, when I was alone. I never wanted a dog of my own after that. The sense of loss was too much to bear.

In my loneliness, I found consolation in my comics and my collection of lead soldiers. I used to fight pitched battles on the hearthrug before the fire during the autumn and winter months. In these battles, I provided the dialogue for every single soldier, varying my voice in what was inevitably a restricted repertoire. Perhaps that's how I acquired my love of impersonation. I still fall easily and naturally into the habit of attempts at imitating other people. When I think back to that time, my 'battles' were, for a shy and mild-mannered kid, fairly ferocious affairs. My battles were massacres, with only one man left standing - usually my favourite soldier. Young Ken sometimes got in the way and destroyed the emotional finale when I delivered a monologue about the futility and stupidity of war. Yet I loved it all. Ken would often ask me embarrassing questions when he surveyed the devastated battleground of dead men. For example, he would ask why I 'saved' one particular soldier.

'Because he was the bravest and the best. He fought better because he was alone.'

Telling words. I imagined I was that little soldier. Alone. I believed then as I do now that the brave are often lonely.

It is true that every child has dark recesses in his or her mind no matter how well they manage to conceal them; and there is an inherent craving to confide in another about these shadows that remain, hopefully under control. Adults are no use as confidants. I knew from an early age that between adult and child is an immeasurable distance, no matter how much they love one another. Adults have different perceptions of life than children who harbour feelings based on misunderstanding or misrepresentation; children have - or should have - a rich imagination, but they invariably see things in a different light from that of their elders. That is what makes them children. I think some adults of today are better at empathy than those of my generation; the same applies to some children. And today's children are better able to express themselves, although I don't believe they are necessarily kinder; often, their self-expression is hedonistic and selfish, narrow and self-seeking. I also feel that today's crop of little darlings have less perception in an imaginative sense; they also lost their innocence two or three generations ago. I blame their parents for pandering to their whims which are almost exclusively materialistic. But such is the nature of progress.

The worst unhappiness of all is caused by a feeling of rejection that often masquerades as something else. More than Norman or myself, my brother Ken desperately wanted a father to look up to; however, he found a surrogate in Uncle Jimmy, whom he loved as if he was his male parent. And he hated it when my mother began a relationship with a local man several years younger than herself in the 1950s, by which time communication between her and my father had been over for about seven years. (Was the timescale significant? In those days - and perhaps even today - after seven years of silence, a spouse was legally entitled to regard a marriage partner as deceased).

Even in my so tender years, I felt my mother was entitled to have a life of her own. In 1954, she had just turned forty, she was still young, still attractive; she worked hard and needed companionship and love. Adam gave her both, even if on his own terms. He was a signalman, lived with his parents in Summerfield Road - he had a domineering mother, of whom he was inordinately afraid - and he liked his drink. At first, the relationship was purely platonic; they would meet on a Saturday night, go to the cinema and maybe have a drink afterwards. My mother hated drink then, but Adam persuaded her to have what she called ' a wee refreshment.' After ballroom dancing - which Adam was inept at - her love was the cinema. I think she could lose herself in a romantic film the way I lost myself in literature.

However, Ante Adam (I used to call that period AA), there were two 'uncles' who visited our house. One visited monthly, the other annually, sometimes biannually. The first was Tommy, who had visited my grandmother's house in Castle Place and lodged with her, which is how he met my mother. Tommy was a painter and decorator who after he went to live permanently in Edinburgh would arrive on a Saturday afternoon and offer to 'slosh your ceiling, Ma.' He called Granny Cockburn Ma because he felt close to her. He had a soft spot for my mother but she thought he was too silly, although they were dancing partners. Eventually he gave up on her and married someone else. But he couldn't stay away from Dunbar and visited us regularly, bringing his wife Eva and son Stuart in his van. He decorated our house in Lammermuir Crescent many times; it was his excuse for coming to visit. I think he had always loved my mother but when she turned him down, he hid his disappointment by clowning, which endeared him to my brothers and myself. Uncle Tommy was FUN.

Tommy rose in the world. He hated the painting business and joined the Slateford-based firm of *Waddie*, a printing firm which specialised in labels advertising various commodities. These labels were fine art work. I began collecting them - well, Tommy got me interested and would bring stocks of them in his black *Waddie* van on summer Saturday afternoons. Sometimes he came with his wife Eva and son Stewart but most times he came alone. Maybe he and my mother had cuddling sessions for when he came alone, he used to let me into the driving seat of his large van, where I sat for hours making driving noises and turning the steering wheel.

The labels he gave me were works of art. My favourite was a Red Indian chief in full headdress, crawling on all fours with tomahawk and advertising *Pioneer Matches*. (Why a Red Indian? Why not some buckskinned scout like Kit Carson who'd more need of Pioneer matches than a redskin who could make fire by rubbing sticks together?) Tommy had countless labels and I dutifully pasted them into the big book he brought me. Other kids collected what were called 'scraps' - effeminate pictures of angels and fairies and flowers. I felt superior with my adult 'scraps'; later, I would add to my collection with cigarette cards I got from Adam. My interest in label-collecting was dealt a death blow after the Race Relations Act 1967 was passed; it outlawed the little golliwog on the *Robertson's* jam labels, which in my view was a piece of politically correct nonsense. Racial prejudice of a different bias had arrived.

Before Tommy and Adam came George 'Sonny' McCall. Sonny had wanted to marry my mother in 1936 but his mother objected to his marrying what she called 'a commoner'. Sonny's father John managed George Boyd's stables at West Barns. Sonny's grandfather was a champion jockey who rode for famous horse-owners like the Rothschilds; he won the Lincolnshire Handicap against all the odds in 1902. It was agreed that golden-haired Sonny, the apple of his mother's eye, would join the Royal Navy. His snooty mother forbade him to come home until he had become a junior officer and had discarded the ridiculous 'bell-bottom' trousers of the ordinary rating. Only a peaked cap with scrambled egg on the front and gold rings on his sleeves would do; anything else was *de rigueur* to his mother. When he qualified and was able to come back to West Barns, he started courting my mother. In 1937, when he announced to his mother that he wanted to become engaged to mine, she hit the roof. His mother, that is. Mrs McCall visited Lammermuir Crescent unbeknownst to her son; she told my mother that she would regret marrying Sonny as he was an atrocious flirt, a philanderer who would quickly tire of her. The truth was that my mother wasn't considered 'good enough' for Mrs McCall's golden son. He thought differently. He even went as far as to buy an engagement ring. My mother handed it back, telling him she would never be good enough for him in his mother's eyes, a fact my grandmother reinforced or perhaps prompted my mother to say. He gave her the ring and said he'd never take it back. He never married.

Sonny was a fanatical rugby fan and whenever England played Scotland at Murrayfield, he came to stay with us that weekend. He always brought me a box of lead soldiers, so I looked forward to his biennial visits. When I think of him, I am reminded of Alan Ladd, the actor. Sonny had the same lovely hair and sleepy eyelids. I still possess some of his lead soldiers although most have lost their heads. Sonny was my golden uncle. One or two of my mother's sisters said he was my father, as I had a head of golden hair for the first two years of my life. I have seen a photograph of my biological father and we could have been twins. The years and the ale took their inevitable toll of Sonny's face and lithe figure; the last time he came to Dunbar, he was bald. His visits stopped in the late 1950's so I assume he died at some point then. I liked him immensely, for he treated me more as a young adult and he told me fascinating stories about the Second World War. I have so many fond memories of him, a very handsome, lovable man.

In those days, children were 'seen and not heard' and were expected not to be a 'notice box' - my mother's phrase for those who were inclined to 'show off'. Sonny was great because he always included me in his conversations. When he got me 'over-excited', my mother would tell me I was being 'facey like the English'. Sonny always encouraged me to express myself and I liked him for that as well as his welcome gifts of toy soldiers. My mother should have married him.

So now I go back to Tommy who lived well into the 1970s. After a spell labouring in the sweatshop of *Waddie's*, he got a prestige job as the company director's chauffeur. He had arrived. He was proud of his position but in his typically self-effacing way, he shrugged his shoulders when we congratulated him on his promotion. Like the chauffeurs I'd seen in Laurel and Hardy films, he looked natty, cool, his natural good looks; his well manicured moustache was set off by his breeches and gauntlet gloves, his peaked cap and polished patent knee-length boots. The greatest moment came one brilliant Saturday afternoon in summer, when he drew up in his employer's *Rolls Royce Silver Ghost,* stepped outside and saluted us children at the front room window. He made a formal bow to my excited mother and asked her whether 'madam and the children would care for a spin'. He drove us into Dunbar High Street where we waved like royalty - I am ashamed to say it - to anyone we knew and saw there that hot August afternoon.

Tommy McDougall was fine in small doses. He was a buffoon who never knew when to stop; what is worse, he committed the unpardonable sin of laughing at his own jokes. He never grew up. In common with many men who are naturally ebullient and fun loving, his wife Eva was a staid woman, forever criticising her juvenile husband; my mother said she'd sucked lemons all her days. Eva came to our house occasionally just to make sure Tommy didn't 'forget himself' when he visited us. Of that, there was never any danger. My mother thought of him as an amiable fool, a jester. At least when his wife and his boring son Stewart came with him, he was manageable. On his own, he was incorrigible, especially when he was painting this room or that in our house. One of his favourite ditties was the then popular ballad 'I didn't know/ the gun was loaded/and I'll never, never do it again.' He blew raspberries like Harry Secombe, farted and made clicking noises with his tongue. A typically meaningless aphorism was 'If cabbages is cabbages, let rhubarb stick up for itself.' It fell far short of the *Goon Show* I was later to adulate. I gradually grew embarrassed in his company; he died in the mid-seventies though he lived long enough to visit my first wife Julie in our Balerno flat. She was very ill at the time. (After my mother and he and his wife left, Julie thanked me for arranging a comedian to welcome her home from hospital....)

If there is an after-life, Tommy McDougall will be present, laughing, clowning, blowing his famous raspberries; during his time on earth, he relieved the monotony of many a wet Saturday afternoon.

The years from 1948 to 1958 were lean years, especially between 1951 and 1954, when Norman went off to do his National Service in the RAF, serving an extra year voluntarily. He managed to send home a few shillings a week however. Ken was growing fast, his appetite almost matching mine. My mother struggled to make ends meet by taking on jobs in boarding houses in summer and *tattie howkin'* in autumn. The law prevented me from taking a job until 1954, when I managed to secure a paper round shortly after reaching age thirteen, the statutory age for young wage earners. My paper round was the largest in Dunbar then; it paid thirteen shillings (65p) a week. During the years 1948 and 1958, I never missed my father except on rare occasions like school prize-givings. As I didn't win many glittering prizes, the loss was never acute. And I didn't relish his birthday present when I reached age fifteen; he sent my mother an application form for me to join the Boys' Service in the Royal Navy. In his letter, he told my mother it was the best thing I could do; he said he didn't want his son working in a shop or other mediocre employment in Dunbar. My mother told me this, then I watched her throw the papers in the fire.

I have to confess I wasn't unduly worried about being fatherless. For me, Dunbar was a paradise and you could keep Germany or anywhere else for that matter. My father was welcome to his foreign home. We had so many places to play, so many to explore. We mounted sieges in the old castle at the harbour; I was always on the besieging side because everybody knew I was half-English, so it wasn't right that I should defend a Scottish castle. I didn't mind. More often than not, my side gave a good account of itself. One day, one of the defenders hit on the brilliant idea of barricading the fore work with a wall of fish boxes until the fisherman appeared to reclaim them, kicking English and Scottish backsides without discrimination. He was anxious to catch the tide and we watched his little boat chugging out of the harbour. As he passed below us on the quayside, he shook his fist.

'An' Ah'll kick the erses o' ye and yir pals if Ah catch ye muckin' aboot' wi' ma boxes iver again.'

We only needed one telling but we answered his threat with raspberries and catcalls from the safety of the quay!

One part of the castle unofficially off-limits to children and adults alike was the old Blockhouse or *Gunholes*, as it's known locally. Towering above the sea to the west of the castle, it was difficult to access and dangerous to climb for strategic reasons. The Blockhouse used to house the heavy ordnance and had to be impregnable, since an enemy storming it would have turned its guns on the castle. But people - mainly young men - went up there to play games of *Crown and Anchor* or whist, betting money on the dice and the cards which was illegal in the 1950s. The gamblers always employed a lookout for the police, paying the boy - notably, Bobby Cameron, a good friend of mine today - a few pennies for his trouble. I was never a lookout for the pure and simple reason that my knees buckled at the thought of attempting that scary walk, inching along a narrow path to the inside, looking down at a dizzying drop of thirty or forty feet into the sea.

Considering my still innate fear of heights, I am still surprised by and have nightmares about the only time I ever negotiated that deathly height in 1960. It was a summer Sunday and I was challenged to climb the rock. In dogtooth check sports jacket and immaculately creased flannels, wearing a white shirt and a *Munrospun* tie, I went up there. I inched my way round the narrow path - it was all of six inches wide - to finally fall gratefully into the broad compound of the *Gunholes*. I walked around, noting the embrasures, the gun-ports and the quarters of the medieval gunners. I was fascinated. But then I realised that somehow, I would have to get back to *terra firma*. There was no way I would go back the route I'd come. In those days, the remains of the covered walkway were such that I could walk down the steps to reach the end of what was in effect a tunnel; the height from the walkway to the beach was about ten feet, so I could *dreep* [hang down] from the mouth of the tunnel, which I did. I still have shivers today thinking about that awful climb. Wild horses or the promise of vast sums of money wouldn't entice me to repeat the performance today.

Another favourite haunt was the West Promenade, gifted to the burgh of Dunbar in 1893 by one of the Hays of Belton. The Baird Esplanade follows the line from the *Men's Old Bathe* to the first green of Winterfield Golf Course. Despite the fact that the Prom, as it has always been called, skirted steep and dangerous cliffs, nobody - not even a drunk - has ever fallen over it. At the other end of the town, near the East Links golf course, there was another though less well-frequented promenade known as the East Prom. It was the scene of a sadly successful suicide pact between two lovers in the 1940s. The woman was pregnant and her lover wasn't free to marry her. The man shot his lady, then himself. As boys, we walked past the alleged spot, some swearing they could see the bullet holes in the golf course boundary wall. I never believed them. I was just so sad that two young people were driven to destroy themselves. Even today, I feel depressed when I walk there. I think of who of they were, what they might have become

But perhaps the most loved of all the places of my heart was - and still is - Belhaven Bay, with its long, flat beaches and mysterious nooks and crannies, its little islands of trees and its sand-dunes. I still love to walk there, examining the flotsam and jetsam, the driftwood cast up by the sea; in those days, many a poor man or woman used the driftwood for fuel, although my mother swore that it 'sparked' so she refused to burn it. Today, the driftwood fuels barbecues and bonfires on the beach. Belhaven was Dunbar's medieval harbour, then it became an armed camp to resist Napoleon's legions, then Hitler's Storm Troopers. There is still a haunting, haunted air about the place. It was reputed to have quicksand near the basin of the river Tyne; there is an apocryphal tale about a horse-artillery team disappearing, gun, horses and men one afternoon before the Great War but I have been unable to substantiate the story. That quicksand existed isn't in doubt because I once watched my brother Norman sink up to his armpits one Saturday afternoon at Seafield Bridge. He had to be hauled out by our friends, the Fawcett brothers – more of them later - who sensibly knotted their shirts together to drag him free. The boys had been diving into what was then known as *The Fluke Dub* (fluke was our word for the flounders or flatfish that abounded there), a deep depression under the bridge; the Dub no longer exists, having silted up over the intervening years.

We spent many a summer afternoon at Belhaven during the school holidays. The view is breathtaking, especially of the Bass Rock, which I used to think resembled a giant snail in the Firth of Forth. For years, I couldn't understand why Frank Bonar, my second year English teacher described it as the 'lion of the Forth' until I visited North Berwick and saw it from a different perspective. It does resemble a sleeping lion from that shore. This taught me a valuable lesson - that life offers different perspectives depending on where you are or the view you have.

Whether we like it or not, we can't ignore the fact that to a great extent, we are what we are because of our parents' influence. My parents ensured I would grow up to have a divided nature. From my English father, I inherited a desire for learning, book-reading, the need to talk 'proper' English which set me apart from the ragamuffin kids with whom he didn't like me to mix. My mother stood for tradition - the Scottish version - the Protestant work ethic that deemed that a man wasn't a man until he took up remunerated employment. In Dunbar, that usually meant using your hands rather than your head. You either learnt a trade or went to work in the farms. I was fitted for neither. I was useless with tools other than gardening implements - I still am to this day. As for farm work, it was idyllic in summer but miserable in winter and the pay was poor. I know that money can't buy happiness but I wanted more than what many in Dunbar settled for in their lives. I wasn't ambitious but I didn't want to earn my daily bread as a serf. Few children nowadays grow up to make their living in the town where they were born; those like my mother who did were either proud of it or despised it. Those who stayed put are sometimes envious of those who left and made their living elsewhere and consider themselves 'better'. I don't consider myself 'better'; ironically, I became a city-dweller and made more money there than I would ever have made in Dunbar but I've always had a secret yearning for a simple, rural life.

Sometimes, when I was writing this book in a small flat in the outskirts of Edinburgh, I imagined I could hear the sound of the sea. It was only the muted noise of traffic but I dreamed myself back in Dunbar - or more precisely, Belhaven. Living close to the sea for so many years, important years, I never lost my love of it. I never forgot the clear, leaping brilliance of the waves, the changing moods, the eternal cleaving of water and the invasions of the shore. I wanted to swim early in life, unlike my mother who loved it but didn't want to get too close to it; when she walked by the harbour, she would grow giddy and had to walk away from it because she said it 'was drawing me in'.

Water is of course fascinating to the young. While I never had any inclination to go out in a boat, I preferred swimming in the sea to the local swimming pool. In those days, there was no pollution in the sea and ironically, the swimming pool was the cause of many ear, nose and mouth infections, probably because it wasn't cleaned properly or regularly. One winter, I decided I would learn to swim by the following summer although I couldn't afford the swimming lessons that cost sixpence [2.5p]at the time. There was no way the restricted and strained family income could stretch to that luxury. So I began to study frogs. Frogs are great little swimmers and in next to no time, I found I could imitate their leg movements. The only problem was, how to co-ordinate the arm movements? Frogs seemed to get by without their short front limbs. I studied them for weeks and finally had to admit defeat. Then I hit on the solution; I would watch the trainee swimmers in the swimming pool without joining them and having to pay the required sixpence per lesson. (It was sixpence to get into the swimming pool and I couldn't afford another sixpence for the lesson!)

I kept my distance, affecting bored indifference while taking it all in. I listened to the pond master's instructions – he was a lovely hirsute man of golden hair, a man called Eric Bradbury, whose daughter Rosemary sometimes comes back to Dunbar from her home in South Africa, a lady I love unreservedly and look forward to her occasional visits to Dunbar. After listening to Mr Bradbury's clear and clipped instructions, I went along the beach, where I chose a flattish rock in the sea to test my co-ordination. To my surprise, I found I could synchronise both ends with disgusting ease, without panicking. Not only had I learnt the art of staying afloat, little by little, I mastered the way to propel myself along; by the end of that summer I could do the breaststroke and felt confident enough to attempt the crawl, although bad weather prevented further experiments. The crawl had to wait until the following summer.

Even if I wasn't a fast swimmer, at least I was better than Norman. He was an excellent diver and thought nothing of plunging into the diving hole from the top diving board; the only problem was that he couldn't swim a stroke and had to be pulled out the water by a friend every time he dived! To plunge into the deepest part of the swimming pool and trust in natural buoyancy was, in my opinion, the height of foolhardiness. But eventually, he too could swim and his diving skills attracted the praise of Peter Heatley, the international diving champion from Musselburgh.

Looking back over the years, I admit I occasionally felt the lack of a father at times. Mine was never one to join in his children's' games. We welcomed his being there one Easter Sunday before the Break occurred; he came with us on our Easter picnic to Oswald Dean, or *Osie Dean* as we knew it. There was a large herd of cows in the picnic area that year; having your Dad around gave you a feeling of security when the animals grew curious and strolled near.

In a later chapter, I discuss the red-letter days of the year, including the Easter picnic. Spring had few red-letter days but one day - or to be precise, one week - we never looked forward to was Spring Cleaning Week. All that miserable, chaotic week, the house was literally turned upside down; furniture was moved, carpets were put out on the washing line to have the winter's dust beaten out of them, blankets and curtains bubbled away in the large copper boiler in the scullery, then they were rinsed in the deep sink, mangled and hung outside. When they were dry, my mother brought them indoors and *beetled* or pounded them with a wooden instrument not unlike an Indian club. (I wonder if my mother's wooden beetle - for I imagined it was spelt that way- was in fact manufactured by *Beetall*, a London-based ironmonger that specialised in laundry aids, including the eponymous Gas Laundry Iron? Perhaps the wooden club was known as a *beetall* – should that be 'beat-all'?*). Every night, hot irons were placed on the stove - no electrical versions in those days - and my mother cursed under her breath while she was 'dashing away with the smoothing iron', a song I used to sing to her until she fetched me a clip round the ear for (as she thought) making fun of her.

All that week, our meals were 'patch-ups' as my mother called the hastily prepared food which she and countless others threw together during the madness that was Spring Cleaning Week. Thankfully, by Saturday, things were almost back to normal; we were chased off to the matinee in the *Playhouse* while my mother completed the finishing touches, then struggled out in the afternoon to buy groceries. On Saturday night, my Uncle Jimmy came home from his job with *Wimpey's* in Grangemouth, then Gilmerton, Edinburgh. Jimmy believed in travelling light, with a brown paper parcel tucked under his arm containing his week's laundry, his other possessions carried in a small wooden suitcase. He would have a quick meal, wash and brush up and then off he'd go to his favourite pub, the *Black Bull* in the High Street. We liked his weekly visits for when he came home a wee bit the worse for wear, he always brought Ken and I a packet of crisps each, a rare treat in those days. Sometimes, he'd bring home a fish supper and extra chips for us and we had a feast before the fire for he didn't have much of an appetite, even after several whiskies.

On Sunday we were allowed a lie-in, reading the *Fun Section* in the *Sunday Post*, enjoying the antics of *Oor Wullie* and the *Broons, Nero and Zero*, the comical Roman duo and other characters in the comic strip. Then it was off to Sunday school in our best clothes and with an order not to come home until teatime. If the weather was fair, Sunday was often her washday, despite her having been brought up to believe that the Sabbath or Lord's Day was a day of rest. She argued that there was 'no rest for the wicked' which to a certain extent salved her conscience. To her critics, she used to say - if it was fair ( ie not raining) - 'The Lord'll no' mind me doin' the washing. That's why He's sent me good weather.' It was probably the only day she didn't dust or sweep or cook much, the only day in the week when she could 'catch up'. Maybe she just wanted the house to herself, so we were packed off to the Sunday school, then walked in the hills or along the beach until it was safe to go home. The Sunday evening meal was a bit of hit-or-miss or 'patch-up' since my mother spent the entire day at the washing tub and ironing. Proper Sunday dinners didn't come until the introduction of washing machines and fridges in the late 1950s. Until then, washing was a major, labour-intensive chore and fresh food had to be bought every day, stored in the stone-built scullery pantry with its small window to let in air and keep milk and other commodities fresh. Housewives were therefore forced to shop nearly every day except Sundays, as shops were closed on the Sabbath. The scullery pantry was a veritable cornucopia, with shelves designated for various foodstuffs, the perishables stacked on the shelf next to the wire-mesh covered window. The stone floor was used for storing vegetables like potatoes and cabbages. I recall that pantry with pleasure, for we could walk into it and steal the odd morsel, raid the condensed milk tin or spoon out mouthfuls of *National Dried Milk* powder which reduced our craving for strictly rationed sweets. Sometime in 1956, my mother bought a small fridge, a little box-like affair with no freezer; the following weekend, my Uncle George demolished the larder or pantry so that we could fit a small table in the scullery and eat in there. Life was gradually improving in the grey, post-war years.

# Altered States

We always had clean, ironed grey shirts, that colour being worn by nearly every boy at that time, probably because they didn't show the dirt as easily as white. In any case, white shirts were for the men, when they went out for their Saturday night pint or to church on Sundays. Only people of substance wore white shirts through the week - bank staff, insurance agents, railway clerks, the police and other like folk.

Like most women of her generation, my mother spent a fair proportion of her week shopping and cooking in the scullery. When she wasn't washing, she was baking scones, rock buns, biscuits, making soup and preparing vegetables for the evening meal. I have this everlasting image of her up to her elbows in soap suds on Sundays, flour on weekdays; I used to watch her check the gas oven for her baking and cooking, lifting pot lids to stir whatever happened to be simmering away - usually soups, mince and stews, including, in those meat-rationed days, rabbit, the poor man's chicken.

Despite our altered state, my mother 'kept up appearances' like Mrs Bucket in the popular TV comedy series. She considered herself a cut above the average woman of her age. She spoke mostly to the older women in the street, possibly because she missed her mother and respected their views on all things domestic. Often, small knots of women her own age would congregate at somebody's garden gate or round a delivery van to gossip; my mother rarely ever joined these groups, which she called 'scandal-mongers'. She used to say they were *clashing* - meaning they were gossiping about some poor woman, probably herself, as she was without 'her man'. Worst of all, they smoked in the street - a terrible stain on a woman's character - and fingers - in those far-off days. She thought them sluttish, especially when they wore their nylons rolled down to their ankles, showing what she called their 'fireside tartan' or 'corned beef legs' - her words for the mottled patterns they got from sitting bare-legged in front of the fire. *Fireside tartan* was the mark of a slothful, lazy housewife who spent much of her time smoking and reading cheap magazines. As my mother rarely ever joined these groups of bored housewives, she was considered *stuck-up* and too good for the likes of them. In many respects, they were right. For most of her life between 1933 and 1958 - a quarter of a century - her priorities were her home and her children. The street philosophers with their fag-end logic were deliberately, studiously avoided. She would refuse invitations to join these street slander-ins by saying she'd 'something on the stove'. She was always smartly dressed, never wore the ubiquitous turban or headscarf of the Dunbar housewife, never ventured over her front door without makeup and stockings secured as they were meant to be. She was often accused of being *dolled-up* and on the lookout for a man, when all she wanted was to be smart. It's no bad thing to take care with appearance and until her death in 2002, in her late eighties, she could still take the shine off many a younger woman.

My mother never learnt any trade or occupation. In her early years, she tried working as a dentist's receptionist-cum-assistant. She didn't last long as she couldn't stand the sight of blood or the moans of pained patients. Then she tried working at *Yorke House*, as the former East Links Cottage Hospital was known. Her aversion to the blood and pain she saw there was even more acute, so she didn't work for long in the place. Her next and most pleasurable job was with a Mrs Shearlaw who ran a boarding house (guest-house in those genteel 1930s years) in Marine Road. She and my Aunt Maggie were employed as maids. In those days, guests were treated like royalty, provided with a 'silver' service - the cutlery was genuine silver, or at least electro-plated nickel silver. The waitresses or maids wore black dresses, stockings and little white lace caps like tiaras. These were Dunbar's *Belle Epoque* days, when the town was the favourite holiday resort of the middling sort, people who considered themselves a cut above the *hoi-polloi* who went to 'common' places like Blackpool and Scarborough, with their rock emporiums, kiss-me-quick hats and cod-and-chip suppers.

In winter, my mother took work in the small kiosk at the *Playhouse Cinema*, where she sold confectionary, popcorn and cigarettes until the start of the last evening performance at about 8.30pm. Her friend Maisie Watt worked in the cash desk. It was in the kiosk that she met my father in 1938, when he was stationed at Castle Park barracks. He started dating her at Christmas 1938; he asked her to marry him and she said she would marry him on her birthday on 31st March 1939 if he were still in Dunbar then. (Perhaps she remembered her first aborted marriage to Norman Hall in 1933). At any rate, they married; the cinema staff presented them with a fine clock that kept good time until she died in 2002, when it stopped ticking. Symbolic? Coincidence? I wouldn't care to say....

After my mother and father separated, she had to take the jobs that were available, mostly on the farms where she worked in the afternoons. The work was hard and demanding but the crowd she worked with were a jolly bunch. Often, she took them shop-bought cream buns from *Smith* the bakers, as the country folk rarely saw these except at weekends - or Saturdays to be precise. During the week, they baked their own confectionery. My mother was popular and often received in exchange for her cream buns the odd bag of potatoes, a cauliflower or a cabbage, which she valued after our own garden was stripped of vegetables.

My mother was particularly attentive and kind when any of us fell ill. Rarely did she take to her bed when she was unwell - she couldn't afford to - but she was a good nurse to Ken and I when we fell sick. She would often offer advice to other mothers in the street, remedies she'd learnt from my grandmother, a great old lady who knew about country cures and remedies. We had a boy in our street with warts like the rest of us had dandruff. My mother told his mother about Granny Cockburn's cure. It was simple; he must spit on the warts first thing in the morning and repeat some incantation. (I suspect that the added application of a moistened styptic pencil was more efficacious but there you are. What once was regarded as witchcraft was still thriving in Dunbar in the 1930s). My mother also dropped cold keys down our backs when we had nosebleeds or hiccoughs. These remedies worked. Bread poultices or gentian violet were the normal treatments for boils. A woollen sock filled with sand and warmed in the oven could cure a sore throat.

And if nothing else worked, there were the ubiquitously used *Milk of Magnesia* and something horrid called *Gregory's Powder,* a vile-tasting concoction which claimed to be a wonder drug that would cure everything. It was the alternative to castor oil dispensed out of large bottles suitably labelled and featured prominently in our comics. Perhaps the *Gregory Powder* which tasted very bitter shocked you out of your illness. There were other folk remedies in those pre-NHS days but I have forgotten what they were. Perhaps best of all were simple rest and care and the sturdy soups made from natural ingredients. My mother never left us alone when we were ill and the gas fire in the bedroom was always lit and kept burning through the long hours of the night. We were plied with hot drinks, our pillows were plumped up at regular intervals, kisses were pressed on our foreheads. Love rather than medicine made us well. And when we got better, we were allowed to sit up and read our comics while Mum soft-boiled our eggs and cut the crusts off our toast. To be ill was proof of our mother's love for us....

One winter, I had a bad case of flu'. Today, that ailment would be cured by antibiotics within a week, but in the days before the NHS, flu' could be and was a killer. Care, warmth and good food were all that was on offer; they invariably worked. The important thing was to sweat out the fever no matter how hot you became. That winter, I lay for over two weeks, often half-asleep or delirious. Nights were the worst times. I would look at the gas fire flames that burnt blue, or the paraffin lamp flame wavering at my bedside table, caught in the draught from the slightly opened window. The flames cast shadows on the walls, and sometimes, when I stared at it too intensely, the wallpaper took on grotesque shapes and faces. The room wobbled and swam as if under the sea and for the first time in my young life, a hand came out of the wall to grab me. It was Desperate Dan from the *Dandy* who tried to throttle me instead of *Korky the Cat* this time. I woke up screaming and my mother was instantly beside me with a mug of *Ovaltine* to help me get back to sleep.

Then the fever broke and you would waken up one morning, stiff and sore and hungry. That was always a Good Sign. After food, sleep was the next best thing. Doctor Anderson came to look at me, take my temperature with a funny little glass rod, then he would nod in approval.

'He's past the worst, Jean. If he's eating food, he's fine.'

What did doctors really know then? Not a lot I suspect. Dr Anderson used to say to me that when a white speck on my fingernail was nearing the top of the nail, I was losing an illness.

# Altered States

'It's when the white speck's at the base of the fingernail you should worry, laddie.'

In my bedroom, there were four large prints or engravings. Two illustrated Biblical scenes with figures dressed in what I supposed were nightgowns. One was a drippy-looking angel with her eyes turned heavenwards, her breasts only just detected through the thin gauze of her *goonie* [nightgown]. The other was the boy David whose eyes were fixed in the same upward stare, his hands clasped in prayer. Norman used to say he was praying for a decent cup of tea. The other prints appealed to my growing awareness of the earthly things of life. One pandered to my love of history. It was entitled *The Boyhood of Raleigh*, a popular print of the time. The picture contained three figures, a man and two young boys. The man was bare legged with trousers cut off at the knee; he wore a broad-sleeved shirt with the sleeves rolled up to his elbows. A battered straw hat completed his ensemble. He was clearly telling the boys some nautical story and he was pointing out to the sea at their backs. The small boys were better dressed and they rested their chins on their hands, indicating their fascination with the old salt's tales. They sat on a stone pier wall; the composition made me think of the Old or Cromwell Harbour.

The other print was sensuous and perhaps appealed to my growing interest in the opposite sex. Its subject was a very beautiful lady showing only head and exquisitely bare shoulders. She wore a broad-brimmed straw hat festooned with cherries. Her enticing almost Mona Lisa-like smile hinted at promised delights. In her slender, long fingers, she held a bunch of ripe cherries to her half-open mouth, her lips painted as red as the fruit itself. I fell in love with her because she seemed to be smiling at me. Now, when I see cherries in *punnets* in a greengrocer's shop, I still get a slight surge of feeling, nostalgic, excited by the thought of my long-lost cherry-eating *coquette*.

My mother never stopped working for us. I am sure I inherited my love of the earth from her and Granny Cockburn, who had made her living from the land. Perhaps such traits are passed on; even today, I can't resist putting my hands into the soil, for I have never lost my feel for it.

Despite our altered state, my childhood was solid enough. We never went hungry, nor did we go to school with holes in our clothes like some of our poorer contemporaries. Darned we might be, our shirt collars 'turned' i.e. detached and reversed when they became worn and frayed. Our boots and shoes - ever the bane of my mother's stretched purse - never let in water. Of those who went to school with holes in their jerseys, my mother would shake her head sadly, then describe these unfortunates as 'more holey than godly'.

In our daily lives, there were taboos to be avoided, things that Must Never Be Done in case we were visited by bad luck. For instance, placing shoes on a table spelt dire disaster, as was the breaking of a mirror; a shattered mirror brought you seven years' bad luck. To cross knives meant a quarrel was imminent; a dropped knife meant a gentleman would call, a fork warned of a visit from a lady. Two teaspoons placed on the same saucer meant a baby was on the way. Cutting your nails on a Friday brought you bad luck. The stopping of a clock heralded a death. Uncannily, this happened more often than not, probably because it was statistically likely and the clock required regular winding. Sometimes, the clock would stop because of dust in the works and my mother would run to fetch a seagull's feather which she dipped in fine oil and twist around inside the mechanism through the keyhole. It usually got the clock going but by then she said it was too late. Someone was about to meet his or her Maker.

'That's a death'

She'd sigh the words in her most dramatic, doom-laden voice, sad because she'd been too late to prevent it. She actually believed her failure to attend to her duties spelt death for some poor soul. As I mentioned earlier, when she died, the clock refused to go again. Even today, I have a momentary morbid fear when a clock stops....

Luck was always a capricious element in our lives. My mother swore we had more than our fair share of bad luck, less of the good. Friday the Thirteenth was one day my mother feared and she did practically nothing that day. (It was many years later that I learnt the truth about Fridays that fell on the thirteenth. The French Knights Templar, a body of warrior knights who were dedicated to sustaining Christianity in the Middle East were outlawed by Pope Clement V on Friday, 13th October 1307 because they had become over mighty).

There were ways whereby you could take action to avoid bad luck. The classic was not walking under a ladder, which must have its roots in the fact that if you did, something might fall on your head. You invited bad luck by talking in a tunnel. If you bought a purse for someone and didn't put a coin in it - a practice known as *hanselling* which derives from Hansel Monday, an old Scottish custom held on the first Monday of the New Year and in lieu of Christmas which in Scotland was once considered a Popish festival until the twentieth century. If you inadvertently spilt salt, you could avoid the ensuing bad luck by throwing a pinch or two over your left shoulder. You never said 'thank you' to someone who picked up your dropped glove, never picked dandelions in flower as folklore had it that you would pee the bed that night. Another forbidden flora was holly; bring it into the house at Christmas and you'd have bad luck for a year. My mother would never use the word 'pig' when she spoke of bacon or pork. She would always speak of the 'grunter' that had been killed. Even in the last year of her life in 2002, she refused to use the word 'pig'. In my youth, I was ordered never to look at a full moon through glass and turn a silver coin - if you had one - when you looked at a new moon. There are countless others which I have forgotten.

Good luck came with a rainbow over your house, finding a silver coin in the street - silver being a lucky colour - avoiding the cracks in the pavement, spitting on a sliver of wood broken from the *Wishing Tree* that grew beside the path to *Lochend Cottage* and has long-since disappeared - then throwing the wood over your left shoulder. The *Wishing Tree* was popular with hopeful lovers and schoolchildren about to sit exams.

There were also popular sayings like the following:

*Happy is the bride that the sun shines on.*

*Happy is the corpse that the rain falls on.*

My mother could also predict the onset of wet weather when her bunions hurt.

'Aye, there's rain on the way. My bunions are giving me gyp.'

If you said something simultaneously with someone else, you linked your little finger in that of the other person and made a wish. Looking back, I am sure there were more taboos than good luck charms; even my practical, down-to-earth father carried a Joan-the-Wad charm during the war, Joan being a Cornish pixie....

It was about my eleventh birthday I was obliged to take an interest in the local shops as I'd to run errands for my mother and carry her bags of 'messages', as shopping was known then. The shops in Dunbar mostly belonged to families who'd been traders for several generations. There were one or two chain stores like *Lipton's* and *The Buttercup,* the latter owned I believe by the Ayrshire firm of *Maybole Dairies.* Both had their distinctive insignia; *Lipton's* lettering was white on a green background and the delivery bikes were painted green with white lettering. *The Buttercup* had a tastefully tiled panel in the doorway, a panel that still survives today, the premises presently occupied by a surveyor. The tiles are a delightful composition of rural bliss; depicted on the right-hand side of the entrance is a sweet young milkmaid feeding a sleepy cow with a bunch of buttercups.

I never cared much for shopping at the local butchers. The sight of dead animals and poultry suspended from hooks in the ceiling made me nauseous although not quite enough for me to turn vegetarian; I also abhorred the wooden floor covered in blood-soaked sawdust. But I did enjoy the smell of sausages, hams, corned beef and black puddings. In those days, butchers and grocers wore the ubiquitous white apron that reached down to their feet. One of the butchers, a special man in my early years was Victor Young; he was kindly and cheerful to all his customers. Yet when I watched him dig out handfuls of mince from a tray, I used to think his fingers were like the fat sausages he sold. Such are the lasting images of the young....

Then there was the dairy in the West Port. Who now remembers the *Renton Dairy* owned by Mr and Mrs Ellison? The shop contained mostly bottles of milk and cartons of cream. They employed a poor man whose name I seem to remember was Winnie - short for Winston? - and I recall that he had no ears; maybe he was their son. The dairy bottling shop was situated next to the shop, premises today occupied by a pet shop; directly opposite in the West Port was the bottle - washing shop where today there is a small plaque of six tiles depicting contented cows ruminating by a gentle stream. Mrs Ellison used to emerge from the bottling shop in her rubber apron to sell you milk or to receive payment for deliveries. The place emitted a sickly-sweet smell that put me off milk for years; I liked it in tea and coffee and poured it on my porridge in winter, cornflakes in summer. But the thought of drinking it made me almost vomit. I had little occasion to visit the *Renton Dairy* other than to pay our weekly bill for deliveries to our door.

Here are some of the commodities on sale in those far-off days, some of which are still retailed in modern supermarkets:

*Bird's Custard, Marshall's Semolina, Marshall's Sago* which we called frogspawn; *Camp Coffee,* whose bottle had a colourful label featuring a Sikh soldier serving a kilted officer outside a tent with his morning cuppa; *Rinso* soap powder and *Sunlight* soap for laundry, Wright's *Coal Tar* soap and *Lifebuoy* soap for body washing, *Robin Starch, Brasso, Black-leading* for the fireplace, *Pioneer Matches* and makes of cigarettes such as *Gold Flake, Black Cat, Turf* (which smelt like singed grass), *Pasha* both of whose packets contained blue and white coloured cigarette cards which were vastly inferior to the beautiful coloured cards produced by *W D & H O Wills* at the beginning of the century - *Players' Weights, Capstan Full Strength* and of course the famous *Wills' Woodbines.*

Several shops in Dunbar have fond memories for me. The first was *Grahame's* the Ironmongers at No 99 High Street, a veritable treasure trove of junk, cheap toys and household commodities. The place always smelled of paraffin, candles, firelighters, tin and cheap paint. You could pick up fantastic bargains and I usually did my Christmas shopping there.

We had a bicycle shop, *Pettigrew's,* next to what today is the Royal Bank of Scotland; it was owned by Billy Jordan, who also fixed wirelesses and did repair work, assisted by Tommy Young, one of the kindest men I ever knew and who charged as little as possible for mending your bike. Unbelievable as it is today, there were five shoe shops in Dunbar; the best quality could be found in the prestigious *William Mason's,* a shop which sold superior quality footwear then and still does today. *Easiephit* was next to *Hurry's Bakery*; now occupied by *The Tasty Bite. Barrie's Shoe Shop,* where my mother's good friend May Wilson of West Barns was manageress is now occupied by *Victoria Wine.* The equally upmarket *Carr's Footwear* further down the street was until recently occupied by *Kingston Country Bakery.* And incredibly, the fifth shoe shop in Dunbar was situated next door to the *Playhouse Cinema. Shiel's* shoe shop bracketed the cinema along with *Birrel's* sweet shop. I could never understand why anyone would want to open a shoe shop next to a cinema. Yet it seemed to thrive, possibly because it offered a shoe repair service, if I re-member correctly.

But let us return to the High Street shops. Walking towards Lauderdale House on the right hand side, you would have encountered *A P Thomson's,* a newspaper shop now occupied by *Bellfine,* another ironmonger's *R A Robertson* now occupied by *Turnbull's Home Hardware;* next door to the *Cloakroom,* premises occupied today by (for the moment) the local tourist office and *Tippecanoe Gallery,* which in an earlier life was a kilt-maker's shop. The *Co-op* had three shops in the High Street - a butcher's, a grocery with a furniture store above and a drapery (now occupied I think by *Lothian Printers)* managed by my good friend Jean Brunton. I think the Co-op occupied premises now owned by the *Tandoori* Indian restaurant; I also think that the butcher's shop then is now the *Food Hamper.* I am sure many people still remember their *Store (Co-op)* number on which a dividend was paid every year; my mother's is imprinted indelibly on my brain - 12647. The Spartan *Law's Barber Shop* has been consumed by *Umberto's*; Willie Law was a colourful character whose establishment catered only for men and boys; nearly opposite his establishment was *Innes* the Hairdresser's, which catered for both sexes and where my mother felt my brothers and I would get superior treatment than that offered by Willie Law. I recall Ken and I having our hair cut by two lovely sisters who welcomed us into the saloon Innes, now occupied by a modern hairdresser's. Ally and Millie Innes were lovely ladies; they used to sit Ken and I on boards placed over the arm rests of the chairs occupied by their adult customers. Sadly, Ally is no longer with us but Millie survives. Recently, she told me that my wee brother and I were special customers because we were so well behaved. I recall those fortnightly haircuts, when Ken sat on one chair and I sat on the other. Ally used to smoke a lot, even when she was cutting our hair. Millie is still around today and still my friend, often to be seen walking with another good friend of mine, Laura Togneri. I cannot pluck up the courage to tell Millie that when she ran her comb through my hair, I experienced feelings that were definitely sexual. I was always afraid she might see the results of her attentions in my summer shorts.......

Perhaps it is difficult to believe today but in those days there were no fewer than six newsagents in the High Street. I frequented the paper shops more often than the five shoe shops. Starting from the east end of the High Street was Hugh *Ross's* papershop beside what is now the *Barns Ness Hotel*; then *Ward's* papershop – it went under a different name when I was a boy - beyond the *Bingo Café* whose premises now house the modern Post Office. Next to Ward's was Gwen Day's *Photographic Studio,* then *Carruther's Cafe.* Across the street were *Downie* and *Knox* - the former selling newspapers and books from at least 1795, when it was rented by George Miller, father of James, who wrote the first history of Dunbar. Then came *Penney's* which was later incorporated into the Bank of Scotland. The fifth papershop was A P *Thomson's,* now the *Bellfine* gift shop, as I said earlier.

Opposite *Bellfine* was *Leighton's* gift shop which sold a range of bric-a-brac and seaside tat to quite prestigious wares. Nearby was *The Buttercup,* which I mentioned earlier. A little further up that side of the street was *Sinton's*

# Altered States

*Grocery* which later became *Cooper's,* a rival chain store challenging Lipton's; for some years, it was managed by the diminutive Jimmy Young whom I went to school with. Further up the street was *Erinall's Emporium,* which I think is today occupied by a shop selling surfing gear. *Lothian Computers* now owned by my good friend Grahame Smith on the corner of the West Port once housed the eccentric horse-riding Ronald Malcolm's grocery store. At the opposite corner of the West Port/High Street was Big *Tait's* butchershop, now thankfully restored in that capacity; hopefully its current proprietor, Peter Whitecross, is doing well as he deserves to do. Then there was *Purves' Grocery Store*, a quality shop which lasted until the owner, Ronnie Purves, a kind man who married my good friend Audrey Boyd, died. *McCluckie's Ironmongery* was next door, then *Mason's Shoe Shop.* Next to *Mason's* was *Nelson's Greengrocery*. Further up was *Greensmith Downes*, a lady's outfitters where my cousin Dorothy worked until she married and emigrated to Canada. Almost directly opposite was *Daniel Smith's*, a very upmarket tailor who sold high quality suits and other accessories; it was a shop my brother Norman frequented because he said it offered the very best quality. The last elegant shop on that side of the High Street was that of *Louis H Allen*, a china shop which you entered gingerly; there were notices everywhere warning you that all breakages had to be paid for. Today, it is occupied by *Alldays.*

But for sheer audacity and even cheek, my favourite shop was a poky little establishment owned by one of the few Jews I have met in my life. The junk shop at the east end of the High Street, near the *Dolphin* pub will be familiar to those of my generation. I have clear memories of Solomon Winston's dusty little place known to everyone as *Solly's.* Solly was outlandish and foreign in a way quite different from the Scots-Italian Togneri family (owners of the fish-and-chip shop in the West Port, cafe *Lido* in the High Street - now the *King's Palace* Chinese restaurant – *Lothian Hotel*, Johnny Jenneta's *Doric Cafe* (now occupied by a dry-cleaner's) and Greco's *Ice Cream Parlour*). Solly was in a class of his own.

Solly lived in *Abbeylands,* a rambling mansion house at the end of Station Road, now housing a private nursing home. His shop was within spitting distance; it was astonishingly small and *Tardis*-like (afficionados of the *Doctor Who* series will know what I mean) and it was stuffed with junk and bric-a-brac. There were brass and pewter ornaments, nickel-plated silver domestic ware like cruet sets, crockery, pictures and picture frames, mediocre and ghastly cherubic chalk statuettes, famous men of history and anonymous people with large, hooked noses - were they his ancestors? – staring at you from the dark depths. There were busts of Julius Caesar, Sir Walter Scott, famous Victorian politicians like Disraeli, Gladstone and Queen Victoria herself. Most of his wares were pure junk except for the watches which were displayed in glass cases in his front window. The junk seemed to have evolved from the dirty, linoleum-covered floor, rising to the ceiling in places.

## Altered States

Is it a trick of memory or do I see Solly reclining in a lop-sided armchair, sitting like a basking shark, waiting for his next victim?  The area occupied by his overstuffed and decaying armchair allowed a little clear space, an island in otherwise unbelievably cluttered premises.  Sometimes he would stand outside in his shirtsleeves and greasy trilby hat; when anyone approached, he would waddle inside, hoping that by doing so, he might encourage the person to stop and stare.  Then he would come out again and invite any individual who lingered too long at the window to step inside.  He was the male equivalent of Auntie Wainright in the gentle TV comedy series *Last of the Summer Wine*. Sensing a sale, he would put a friendly arm round his potential customer's shoulders, particularly children.

> 'Vat you like, sonny?  You vant to buy for your Mamma a present?  I got chust the thing for her birthday.'

Nervous, you might affect to be interested in some cheap glass salt-and-pepper set in a verdigris-coated brass holder.

> 'Very good choice.  Antique.'

Then you'd try to edge away, saying it was too expensive.

> 'Vun shilling vun veek will buy for your Mama.  I keep for you.  Or you buy now and pay every veek.'

Forever, as my Uncle Jimmy used to say.  Once Solly had you in his clutches, you were his for life because when you paid the price (with weekly interest added), he would sell you something else.  You had to keep going back as you were in hock to him.  First it was a birthday present, then a Christmas gift. Solly made me think of Jacob Marley in Charles Dickens' *A Christmas Carol* except it was *you* who were bound to *him* by chains.

In his exalted squalor, Solly ruled as a king.  Lurking in the dusty recesses of his empire, he watched passers by and children who came to press their noses against his fly blown window, studying the watches in forlorn hope of buying one.  Some lingered longer than others, which brought Solly outside. He knew that the kids couldn't afford his watches so he would chant his mantra:

> 'If you vant to buy a watch, come inside.  If you don't vant to buy a vatch, take your dirty nose off my vindow.'

Is it yet another example of my faulty memory or did Solly always wear a battered, greasy trilby, with a grubby, off-white collarless shirt?  I'm almost certain he did  I never found out how he came to Dunbar.  Was he one of the lucky ones who escaped from Nazi Germany in the 1930s?

Without doubt, the most popular of all the shops were the confectioners, or *sweetie shops*, of which there were several in Dunbar.  Despite the sweet rationing, they all managed to keep open, making a good, steady living for their owners.  The most prestigious was *McDonald's* in the West Port, now the store-room for *Togneri's* fish and chip shop; wee Miss McDonald had a superior and varied range of good quality fare, most of which was out of our price range, let alone the added restriction of sweet coupons; after she retired, the shop was taken over by my good friend Laura Togneri. Another upmarket shop was *Birrell's,* adjacent to the *Playhouse Cinema*; it sold mouth-watering ranges of chocolates laid out in trays. Then there was the small *R S McColl's* next door to *Lipton's Grocers* (both now subsumed by *Ladbroke's*); the shop was tiny, having been created by blocking off a close between the grocer shop and the *Eagle Inn.* Finally, there was *Mackay's*, an odd little *Curiousity Shop* of a place next door to the *Lorne Temperance Hotel,* now *Sweet Occasions*. *Mackay's* sold mainly boiled sweets and homemade toffees. Miss Mackay, another diminutive soul, was eccentric; her fly-spotted window with its faded posters *advertising Fry's Chocolate Creams* must have dissuaded many a potential customer. Her range was limited and the shelves often had gaps, although what she sold, she kept in fly-proof glass jars with fancy tops of the kind popular in Victorian sweet shops. Even the sticks of Dunbar rock and striped candy walking sticks were kept in these jars. She wore woollen gloves with the fingers cut out - shades of Auntie Wainwright again in the TV comedy *Last of the Summer Wine* - irrespective of the season. I used to dread that the wool would contaminate my purchases; there is nothing worse than sucking a hairy sweetie...........

The range stocked by all these shops was astonishing. Brandy balls, aniseed balls, glacier mints, acid drops, pear drops - these smelt like nail varnish remover - rhubarb rock painted red to resemble rhubarb, *soor plooms* (sour plums were green, the colour of Connemara marble), caramels, chocolate eclairs, all the famous brands and delights produced by the giants like *Cadbury, Rowntree, Fry* and *Bassett's.* On sale were novelties like liquorice bootlaces, straps and pipes whose bowls were decorated with red hundreds and thousands (little pinhead-sized sweets used to decorate birthday cakes) *Mars* bars*, Bassett'sLiquorice Allsorts* and *Jellybabies,* sweetie cigarettes and shredded chocolate coconut sold as pipe tobacco; *Wrigley's* spearmint chewing gum (which we called *chingo*) and bubble gum were also cheap favourites. At one time there was a school tuck shop in *Rose Cottage* at Woodbush; it sold cheap confectionary like the bitter liquorice stick which you put in a lemonade bottle filled with water to make *sugerelly* and which gave you the runs; there was another commodity called *sweet wood*, a liquorice-tasting fibrous twig you sucked until it dissolved into shreds; there were gobstoppers which changed colour as you sucked them, barley sugar twists, *Cowan's Highland Toffee,* with its famous cow trademark, mint humbugs, bullseyes and lucky potatoes - the latter being a cinnamon-powder dusted wedge of white sweet stodge with a little gift encased within - if you were lucky - sherbert dabs or *sookers*, with hollow liquorice sticks to allow to suck up the sherbert from the packet. There were cinnamon sticks which could be chewed like cigars or even smoked by the more bold and decadent among us. Favoured by the girls were Conversation lozenges which came in a variety of shapes, sizes and flavours; they had little homilies carved on them – like 'I love you' and 'You are my sweetheart' as well as the less romantic 'You have cold feet'. The range was endless. When sweets went off the ration and I won two sixpenny vouchers at the School Sports on Coronation Day, 2nd June 1953, I blew the lot on *soor plooms, brandy balls* and a stick of rhubarb rock...........

When money and sweets were in short supply - which was often - we resorted to *Ovaltine* and *Horlicks* tablets; in extreme desperation, I made a kind of toffee basically consisting of syrup, sugar and margarine. My efforts (when my mother was out at the cinema, for she would have flayed me alive for using her cooker) ranged from the quite good to the greasy, soft messes which had to be strained through grease-proof paper, then patted into slimy balls which for all their nauseous appearance, Ken and I avidly consumed. I can still here him saying this when my mother went to the pictures:

'Make toffee, Loy. Make me toffee.'

I got the recipe from one of Ken's Christmas annuals, something to do with a squirrel if I remember rightly. What on earth was a squirrel doing making toffee?

Two other shops which deserve particular mention are Greco's *Ice Cream Parlour* and *The Bingo Cafe;* the former is still there, at the north end of the High Street, near Lauderdale House; the latter's site is now occupied by the modern Post Office. Greco's made what I considered the best ice cream in Christendom; the *Bingo* was famous for its ground coffee, cream buns and excellent cakes. You could order coffee beans there and watch them being ground into powder. When I walk past the GPO today, I can still imagine the rich, heady scent of roasted coffee beans that wafted down the High Street on summer days. Alas, such exotic places which erotically teased the taste buds disappeared before I was able to sample their delights as a young man; we had to make do with the *Doric Café* - usually known as *Johnny's* after the proprietor Johnny Jenetta – and next to Peter Whitecross' butcher's shop at the corner of the West Port). *Johnny's* was popular with the young folk as it had a juke box and sold *espresso* coffee which for me was a pale imitator of real coffee flavour, a warmish bland drink with the consistency of cotton wool.

So the years passed. Gradually, I grew more aware of what the small world of Dunbar had to offer. The 1950s were gritty and grey but in some respects, they were the happiest years of my life. We were no different from other families struggling to survive, some adept at keeping up appearances like my mother. There was little to go around, so there was less jealousy, less envy in those days. There was also more community spirit, more genuine friendship; neighbours helped one another. The 1950s were good because they instilled in the people a sense of 'bearing up and seeing through'; the war years had taught us that. The 1960s introduced the acquisitive society which would divide and destroy that fine sense of community spirit and comradeship.

I think that 1956 was the most significant year for me. At that time, I was about to enter my Fourth year at the school. Politics entered my life for the first time. Russia invaded Hungary and quelled the rebellion there; I hated the regime that sent us scores of refugees to *Whittingehame House* and brought my friends and I on bicycles to deliver bread to these 'useless' mouths. Hungarian being an extremely difficult language, we communicated with them through interpreters or sign language. Thus I was beginning to be dragged into the real world. I hated it. For me, the world was a lovely place of beaches and hills; why should something called politics and war be allowed to interfere with what I believed was every person's right to enjoy?

In 1958, I wrote to my father and asked him to come home. He was a stranger the day he stepped off the train in his white, belted raincoat which showed his paunch. He stayed with us when he was retired from the army in 1960; he shared my bedroom one night a week from then until his death in 1967. My mother couldn't love him any more; the years in between had soured her. One altered state had been replaced by another. And the other had little, if any, love in it.

# 4

## Funny by Gaslight

This chapter derives its name from *Fanny by Gaslight,* a 1944 film originally called *Man of Evil,* starring Phyllis Calvert , James Mason and Stewart Grainger. I saw the film, yet I was unable to appreciate the menace it portrayed.

Gas. That three-letter word conjures so many images from my childhood. Until the early 1950s, it was the main source of light, cooking and to a certain extent, heating. The word gas has no obvious poetry about it; it doesn't in the least sound romantic, yet the effect it had on my early years was both emotional and to some extent, even inspirational.

In those days, most Dunbar homes were lit by coal gas; cooking was done on gas stoves and in ovens and some of our bedrooms had gas fires. The gas mantle used for lighting was a fragile device designed to increase the illumination of a naked gas flame. Invented in 1885, it served the bulk of the British (well, Scottish, as electricity was introduced earlier in England) public well for almost seventy years. The gas mantle was a tube of loosely woven fibre, sometimes rayon but more often cotton. A coating of oxides was impregnated onto the fibre base and the rayon and cotton burned off at the first firing leaving a fragile matrix that became incandescent when hot. Installing a replacement mantle required care, as the material was so thin and fine it could be easily broken, so every home kept spares.

The *Dunbar Gas and Light Company* was formed in 1826 to provide street lighting in the High Street; before that, the street lights probably burnt whale oil, Dunbar being a whaling port between 1750 and 1810. Retail and domestic premises at that time were lit by oil lamps, candles also being in common use, as ordinary families couldn't afford the cost of lighting their homes with gas. Gradually, as pipes were extensively laid near the end of the nineteenth century, most homes were served by gas for lighting and cooking. In 1886, the Burgh Council took over the *Dunbar Gas and Light Company* and formed the *Dunbar Gas Company*; the company offices were situated just beyond the road-end at Doon Avenue, adjacent to the first dwelling house there, that of the gas manager. As can be seen today, the doors and windows of the Gas Office were bricked up, the entrance to the gasometer area closed by a high wire mesh gate after the company was abolished when electricity became the main source of heat, light and cooking in the 1950s. Inside the gate were two massive gasometers - more properly gasholders - one constantly in use, one maintained as a reserve or holding tank when the main gasholder was empty. Encased in a water tank, these massive structures emitted rumbling sounds as the gasholder within moved up and down. It was a place where we played games in the square compartments of earth tinted blue - we thought they were small forts or redoubts created for our play - much to the chagrin of our mothers when we came home with knees and clothes stained with the colour.

Town Gas was a by-product of coal. It had a strong smell, unlike modern natural or North Sea gas. It lit our rooms and was used for cooking, coal providing our heat and hot water. Coal was king in those days, the British coalfields enjoying their heyday until the use of fossil fuels gradually went into decline. Near our house were the gasometers, snoring like the sleeping giants they were; they creaked and groaned and rumbled, making odd sounds that we children used to listen to, pressing our ears to the metal. Gas manufacture was a mystery to us. All we knew was that it provided a relatively cheap source of light. As long as you had a penny for the gas, it never let you down. Coal fires were universal and the older houses had large ranges on which pots simmered away, cooking soups and stews. Although my mother never cooked on our coal fire, it was the focal point in the living room, like the TV set is today.

Being the daughter or handmaiden of old King Coal until the advent of electricity, to have gas was to be modern; it was supplied by the Burgh Council first to the High Street, then the Harbour areas and finally the new housing estates built to the west of the town between the two World Wars. For an old penny, you could light your living room for half an evening, depending on the season. In winter, a penny would give you about two hours' supply of gas, less if the family was large and more than average cooking was done. When electricity finally came to Dunbar, we were wary of it; gas was alive, a living flame, whereas electricity was invisible. There was something decidedly sinister about it. Some of the older generation in the 1950s were suspicious of it; at least one old lady in our street said she always kept the electric plugs in their sockets

'For the electricity micht rin oot o' the holes. Ah cannae afford tae lose it when Ah'm no' usin' it.'

Electricity certainly lacked the character and warmth of gas, even if it was a brighter, cleaner form of fuel supply. There were some who said it would weaken your eyes.

As I said earlier, the coal fire was the focal point in the sitting room - more commonly and aptly called the kitchen or living room, since it was the room in which families spent most of their waking lives. Coal fires were rarely found in bedrooms for obvious reasons; gas was safer and cheaper. Besides, a coal fire required the daily ritual of clearing out the ashes from the previous day and night. After these were removed in a tin pail, the hearth was swept clean, then the new fire was 'laid'. A layer of newspapers which were sometimes called 'sticks' - strips of paper cut into short lengths and twisted together

- formed the foundation on which a few sticks of wood kindling were laid, with a firelighter, or short stick of a crumbly substance which contained paraffin was broken into small pieces and scattered on the small pyramid of paper and kindling. Finally, a few small nuts of coal or cinders were placed on top of the pile. The paper was lit and on cold mornings, something equivalent to prayer was silently mouthed to assist the fire to 'take'. In those days, there was a hint of the primeval about the combustibility of an open fire, even if I didn't know it then. The hearth was literally worshipped - you had to kneel before it to get the fire going – and it was revered as the home of what you hoped was the benevolent god of fire.

Winter fires smoked when the wood kindling or coals were damp. Sometimes, a draft had to be manufactured by placing an open newspaper over the grate and flue; the fire was thus coaxed into life. When it burst into flames and larger pieces of coal were laid on, everyone sighed with relief. The range was black-leaded once a week, a chore that took up a fair slice of a housewife's time. Day didn't officially begin until the fire was lit; night began when the gas mantle was extinguished, when the last person in the household - usually when parents - in our case, my mother - went to bed.

Every fire had a personality of its own, possessed of its own peculiar quirks. My mother used to say that our fire was stubborn in February and March, possibly because these were damp and cold months. Some mornings, her fire would 'play up' as she would inform us sleepy kids who hoped to warm ourselves before we went off to school. She would curse and swear when the fire spluttered and emitted too much smoke; she'd blame the damp kindling or accuse Hughes, the local coalman, of putting too many 'stones' or poor quality coal in her weekly sacks because she had no husband to fight her corner. Even so, I heard her criticise him on many occasions, warning him she'd take her business elsewhere if the supply didn't improve in quality. Hughes wasn't the only coal merchant in Dunbar at the time; my mother could have changed her supplier to *George Foggo and Son* of Innerwick, whose son Tommy later married her great niece Moira. For some reason, she stuck to Hughes. Her threats fell on deaf ears.

A sullen fire is an obstinate, frustrating creature; without a good going blaze, life lost its joy and the living room was a cold and miserable place in those far-off days before electricity. When all went well, a coal fire under gaslight was lovely to watch and sit beside.

At about 4.15pm on a winter's afternoon, when Ken and I came home from school, my mother would turn the flat handle on the gas bracket in the wall above the fire and apply a lighted 'spill' - a strip of cardboard - to the mantle. The light plopped in, then it settled down to a slow, hissing sound. It stayed on all evening. As I said earlier, a penny lasted about two hours; the light would go out without warning unless you could judge what you'd used from the night before - an impossible task except amongst the very thrifty - and one of us would run to the scullery where my mother kept a pewter jug containing a ready supply of pennies beside the gas meter.

The streets then were also lit by gas. I can remember Wattie Hutchinson, the gaslighter or *leerie* coming along Lammermuir Crescent on his bike, carrying two long poles. Wattie turned on the gas with a pole which had a hook on the end to switch on the gas, then another with a heated tip which ignited it. You could follow *leerie's* progress along the street in the growing gloom. House by house, Lammermuir Crescent came alive as he made his way along it. It was fascinating to watch the lamps come on, one by one. He did the same in reverse later in the evening; street lamps were usually put out by 11pm, when respectable people were expected to be at home, if not actually a-bed.

Our house had its quota of paraffin lamps and heaters; the lamps were for emergencies, when the gas supply ran out and we'd no pennies to feed into the meter, or when we needed to be lit to bed upstairs, there being no gas lamps there. A paraffin heater was lit in the bathroom in winter since the water tank was situated in the loft above it and my mother was terrified of frozen water pipes. We used to get dressed in the bathroom in winter as it was always warm there. To keep the house as comfortable as possible, my mother stuffed knitted 'sausages' or 'snakes' at the foot of the front and back doors, with small rectangular pieces of carpet placed against the interior doors, crude but effective draught excluders. The 'sausages' or 'snakes' were a nuisance when you had to open the front and back doors as they opened inwards, unlike the interior ones.

As I have already said, the coal fire was the only source of heat; it also heated the water as behind the fire, there was a boiler that fed hot water into a holding tank in a cupboard in the living room. The fireplace consisted of a black-leaded grate with a tiled base and a brass fender to stop coals jumping out of the fire on to the carpet. At either side of the fire stood two *wally dugs*, the jolly ceramic dogs found in almost every household of the day. Beside them was the almost ubiquitous shell canister from the Great War serving as a receptacle for the pokers until proper custom-made 'fireside companions' came on the market to accommodate pokers, tongs and stiff-headed brushes to clean the grate. Being the focal point of the living room, the furniture was arranged round the fireplace so that everyone could share the warmth.

The fire was never allowed to go out until late evening, when the damper was pulled and allowed it to 'die down'. Woe betide any of us who, left on our own, allowed the fire to expire by failing to lay on more coal before it was time to 'die down'.

In the 1940s and 1950s, while coal was the main fuel burnt, many families supplemented their supply by burning logs bought for about half a crown [12.5p] the sack; *briquettes* which were brick-sized and consisted of small coals and coal dust were also cheap and popular. But the mainstay of many families was coke or cinders, in reality the slag or residue of coal used in the gas manufacturing process. Cinders still retained a measure of combustibility and they and *briquettes* were very cheap. *Briquettes* and cinders were bought from the gasworks. The gas company was a very important utility, its manager having considerable standing in the community. In 1948, the manager was a Mr Morrison, whom I recall as a well-respected, kindly man with an even kindlier wife. They lived in the large company house on the corner of Doon Avenue, Mr Morrison's office being next door to it. You paid your gas bills at a small counter behind which sat a female clerk.

Coal was delivered to your house every fortnight; like other houses in Lammermuir Crescent and elsewhere, we possessed a small brick-built coal shed at the rear. The coalman would lug his sacks down the path at the side of the house and empty them on the floor. It was my job to sweep the coal into a pile which allowed us to open the coal shed door. After my brother Norman went off to do his National Service, I had to go to the gasworks every Friday afternoon after school to collect our weekly supply of cinders and *briquettes*. I hated and feared that job. In the winter months, I made an extra weekly trip on a Tuesday. You had to supply your own sacks begged from the coal merchant; the sacks were invariably holed and threadbare- which is why you were given them - threatening to burst when you filled them too full. I also took a heavy grape or fork to scoop up the wet, steaming cinders often newly drawn from the furnace and dampened down with water. Most families used *bogeys* or carts to collect their supplies; all we had was the base of the pram which I, then Ken, had been wheeled about in as babies. It was virtually a wooden board on wheels, with no sides to contain the bulky sacks of cinders. I attached a rope to the front but it wasn't very effective for steering. I went off cheerfully enough but my heart sank when I entered the inferno of the gasworks furnaces; as I said earlier, the land around the gasometers – they were my generation's idea of great castles or towers - was tinged blue from the gas, a wasteland where only coarse weeds thrived in the sooty soil. If you fell in that tinted earth, your skin was stained a faint bluish colour. Some folk said it gave you impetigo, others insisted you would get more serious ailments. I am sure there was more than a hint of propaganda in this, put about by women who had to scrub clothes on a washing board before the advent of robust detergents that removed 'stubborn' stains. The washing board was a vital piece of equipment in the housewife's scullery; it harked back to the days when women washed clothes at the side of a stream, on the stones. It had a brief and romanticised career in the skiffle groups of the day, chiefly that of one Lonnie Donegan.

I knew most of the furnace men by sight if not by name; they were usually friendly, although one or two of the stokers were bad-tempered and ignored kids like me, serving adults who came after me. The more thoughtful men like Wattie Hutchison shovelled the cinders into the sack I held open, hoping that I wouldn't make a fool of myself by letting the mouth sag. I was very shy and 'handless' in those days, a trait that still inflicts me fifty years on.

# Funny by Gaslight

Once the sack or sacks were filled, the stoker would take the money and put it into his overall pocket, then he'd tie the sacks with a piece of twine and load them onto my cannibalised pram. The nightmare began at this point. I usually managed to get out of the gasworks gate without mishap, but the next part of the journey terrified me.

Once out of the gate, I hauled the heavy weight along the uneven pavement and managed to negotiate the Doon Avenue intersection with the main road. Doon Avenue was fine for about a hundred yards, then it sloped down towards Lammermuir Crescent; the trick was to walk behind the pram, holding on to the rope attached to the front axle. The pram had no brakes and the rope was useless for steering, so I had to physically restrain it from running out of control. Today, it doesn't sound a tough job but to an eight or nine year-old boy, it was frightening. I was always scared a wheel would fall off or the sacks would shift, thus throwing the balance out of kilter. My greatest nightmare was that the whole lot would tip over in the road, as I hadn't the strength to lift the sacks back on board. Fortunately, this happened rarely but when it did, I had to wait for a kind adult male - preferably one wearing dungarees or working clothes - to give me a hand. The likeliest spot where I would come to grief was the corner where Lammermuir Crescent cut across Doon Avenue; after negotiating the bend, I knew I was safe because the Crescent was flat all the way home. I was always pleased to reach our garden gate and haul the pram down the path to our coal shed. Mission accomplished, my mother would grumble at the time I'd taken, then she would haul the sacks into the shed for Norman to empty on the heap inside. In those days, bags of coke or cinders and logs were the mainstay of those families who couldn't afford enough good quality coal during the long winter months. Coal was graded then and probably now; the best was Grade A, the cheapest being *slack* which contained a high proportion of stony fuel which spat and spluttered and occasionally shot out of the fireplace and landed on the hearth rug. My mother would buy equal quantities of Grade A and poor coal, then mix them in the shed to make the whole supply burn reasonably well; as a consequence, she'd to tend the fire closely, ready with the tongs to retrieve 'rogue' coal shooting out of the hearth.

Gas was vital. As I said earlier, our streets were lit by gas. The lamps were alive, the gas popping and hissing away as we played under the intimate light they shed, warm, comforting little islands in the darkness. Modern streetlights are cold, impersonal, anonymous and in my opinion ineffective. Gas lamps may have given off a limited light but it was bright for all that. Gaslight was friendly, the lampposts were popular gathering places for the young and we played many games under the circle of light cast by these golden torches that held the beleaguering night at bay. As indicated earlier, the lamps were put out at about 11pm; well I recall looking out of my bedroom window on a winter evening at a pitch-black world - unless of course there was a full moon. I also remember with fondness the rain-washed street paved with the silvery traces of the full moon hanging above Doon Hill. Even now, I can see myself dressed in pyjamas, chin resting on hands with elbows on the window-sill, mesmerised by the moon which changed or redesigned shapes familiar in daylight. It was a silent, beautiful world and it was safe and secure, infinitely more so than today's night streets which are lit from dusk until dawn. There were few crimes in those days - burglaries did occur but on a much smaller scale than today simply because few families had anything worth pinching.

Someone wrote recently that childhood memories are as frail and dis-torted as clouds or spindrift; mine remain remarkably clear, especially of the house where we lived. As you entered the front door, there was a staircase to the upper storey; on the wall facing the living room door (in those days, we called it the kitchen), there was a row of hooks to hang wet coats and a sort of tin bucket for wet brollies.

Entering by the living room door, your eyes were immediately drawn to the hearth or fireplace on the wall opposite. It had a detached brass fender that could be removed so that the hearth could be swept. The hearth was tiled with brown tiles; the grate could also be removed for clearing away ashes. The grate and its surrounds were made of iron, regularly black-leaded and a tiresome job. My mother had a kind of fender stool set beside her armchair; it had a hinged top where she kept her knitting and wool for darning socks, almost beneath the gas mantle for maximum light. It doubled as a handy little seat for me, then Ken. Coal was brought in by the bucket from the coal shed at the back of the house, stored in the under stair cupboard in the scullery.

In those days, before fitted carpets, there was usually only a hearth rug that lay on the wax-cloth or linoleum. The dinner table was usually set in the centre of the room in winter, before the fire and at the window in summer. Various carpet 'runners' were placed strategically to deaden the noise of foot-wear on the floor; the positioning of these runners was determined by the posi-tion of the table.

Above the fireplace was a mantelpiece containing a few ornaments. Pride of place was given to the plain clock set in a wooden casing, a wedding gift from the staff at the *Playhouse* cinema, where my mother had worked in the sweet kiosk in 1939. Another important receptacle was the small cylindrical spill-holder coloured green and decorated with a lady in a bonnet and pink and blue crinoline. The spills were lit from the fire to ignite the gas mantle My mother hated clutter on the mantelshelf and we were never allowed to leave toy cars on it. She would put birthday and Christmas cards on it; she also put bills and other important documents behind the clock, knowing she would find them there when she needed them.

Above the mantel was a heavy mirror; it hung from a stout chain to keep it secure - we all knew that a cracked or broken mirror meant seven years' bad luck. My mother used to fix little paper flowers, ribbons from birthday presents and in November, Haig poppies to the hinges that held the mirror in its wooden-backed frame. On each side of the fire were two heavy armchairs of a kind of plastic material (for ease of cleaning) and a matching bed-settee-cum-sofa whose position in the furniture arrangement depended on the time of year; in winter, it was placed under the window, in summer before the fireplace, alternating its position with the dinner table.

On the wall opposite the fireplace, next to the scullery door was a small table on which stood the wireless; it was placed there so that my mother could listen in even when she was in the scullery cooking or washing. Next to it was a long sideboard with a drape of fringed velvet on which stood some of my mothers prized ornaments – a pair of white matching vases with flowers, *Little Nell* and a bespectacled little man wearing glasses which she swore was Mr Brownlow from *Oliver Twist.* (She knew of Mr Brownlow not through Dickens' book - she rarely read much in those days – but from David Lean's classic film adaptation in 1948). Also prominent were a small tray featuring four little Dutch boys in hats and clogs dancing in a ring and its matching bowl showing four little Dutch girls in headdresses walking in single file, three staring ahead. The fourth one smiled out at you, pointing a finger whimsically at the back of the one preceding her as if she were poking fun at the well-behaved trio or sharing some private joke with us. The sideboard had drawers and two cabinet-style doors; the latter kept the best crockery. One of the drawers contained an odd assortment of necessaries - our ration books, insurance policies, hire-purchase payment books, the wireless licence, string, sealing-wax and much else. One was used for cutlery and was compartmentalised for knives, forks, soup and dessert spoons; they lay gleaming on the velvet cloth placed in each compartment. Also in that drawer was a small leather-covered presentation box with purple velvet on which rested six silver teaspoons and a matching pair of silver sugar tongs; these were dutifully and regularly treated with silver polish, brought out only on special occasions, when someone important was having tea with us.

In winter, my mother hung thick, heavy crimson curtains at the window, to keep out the draughts. In spring, these were washed, ironed and put in a drawer, replaced by light linen or floral patterned ones.

Off the living room was the back bedroom where my mother slept, with a cot for me, then Ken, until we were old enough to sleep in an upstairs bedroom. There was enough room for a double bed, a bedside table, a wardrobe and a dressing table with mirror. (By way of illustrating the affluence of fifty years on, in the year 2000, my mother's bedroom in her sheltered housing complex in Summerfield Road contained no fewer than three wardrobes, a built in cupboard and a dressing table to store her range of clothes, shoes and underwear!) Through the wall from her bedroom was the scullery or back kitchen; it contained double sinks side by side. The smaller sink was used for washing dishes; its deeper and larger neighbour had a removable top which served as a work surface when the sink wasn't being used for washing bed-linen, clothes etc). Beside the deeper sink was a copper boiler in the corner next to the gas cooker; it was heated by gas and was used for boiling whites. The two sinks were separated by a wooden strut on which was clamped the wringer or small mangle on wash days. On the wall opposite the cooker was a brick-built pantry with a small unglazed window covered with fine mesh; this was to allow fresh air in and keep flies out. The pantry or larder was used for storing food in those pre-refrigerator days. On its stone floor were placed sacks of potatoes, vegetables, sugar and other less perishable foodstuffs. The two or three shelves were used to store comestibles in ascending order of per-ishableness - tinned food, dried milk, flour, rice, lentils, barley, split peas and salt - the topmost shelf containing the really perishable goods - eggs, butter, milk, fresh meat, cheese etc which were stored directly under the small win-dow.

In the scullery and under the staircase was a small walk-in cupboard where we stored brooms, brushes, the shovel and ashpan used to empty the fireplace ashes, cleaning materials, the wringer, bootbrushes, shoe and furni-ture polish, old clothes and newspapers, a bucket of coal and firelighters used for lighting the fire. The smells in that restricted, cramped cupboard remain in my olfactory sense; like Proust whose childhood memories were triggered by the taste of a particular cake, the dubious *potpourri* of sweat, grease, polish, candles, paraffin, damp paper, old clothes - my mother kept an old raincoat in there which she wore when hanging out her washing- is powerful enough still to send me back to those early years.

The scullery lighting was of course gas. It differed from the living room or kitchen in that the gas bracket was set in the centre of the ceiling, thus allowing maximum light into every corner. It also had to be as far away as possible from the wooden pulley slung above the cooker, where my mother dried clothes in winter. Pulleys were great things; they were rungless ladders fixed to the scullery ceiling; the frame was lowered by ropes to allow clothes to be draped on the struts, then hauled up to the ceiling. On washdays, my mother did her main wash in the deeper of the two sinks, scrubbing clothes on a ridged washboard, scrubbing the washing with a large bar of *Sunlight*? soap. Then she would clamp the wringer onto the strip of wood separating the two sinks and order me to ca' [turn] the handle. I hated ca'in the wringer, espe-cially when thick or heavy items were being squeezed through. Washdays were hell personified, what with the copper boiler clouding the small scullery with steam - good for nasal blockages but bad for condensation. The scullery walls literally ran with water, even with the back door open.

Now we go upstairs. The staircase was carpeted in part by a long strip of carpet set in the middle of the stairs; the exposed wood on either side of the carpet was painted with a dark varnish. The stair carpet was held in place by brass rods fixed in every step. The stair 'turned' at the top, where my mother placed a pot plant in a large receptacle - was it an aspidistra? Immediately to the right at the top of the stairs was the small bathroom, consisting of a bath with clawed feet - it would be another ten years before my mother 'boxed-in' the bath. At the drain end, a small basin or sink was attached to the bath so that you could perform ablutions with a facecloth and brush your teeth. The WC had a wooden 'pan' seat above which was the cistern to which was attached a chain with a wooden handle that you pulled to flush the toilet.

There was a stout banister on the landing, to stop you falling over and used mainly to dry clothing. Next to the bathroom was a small bedroom in which I slept when Uncle Jimmy and Norman weren't using it. I had mixed feelings about that wee room; in autumn, I could open the window to listen to the swallows screaming about the spire of Belhaven Church and I could hear the sounds of the sea at Belhaven. But on balance, I preferred the 'front' room, with its view of Lochend Woods and Doon Hill. When Uncle Jimmy and Norman were at home, they shared the room; it contained two single beds, a bedside table, a wardrobe and a small one-drawered receptacle topped with a mirror. The drawer contained baby teeth extracted over the years. Why my mother should want to keep these grisly relics was a mystery to me - until as I later discovered, could be a source of income.

Next door to the west-facing bedroom was the main one whose windows looked out on a section of Lochend Wood and Doon Hill, through a gap in the street which gave access to Summerfield Road. When you entered the room, there was a deep walk-in cupboard to your left. It was used to store old clothes, toys, Christmas annuals and junk. At first, Ken and I shared a double bed, then we were given the luxury of single beds. We shared a wardrobe, a dressing table and a small, folding table with a green felt covering -often used as a card table – for our homework or for play. Again, our floor boasted strips of carpet on either side of the bed so we didn't get cold feet in the morning.

Although we had gas fires in the bedrooms, these were lit only when we were ill or when it was intensely cold. My mother was always afraid they'd go out - always a possibility if you didn't feed a few pennies into the meter - and that we'd be gassed in our sleep. (How could we have been asphyxiated? When the money ran out in the meter, the gas supply automatically shut off!).

As I said earlier, the coal fire in the living room dictated how the furniture was arranged, just as today, the television set is the focal point. I loved the fire and spent hours before it, watching the flames and the embers forming shapes that existed only in my mind. Identifying faces in the fire was a favourite winter pastime. I would sit before the fire, my knees drawn up to my chin, my arms round my knees, watching the embers in the darkness, when Mum was at the pictures and didn't come home until 10.30pm, the best time for seeing the fire faces.

The only problem with gaslight was that it could go out without warning, much in the same way as an electric light bulb blows its filament today and plunges a room - and even a whole area of the house - into darkness.

# Funny by Gaslight

(Despite modern sophisticated technology, we still can't predict when a light bulb will blow). However, in the days of gas, there was always the fire to offer some light and one of us would reach up to the mantelshelf to fetch a spill or taper from the little wooden container I described earlier. The spill-carrier would light the way to the scullery and reach up to the shelf where the gas meter stood, then rifle the pewter mug for a penny which was inserted into the meter. If you were quick, you could use the same spill to relight the gas mantle, something at which I became adept.

As I wrote earlier, the dinner table was moved from its summer place at the window, where we ate our meals and enjoyed Granny Cockburn's array of roses that leaned against the window. In winter, we ate at the table before the fire. Those winter teatimes are fixed forever in my memory. Tea as opposed to dinner or supper was a fairly light meal, with slices of bread toasted on a long fork before the fire. We often had boiled eggs or *Shiphams* meat paste sandwiches. *Shiphams* was the poor man's *pate*; even now, a whiff of meat paste can send me into paroxysms of nostalgia as I relive these long lost early dark winter evenings. Tea over and table cleared, Ken and I would play with our toys. Ken had his beloved *Dinky* toy cars, I had my lead soldiers, each of whom I gave a first name – *Shorty* for the smaller soldiers kneeling down, *Leader* for the general in charge of the army and so on. Ken preferred to play with his toys on the table with its protective felt cover; I conducted my battles on the floor, which provided the space I needed. Serious battles cannot be fought in restricted places like table tops....

Playing on our selected and preferred sites, we couldn't help overhearing the conversations between my mother and Norman or Uncle Jimmy. Often, the talk with Jimmy turned to events that had happened in the family before Ken and I were born. Occasionally, I would interrupt their conversations with some question or other.

'Mind your own business, nosey-parker' my mother would chide. 'This isn't for your ears. Get on with your game.'

Before winter arrived, most families had the chimney swept. It was considered a mark of downright irresponsibility if you allowed your *lum* [chimney] to go 'up'. Some poorer households did this on purpose; it was a cheap way of cleaning the lum for nothing; the local council put a stop to this by fining people five shillings [25p] for calling out the local fire brigade. The chimney sweep Matthew Boyle - *Mattie Bile* as he was known to us and whom we encountered in Chapter 2 - did a brisk trade in the months of September, October and November and in the spring months. *Mattie* was a familiar sight with his small handcart piled with the distinctive flat circular flue brushes of his trade and his grubby dustsheets. For obvious reasons, he wore a black jacket and trousers to match, black sandshoes and black socks; incongruously however, his shirt was always white - well, almost. His face was soot-encrusted, his greasy *bunnet* blackened by years of peering up or down chimneys. He never used a ladder to gain access to a roof; he would shin up drain-pipes, agile as a monkey and as far as I know, he never once came to grief.

I hated it when the chimney was swept, hated it almost as much as the Spring Clean Week. The fireplace was cleaned out, the furniture pushed into the furthest corner from the fire and covered with dustsheets. In would come *Mattie*, grinning his toothless smile - he rarely wore his false teeth when he worked in case they fell down the chimney when he peered down from the roof. He would first secure his dustsheets across the fireplace, anchoring them with stones on the mantelshelf, then pin the sides to the walls so that no soot could escape. Mattie knew his trade well. When he was satisfied that every-thing was securely in place, he shinned up the drainpipe like a monkey. The first thing he did was to shout *Halloo!* down the chimney he was supposed to be sweeping so that someone below could go outside and confirm he had the right chimney and not the next door neighbour's. Then he'd plunge the flue brush with its heavy lead weight into the chimneypiece; I used to listen to it bumping and scraping the sides of the chimney walls as it raced to the bottom. He had the exact length measured so that the brush never hit the hearth; all you heard was a *Whoosh!* Which told you that the soot had landed in the grate; all you saw was a slight puff of soot escaping from the sides of his dust sheet covering the mantelpiece. He repeated this operation three or four times until he was satisfied that the chimney was clean. The last job was done gingerly; removing the light, powdery soot from the fireplace was a delicate operation, but *Mattie* was an expert. He'd ask my mother where she wanted the contents of his sheets dumped, which in our case was the back garden. *Mattie* swore that soot was great for growing rhubarb and strawberries, fruits we never grew. But soot was a good general fertiliser on its own and even better when mixed with sheep manure. *Mattie* let us keep our own soot for the garden; if we didn't want it, the sack was emptied over the wall in the Sailors' Park. Re-cently, my good friend Betty Jeffrey reminded me of this practice. She recalls playing in the soot in the field with one of the few 'coloured' boys in Dunbar; that day, her mother ordered her into the house to get cleaned up. As she was climbing the garden wall, she said to the coloured lad whom she'd just met:

'You'll have tae gaun hame to get washed as weel. You're as black as me.'

In these politically correct modern times, that would be considered a racist remark. It was completely innocent, as we were in those days.

Despite my mother's meticulous attention to the times when the chim-ney should be cleaned, one year she got it badly wrong. As a result, our *lum* went 'up' on that occasion. Once was enough. One autumn afternoon, she lit the fire as usual, let it take and went into the scullery to start the evening meal. She heard a roaring noise coming from the chimney half an hour later. By this time, Ken and I were home from school and she grabbed us and ran into the front garden from where she saw flames shooting out of the chimney. She stood there horrified, fascinated by the flames; it was a serious fire as most *lums* that went 'up' emitted grey or brown smoke, then petered out. She had to get me to run to the phone box in Summerfield Road and call the Fire Brigade; when I got back, there was a small crowd gathering in front of our house to enjoy the spectacle.

My mother was mortified more by the tacit criticism of her neighbours who clearly thought she kept a dirty house; she swore at the people - mainly kids - peering up at our roof. I went into the garden and told them to go away, the fun was over. I was boo'ed by the kids whose mothers refused to budge; to my mother they were judge and jury both, wearing their turbans and wrapover *pinnies* [pinafores] their arms folded across their chests. Phrases like *Aye, Ah kent she wis dirty for a' her airs and graces'* and *That serves the stuck up bitch right.* And then my mother's good friend and protector came striding from her house across the road. It was Annie Lough, her own arms folded over her *pinnie*, puffing indignantly on the cigarette in her mouth. She walked in our garden gate and rounded on the assembled company.

'A' right, a' right. The show's over. Away hame tae your ain fires and see that you're no' the next fur the Fire Brigade.'

The Fire Brigade men were sympathetic and kind, but they told my mother she'd be liable for a fine for causing an unnecessary fire; that was how it was in those penny-pinching days. My mother never really lived that episode down, though when remedial work was done on the chimney later, it was discovered that both ours and the next door neighbours' chimney had crumbled over the years, so the fault wasn't solely ours.

Annie Lough never came into our house, nor did we ever enter hers. She stood on our doorstep puffing furiously on her cigarette, saying my mother needn't worry for she wouldn't be the first to have a chimney go 'up, nor would she be the last. Annie was a lovely lady, the salt of the earth.

Nights, especially those at the height of winter, were reserved for ghost stories and lurid tales whose horror was amplified by gaslight and firelight. Reality could also be frightening. In the 1950s, there were three unforgettable cases resulting in murder, one of which was particularly morbid. In these gas-lit evenings, my mother was accustomed to reading aloud to Ken and I from the Daily Express. The first of these cases occurred in 1952, involving two young men called Derek Bentley and Christopher Craig. Bentley was an impressionable epileptic of low IQ aged nineteen; Craig was a brash, cocky sixteen year-old thug who manipulated the older, less intelligent boy. 'Boy' is the appropriate description because in those days, a male didn't become a man until the age of twenty-one, the age of consent. Craig was a seedy little teenager who fantasised about becoming a big-time crook; at sixteen, he was wearing a trilby and overcoat - what my mother called 'an old man cut down,' her expression for young men attempting to be adult before their time. Craig would have found many companions in today's generation but few would have matched his thirst for violence; Chris Craig carried a gun and he intended to use it at the earliest opportunity.

Craig coaxed Derek Bentley to join him in robbing a Croydon warehouse. On the night of 2nd November 1952, Craig and Bentley were spotted on the warehouse roof by a man who immediately called the police. Shortly afterwards, the police surrounded the building and Derek Bentley was apprehended. Chris Craig fired at the detective holding Bentley, wounding him in the shoulder. In custody and completely harmless, Derek Bentley shouted to young Craig, pleading with him to give himself up. Meanwhile, Police Constable Sydney Miles was edging along the roof to take Craig into custody, imploring the young gunman to surrender. Then Bentley shouted this to his accomplice:

'Let him have it, Chris!'

Chris Craig shot PC Miles between the eyes and jumped off the roof. In those days, killing anyone, especially a policeman, meant the death penalty.

To this day, the argument continues as to what Derek Bentley meant when urged Craig to 'let him [PC Miles] have it'. Did Bentley mean that his confederate should give the gun to the policeman or shoot him. Maybe Craig himself was confused as to what his friend meant. The prosecution argued the latter successfully; Derek Bentley was hanged on 28th January 1953 for his implication in that crime. Despite a good fire, I recall shivering that night, when my mother read us the details

That same year, we had another nightmarish experience – that of the serial killer John Reginald Christie. Christie was a sick mass murderer who raped several women after he had murdered them. Ken and I were spellbound and scared at the same time as my mother read out nightly accounts of the trial – reports of strange smells emanating from No 10 Rillington Place, London. A body was found. Then another. And another. Three female cadavers were found in a small cupboard whose door had been papered over. Then, beneath the floorboards of the front room, the police found the remains of Ethel Christie. This sparked off a general hunt in and around the house. In all, eight corpses were discovered; there may have been more.

It got to the stage that Ken and I could hardly eat our supper without first hearing of the daily trial proceedings. We jumped nervously every time the gas mantle popped. When it went out, we pretended to be indignant rather than scared. The truth was we were more scared than annoyed. It was a raw fear that never left me, even to today. Ken and I were scared silly

Recently, I read an account of the murders. The first had occurred during the Blitz, in the Blackout. Then in 1949, Christie had taken in a couple of lodgers, Timothy and Beryl Evans and their baby. It seems that Timothy Evans had in fact murdered his wife Beryl during a violent argument and that Christie despatched the baby. Today, Evans would have been convicted of manslaughter. Eventually, he was granted a posthumous pardon. I was glad when the authorities hanged him on 15th July 1953. He remains the bogeyman of all my gas-lit evenings. John Reginald Christie was chillingly brought to life by actor Richard Attenborough in the 1971 film 10 Rillington Place, scripted from Ludovic Kennedy's book. John Hurt played the part of Timothy Evans, imbuing the character with all the flaws so obvious in that poor young man. The Evans' trial was used in the campaign to abolish capital punishment; I felt that this was and is a mistake.

Two other events from my gas-lit memories of the mid-fifties arose as a result of the Cold War with Russia. The first was the disappearance of the frogman Commander Buster Crabbe who was spying for M15. He was investigating a Russian destroyer in an English port; he was never seen again. It is almost certain that he was caught and executed. The other memory is even more poignant; I can't recall the precise year but I recall my mother reading accounts of the loss of the submarine *Thetis* in home waters. The submarine was undergoing trials when, for some reason, it failed to resurface. Most of the crew died of asphyxiation; a few were saved by escaping through the submarine's conning tower and its torpedo tubes. The agony of selecting those who were to remain behind must have been dreadful and the thought of it haunts me to this day.

After listening to lurid tales, I climbed the stairs each night with a paraffin lamp that cast menacing shadows on the walls. I had a few nightmares, but children have great powers of self-healing and it wasn't long before Norman and I were telling each other - and young Ken - ghost stories once more. Gaslight certainly encouraged the spinning of yarns, much more so than electric light. Better still was the kitchen lit only by the flames of a living fire. My mother often sat with us, recountig stories of her childhood as she knitted. She loved ballroom dancing and regaled us with the times she went dancing to the Gymnasium, or *Gym*, in Castle Park barracks, later known as the Victoria Ballroom. We were fascinated when she told us that between the two World Wars, the young officers wore spurs as part of their dress uniforms. My mother's love of dancing was legendary. An expert in most dances of the time, she unconsciously taught me that the love of dancing is indicative of a personality with a spark of gaiety, romance and shared human responses. I shall never forget her stories about the manners of these young men.

> 'They were gentlemen as well as perfect dancers. Their spurs never caught a girl's dress. We wore long dresses in those days. They were absolute gentlemen. And so handsome.'

She would chuckle as she recounted her memories of a girl known locally as *Tattie Soup* but known to the soldiers at the Barracks as *Chinstrap* on account of the fact that she always wore a straw hat secured under her chin by a broad elastic strap. Another name she went by was *The Sandshoe Queen* for obvious reasons. Mum had us in stitches with her tales of the old days. Like when she was dancing with the young officers who would buy her several sherries and which she would pour into the aspidistra plant nearby.

# Funny by Gaslight

In the gaslight evenings, we listened to creepy and chilling plays on the wireless. The radio and gaslight made these more atmospheric, more menacing. But fact is invariably more bizarre and even more frightening than fiction. I recollect two gaslight incidents that still give me the shivers. They are indexed in my memory under the headings *The Face at the Window* and *The Rustling Ghost.*

*The Face* incident occurred one stormy autumn night of lashing rain. I think it was either late September or early October, since the dining table was still in its summer position at the window. The gas suddenly went out and Ken and I were waiting for my mother to put another penny in the slot. It was dark save for the flickering firelight and we wanted to get to the fire as the room was chilly. My mother was very strict about us leaving the table before we'd finished the meal, so we had to wait until she returned and let us sit by the fire. The gas plopped on again; at the same moment, we heard a tapping on the windowpane. Gentle at first, I thought it was one of Granny Cockburn's roses nodding against the glass. Then the tapping grew to an impatient knocking. My mother made some comment about damned kids starting their autumn night tricks early and pulled back the heavy red curtains that were put up after summer ended.

She gave out a loud shriek as she drew the curtain back. There, framed in the rain-streaming window was a gaunt, white, skeletal face bracketed by wild straggling hair that blew over its eyes. The mouth was one of bared teeth, wide open as if emitting a silent scream. My mother yelled again and we jumped off our chairs, as scared as she was. The apparition raised its hand with palm upward, indicating that it was raining, then lowered it again to grasp the other as if in supplication. The voice wailed, imploring my mother to open the front door.

It was none other than Alice Gillon from across the street. She was tallish, thin, worn to the bone with years of drudgery, her face ravaged with lines as she struggled to make ends meet. At times she looked half-starved and probably was. She tended to save on food to pay some bill or other. In those few seconds, she'd been totally unrecognisable, her face distorted by rain streaming down the window, her hair plastered to her skull, even more lopsided than usual, like one of last year's collapsed nests.

With a cry of relief, my mother went to let her in. Alice had been soaked to the skin walking the few yards from her house to ours. She'd knocked at the front door but we hadn't heard her because of the wind and rain. In those days, neighbours locked their doors at night and when they went out but they always left the key on a string that could be pulled through the letterbox. Gone are those innocent days.... However, not even a close neighbour would have dreamt of retrieving the key and letting themselves in. All Alice could manage was this:

'Och, Jean. Ah'm that sorry Ah gien yis a' a flegg!'

# Funny by Gaslight

Her apology for having given us a fright was hastily accepted – on the surface!

Alice had come to borrow a cup of sugar for her husband Jockie's tea. My mother sat her down by the fire and got a towel to dry her hair. We sat at the table just staring at her, still unable to take it all in. We were also told on pain of a skelp [cuff] round the ear not to speak broad dialect in front of adults. I remember thinking why shouldn't adults afford the same consideration to us children? Alice was typical of the adults in our street who made little or no concessions to bairns.

'Whit weel-hannelled laddies yis are. Ah wish they wis mair like yis.'
Well, we were well mannered, for that was flogged into us!

My mother spoke dialect readily, especially when in the company of an older woman but rarely in front of us. Perhaps she too was still suffering from the shock of Alice's arrival.

'Och, ye should come visit us mair often Alice. They've no' been sae quiet for ages.'

After that, we called Alice Gillon *Mrs Face-at-the-window,* abbreviated to *The Face.* But never to her own....

The second incident was known as the *Rustling Ghost.* It too took place on a windy autumn or winter night. Again, the gas went out at a crucial moment. This time, it occurred during the course of one of the weekly *Man in Black* stories on the radio, tales which lasted about fifteen minutes and left us begging for more. These ghost stories were told by a man called Valentine Dyall - his very name conjured up an image of a dark silhouette dressed in trilby hat and cloak, something like the outline on the bottles of *Sandeman Sherry,* one of which my mother allowed in the house at New Year. Dyall had a rich, velvety voice with just a hint of menace; it wasn't unlike that of the hammier Vincent Price but Dyall told ghost stories like nobody else before - or since. He always introduced himself thus:

'Good evening. This is your Storyteller. This is the Man in Black....'
(You could almost hear the dots after his name, for he would pause after the last word, letting it sink in).

I can't recall which of the stories Norman and I were listening to but they were never dull and invariably left you with an odd, shivery feeling which some say is the hair standing on the back of your neck. (Personally, my hair has never stood on end but you get my meaning). That night, Dyall excelled himself - or was it the wind booming in the chimney that added to the atmosphere created by his soft, menacing voice? At any rate, Norman and I moved closer to the fire as the tale unwound. Then the gas went out. Neither of us was keen to go into the dark scullery to put a penny in the meter. We sat still until the broadcast ended. Then Norman said this:

'Right. The gas needs a penny. You go. You're youngest.'
Somehow, I sensed that Norman was as scared as I was.

'No. You go. You're older than me.'

# Funny by Gaslight

We tossed a button as we didn't have any money. Norman lost. He went into the scullery to find the pewter cup bereft of pennies. Our mother was at the pictures and wouldn't be home until 10.30pm. So we lit a paraffin lamp and settled down to read by its dull light. After trimming the wick, Norman was replacing the globe on the lamp when a gust of wind blew a cloud of smoke down the chimney. The living room door swung open at the same time. Norman went to close the door, but as he was doing that, he stopped, turned to me and put his finger to his lips to shush! me. He came over to the fire where I was sitting with my comic.

'There's a noise up the stairs.'

He was whispering and looked scared. He coaxed me out of my armchair and led me to the door. At first, I heard nothing, then after what was probably no more than a few seconds, I heard the Noise. It was quiet, then it gradually got louder, a rustling noise which seemed to rise and fall. Someone - or something - was upstairs. It stirred slowly, grew to a crescendo, then died away. My anxious brother's chalk-white face remains in my memory to this day. He whispered again.

'Ah think there's somebody upstairs.'

We went back to the fire. He said it was probably young Ken getting up to go to the bathroom. No chance. Ken had a *pottie* [chamber-pot] under the bed and I knew he'd use that rather than venture along the cold landing to go to the even chillier bathroom. I said as much.

'Norrie, that's not Kenny. He's too wee to get up and go to the bathroom
on his own. You'll need to go up the stairs and see what it is.'
He snorted.

'Nae fears. Ah went to the scullery in the dark. It's your turn.'

I protested that he'd gone to the scullery because he'd lost the toss of the button. Norman wasn't afraid of anything physical but that night, he was scared of the unknown. His face was drained of any colour and he kept looking behind him for some reason or other. Then he pushed me to the door of the living room.

'We'll baith go. The gither. And ye'll hae to carry the lamp so's ma
hands are free.'
'Why d'you have to have your hands free? You're bigger than me. You
should take the lamp. Why can't you go first?'
'Because.'
'Because what?'
'Because if it's a man, Ah'll hae tae grab him.'
'What if it's a ghost?'
'Yir daft, wi' yir talkin' o' ghosts. That's only on the wireless.'

Logic at last penetrated my addled brain. But I felt vulnerable when I grasped the heavy lamp and walked through the living room door into the dark stairway in front of my heroic brother.

# Funny by Gaslight

Step by agonisingly slow measured step, the pair of us crept up the stairway, our shadows weaving on the wall like in the famous *Adventures of Robin Hood* film when Basil Rathbone and Errol Flynn engaged each other in that fatal sword duel. So I imagined it.

The Noise began again as we were halfway up the stair. Outside, the wind was moaning round the house. I stopped. Then Norman dug his forefinger into the small of my back.

'Get a move on!' he hissed.

At the top of the stair, the Noise was loud. We were both shaking. The leaping shadows cast by the paraffin lamp terrified me and I was gripped by a sudden, terrible thought. What if I dropped the lamp? What was worse, what if it went out? I stood aside at the top of the stair, all goose pimples and cold.

The Noise came from the bathroom. Norman stood by the half-open door. The Thing that made the Noise was in there and there was no light for us to see it. Summoning his last reserves of strength and with the fireside poker in his hand, Norman pushed past me, kicked fully open the bathroom door and yelled out this:

'Got ye, ye bugger! Quick, Roy, the lamp! Let's see his bloody face!'

I followed him into the bathroom, my hand shaking and aching from the lamp's weight. Then I heard Norman laughing. He turned to me, a huge grin on his face.

'It wis the lavvy paper that wis flappin'. That wis the rustlin' noise. The windae was up at the bottom tae let oot the smoke fae ma last Woodbine.'

The rustling had been caused by the wind shaking the toilet roll fixed to the wall just below the window ledge.

Nervous but glad, I joined in Norman's wild chortle. But it was a long time before I could listen to Valentine Dyall's weekly story without first checking the gas meter and the pewter cup for pennies. I also made sure the bathroom window was always closed....

Coal gas served us well for another year or two after this incident. When electricity was installed, gas still provided our cooking and the coal fire still heated our living room and the water supply until at last in 1958, my mother went 'all electric', as they used to say with a certain measure of pride.

The passing of the Gas Age left me with ambivalent feelings. The streets were undoubtedly brighter but it was a sodium glare and unnatural. Also, the improved lighting meant you could be detected easier when you hid from your street pals or your parents and neighbours. The Gas Company laid off some of its employees and while I continued to collect cinders and *briquettes* for the open fire, I knew these days were numbered when my mother talked about 'going all electric.' An era was passing before our young eyes. We protested in vain to our mother.

'Ach, the fire's a herber [harbour]o' dirt and stoor [dust]. Ah'm no gonnae blackleed [blacklead] it and set it in the cauld mornins'. No. An Ah'm niver goan tae haul buckets o' coal frae the coalshed again. Coal's gettin' dearer every year onyway[anyway].'

Uncle Jimmy who was living with us first at weekends, then all week after 1958, tried to reinforce our argument by reminding her that an open fire burnt a fair proportion of household waste. Mother was unmoved by his pleas.

'Aye, weel the Cooncil will hae to put on extra rubbish collections. Yir oanly takin' the bairns' side on accoont o' ye like tae heugh [spit] into it. That'll need tae stop, it's a filthy habit.'

My mother won. The electric fire with its cream and light brown tiles was clean but clinical. I had to admit that the electric fire did away with black-leading, chopping kindling and laying coal nuggets which took a long time to offer warmth on cold winter mornings. There were also no more capricious gusts of wind that sent blue smoke into the living room. In time, we got rid of the gas that had so entranced me in my childhood. In doing so, we spelt the death-knell of coal mining and the weird but wonderful gasworks which in later years would remind me of Dante's *Inferno*, with all its graphic imagery. An era had passed and I didn't realise it was gone until many years later.

Funny by Gaslight is the appropriate title for this chapter. In this context, the word 'funny' means both humorous and strange or peculiar, even frightening. After the gaslight was replaced by electricity, life for me was never the same again.

# 5

## Street Rhymes and Games

Our street was a place where most neighbours looked out for one another. And our street was a communal public space where kids could play safely. Today, Lammermuir Crescent still holds happy memories for me, for it was the first place – the only place – I consider my home. I am tempted to think of generations of salmon that are spawned in one stream, then wander the waterways of the world only return to spawn again where they born, then die there. This book is as much dedicated to the people I knew and lived with in that street as it is to my brother Ken. I have always believed that all lives are important and the stories of those that are gone are worth remembering. There is in my view, no human being who is unimportant or 'ordinary'. The street where I was born and still survives has changed in many ways – not all for the better – but it is history. For what is history but the record of human lives and how they lived these lives. Gone are most of the people I loved, argued with, fought (only occasionally) and played with. I am still friends with those that survive today. I miss those that I knew and are gone, for they were part of me, part of growing up in the street I loved.

Like all generations of children, in Lammermuir Crescent, we had our rhymes, games, customs, rituals, sayings and Red Letter Days. Through these activities, we bonded, learning to inter-relate with other children - well, at least that was the theory. Being something of a loner and even a misfit, I chose games I could play on my own a good deal of the time, eschewing the communal ones except in the autumn and winter. In summer, the beaches, the woods, fields and hills were our playground; in autumn and winter, the streets were where we congregated in small groups under the lampposts. This chapter describes the pursuits and important days that made the childhood of my generation memorable. Children then made their own amusement and in my opinion, benefited from the consequent exercising of their imagination, which is surely a child's most effective way of coping with reality, with its limited experience of life. Today's kids have lost that magic; they need expensive toys and equipment like computers and play stations to pass their time; my generation had none of those dubious accessories and as a consequence, I believe we had a more enjoyable and fulfilling childhood.

I sometimes wonder what the children of the present century will make of our innocent, unsophisticated pursuits and beliefs, our simple, less complicated lifestyles. Will they enjoy the same things as we did? I doubt it. They may look back and wonder at pursuits that will seem naive, even silly to them, with their sophisticated computer games and play stations. It's doubtful whether they will be able to appreciate the simple pleasures those of my generation enjoyed. Some will care less about the mystery of the world, the wild beauty of seashore, wood and meadow, although the efforts of the staff at the *John Muir Birthplace* have already proven valuable in redressing the balance. To be fair to modern children, fewer places prominent in our landscape are accessible to them today, sites like Dunbar Castle, although this may change in the future. Their playgrounds are increasingly becoming rigidly controlled areas that have to meet stringent health and safety standards, supervised by adults to protect them from predatory individuals. That sadly is a reflection of the society in which we live; in my opinion, it will get worse as the new century progresses. I sincerely hope I will be proved wrong, as it's a depressing thought.

I have arranged this chapter in sections describing the street games, pursuits and their accompanying rhymes we enjoyed in the 1940s and 1950s. I cannot claim it is an exhaustive list but hopefully, it will offer a glimpse of the way we spent our leisure hours half a century ago. That age of innocence has disappeared, although the children of that time who found so much joy in the simple pleasures of that time, playing in safe streets, pollution-free beaches, open fields and safe woodlands.

### *Rhymes and Riddles*

Children the world over inherit much by word of mouth from the generations that preceded theirs. Many of the rhymes and riddles we learnt were passed down to us by older brothers and sisters who learnt them from their antecedents. Boys relied less on street rhymes than girls, with their ball and skipping games. Boys tended to play games that required physical attributes rather than words, although they had their own word games.

The first rhymes I heard were little songs and poems meant to help children fall asleep. The clearest and earliest memory I have is of a little poem my mother chanted, first to Norman, then me and finally Ken; she said she'd been taught it by her own mother. It is an endearing, though perhaps not enduring little piece; I certainly haven't heard it since Ken's childhood. It's called *Wynken, Blynken and Nod,* recited to the Very Young at bedtime.

My mother used to rattle off this cautionary tale when we sat too close to the fire on winter nights:

*Little Polly Flinders*
*Sat upon the cinders*
*Wearing her pretty little dress.*
*Her mother came and caught her*
*And spanked her little daughter*
*For spoiling her nice new dress.*

'Let that be a warning to you. If I catch you singeing your good jerseys, watch out.... ' she would say as she wagged her finger at us.

Riddles were less common but my brother Norman was fond of trying out his repertoire on Ken and I.  He succeeded in baffling both of us with the following:

> *Round and round the Radical Rock,*
> *the raggedy rascal ran:*
> *If you can tell me how many r's are in that,*
> *You'll be a clever man.*

The answer was none - in the word *that*.

In the same idiom was one popular in the school playground:

> *Constantinople is a very big word,*
> *A very big word to say;*
> *If you can't spell it, you're a very big dunce*
> *And you are a fool today.*

The answer was *it*, the not-so-obvious key word.


### *Skipping, Ball and Counting-Out Rhymes*

These were popular with the girls, skipping rhymes being the most numerous.

> *On the mountain stands a lady,*
> *Who she is I do not know*
> *All she wants is gold and silver,*
> *All she wants is a nice young man.*

A skipping rhyme which allowed a friend to join in - more than one when two girls *cawed* [cast] a long rope, one at either end, went like this:

> *I like coffee,*
> *I like tea,*
> *I like* [name of girl]
> *In with me*

That was the signal for her friend to join her without breaking the rhythm of the rope.

The girls in Lammermuir Crescent used to play a ball game called *doublers* with two balls; some like my good friend Betty Jeffrey were extremely adept at it, bouncing the balls off the air raid shelter wall at *Paylor's Corner.*

A favourite rhyme was *Katie Beardie:*

> *Katie Beardie had a coo,\**
> *It was yellow, black and blue,*
> *Wasn't it a bonnie coo,*
> *Dance, Katie Beardie.*

*\*Coo = cow

An alternative to the last two lines went thus:

> *All the monkeys in the zoo*
> *Laughed at Katie Beardie.*

# Street Rhymes and Games

This rhyme is very old and is quoted in Sir Walter Scott's *The Fortunes of Nigel*

Girls were fond of the following rhyme:

*I wrote a letter to my love*
*And on the way I dropped it,*
*I dree, I dree, I dropped it*
*So somebody has picked it up*
*And put it in her pocket.*

Another favourite with us was this:

*Iddle diddle, my son John*
*Went to bed with his clothes on,*
*One shoe off and one shoe on,*
*Iddle diddle, my son John.*

A rhyme frequently heard on winter nights, when we imagined the road between the pavements as a river, went like this:

*Ah\* came tae a river and Ah couldnae\* get across,*
*Ah paid a shillin' for an auld\* blind horse;*
*Ah jumped on its back and its bone went crack*
*And we a' played the fiddle till the boat came back.*

\*Ah = I; couldnae = couldn't; auld = old; a' = all

A short rhyme popular on Sundays was appropriate for that day, usually chanted just before Sunday school began:

*Matthew, Mark, Luke, John,*
*Haud\* the cuddy\* till Ah get on.*

\*Haud = hold; cuddy = horse

A taunting rhyme often doubled up as a skipping one, as in the following:

*Tell-tale tit,*
*Your mammie cannae knit,*
*Your daddie cannie go to bed*
*Without his dummy-tit*

Nonsense rhymes were favoured by boys; favourites were:

*One fine day in the middle of the night,*
*Two dead men got up to fight,*
*Back to back, they faced each other,*
*Drew their swords and shot each other.*

Another example of a nonsense rhyme was sung whenever anyone wearing a kilt hove in sight or when a pipe band marched in the High Street:

*Hear the monkeys kickin' up a din,*
*Tooral-addie, Tooral-addie,*
*Hear the monkeys kickin' up a din,*
*Still a pudden, still a pudden\*.*

\*Pudden = pudding, meaning a stupid person

Another taunt shouted after a kilted boy or man – my generation were

85

Lowlanders who eschewed the wearing of such outlandish wear - was brief but to the point:

> *Kiltie, kiltie cauld\* bum,*
> *Never had a warm yin\*.*

\*Cauld = cold; yin = one

This rhyme was invariably sung when boys of my generation encountered a string of pupils from Belhaven Hill School, out for their Sunday walk; the boys were extremely well-mannered and usually wished us Good afternoon which we thought was the mark of the *sissie* or *jessie*. Today, I wish I could turn back the clock; these kids were polite....

If a boy found something belonging to somebody else and was challenged for it, he would chant to the loser:

> *Finders keepers,*
> *Losers greeters\**

\*Greeters = weepers

A boy might show appreciation of or disdain for a girl's anatomy by chanting the following little ditty:

> *Skinny-ma-linky long legs,*
> *Umberella feet,*
> *Went to the pictures,*
> *Couldnae find a seat.*
> *When the picture started,*
> *Skinny-ma-linky farted,*
> *Skinny-ma-linky long legs,*
> *Umberella feet.*

A rhyme popular with sniggering boys waiting for the *poor oot* [money thrown from the wedding car by the bridegroom at weddings], aimed at the bride if she were fat or suspiciously stout round her middle:

> *Here comes the bride,*
> *Fifty inches wide,*
> *She couldnae get in the front door*
> *So she had to go in the side.*

From a healthy distance, boys got even with stronger detractors by singing this ditty:

> *Sticks and stanes*
> *Will break my banes*
> *But words will never hurt me.*
> *When Ah'm deid*
> *And in my grave*
> *Ye'll rue the names ye called me.*

[Stanes = stones; banes = bones; deid = dead]

# Street Rhymes and Games

### *Counting-out and Counting-in Rhymes*

These were games involving a group of children, mainly girls but occasionally boys and sometimes both. The object was to eliminate all but the winner, the last in a circle. The following rhymes were popular and used all over Scotland:

> *Ip, dip, dip,*
> *My little ship*
> *Sails on the water*
> *And you are IT*

which meant that the person pointed at had to leave the circle.
There was also the ever popular *Eenie, meenie, miney , mo:*

> *Eenie, meenie, miney, mo,*
> *Catch a baby [or nigger] by the toe,*
> *If he squeals, let him go,*
> *Eenie, meenie, miney, mo*

A favourite with girls was this quartet:

> *Red, white and blue,*
> *The cat's got the flu',*
> *The dog's got the chickenpox*
> *And so have YOU.*

Another popular rhyme involved a circle with one person appointed as the counter and everyone offering clenched fists for the counter to hit with his/her own to eliminate everyone save the winner:

> *One potato, two potato, three potato, four,*
> *Five potato, six potato, seven potato MORE*

Every player had two 'lives', one being lost when the player's fist was struck as the word MORE was uttered.
The shortest counting-out rhyme was the popular

> *Eetle, ottle, black bottle,*
> *Eetle, ottle, OUT!*

There was of course an official day for jests and jokes on 1st April which is April Fool's Day or *Huntygowk*, literally meaning hunt-the-fool or cuckoo, known as a *gowk* in Scotland. The custom originated in the Middle Ages and involved a stooge who was sent to hunt the cuckoo, or *gowk*. In its earliest guise, someone would prepare a sealed message and hand it to the unsuspecting messenger ordered to deliver it to the recipient. The message informed the recipient to re-direct the messenger elsewhere and the message was re-sealed. The poor *gowk* was sent all over the place until someone took pity on him or her and finally confessed the trick. That was supposed to happen before noon on 1st April.

One of our tricks was to up-end an empty eggshell in an egg-cup, thus making it appear as a genuine boiled egg. When the victim cracked the shell with a spoon, he or she would be greeted with cries of 'Huntygowk!'. But in my time, as in the Middle Ages, it all had to stop at midday. If you went over the deadline of noon, the person you'd tried to trick was entitled to chant the following rhyme:

*Huntygowk's past,*
*You're a fool at last,*
*You're a fool an' no' me,*
*You're a fool an' up a tree.*

### *Outdoor Pursuits and Games*

Children of today are rarely seen playing outside; they are in their bed-rooms watching TV or playing computer games, which I think is a great pity. The children of my generation probably played more out of doors even in the dark autumn, winter and early spring nights. While we loved the fireside's bright glow, we first looked forward to a night's entertainment in the open air. The games we played in the playground and after school, in the dark streets, are rarely seen today. The generation of the 21st century appear to have little enthusiasm for the use of that most valuable asset, the imagination. We see groups of kids at various places but they seem bored and admit they are. I can't fathom that. I was never bored in Dunbar, no matter what the state of the weather. We had little by way of play toys, let alone educational toys and we made our own - articles like *bogies* or carts fashioned from the cannibalised bits of prams; there was also the ubiquitous *girds* or old bike wheels from which the rubber tyre had been stripped; and various missile-firing weapons made from odds and sods - more of which comes later. On balance however, we played innocent games handed down by earlier generations.

As already mentioned, girls had their skipping and ball games. Boys favoured marbles, chestnut bashing, carts and *girds* [a *gird* was a bike wheel bereft of its rubber tyre]. The expert girder *cawed* [drove] his *gird* with a wooden stick, directing it skilfully along roads and back streets, taking added pleasure from steering it into a group of girls sitting at the kerbside playing with dolls. The young chauvinists among us would cry out 'Mind yirsel" as they disrupted these groups of girls, taking malicious delight when the girls drew their feet and legs from the road to the safety of the pavement.

An evergreen game enjoyed by boys and girls was *rounders,* based on the American baseball game devised during the American Civil War to keep the Union troops of the Northern States occupied when they weren't being whupped by Robert E Lee, the brilliant Confederate general in the South . *Rounders* was a game played by both sexes –and not only children. At Easter, when we all went to *Osie Dean* to roll our Easter eggs, adult men and women eagerly joined in. Another popular pastime was *plaws* or *peevers,* known I believe in England as *hopscotch* – the word *scotch* implies that the game originated north of the Border.... Whatever its origin, the game was played by chalking a column of squares in the road or pavement; the squares were numbered one to ten, with numbers four and five, then seven and eight placed side by side so that the effect was like a French, or Lorraine Cross. The *peever* or puck was usually a smooth, flat stone or an empty *Cherry Blossom* polish tin. The first player slid the *peever* into square one, hopped on it and retrieved the *peever* in the process. (There were many invigilators who watched the player's feet to see if he/she stood on the chalked line; those who did were declared 'out'). Anyway, the player would then progress up the column to the top number ten - providing he/she hadn't landed the *peever* on a chalk line or stepped on one.

Games were spontaneously played as soon as there were enough young people gathered round the foggy street light on autumn and winter evenings. Among our favourites was *What's the Time, Mr Wolf?* One of the kids would be appointed the wolf and the others walked round him/her in a circle, frequently asking the wolf what time it was; the wolf would answer a few questions, then shout 'Dinner time!' which was the signal to start chasing the others, the first to be caught becoming the wolf. Another favourite was *Farmer, farmer, may we cross your Golden River?* This was an alternative to the game *Mother may I?* In the 'farmer' game, the boy selected for the role was asked for permission to cross the river and he might answer 'Yes, if you are wearing the colour red' or some other qualification (girls didn't care for this game because they would be asked to show their knickers to prove they were wearing red/ white or whatever other colour). The *Mother* game required the players to ask the 'mother' if they might do something or other, which allowed the questioner to step nearer to her. In that game, the trick was for one person to touch 'mother' before she could answer. The winner thus become the next 'mother'.

Another game was *Statues*; this involved a person standing with his/her back to the players and turning round after counting to ten – slowly or quickly, so that the players never knew when the count was completed. The counting person could walk among the 'statues' and try to make them snigger or move - sniggering and moving meant you were disqualified or 'out'. The player who won the game was first to reach the base or hedge and for some reason lost in the mists of time, shout out 'White Horse!' That player was then elected to replace the person who had judged the 'statues.'

Extremely popular were the physical games like *Hide-and-Seek* or *Kick-the-Can.* The first is self-explanatory and is played today. The second was a more sophisticated version of *Hide-and-Seek* and was usually played by boys. A tin can was placed in the centre of a chalked circle in the road and a 'keeper' was appointed. One player started the game by kicking the can as far as he could, the signal to allow the others to run away and hide while the 'keeper' counted to a hundred with his hands covering his face and usually standing at the nearest lamp post. He then replaced the can in the chalk circle. The trick was to emerge from your hiding place, kick the can and return there without being caught by the 'keeper'. If you were caught, you were a prisoner. Anyone 'captured' could be set free by another player running out and touching him/her, then kicking the can and returning to his hidey hole without being caught. Hidey holes were usually nearby gardens, a fact which infuriated the keen gardeners in our street, particularly one elderly gentleman who was a dead ringer for *Grandpa Broon* in the *Sunday Post.*

Another lively game was *tig,* sometimes known also as *catch.* The players ran about the street, endeavouring to evade the 'catcher' who simply had to touch one player and call out 'tig!' so that the player became the 'catcher'. A game usually played indoors was *Blind Man's Buff* but out of doors, it was made more lively by blindfolding the victim in a dark part of the street - usually between two lamp posts - then spinning the person round three times to allow the other players to find themselves 'safe' places. In this game, players weren't allowed to leave the street but they could stand where they wanted to - against a lamp post/garden gate/hedge. If the blind man found and identified you, you were the next victim.

Not unexpectedly, the school playground provided us with a spacious area for games played at morning and afternoon playtimes known as 'leavetimes' ie. leaving the classroom for a few minutes' play. We called both periods the *leavy* or *leafy,* when you ate your play-piece, then horsed around in the playground. Some of the school playground games were dictated by the seasons; snowball fights in winter, *Huntygowk* on 1st April, chestnut bashing in autumn; a variation in Dunbar on chestnut bashing was *tangle-bashin'.* Usually played after school, we went to the beach and selected oar weed stripped of its fronds so that it resembled a club; you then laid your club on a rock for your opponent to smash, then you tried to smash his.

The most common playground pursuit for boys was marbles, played through the whole school year. At Woodbush, where Dunbar Grammar School used to be, there were a few square yards of barren, hard earth next to the Special Class Hut (we said it was for the *loonies,* now more kindly called the mentally handicapped) where in that blasted earth and under an equally blasted tree, we dug *puggies* - holes for tossing in your marble before you could attack those of your opponents. These games were often played to arbitrary rules which had to be agreed before the game began. Games might be for *keeps* - meaning every marble you hit was yours - or *nae keeps,* which is obvious. Another rule was that there were to be *nae hunchies* - which meant that no player was allowed to bend too far forward and thus get his marble into the *puggie.* Complaints were shouted loudly and marble games could become quite animated, with perhaps two boys staring each other out, one accusing the other of cheating ('I did nut' [not]. 'Ye did sut '[so]. 'Did sut'. 'Did nut.' 'Sut'. 'Nut'. And so it would go on until the protagonists degenerated into a fist fight. At Dunbar Grammar School, I was known as *Puggie* but not, alas, for my skill with marbles. My surname said it all....

In autumn, we had the craze called *chessies.* At weekends, gangs of boys would scour the countryside for horse chestnut trees, knocking the nuts off by throwing sticks into the branches. My favourite place for this was *Bowerhouse* or *Boorhoose* as it was popularly known locally. The chestnut trees are no more today.

The nuts were hardened in the oven, pierced with a nail, then strung on a piece of string or twine so that you might have six on your string, although you only used one nut at a time. The game was simple; all you did was challenge another boy to a duel and the challenger offered his first chestnut. This went on until one or other chestnut was smashed or cracked. When one nut had 'killed' four others, it was regarded as a champion and its owner was carried shoulder-high round the playground.

We also made crude weapons that could fire missiles. Most common was the peashooter made from the hollow stem of the hogweed plant; you cut your stem to the required length, blew through it to remove the usual earwigs lurking inside, then washed it out with soapy water. A supply of dried peas for 'bullets' was usually to be had in my mother's pantry, although some boys gathered berries from the hedgerows in autumn. A good marksman could hit a chosen target at 10 paces, an expert one could annoy a cat at 30.

Another lethal weapon in our armoury was the catapult or *guttie*; most versions were home made using a Y-shaped piece of wood, the stem of the Y being reinforced with rubber to give a good grip. A strand of strong rubber was fixed to the arms of the Y with a leather patch threaded through it to hold the missile. These weapons could be deadly and many a poor unsuspecting rabbit met its end at the expert *guttie* marksman's hands. Some devotees would buy metal Y-shaped catapults, boys like Jock the Wild Man, one of my childhood heroes even though he was about the same age as me. Jock also owned an airgun. We shall hear more of Jock in due course.

The most popular of all was the matchstick gun, a fairly innocuous weapon which as the name suggests fired spent matchsticks and could sting when meeting with unprotected flesh. It was made from a six or eight inch piece of kindling wood, with heavy-duty rubber bands to provide the propulsion. The trigger was a simple *kirby* [hair] grip used to keep girls' hair in place; with its legs splayed out on either side of the wood, the *kirby* grip head passed under the rubber bands and was drawn back towards the firer. The matchstick was then inserted and the crude trigger was held by the thumb until a suitable target presented itself. This juvenile version of the crossbow could be quite effective at close range; a competent marksman would hit what he was aiming at, provided it was no further away than about 10 to 15 paces. Very soon, boys were improving on the basic design by reinforcing the rubber bands by using more, or adding a second hairpin to the underside so that they could have two shots. A few boys even carried two matchstick guns, thus emulating their cowboy heroes and firing both simultaneously – two-gun embryonic John Waynes in effect.

Another martial game we played was *soldiers* using *lamb's tongue plantains* that grew in profusion along the country roads. The plantain is a weed whose flowers are borne on a tall cylindrical spike rather than a stem; after flowering, the head resembles a busby - hence the name of the game. You simply held out your plantain spike and invited a challenger to knock off its busby with his own plantain spike.

The game most favoured by boys was WAR. Having recently lived through the Second World War - but not experiencing hostilities to any great degree other than the two bombings and the inconvenience of rationing and the Blackout - the boys of my generation were predisposed to fighting mock battles, capturing home-made castles or camps. In these sieges, the favoured weapon was the *divot*, or clump of grass pulled out by the roots, the soil clinging to the roots being moulded into an arrowhead shape. These fights could become quite vicious and usually ended when blood was drawn by a stone often deliberately concealed in the earth-head of the divot. Autumn was a popular time for these battles as corn stubble pulled out by the roots made excellent missiles; when shaped as above, they could be propelled with uncanny accuracy. Many a late Saturday afternoon I went home with my clothes stained with clay or dirt from these epic encounters.

Once during a particularly vigorous conflict in what was the cornfield now occupied by the modern Tree scheme - so-called as all its streets are named after trees - I was forced to take shelter in the thorn hedge that marked the boundary of the cornfield and land owned by the Usher family and the wall that enclosed the south boundary of *Summerfield House*. As I lay in the roots of the thick hedge, I noticed a perfectly shaped little nest supported by a few stalks of corn that had escaped the reaper. I peered in the little opening and to my surprise found a small field mouse peering back, sitting on its small pile of acorns and berries, clearly its winter store. I forgot the world I lived in for a moment and entered the other world of nature that exists alongside our own. I think that day I discovered a lasting love of nature and small creatures. For a few minutes, I was oblivious to the war cries, screams and sobbing of small boys hurt by corn missiles. Then someone broke the spell by screaming at one wounded kid to 'stop yir bluidy peengin!' [whining]. I quietly tiptoed away, leaving the quivering little creature to its peace. The *peenger* was later consoled by a trip to see the field mouse nest on his promise not to reveal its whereabouts to the others. He stopped his sniffling and was as enchanted as I'd been, forgetting for a while the pain in his head.

Some of our pursuits were lucrative. The most common was the *pooroot* [pour-out] at weddings. Most weddings took place on a Saturday which meant that there was always a knot of boys and girls hanging outside the various churches, be they Kirk of Scotland, Episcopal, Methodist or Roman Catholic

- we were ecumenical in the sense that we took anybody's money- around three pm. We pretended we wanted to see the bride and groom, but all we were interested in was the money from the *poor-oot*. When the happy couple emerged from the church and had their photographs taken, the throng of children grew restless and jockeyed for positions near the taxi waiting to whisk the recently joined pair to their wedding reception. The formalities over, the happy couple made a dash for the taxi festooned with white ribbons. Then, when they were comfortably ensconced, the bridegroom traditionally sitting at the side of the taxi nearest the road, the vital moment came. Down went the taxi window and the grinning groom thrust his head out - no doubt he was remembering his own *poor-oot* days - and then he threw out handfuls of halfpennies, pennies, threepennies [about 1p] and the odd sixpence [2.5p]. The effect was incredible. A boiling, bubbling mass of upturned faces were soon turned to the pavement as the coins fell on the road. It was like a rugby scrum but much dirtier as the kids pushed and pulled each other, standing unashamedly on each other's fingers as they scrabbled for the loot. To win a sixpence was the greatest kudo.... In a Dunbar *poor-oot,* there were no holds barred, no rules and definitely no referee. It was rare for me to come out of the scrum without some coins - and skinned knuckles and knees.

Other money-making schemes were hunting for empty lemonade bottles which carried a tuppenny deposit and jam jars which earned us a penny each. We used to forage for empties at Belhaven's Seafield Dump; it was a sad day when we didn't come home with something or other. (It would later give a new meaning to our school motto devised by J I W Milne, the Latin Master - *Non Sine Pulvere Palma*, meaning *No Prize Can Be Won Without Effort*). And one memorable day in February 1953, I had an unexpected bonus; rummaging about in the empty cardboard boxes, I found an intact *Mars Christmas Selection Box*, probably thrown out inadvertently from one of the local sweetshops. So Ken and I had a feast, gorging on the lot. (Some doctors today might turn up their noses at two young boys eating sweets found on the municipal rubbish tip; what do they know? In this clinical age, with its viruses and complaints, I often think we are mollycoddled to an extent that we will succumb to even the most mild diseases simply because we have no immunity to them. We had been deprived of sweets for so many years so we weren't fussy. What is more important is that we were none the worse for eating the stuff. Word got about of my find, so the following Saturday the kids outnumbered the seagulls on the municipal dump!

But the most lucrative of all our money-making ventures was the annual Gold Rush, or *Klondyke* as we called it. The summer which had brought hordes of visitors to bask in the capricious sun at the East or Coastguard Beach gave way to the autumn, with its violent equinoctial gales and high tides which stripped the sand from the beach in September, exposing the rocks underneath. There it was we mined for our gold - or, to be precise, silver. During the summer months, men on holiday lost money out of their trouser pockets when changing into their swimming gear; women dropped some of the contents of their purses as they doled out coins to their children for ice lollies and ice creams. The money slipped into the sand and was lost forever - or so they thought. We knew better. The rocks trapped the coins and when the severe winds and high tides came, the rocks were exposed. It was a mini -*Klondyke* for us kids.

After school, hordes of kids would descend on the stony beach to scrape among the loose stones and small rocks to retrieve the summer tribute. It was a rare occasion when I came away empty-handed. Even when we had only thirty minutes' daylight left after school, it was surprising how much you could excavate in that short time. My best find was a half-crown [12 or 13p], a small fortune for a boy accustomed to sixpence [2.5p] pocket money each week. The most common finds were halfpennies and pennies but fairly often, there were threepenny bits and sixpences. I doubt if the practice continues today as the beach is empty all summer long.

Sometime, Dunbar schoolchildren were gripped by 'crazes' - like spinning the silver foil tops off milk bottles. You held the top gingerly between crossed index and third fingers, then by flicking it gently, you made it spin through the air like a flying saucer in miniature - perhaps today's children would recognise the article as a *frisbee*. 'Collecting' crazes were also popular - matchboxes, bottle tops, gaudily coloured marbles, ball-bearings or *steelies,* as they were known, cigarette cards from the *Pasha* brand of cigarettes, vastly inferior to the beautiful, glossy coloured cards produced by *W D & H O Wills* depicting railway engines, British Army uniformed men, the seashore, wild flowers and trees. I still have some of these which were in circulation from the First World War until the 1950s and are prized today for their rarity. The aim was to collect the complete series of 50 cards and paste them into books you could get from any stationer or tobacconist. I think I learnt more about nature from those cards than from books.

Ken and I were great on games played in the back garden which, although they had to be restricted and not too boisterous because of lack of space, were nonetheless good fun. A couple of doors away lived Jenny Herkes whom we knew as Jenny Crow or Craw - Crow being a nickname for one branch of the ubiquitous Herkes (also spelt Harkes, Harkess, Herkess and about another ten ways) family. Old Jenny was known to me as Gramma; she was renowned for wearing large, gypsy-style earrings and for her habit of sitting in the front garden every afternoon devouring her beloved *poos* [crabs], picking the meat out of the claws with a pin. Her daughter Euphemia - Effie or 'Fame' - who, with her husband Sid Fawcett and their family, came from Edinburgh to stay with her mother for a few years in the war years. 'Fame' was lovely, Sid looked like Clark Gable. The Fawcett children numbered six; the boys were Billy, the eldest boy in the family, competent with the boxing gloves and my brother Norman's friend and sparring partner; Ernie, my favourite, was happy-go-lucky and bore an uncanny resemblance (in my later opinion) to the actor James Bolam who played Terry Collier in the TV comedy *The Likely Lads*. The girls were pretty, taking after their mother; Norah was the eldest; then came Brenda on whom my brother Norman had a crush - unknown to her as she recently complained; I had a crush on Ann, the next one; Norma was little more than a baby. (In the summer of 2003, I met Norma and her husband Ken on holiday in Dunbar; I hadn't seen her since she was a button. Needless to say, we didn't recognise each other at first but as I was working in the Town House Museum and wore a name badge, she immediately knew who I was. We swapped many happy stories and memories that afternoon).

Many a Saturday afternoon was spent in the Fawcetts' company, usually in our drying green, when the clothes' poles were roped off to make a boxing ring. Ernie provided the bell for each round, the 'bell' being a tin can struck with a stick; I think both he and Billy had watches - unheard of in my family - so the rounds lasted the official four minutes. The boxers wore proper boxing gloves and neither - literally - pulled their punches. These matches usually ended with a win for Billy as he was bigger than Norman, but even if Norman ended up with a bloody nose, split lip or black eye, his opponent was rarely unscathed. Like Ernie, I preferred play-acting to blood sports and such-like.

At one time, Norman was interested in archery, having seen all the Errol Flynn movies about Robin Hood. Somehow, he acquired a real longbow, made of ash; it was six feet in length and he made arrows for it - long shafts of ash wood with goose-feathers at one end and a nasty sharp steel tip at the business end. He soon became an expert marksman after a bit of practice in the field beside our house. He used to position tin cans on the coal-shed roof, then climb over the wall into the field and fire at them; if he missed, the arrow ricocheted off the house wall. Very soon, he was astounding the neighbours with his skill. Sometimes, he'd stand in the street and fire an arrow into the air and it would disappear from sight, then falling earthwards, it landed almost inches from where he stood. Some local lads were jealous of his prowess and they stole the bow one night. Finding they couldn't break it, they burnt it in the field, where Norman found the remains. The bow was a work of art and Norman broke his heart over it, as it was his most treasured possession.

The Fawcetts were a lively bunch. One Saturday afternoon, I went through a mock-marriage with Ann in our back garden. I think it was old Gramma Craw who suggested it as she'd seen Ann and I chatting at her garden gate a few times. She said we were lovers and ought to be wed. So they dressed her up in one of her mother's frocks; with a net curtain for veil, she was solemnly led into our garden, her sisters Norah and Brenda acting as brides-maids. Norman offered to be my Best Man. I wore my short trousers and a blue jersey; someone managed to provide a top hat for me, which kept slipping over my eyes so that I literally married Ann blind.

Ernie acted as the minister and did a great job, as he is a born comedian who can still put on a sombre face; that day, he excelled himself, intoning the marriage service words with a straight face. After being allowed to kiss the bride, I led Anne to the coal shed wall, where there was a bench laden with the wedding breakfast, which consisted of *Bourneville Cocoa, Ovaltine, National Dried Milk Powder* - all in their tins, the latter probably courtesy of baby Norma - and a couple of sherbert dabs for the bride and groom. The ceremony was solemnised by my placing a brass curtain ring on Ann's wedding finger; she proudly displayed it to her chums in the street.

I recall once in those few years, my brother Norman fell into quicksand at Belhaven Beach, not far from Seafield Bridge. It was incredibly close to where people walked. That day in 1946, I saw my heroic brother sink up to his armpits in sand; the two Fawcett lads took off their shirts to make a rope that they used to drag him out of the sink hole. That day, they all walked up the Back Road from Belhaven, swinging their shirts and shorts to dry them, for none of them wanted my mother to know what had happened.

When 'Fame and Sid Fawcett took their brood to England, I wept buckets. In some ways, Sid could have doubled for James Walker, the spiv in *Dad's Army*; Effie was very attractive and as straight as they come. Brenda took after her father but Ann was her mother's daughter, though quieter. For years afterwards, old Gramma Craw would report the arrival of a Fawcett letter, reading bits of it to us, cackling at the end that my 'wife' was pining for me. Years later, I met Ann on a rare visit to Dunbar; still a pretty blond, she informed me that she was about to commit bigamy! Ernie came back a couple of times and we blethered about the good old days in the back garden of 75 Lammermuir Crescent. Visiting Dunbar in 2003, his sister Norma told me he hadn't changed. Then in August 2004, Ernie arrived here with his lovely Chinese lady Lisa and again we reminisced over the old days. He told me he was staying with Ann was now a widow and I asked him to pass on my regards – and my apologies for being such a rotten husband. Subsequently, Ann came to Dunbar and we spent some time together, reminiscing about the good old days.

Ken and I used to love playing 'shops' in the back garden. I would set up a small counter - a bit of plank supported on a couple of bricks. We used seeds from the garden for imitation tea and tobacco, usually the seeds of the *docken* plant; we used bits of rhubarb as itself, the leaves of weeds for cabbages or lettuces and we gathered various coloured stones from the beach at Belhaven, crushing them into pink and white powder which served as sherbet, sugar or flour. Ken had a set of toy scales which he'd added to his 'tooker' - more of that mysterious instrument later - and he would ceremonially and reverently place them on the shop 'tounter', another of his pet words. The imaginary shop bell would ring (he as shopper made the tinging sound) and he would enter the imaginary premises looking solemn and determined. He would greet me as the shopkeeper with a cheery 'dood morning' or 'dood afternoon' and ask for various bits and pieces. He would insist that the plasticine bacon or beef was lean - 'no fat please' and that I should ensure that the 'take' or 'tream tookies' weren't stale. He always bought prodigious quantities of 'tocoa' because he loved to watch me ladle spoonfuls into a small paper bag and weigh it on his scales, an operation which took a tediously long time. All the while, he would chunter on about the weather, the price of 'toal' and such-like - all eavesdropped from the housewives he'd heard in Dunbar shops where he went often with our mother. His problem with the letter 'c' continued for some time, as did his mispronunciations, most common of which were *lipspick* and *hobspital,* the latter being a place he dreaded because someone had once told him people went there because they were ill and sometimes never came home again. (In later life, Ken would proudly remind me that he alone of the three of us had had a nursemaid – Jan Henderson from West Barns – and that she had reassured him he'd never go into *hobspital* because when he was a baby, she took him for long walks in his pram to enjoy the fresh sea air).

Although the Fawcetts left Dunbar in the 1940s, the kids came back for summer holidays from time to time. We also kept up with their cousins, the Lunams who lived in *Lochend Cottage*. They came to visit Gramma Herkes regularly; the girls May and Norah played in our back garden on many occasions. May is more my age; she recently reminded me that we had many fun afternoons; Norah, who is closer in years to Ken remembers playing with him. The Lunams are descendants of John Muir, the famous conservationist who founded the National Park system in the USA.

When we tired of playing 'shops', there were other diversions involving insects. We had snail races as we had clusters of the creatures nesting in our fuchsia bushes. The game was to put half a dozen in a chalk circle with numbers chalked on their shells; we chose our numbers and the first out of the circle was the winner. Another popular pastime was annoying the ants that lived in the spaces between the kerbstones on the pavement. You poked a thin stick between the kerbstones, infuriating the insects to emerge. A more useful game was catching *clippieshears* or *clipshears* [earwigs] inhabiting the rose bushes, then putting them, slugs and caterpillars into a pail into which we poured paraffin and set fire to the lot. We caught butterflies and bumblebees in jam jars - separately - to observe them because we were fascinated by them. After a few minutes in the jam jars, we set them free.

Red letter events in any child's life of that time was when circuses and the *Shows* came to town, but I remember an even more momentous event - the coming of electricity, which meant digging up the streets and pavements, the kind of upheaval that only small boys enjoy. For weeks, the pavements were excavated and trenches dug in the roads for laying the cables to each and every house. We had to walk over a plank drawbridge - well so we imagined it - to get from the garden gate into the road. Although each temporary access was roped for safety and supporting pedestrians, Ken somehow contrived to fall off one morning and almost strangled himself, hanging helplessly by his neck until a vigilant navvy set him free.

But by far the main attraction was the company's steamroller. Even if it interfered with a summer habit, when we popped the tar bubbles in the road, a favourite pastime when the weather was hot, we were mesmerised by the steamroller, falling in behind it as gulls follow the encroachment of the plough in spring and autumn. Children to its Pied Piper, we ignored our mothers' warning us to stay away from it. For housewives, steamrollers were Bad News. Stinking, dirty, noisy, emitting clouds of steam and smoke that carried sooty flecks that ruined their snow-white linen hanging out on the clothesline to dry. We small boys marvelled at the great cast-iron wheels and the way the driver steered it by furiously spinning the handle in his cab; to us, he was a hero. The steamroller was a never-ending source of fascination, a great hulking leviathan that clanked and smoked and puffed away like an iron dragon. A favourite trick was to place some small object in the steamroller's path - a toy soldier for example - and watch it being crushed. I loved the smell of boiling tar; it cleared your nostrils of any lurking head cold. The pungent treacly smell opened your nasal tubes in a way no proprietary brand of inhaler ever could. We loved to watch the workmen spread the black, molten porridge on the roads, then the steamroller flatten it out. To this day, whenever I smell creosote or hot tar, I am like Marcel Proust who could remember incidents from his childhood triggered by the taste of a particular cake. So these remind me of the day that electricity came to Dunbar.

While I had little or no enthusiasm for joining any of the local 'gangs' which held sway over certain designated territories, I did have one or two good friends with whom I shared my outdoor pursuits. Jim Cockburn, my cousin and his next door neighbour, Willie Tear were member's of Willie's Summerfield Road gang but I was never more than a casual member, a fellow traveller on occasions like collecting waste paper for Bonfire Night on 5th November, or going off on expeditions to gather chestnuts/mushrooms/brambles/rosehips. At the time, my best friend was Jock Gardiner - I referred to him earlier as the Wild Man – followed closely by David Barry and Jim (*Skinny*) Hammond. The last two were the sons of Coastguard officers and lived in the row of Coastguard houses overlooking the East Beach. But my hero was Jock the Wild Man, a brave but foolish lad - the two often go together - who was pugnacious and considered himself 'worldly'. I guess he was a young version of the actor Steve McQueen, whom I admired later in life. Jock was up to all kinds of wheezes, dodges and tricks. He had a unique way of spitting - with uncanny accuracy - at dogs and cats. He would gather a gob of phlegm in his throat, work it into his tongue which he formed into a funnel, then he puffed out his cheeks and let fly at his victim. He rarely missed.

At school, Jock was viewed with mixed feelings - not because he was a

Roman Catholic, but because he was Glaswegian by birth, an interloper in some eyes. Everybody agreed he was wild and unusual but he drew censure on himself by 'showing off'. It was no more than high spirits. A natural anarchist, he liked to attempt feats of daring which nobody else had thought of before. He knew all the best places for birds' nests and eggs; he would collect the eggs and blow them out by inserting a pin in either end of the shell, a popular pastime he shared with my brother Norman. Norman specialised in the eggs of seabirds, possibly because he'd to climb cliffs to get them, making them more valuable in his eyes. Norman and Jock were separated by eight years, so they never became friends but I told them both of their mutual interest in birds' eggs. By its competitive nature however - every boy wanted to own the best collection – bird nesting was a necessarily solitary and secretive hobby. Today, robbing nests is forbidden by law - and rightly so. But in those days, I used to marvel at the range of eggs Norman kept in glass bowls in my mother's china display cabinet - clutches of blue, white, cream and mottled greenish-brown prizes.

Jock carried an impressive range of artefacts in his pockets. He made me think of Huckleberry Finn in Mark Twain's *The Adventures of Tom Sawyer*. His pockets contained a penknife with a corkscrew, a handkerchief covered in a myriad of questionable stains, some which were bloody - his or some animal's? - wine gums which had escaped from their tubes and were covered with the fluff in his pocket - how did all small boys' pockets contain fluff? – lengths of string, a stub-end of red sealing wax, stubs of pencils, used chewing gum wrapped in bits of newspaper, a home-made *guttie,* marbles, a box of *Bluebell* matches, a battered pack of five *Woodbines* missing three, a half-smoked end of cinnamon which we smoked instead of cigarettes and a candle-end. On summer nights, he roamed the fields and woods when we were expected home at 9pm. In winter, we had to be in an hour earlier but Jock was always last to go home. Often, lying in bed on a winter's night, in the stillness of a frosty, moonlit November or December, Ken and I would hear his ear-splitting, blood-curdling war cry *Kreeeee-Gaaah*! He told us he'd learnt it when on holiday in the African jungle. Later, we discovered he'd pinched it from one of the *Tarzan* comics he'd read before us. (He did go to Africa however, when he started his adult working life).

His indiscipline at school was legendary. Despite his religious background, he kicked against every form of adult authority, be it religious or secular. When we asked him how he squared his pursuits with the local priest at confession, he was audibly insulted.

'Confession? Ye dinnae think Ah'd tell yon auld bastard ma secrets. Kee-Rist-All-Bluidy-Mighty! Are youse aff yir feggin' heids?'

Jock was bold, brash, fool hardy. He climbed the tallest trees, the steepest cliffs round the Promenade, challenged the tide to cut him off and once let himself deliberately be marooned on Spike Island at the mouth of the river

Tyne so that he could watch the ducks fly over at dawn. He once rescued a jackdaw that had been injured flying into a telephone wire, claiming he taught it to speak.

'His name's Chack He kin say it a'ready. G'wan Chack. Say yir name, boy.'

The bird replied quite distinctly and we were impressed until another boy pointed out that all jackdaws said *Chack* - that's how the bird got its name. No matter. To me, Jock was a hero.

I have two fond memories of Jock. The first was his announcement to a group of boys at *leafy* - the name I said earlier was given to the playtime in between classes, when we were allowed a break in the school playground - that he was going to make his Big Run down the Kirk Hill, near the school. Holding his play piece in one hand and a banana in the other, he said he would ride his bike down the steep Kirk Hill without using his brakes. The Kirk Hill then and today is a steep grassy slope next to the *Hillside Hotel* which ends in a small drop into the East Links Road. Everybody said he was nuts and that he'd have to use his brakes. He shook his head and bet several boys he'd honour his promise in exchange for their marble collections or a few comics. To show good faith in his intentions, he turned up on the day of the *Kirkie Hill Run* with the brake blocks removed from his bike. With Jock, you got what he promised.

The *Run* took place on a Monday morning, Jock confessing afterwards that if anything had gone wrong and he'd been hurt, he'd have won anyway, getting a week off school. The *Kirkie Hill Run* was an unqualified success and Jock duly collected his winnings. Then some poor loser challenged him to repeat the feat, this time down the school Quadrangle steps. He agreed to do it. On the appointed day, Jock came screaming through the school gates, scattering boys and girls in all directions as he cried out

'Nae brakes! Get oot the wey! Nae brakes!'

as he headed straight for the Quad. Down the steep steps he careered but this time, the Gardiner luck deserted him. He landed at the bottom of the steep steps, his bike wheels buckled, the handlebars twisted; the bike was a write-off. He was lucky to get away with only a broken arm. Years later, when watching the film *The Great Escape* for the first time, I thought of Jock lying there like Steve McQueen entangled in the barbed wire after his spectacular motor-bike ride to escape from a German POW camp. Unlike McQueen, Jock fought back the tears after what was undoubtedly a painful break. That day, he looked up at the boys and girls gathering round him, managing a weak smile as one of the teachers broke through the crowd to attend to him. I seem to remember him saying this:

'If Ah dinnae laugh, Ah'll greet [cry]!'

Jock did get to Africa, where he worked on some no doubt dangerous outdoor job. Sadly, he was killed when he fell from a high-speed train when the door unaccountably opened. He was travelling up from London to Dunbar to visit his children from marriage to his wife Anne, who had died of cancer. It was a tragic end to an endearing and unique character, but I know Jock would never have wanted to die in his bed.

### *Summer Diversions*

A fair proportion of the school summer holiday was spent at the East and Belhaven beaches, or if we were flush, the open-air swimming pool at the foot of the *Glebe* in Bayswell Road. Our mornings were usually spent playing in the back garden, afternoons were reserved for the seaside. In those seemingly endless sunny summers, boys wore practically nothing, the same uniform being adopted by most. The outfit consisted of a T-shirt - we called them *Sloppy Joes* - canvas shorts and either black sandshoes or sandals or even bare feet and nothing more. So all summerlong, vestless, pantless and sockless ways we'd go. Mothers were glad to reduce their laundry baskets considerably in summer....

The East or Coastguard Beach was a veritable paradise, not only for swimming or making sandcastles with moats for the incoming tide to fill but also provided an ideal scenario for social historians and those interested in mass observation. Children are great imitators and we had a field day, copying the unconscious eccentric habits of adults at their off-guard moments. We soon learnt to enjoy a surreptitious pee by watching a man dig a hole in the sand, then place his body face downwards strategically over the hole and relieve himself through his *cossie* or bathing costume!

There was also the added attraction of the *Seaside Mission* laid on by the *Salvation Army*. Every summer, two buxom young lasses would appear on stipulated afternoons wearing their serge *Sally Ann* uniforms complete with bonnets, black stockings and sensible, flat beetle crusher shoes. The rules were somewhat relaxed in summer however; the girls were permitted to remove their jackets and the sight of their crisp, white starched blouses straining to fetter their ample bosoms remains a fond childhood fantasy. They didn't think of themselves as sexy, nor did they dream for one minute we - or at least I - would dream of it either. (I didn't know what 'sexy' meant; all I knew was a strange excited feeling in the pit of my stomach). I am not ashamed to admit the fact, although I suspect I wasn't the only boy to harbour thoughts of what they looked like underneath their clothes. These girls worked hard at trying to instil us with religion and a conscience; they would have been shocked if they could have read our minds.

It was shortly after lunch (dinner in those days) that these two beauties would venture down to the beach, picking their way through the recumbent bodies and deck chairs with their small portable organ. Up would go the cry from kids with towels tucked under their arms like Swiss Rolls:

'C' moan, c'moan! The feggin' Happy Praises is here!'

# Street Rhymes and Games

These girls were good for a laugh as well as an innocent fantasy or two. We also got an opportunity to bawl out a few hymns without censure from any nearby adults, for to the lassies, we were their little dears, trainee Christians who would embrace the faith in God's good time. Of course, we mercilessly parodied some of the hymns with different words. The girls gave out transfers with a gummed back; slightly bigger than postage stamps, they depicted a religious scene like Jesus holding a lamb, or him seated with a group of adoring children at his feet. The idea was to stick - or imprint - the transfers in a small notebook but as most of us couldn't afford one, the transfers ended up on the backs of our hands.

'No, no, dears! They're for you to keep in a little notebook, to remind you that Jesus loves you.'

Somebody behind me muttered that if he loved us that much, why didn't he send us a bloody notebook?

One of these well-meaning lasses would sit at the small organ and pedal away with her black-stockinged and (tremble, tremble) shoeless foot. The other would hand out small hymn sheets she collected after the service. The hymn sheet lady would start with a short sermon, while her partner played appropriate background music. In their heavy clothing - even minus the thick serge jacket - the girls sweated mightily for Jesus, as we could see from the damp patches under their armpits when they raised their arms heavenwards in praise of their Saviour.

These buxom, red-necked, muscular Christians and perspiring girls wore no make-up, had legs like dinner tables or pianos and were honest - and naive - to a fault. They never lost their tempers, never scolded you as a teacher would and gently pointed out the error of your ways when your attention strayed. They exhorted us to come to Jesus. They taught us to do actions to some hymns, the most memorable being the one where we were shown how to spin one arm over the other quickly in a rolling motion when we came to the line in the hymn that announced that

'My cup's full and runneth over!'

Naturally, in a community where fishing was still a viable occupation, the hymns tended to be those with a seafaring theme for those whose fathers were in peril on the etc etc.... One particular favourite of mine was *Throw Out the Lifeline* which went something like this:

*Throw out the lifeline, throw out the lifeline,*
*Someone is drifting awaaaaaay!*
*Throw out the lifeline, throw out the lifeline,*
*Someone is drifting todaaaaaay!*

Then one of the girls would exclaim:

'Who is on the Lord's side?'

Back would come the predictable answer:

'No' me! Ah'm wi' him!'

as he pointed to his neighbour and giggled. But they wouldn't be put off, these strapping, sweaty, muscular servants of Jesus.

They would get us to sing children's hymns we knew from Sunday school at Belhaven Parish Church, like the evergreen

*Jesus loves us this I know*
*For the Bible tells me so*

       or

*Jesus bids us shine with a pure, clear light,*
*like a little candle burning in the night.*
*In this world of darkness, we must shine,*
*you in your small corner and me in mine.*

Except that in the above example, the first line came out as this:

*Jesus bits* [boots] *are shinin' wi' a rare clear light*

and the last line invariably went like this:

*Keep tae yir ain corner or ye'll get a punch o' mine*

Another favourite hymn was

*I'm not shamed to own my Lord*

Except that we invariably sang

*I'm not shamed to owe my Lord.*

When Catholic kids wandered by, pretending to ignore the proceedings but dying to join in, we would call to them, inviting them to come worship Jesus. If Jock the Wild Man was among them, he'd shake his head and shout back

'Wir no' allowed!'

Then he'd park his bum a short distance away, just enough to hear our singing and blow raspberries and imitation farts to put us off. Being broken reeds and weak vessels, we were easily distracted.

After about half an hour of this charade, concentration would falter and one by one, we drifted away, more interested in the fat man trying to struggle out of his *cossie,* attempting to maintain decorum by wrapping himself in a large bath towel, then wriggling his bum so that the article finally lay at his feet. Tiring of the Christian propaganda often came sooner; on a sunny beach, the indoctrination had little chance of lasting effect. So surreptitiously, as opportunity presented, we sneaked away, leaving the sandy - and temporary - converts (usually the girls) to sit it out to the bitter end. The lure of the sea was more exciting and we longed to strip off and reveal the bathing costumes we almost wore under our canvas shorts. I use the word 'almost' advisedly - why will shortly become evident.

The East Beach was the place to be seen, even in your homemade *cossie.* It was always crowded in the months of July and August and we locals had to fight for a space between the deck chairs and windbreaks made from travelling rugs; we were indignant and silently resentful. After all, we *lived* in Dunbar and felt we were entitled to our little slot in the summer sun.

Finding - and defending - your space was essential. We always donned our *cossies* at home so that when we got to the beach, all we had to do was strip off the few clothes we wore and spread our towels on the coveted piece of sand - often no more than a towel's length and breadth. The Bathing Costume was well named in every sense, particularly the second word. Costume was what it was. Mine was like most of the others - a navy blue or green wool affair, a hand-me-down from Norman, who'd moved on to the deluxe elasticated version, as he was older. My *cossie* was baggy and shapeless, being a size or three too big for me; also, as it was knitted, it was already sagging and threatened to expose bits of me that the law required me to keep covered. The version I wore had crossover straps at the back but these only ensured it remained attached to your body. Every year, the *cossie* would be ceremoniously dragged out of its winter quarters and inspected for moth holes, then darned - yet again. When you first hit the water, it sagged even more and you emerged from the sea, drawing its baggy folds about your person, hoping that no one could see the real you.

The dreaded knitted costume was often filled with sand cast about by the waves and breakers that made it sag even more. Big boys used to grab smaller ones and thrust handful after handful of damp sand down the front and back so that when you got to your feet again, you looked deformed. The only way to get rid of this excess ballast was to dive back into the sea, by which time the *cossie* was hopelessly out of shape. Again, re-emerging from the breakers required you to clutch and draw it from behind to make it look as though it fitted your scrawny body from the front.

We did ill-advised things in our knitted *cossies*. For example, it was inviting trouble to do handstands while wearing it, particularly when it was wet. The sodden wool rode up your body when you were upside down so that bits of your private parts were revealed by the sagging crotch. If the Americans coined the expression *beach bum,* Dunbar children could have been the inspiration. In the 1950s, because of woollen swimming costumes, beach bums were 'out' rather than 'in'. All summer long, we inspected our costumes thoroughly for signs of damage in the forlorn hope that we might qualify for a new one before the season was over. After the beginning of August, you knew you were doomed to suffer the indignities of your old *cossie*, as mothers would say it wasn't worth their while knitting new ones, the summer being nearly over. It was great fun, going for a *dook* [a swim], as Ernie Fawcett reminded me in July 2004, when he visited Dunbar after an absence of over fifty years.

The rock pools at the East Beach were a never-ending source of entertainment. We studied with wonder and sometimes tried to catch the minute life that lived in these pools. In those pre-pollution days, a rock pool was a world in miniature, teeming with small sea creatures such as hermit crabs that lived in whelk shells, comical little creatures that staggered about drunkenly on the floor of the pool until you touched them and they withdrew into their temporary homes. There were elusive shrimps that darted away as soon as you put your hand in the water, small brown, minnow-like fish and *podlies,* as we called them; all head and no body, these fierce-looking little fishes are part of the *genus goby;* they have small 'horns' on their oversize heads that give them their aggressive appearance. Fronds of brown kelp, olive wrack with their bubbles, red seaweed and the delicate tissue-thin lime-coloured sea-lettuce was home to all kinds of small sea creatures - small soft-backed green and brown crabs weaved their sideways walk, sea-snails, immature sea urchins and starfish. No rock pool was complete without the exotic brown and blood red flower-like anemones; clinging to the side of the rock underwater, they waved their tentacles about like Salome's veils, hoping to catch minute mites and plankton for their sustenance. A favourite trick was to feed tiny bits of shell into their ever gaping mouths, only to watch the creature spit out the useless pieces a few seconds later. Another ploy was to tickle them with your finger and they would grip you lightly with their small tentacles.

When we tired of the beach and the embarrassment of the benighted *cossie* - we often wished night would indeed fall and cover our shame - we would get dressed and make off to the harbours or the old castle. The castle was my favourite playground where we fought pitched battles against imaginary English hordes. Few artefacts were discovered in or beneath the ruins but every bone we found was pronounced that of a dead Englishman or a brave Scottish warrior. One place we hung about was the *Beach House Hotel* - it survives today as a block of flats - which incorporated the *Cosmo* dance hall, the haunt of Teddy Boys and ne'er-do-wells. We didn't go there for the dancing; during the day, the *Cosmo* was disguised as an ice cream parlour-cum-coffee-shop, quite respectable. It had a bit of a reputation for fast women and their escorts, gum-chewing James Dean lookalikes, with hair slicked back with *Brylcreem.* For the wilder elements, it was The Place to go, as jiving was all the rage. Did I first hear Bill Haley and the Comets' *Rock Around the Clock* there? I must have, as the dances were of that vintage and records rather than a live band entertained the patrons. The place buzzed in summer, open to 11.30pm on weeknights and midnight on Saturday. The guys in their long black jackets, white shirts with bootlace ties, shocking pink or green socks and thick-soled suede brothel creepers rocked and rolled their girls who wore several layers of frothy material to make their gaudy dresses flare a few feet from their bodies. Fuelled by a few pints from the nearby *Forresters'Arms*, the guys whirled and threw their dolls about, young teenage girls already dizzy from a combination of cheap scent, hair lacquer that kept their beehive hairstyles intact and maybe a shot or two of rough cider and lager shandies. Reputations of all kinds were won - and lost - within the confines of the *Cosmo*; we couldn't wait to grow up and join our older brothers and sisters in that den of iniquity.

But when I was a boy, you had to make do with an ice cream cone which you could eat on the premises; we would stare around at the shadowy corners, wondering what went on there after dark. You entered the *Cosmo* by descending a few steps - they are still there today - and you felt you were entering the bowels of Hell as you gasped for breath in the thick cigarette smoke. I think the owner of the *Beach House Hotel* and the *Cosmo* was called Henderson and he had an ice cream stall near St Anne's Episcopal Church in the Westgate; I also think he employed a man to ride the streets and the East Beach promenade on a tricycle with a candy pink-and-white-striped awning, selling his wares. Or am I confusing him with a gentleman we knew as Enzie Lonzie, a wee, moustached Italian with a Charlie Chaplin waddle?

Another establishment we frequented was *Eildon Cottage* - known to us as the *Eildon Cafe* on the corner of Brewery Lane, Belhaven. Well, frequented is perhaps not quite appropriate; we never went inside, as there was a little window where boys and girls could order what they wanted. (Adults entered the front room where they could partake of coffee and biscuits or chocolate cake, one of the specialities appearing on the chalk slate board at the gate). The cottage stood beside the *Masons' Arms* or as it was better known after its proprietor's name, *Bungie Wells'*.

Us kids were served at a small hatch in the front garden; the usual fare were bottles of pop and bricks of hard *Walls* ice cream sandwiched between two - invariably soft, as they were past their sell-by date - wafers. Two spinster sisters owned the cottage, the Misses Land who lived there in 1947. The Town Council granted them a licence to sell soft drinks and jellies in waxen cartons at the East Beach and Belhaven in the summer months. Their jellies went mushy by the time you carried them from her cottage to Belhaven Beach so you'd to suck them through a straw they provided. They were delicious for all that. One Miss Land was a strange old bird; some said she was a spiritualist-medium, while others called her a witch - she did bear a slight resemblance to Margaret Hamilton, the actress who played the Wicked Witch of the West in *The Wizard of Oz*. The more charitable simply described her as 'not quite right in the head.'

Of course my greatest hero was my brother Norman. Like Jock the Wild Man, he was reckless to a fault and performed scary feats - like exploring the dangerous areas of Dunbar Castle. One day, he announced he'd investigate the staircase which at one time had given access to the remains of the 'camel's eye', as the sole remaining stack is known locally. Billy and Ernie Fawcett and one or two others lowered him over the edge of the rock, then he swung himself into the narrow entrance, oblivious to the dizzying drop into the sea below. When he'd seen enough, he shouted to the lads above to swing the rope into the aperture so that he could grab it and thus climb back up. Vertigo wasn't a word in his vocabulary. I hung over the edge, lying on my belly, terrified he'd fall and be killed. Somehow, he managed to grab the rope and launched himself into space, the lads above taking the strain as he climbed up, hand-over-hand to safety. Norman examined every hole, cellar, nook and cranny in much the same fashion. He pronounced the castle 'boring.' Boring!

# Street Rhymes and Games

The *Gunholes,* or Blockhouse, one of the earliest artillery emplacements built in Scotland, just after Flodden, was virtually inaccessible. Well, almost. Norman climbed it, as did others seeking refuge from the prying eyes of the local constabulary who were on the look-out for illicit gambling. Yes, in those days, to play games for profit - cards, horse-racing - was against the law. Hidden within the *Gunholes* compound, a few young men played cards or *Crown and Anchor* for pennies, posting a lookout on the Castle to warn them of the approach of the police. (My good friend Bob Cameron tells me he earned many a sixpence keeping *keppie* [watch] for the *polis*). Before betting was legalised an unofficial betting industry existed, the Dunbar version being run from a house in Castle St. Jock Bowie ran it and employed my friend Ally Knox to act as his 'runner'. Until legalisation, men wanting to bet on a horse/ greyhound had to place bets under a *nomme de plume;* my Uncle Jimmy's was JDCX - James Dingwall Cockburn plus that X. If you were naive enough to give your real name, you could be fined for illicit speculation on games of chance - horse and greyhound racing, a crime in those narrow-minded days. Doing the football pools was, however, legal.

The castle was a constant source of imaginative enjoyment but there were other places equally fascinating. One was the *Fluke Dub - flukes* are flounders or flatfish. Not particularly deep, the *Dub* [puddle] was a large landlocked pool beside the East Links Golf Course, where we once built a raft of railway sleepers cast up by the tide. Needless to say, we got stuck in the middle, our poles unable to shift the cumbersome craft; those wearing *wellies* had to tow the raft back to shore. Another place we frequented was known to us as the *Three Rocks* – near a one-time fishing settlement known as *The Vaults*. We called these rocks in the way imaginative children will. In childish obstinacy, we misnamed them, as there are actually four rocks; the fourth was so small we ignored it. The sea had carved them out of the coast thousands of years ago; they are composed of a slate or flaky honey-coloured sandstone; they are isolated from the shore at high tide, although not dangerously so. They have grassy surfaces and today remain as the strange sculptures we thought they were half a century ago.. Many a Sunday afternoon we spent playing at pirates or castaways in and out of these rocks, sometimes bridging the spaces in between with the flotsam of wooden planks scattered along the beach. Further along the coast, beyond the 9th green, was a large yacht which had been beached there. We knew it as *The Boat Ashore* and I believe it was owned by Lord Balfour. It lay there for years, a magic place for kids playing pirates or sailors. Many an afternoon, we enacted scenes from the popular war film about a naval frigate, *In Which We Serve,* starring Noel Coward and other stalwarts of the war-time film industry – John Mills, Richard Attenborough and Bernard Miles. We could get up on deck by means of a rusty iron ladder, then get into the bridge, where we made all the appropriate sound effects of guns firing and hooters hooting. The only people that marred these visits to the East Links

# Street Rhymes and Games

Golf Course were the golfers who in our opinion got in the way of our entertainment. Perhaps that explains why I have never had the slightest interest in playing golf.

Another 'valley' hardly worthy of the name, although we had vague notions of it as such survives at Winterfield Golf Course. *Death Valley* was a steep slope on the course; it ends today at the thirteenth green, near the chalets at the foot of Back Road. It wasn't really dangerous but it was *Death Valley* to us, a place where we sledged in winter. The trick was not to fall off your (home-made) sledge - usually a piece of board to which we nailed runners made from the alloy metal bands stripped from wooden crates we found at Seafield Municipal Dump.

We had Adolf Hitler to thank for what was arguably the most exciting and adventurous playground at Belhaven Bay, with its snaking rows of anti-tank blocks and crumbling trenches which ran above the sand dunes thick with marram grass, or sword-grass as we called it because it could inflict a sore cut on your bare arms and legs. The Army used the site for small arms target practice until about 1955, so the beach beyond the butts was littered with spent bullets, which we avidly collected. Near Hedderwick was the tank training ground but we were never allowed to venture there, it being well monitored when Churchill tanks were on manoeuvres.

We tried our hand at fishing in the Victoria Harbour in July and August. For a few pennies, you could buy a lead-weighted, ready-hooked green line wrapped round an H-shaped frame of wood from *Robertson's* ironmonger in the High Street. Armed with this gear, we went to the harbour hoping it was low tide so we could dig for bait. Some of us favoured lugworm - hairy sandworms - while others swore that limpets or the guts of sprats guaranteed a successful catch. The sprats we fished for were capriciously fussy about their diet; sometimes they wouldn't bite on lugworm, limpet or their own kind and friendly fishermen would suggest crabmeat as an alternative. A fish we often caught was the *podlie* mentioned earlier, with its large 'horned head' and a scaly body. When we caught one of those little creatures, a favourite trick was to throw them back into the harbour with corks attached to their horns, taking malicious delight in watching the seagulls dive-bombing them. This was a trick I learnt from my Uncle Jimmy, who had done the same as a boy.

A fish to be wary of was the conger eel. These frequented the harbour bottom, usually curling up inside the odd hollow and hidden by the seaweed. A mature conger eel will easily bite through a fishing line and even swallow a lead sinker. I once saw a small boy dragged into the harbour from the quayside by one of these vicious creatures; fortunately, there were adults around to rescue the little chap.

I knew most of the fishermen by name; they were a close-knit community and they tended to intermarry, handing on their boats to sons or sons-in-law. Some of the fishermen of my mother's time had colourful names like

# Street Rhymes and Games

*Shie, Traiveller, Boups, Fiddler* (after the crab of the same name), *Aipple* and *Hill 60.* (In my book, *Swords, Loaves and Fishes,* there is a photograph of some of the more flamboyant among them around the turn of the twentieth century; a rum lot, they were characters every one). All fishermen worth their salt are experts at reading the weather from the state of the sea, the sky and the wind directions. We always consulted them if we were planning a picnic or walk in the Lammermuir Hills. They would sit on the bollards mending their nets, chatting to each other as they baited the hundreds of hooks they used to catch the herring. More often, that laborious task was delegated to their womenfolk but in my childhood, the herring shoals had moved north and west of Scotland, so the men did the job themselves out at sea, fishing for cod, mackerel and other whitefish like haddock and sole. Nowadays, the few men who carry on the industry fish for *poos* [crabs], lobsters, mackerel and prawns. Most know that their sons won't follow them in their chosen profession, which is cold, hard work requiring an early start whatever the season. Fishing off Dunbar may disappear as a result of the European Commission bans and all the other arguments about conserving stocks. They were a vital part of the community for centuries and now, like the farmers, their world is shrinking, their livelihood almost a thing of the past. Some of the notorious dwelling houses and cottages of the local fisher folk are thankfully gone; most were no better than slums, like the infamous *Cat's Row* in what is now known as Castlegate/Victoria Street. These slums were gone before I was born but I still recall one or two of the old fisherwomen sitting outside their new houses on summer afternoons, smoking their clay pipes and reminiscing about the past.

One summer attraction which has long-since disappeared were the *Pierrots* or as they were known locally, the *Peer-os.* Every July, the troupe of entertainers - usually no more than half a dozen in number - would descend on Dunbar, giving performances first in the Winterfield *Pavilion,* then the *Shore Hall* adjacent to the modern lifeboat shed and demolished just after the war. They finally performed in the *Corn Exchange* hall, used by amateur dramatic groups and so on. If you were lucky, you got to one of their performances during the summer months. The entertainment was pitched at a fairly juvenile level, although the adults enjoyed themselves too. Or so it was said. To be truthful, many families were driven inside by the bad weather, particularly in July, often a wet month in Dunbar. The performances usually followed the standard routine of tap-dancing, crooning and a comedy act with a stooge or 'straight' man, juggling and finally, a bout of community singing, which I hated. The troupers were dressed in various costumes, the most familiar being the classic white, all-in-one *Pierrot* clown costumes festooned with red buttons and dunce-style hats. The main feature was the 'smart-alec' type comedian and his fall guy, a stereotype music hall act. The comic's patter was usually of the following kind::

*Comic:*      Hello! Hello! Hello! Is everybody happy tonight?

*Audience:*  Ye-e-s!

*Comedian:*  Right. We'll soon put a stop to that. Is there anybody here from Edinburgh? [or Glasgow, depending on which fort night of the Trades Fair it was].

*Audience:*  Ye-e-s!

*Comedian:*  I thought so. Tough luck.

That sort of thing went down well in unsophisticated Dunbar; to my mind, it wasn't worth the stiffness the hard seats in the *Corn Exchange* inflicted on tender bums.... (As I said earlier, years later, BBC TV parodied the *Butlin Camp* holidays in the programme *Hi-de-Hi*, which brought back excruciatingly painful memories to me, particularly as one of the main characters was a neurotic, sexually repressed woman called Pugh....).

The Town Council - or as it was universally known, *The Cooncil* - controlled and organised practically every event during the summer months. Councillors were usually avoided like the plague because they spelt trouble, acting through the omnipotent dictator, the *Toon Clerk,* not a faceless bureaucrat but a Real Presence whose name appeared on every bye-law or official notice forbidding you to do something *By Order.* The Council was hot on preserving law and order all the year round, not just in the summer months. It was good at forbidding this and that but not so quick to repair things or accede to the pressing demands of householders. All summer long, we boys lounged on the beaches or any order-free parkland; we didn't drop litter, didn't stray off the designated paths, did enjoy the sun under what was a *Cooncil Heaven.* Most of these Councillors attracted scorn and censure, perfectly expressed in the Scottish saying - usually applied to writers of books - *Him a Cooncillor? Ah kent his faither.*

The Town Clerk was one man to steer clear of. Another was the Poor Inspector, who doubled as the Registrar of Births, Marriages and Deaths. His was a face straight out of Dickens' *Oliver Twist*; he could have played Bumble the Beadle. Our Poor Inspector was as cold as charity itself; he was a squat little creature who loped along like a ranging wolf, sniffing out trouble. To have to visit his poky little office near St Anne's Episcopal Church (now a day centre for the elderly) was a trial for any adult, let alone a child. I am glad to say that my family had little need of his services other than for the registering of our own *hatches, matches and dispatches*, as they called births, marriages and deaths then and probably still do.

Popular events throughout the summer months included the swimming galas in the pool. On such occasions, the swimming-pool was cleared of its accumulation of snot, mucus, pee and stones cast there by the sea; the cubicles were flushed out and scrubbed, the wooden slats on the floors hosed down in a vain attempt to remove the infection which resulted in *verrucae* - painful wart-like protuberances that grew on the soles of your feet. The pondmaster, the late Eric Bradbury, was a handsome, tanned, blond, leonine-haired creature -

he looked like Michael Heseltine MP on one of his better days - who in his duty whites of shirt, shorts and long socks turned many a female head as he strode about his domain. One summer in the future, my brother Ken would be his assistant for a season.

The summer galas were 'official' occasions, when the Town Council was represented, usually by the Provost and one or other of his bailies. The galas took place in the evening and they were well-attended until the late 1970s, when the pool was hardly used at all, resulting in its closure in 1979; it was then run by the local Traders' Association for a couple or so years until it closed for good in 1981 and was demolished in 1993.

Needless to say, I wasn't one for entering into the gala spirit, chiefly on account of my god-awful knitted *cossie.*

The records played over the tannoy were usually up-to-date, featuring Elvis Presley's famous *Heartbreak Hotel* which echoed marvellously across the water. But the pond authorities were obliged to play a family assortment and we were tortured – or at least I was –by the inane renditions by Max Bygraves and other such like banal 'entertainers'. I remember one of Bygraves' ('I wanna tell ya a story') particularly stupid songs that was popular one summer; it was truly idiotic and went like this:

*Gilly, gilly, Ossenfeffer Katzenallen Bogen*
*By the sea-eeee-eeee-eeee-eee!*

It was popular with the 'bloods' that summer of 1959 and of course those who enjoy 'community' singing; the aforementioned young bloods were always to the fore. They strutted about arrogantly, expecting to be admired and took themselves seriously. They were pratts from the tops of their heads to their toes. One or two are still around and occasionally visit Dunbar, much to my regret. One in particular was called 'Pally' by his small victims which included me, a detrimental nickname as he was anything but. He still affects the same snooty, disdainful expression today. My mother commented that the community singing of that year was typical of the daft English who fervently *sangalongaMax* at swimming pools all over England.

In late August, the kittiwakes that had arrived in mid March left the Castle Rock and the window ledges of the old granary at the harbour. We knew then that the summer season was coming to its end. And when the swallows began to gather in swarms above the chimney pots in the High Street in late August, wheeling and screaming as they acrobatically negotiated the high tenements, we knew the summer season was finally over. The beaches were deserted, the swimming pool closed earlier and the summer bus and train time-tables were changed. It was coming to an end yet again. Our attention switched from the sea to the woods and the hills and we began making forays into the countryside for our late season entertainment. A favourite pastime on these treks into the Lammermuir Hills was to *guddle* [tickle] trout in one of the burns, hoping thereby to catch these elusive fish. *Guddling* was an art; you mesmerised the creature by running your fingers gently under its belly and it would rise to the surface, allowing you to heave it out of the water. I had mixed success with this method of fishing but occasionally I had quite spectacular success so we had trout for tea.

By early September, the days continued warm; folk talked about an Indian summer –whatever that was. Then the nights came in chillier and darkness fell earlier. This confused our body clocks; we resorted to telling the time by looking at the position of the sun and if it wasn't out, we used dandelion clocks. We puffed away the seeds, each puff representing one hour from midday. These 'clocks' were remarkably accurate - or were we really better at guessing the time ourselves? When we grew hungry on these largely weekend jaunts, we lived off the land; we ate the ripening beech mast, brambles, thistle cheese - got from the inside of the flower very gingerly - and *soordooks,* a thirst-quenching plant whose leaves were sourness itself. The plant is properly named sorrel to distinguish it from other docken species

At summer's end, we were treated to pony rides from *Aye-Aye,* a gypsy-type character who lived at Belhaven; he was rarely to be seen in the local housing schemes during the summer as he tended to frequent the beaches, offering pony rides to the visitors' children. These weren't sanctioned by the Town Council, a fact he studiously ignored. He wore a Romany-style neckerchief - am I right in thinking it was red with white dots? - a naturally off-white (dirty) shirt and baggy moleskin or corduroy trousers, all of which needed a good scrub and having seen better days. His old flea-bitten nag was well past her sell-by date and rumour had it that she ended up in a glue factory, which is entirely possible. He stabled the mare in a ramshackle shed in Duke Street, now a fashionable part of Belhaven where modern privately owned houses have largely supplanted the former cottages and stables. We knew summer was really over when *Aye-Aye* appeared in Lammermuir Crescent, selling rides at threepence [about 1p] a time. He hoisted you up into the saddle and sat you in front of him, then he goaded, coaxed and cajoled the poor old brute of a horse to clip-clop slowly along the Crescent to Doon Avenue, where he turned round and brought you back to the starting place. The poor mare nodded her drooping head with undisguised melancholy, threatening to peg out at any moment. However, her droppings were useful, scooped up by my mother with a shovel and used to fertilise our roses.

Summer now over, kids looked forward to the annual visit of *Madam Fossett's,* then *Robert Bros.*circuses, although I never cared much for the *Big Top. Fossett's* came to Dunbar in 1944 - perhaps also before the war - and it or *Robert Bros.* kept on coming until the early 1960s, when circuses seemed to lose their appeal, possibly because they began appearing on television. I loved all the activity of the great tent or *Big Top* being raised in the *Bleachfield* but felt distinctly uneasy about the animals in their cages. None looked happy, particularly the big cats that lolled languidly in their cramped quarters looking bored. I was taken once or twice to the show; after the second time, I had no desire to go back. However, everything was at it should be. The ringmaster wore the traditional red claw-tailed coat, white breeches and gloves; his ensemble complete with top hat and whip - his symbol of office- made him an imposing figure but I didn't care for the way he ordered everybody around, including the animals. There were crazy clowns wearing the appropriate costumes - short bum freezer jackets, baggy pants, funny hats and huge oversized shoes with soles that flapped - and of course the usual red noses, white faces with smiles painted on so that they never betrayed any pain when they tumbled and somersaulted about in the sawdust-covered ring. There were trapeze artistes whose death-defying stunts brought forth appreciative gasps from their audience, especially when the clowns took away the safety net. All eyes were turned skywards, all hearts were in mouths, all sweetie-sucking was suspended as the trio - usually two men and a woman dressed in spangled leotards and tights - went through their routines.

Next came the lion tamer who cracked his whip to encourage the sulky, bored lions and tigers to rise to their feet. There was a strong man in the traditional leopard-skin, a juggler, a fire-eater, a bearded lady - all the stock-in trade characters of the time.

But for me, the queen of the circus was the lady bareback rider - meaning the horse was bare backed or unsaddled although the lady herself wasn't entirely bare backed. She was beautiful and her skimpy and beautifully sequinned costume only just managed to cover her small pert breasts and her sculpted back. (I hope I may be forgiven for this lapse into purple prose but it remains another childhood fantasy). I recall she wore white tights dusted with silver - or so it seemed. I sighed and asked myself why ordinary women didn't wear such neat apparel instead of the stockings that needed corsets with suspenders attached to hold them up. I was light years ahead of my time...

The lady's horsemanship was superb; she adroitly and effortlessly moved from a standing position on one horse's back to the second of the pair she handled, completing a circuit of the ring when she repeated the action. Sometimes she sat astride one of her lovely white horses, then she slid under its belly, rising up again to a standing position on its neighbour's back without batting an eyelid. I don't think I batted one either. I was mesmerised by her. The horses were well trained and kept up their faultlessly measured pace, their plumed heads nodding in time to the tinny music as they danced and pranced about the ring, somehow knowing they were the star attraction. The bareback lady was soft, silky, smooth and stupendous - I didn't know the word 'sexy' then - but I fell hopelessly in love with her.

She ended her act with a so professional flourish, the ringmaster needlessly cracking his whip at the back hooves of her prancing animals. The horses responded immediately, rearing up on their hind legs as the lady gathered the reins in one hand and raised her free arm above her head, showing a shaved armpit to the adoring crowd. I thought she was doing it for me. In another life, she could have been a ballerina. Imagine my disappointment a few days later when I saw her without her make-up, dressed in baggy dungarees, a grubby *burberry* [raincoat] and *wellies*, feeding her horses out of a battered bucket. Even so, the initial impression remains to this day; every time I see sequins on a woman's evening dress, I think of my lovely horse lady.

Another annual attraction was *Emerson's Shows*, which arrived in Easter and at the time of the Edinburgh autumn holiday, usually the second weekend in September. I preferred these tawdry sideshows and their big brothers, the switchback or *Ben Hur,* the *Dodgems*, the *Hobbyhorses,* the *Chair o' Planes* and the *Ghost Train.* (How did they manage to fit all these sideshows into the relatively small Bleachfied?) The switchback was the main attraction with its whirling, swirling chariot-type bucket seats which spun round to the accompaniment of a wailing music. When the switchback was operating and even after it stopped, the music continued, thumping out of a mechanical *hurdy-gurdy* which stood in the centre, its characters looking distinctly Italian with caps and bells, 1930s figures which stared sightless into the night, striking bells and drums which added to the general cacophony which was the *Shows*.

On one particular Saturday night in September, we begged every penny we could and spent the entire evening there, mesmerised by the naphtha flare lights, the smoke, the smell of hot oil, the throbbing of the traction engine and the generators which provided the electricity by means of a veritable spaghetti of cables and wires. All evening, the raucous voices of the stallholders invited you to have a go at hoopla/rifle range/roll-a-penny. The tinny music, the machines, the dry, stale air were essential ingredients of the thick, hot soup which we eagerly drank but left us with a thirst for more. We called out to our chums, our voices throaty and excited; when our few pennies were spent, we played *tig* and *hide-and-seek* amongst the trailers and stalls. On one unforgettable night, I tried to hoopla a goldfish - and was successful. Next, I won a coconut at the coconut shy stall. My cup ran over that night....

The reason Saturday night was so popular was that the young men were paid on a Friday, so they could have a few drinks on the Saturday, wanting to show off to their girlfriends and taking them for rides on the switchback, where they screamed their heads off in mock fear. When the lads had had a skin full, they were careless with their coppers and I found many an inadvertently dropped penny in that field which was promptly squandered at the roll-a-penny stall. The silvery-hot hurdy-gurdy wind-blown sounds of music played far too loud was part of the attraction. Kindly uncles who collided with you bought you toffee apples and candy floss - the latter was wispy and tantalisingly sweet and ephemeral, as insubstantial as were the *Shows* themselves.

Finally tiring of the noise and excitement, you'd make your way home, the brash music fading behind you as you wiped away the last traces of candy floss or toffee from your mouth, smelling the *verdigris* from the much-handled greasy pennies. For me, the smell of pre-decimalisation pennies - there are still some knocking about - is Proustian and it never fails to conjure up images of the days -or nights - when the *Shows* came to Dunbar.

One 'uncle' who was a godsend to me when the *Shows* came was Adam the signalman.

I had a lot of time for Adam. He was my friend and he introduced me to books, real books without pictures. Being a signalman who spent long and lonely hours in the signal cabin, he was an avid reader. He used to enthral me with ghost stories and being a drinking crony of my future Latin teacher Jack Milne, he perhaps learnt many stories from him. Jack was an expert ghost-story teller, as I would find out later, when I went into secondary school in the autumn of 1953.

Adam's and my greatest pleasure was shared in his dedication to - and my growing interest in - books. He introduced me to his hero, T E Lawrence, 'Lawrence of Arabia'; I read everything I could lay my hands on about that famous but flawed idealist's part in the Arab Revolt against the Turks in the First World War. Like Adam, I felt Lawrence got a raw deal but today, his dream of an Arab republic is flawed. The Arabs are a cruel race of people steeped in an antiquated religion that remains rooted in the Middle Ages. The Arab has never developed in seven hundred years; he is frozen in the time of the prophet Mohammed. While I am interested in the medieval period in history, I have no desire to live in it. Also, Arabs are insensitive to women, preferring male company and treating their women as chattels. Perhaps that was why Lawrence felt at ease among the tribes he met. He was notoriously shy and shunned or felt awkward in the company of women, other than Bernard Shaw's wife. I believe Lawrence was a latent homosexual and that he had a hang-up rooted in his illegitimacy, which made him feel an outcast.

However, the relationship between my mother and Adam subsequently cooled and they were never close again. My halcyon days train spotting at the East and West signal boxes and at Beltonford came to an abrupt end after they parted. I missed the trips to get coal for the signal box fire, missed the comfortable greasy armchairs, the mugs of strong tea, the 'doorstep' sandwiches Adam would share with me - and of course, the ghost stories. Adam and his signal boxes are long gone. He came apart when his parents died; the signal boxes were demolished, a casualty of progress when the line was electrified and signalmen were no longer needed.

As I wrote earlier, in 1956, we had an unexpected windfall in the family when my Uncle Jimmy won the football pools. To the end of his life, he lamented that he'd only staked a farthing a line instead of his usual halfpenny; farthings and halfpennies cannot be easily quantified in terms of the modern coinage. Instead of winning £700, he netted half that but it was still a considerable sum for the time. (In 1956, Jimmy was earning about £12 a week, which meant he'd won about 30 weeks' pay; in today's terms, the sum would be about £6-7,000. He was inundated with begging letters; people called at our house seeking loans but he was adamant. His money would go to his family, for as he said to these people and the minister 'Charity begins at home.' We all got gifts. My mother fared best because she'd welcomed him into her house after he became disabled in the 1930s, when none of his other sisters or elder brother had any time for him. Jimmy also liked his dram but despite her hatred of alcohol, she loved him. I think Ken got his first football strip and football; I forget what Norman received but I got a *Rudge Raleigh* bicycle - second-hand mind you, but almost new. It had three speed gears and a dynamo. Painted red, I worshipped that bike, cleaning and polishing it every weekend until I got married in 1970, when I sold it for twice what it had cost in 1956.

The bike opened up an entirely new world for me. I used to disappear early on a Saturday morning or Sunday afternoon, exploring the remote places of the Lammermuir Hills so long as there was a track of sorts to take me there. I made new acquaintances in the outlying farms, was able to visit school friends in the distant villages who welcomed the chance of a chat with someone they knew. Many a piece of homemade bread and homemade blackcurrant jam I enjoyed on these cycle runs. On reflection, I think these days were the happiest of my entire young life.

But somehow, I had a vague sense that it was all slipping away, all disappearing, those habits and customs of over 50 years ago. Who today eats thistle cheese, sucks *soordooks* or seeks sustenance in the bramble patches? Pesticides and car exhaust fumes have ruined the hedgerows and made them dangerous for those used to foraging for their delights.

As autumn advanced, we found new places to play - or more precisely, renewed our acquaintance with old ones. Three popular spots were Lochend Woods, the Curling Pond and the Latch Park. Lochend was favoured for the simple reason that it wasn't popular with adult walkers and we were rarely ever disturbed at our games. Once the site of Dunbar's great glacial loch, drained I believe in the Middle Ages, Lochend Woods still bore traces of its former state in the marshy areas around Sucker Island with its pond which existed in my youth. We used to go into this forbidden part to gather wild daffodils, violets and primroses; we had to jump from one tussock to the next to avoid the treacherous, green scummy pools. The estate once belonged to the Warrender family, famous in Scotland's and Britain's history from the 1715 Jacobite rebellion until modern times. The Warrender presence at Lochend ended in 1859, when the second of their houses burnt down, due it was said to a gypsy curse that the family would lose three houses to fire. The family moved to Edinburgh where the surviving member of the family resides today. However, they owned the estate until the end of the twentieth century and they employed a gamekeeper to manage the wooded area. We knew the gamekeeper as Wullie, so we called the wood at *Lochend Cottage Wullie's Wud* [wood]; he reared pheasant chicks there so it was off-limits to small boys unless they had his permission to go in. We used to go to Wullie's cottage at Hallhill and timorously knock at the door to ask if we could go into the wood to gather fallen pine branches as they made excellent supports for growing peas. In another part of the wood, there once was a sawmill which had produced a great pile of sawdust where we could roll and tumble without hurting ourselves. We played many games of Robin Hood there, in the secluded safety of the wood, within sight of the Lunams' cottage.

I have one everlasting memory of Lochend. The Great Fire. The farmer who owned or was tenant of the land to the south of the railway line - now partly occupied by the Hallhill Healthy Living Centre - decided he wanted to reclaim some land which was given over to the pine wood adjacent to *Lochend Cottage*. He chopped down a fairly large area of trees, then bulldozed the stumps and roots into a massive pile in the middle of the field behind the cottages known as *The Kennels*, occupied by his aggressive gamekeeper Jock Gibson, a man with none of Wullie of Hallhill's gentleness. Anyway, the farmer set fire to this pile and the place smoked away for several days. Being curious and living next to the railway line, Willie Tear and Jim Cockburn, my cousin, invited Ken and I to join them to inspect the conflagration one November Saturday afternoon. We crossed the railway line from the Cockburn cottage in Summerfield Road - a serious offence then and now - and went to play at the fire. It was like Dante's *Inferno*. I recall we walked over the crust of this fiery place; when you stepped on a thin part, you unleashed a column of fire, like a miniature volcano. We spent an hour or so there, fascinated by the occasional bursts of flame. We were about to make our way home when we spied a policeman parking his bike at the railway tunnel and running towards us. We stood still; it was useless to run away as we knew he must have been studying us for a while. He was a pompous, officious fool. He came up to us breathless, unbuttoning his tunic to take out his notebook. We knew he would take our names.

'Right. Who's got the matches?'
Never one to allow authority the upper hand, Willie Tear, the oldest among us, stepped forward.

'Constable, we haven't got any matches. The farmer lit the fire. You can check with him. He started it days ago, last week or the week be fore. We were only playing.'

Undaunted and a little annoyed at one so forward, PC Plod began taking our names, although he let Ken off as he was only about five years old and had been 'clearly led by the other boys who should know better.' In fact, it was Ken who'd got us caught because he'd left his toy six-gun near the fire and I'd gone back to collect it. We were never charged as the farmer subsequently corroborated. What is ironic is that the policeman never asked how we'd got there or how we'd get home. We crossed the railway line again and could have - should have - been prosecuted for that. The policeman's mind is sometimes difficult to fathom.

The Curling Pond was reputedly haunted by the ghost of a man who'd committed suicide there. Was he the poor soldier on sick leave from the Western Front during the Great War who had gone there and shot himself, as I had read in the local paper during my research for my second book? It was a magical place for kids; created by the short-lived *Dunbar Curling Club*, its sunken marshy square was sheltered by pine trees on every side. It was a place frequented by Cowboys and Indians. Sometimes it was also frequented by Girl Guides led by the intrepid Miss Macaulay, our headmaster's sister; there she taught the girls the rudiments of woodcraft, like identifying the tracks of small animals and birds and lighting a fire without using matches. It was an ideal spot for ambushing unsuspecting girls. One Friday evening in summer, a few of us – *Tossle* Smith, Sandy Thomson, Jock Fender and myself climbed the trees that overlooked a clearing, watching the lassies squatting in small groups, rubbing dry sticks together in the forlorn hope of setting fire to their little piles of brushwood. We dropped out of the trees, whooping war cries and scattered the girls in all directions. An irate Miss Macaulay appeared, shouting that she'd have the law on us and that we were not to interfere with 'her girls'. (Later, when I read the brilliant book *The Prime of Miss Jean Brodie* by Muriel Spark, I thought of Miss Macaulay. As soon as her back was turned, we whispered to one or two of the lasses that they were welcome to one of our matches so they could pass their test. A few of the weaker vessels took up the offer.

The Latch Park was another good place for games involving tree climbing. Little more than a path beside a fenced-off field of turnips or cabbages, to us it was a magical place, as the path skirted a slope covered in trees and stunted bushes. There was a bench for those supposedly there to study the moon rising over Doon Hill on summer and autumn nights- courting couples in other words. The branches of the trees - rowans and elderberries - hung over the path, providing shelter from a sudden downpour but more importantly, for swinging among the trees on ropes. It was next to the railway line, separated from it by a high stone wall, although that didn't deter me from visiting Adam in the Dunbar West signal box, just past the graveyard on the other side. There was also a spot covered with a few railway sleepers which, as tradition in our family had it, was the resting place of the old horse which had pulled my grandfather's employer's cart. Sadly today, the Latch Park has been obliterated by a children's adventure park/playing field, although you can still see the boundary wall and the trees above it. The old path has disappeared almost entirely, although there is a stretch still visible, its access choked with brambles and nettles. I wonder if the bench is still there, covered by undergrowth. There was also a pair of sleepers there, reputedly covering the grave of my grandfather's horse, the poor brute that licked his face when he was drunk in the 1920s. I cannot say that is true, but it was a family legend for many years.

# Street Rhymes and Games

Eventually, as autumn progressed, we restricted our games to the local streets. At weekends, a number of vans and carts came round the schemes regularly, selling various wares. In those days, any van or person selling round the doors was fair game for curious boys and girls. We used to gather round stationary vans, carts, bicycles and pedestrian hawkers. Like wasps round a jam pot, as my mother used to say. A good deal of trading was done on the hoof as it were and it was fun to follow a hawker from door-to-door to see how he/she fared. These people have long since disappeared from the streets - the fish-hawkers with their wicker baskets, the knife-grinder with his foot-cranked grinding machine and pet monkey, the rag-and-bone man, the French *Ingin' Johnnie* [Onion Johnnie] wearing a black beret and blue-and-white striped jersey, his bike and person festooned with strings of fat onions. Gone too are the gypsy ladies selling clothes pegs, sprigs of lucky white heather and telling fortunes, the Sikh salesman in turban carrying a battered cardboard suitcase stuffed with gaudy wares - ties, handkerchiefs and everything else under the sun. We wondered how he managed to cram so much into such a small recep-tacle. These were familiar characters in our childhood, usually friendly folk simply trying to make their living.

One winter's day, the rag-and-bone man got more than he bargained for from our house. As I wrote earlier, my father had begun his army service in India where he'd played polo, wearing leather-enforced *johdpurs* and using a crocodile leather whip to encourage his pony. These things and what he called his army dress sword were stored in the walk-in cupboard in my bedroom. On winter evenings, I used to drag them out and inspect them. I liked to draw the sword from its scabbard, giving the latter to young Ken in our mock sword-fencing fights. (Once I stabbed him in the side with the sharp point - thank-fully, the sword had no edge to it - and he kept quiet about the incident, al-though the broken skin left a mark in his side that is still there today. Another time he threw a hot water bottle at me and I ducked; the bottle smashed the glass of a print hanging on the wall. He got the clobbering I deserved for ducking. He held both these incidents against me for years. He said he could have told our mother about the skewering I gave him. 'But you didn't. You stuck me with Dad's sword and I kept quiet about it. You could have said it was your fault that the glass in the painting got broken. But you didn't and I got clobbered for it').

But back to the rag-and-bone man story. What we didn't know was that my father had stored his army service revolver and six live rounds in the same cupboard. When my mother was rummaging in there for rags, to her horror she found the gun. She was scared. Why did her husband keep a loaded revolver in the house? What was it for? She assumed the worst and decided to get rid of it that afternoon. She unloaded the gun and wrapped it in rags, handing the bundle to an unsuspecting ragman. Then she foolishly threw the six live rounds into the *Sailor's Park* at the back of our house, where hopefully, they rusted away and by now are harmless, as the park is used by school kids playing sport. I often wonder what the ragman felt when he discovered the heavy Colt revolver among his acquisitions....

So much that was Dunbar and our unofficial playground has gone - or at least tamed by safety regulations and house building. The swing park at *Winterfield Pavilion*, with its spider-web wheel which spun round and round and made you dizzy, the wooden boat which worked on the sea-saw principle and once gave me a bloody nose when I leant too far forward to speak to my companion and bounced my proboscis off the small funnel that separated the occupants. The Countess Road swings and chute have been moved from their original place near what was once Dunbar United's football pitch - now transplanted to the *Hallhill Healthy Living Centre* - are now sited near the two supermarkets and anaesthetised by a 'safe' wooden enclosure. The swings and the chute were popular on Saturday afternoons by boys wanting to watch the football game but unable to pay the few pennies to get into the pitch. (In my opinion, the local team wasn't worth paying money to watch, but then I have never appreciated soccer, as they called it in those days. They used to open the gates about twenty minutes before the game ended in case folk wanted to leave; it was at that point they would let young kids in for nothing). Gone also is the putting green at Bayswell Park and its welcome drinking fountain, although the latter has recently been rescued from some store and installed outside the *Hillside Hotel.* The grass borders of the West Promenade were lovingly manicured all summer long; now, the weeds grow almost three feet, the borders trimmed by two volunteers in their spare time, providing a toilet area for the dog-walkers that venture round that once-idyllic place. The path beside the wood at Lochend, *Lovers' Walk,* which ends at *Lochend Cottage* is now overgrown and muddy, the Lochend Estate boundary wall on its left broken and cast down. The *Wishing Tree* at Lochend has been cut down; I consider that a particular act of vandalism, for generations of children and young people went there to chip off a little piece of wood and wish for their heart's desire – to pass an exam, gain the affection of a lover, win at sports etc, etc....

# 6

## Firelight and Starlight

Now I will write about the things we did indoors or at least mostly so in those years before television.

### Indoor Games

When the weather forced us to remain indoors, Ken and I had the usual board games to while away the time. In addition to the ever-popular *Snakes and Ladders, Ludo, Tiddley-Winks, Dominoes, Draughts* and card games like *Snap* and *Happy Families,* we were the proud owners of four less common games - *Chinese Checkers, Halma, Steeplechase* and *Lotto. Halma* was a more versatile game than *Chinese Checkers*; the objective in both being to move all your counters into the corner of the board occupied by your opponent. The difference was that in *Halma,* the counters could move in eight different directions - back, forward, sideways and in four diagonals across the grid of squares on the board. *Steeplechase* was, as the name suggests, a racing game played with tin horse-and-jockey counters; there were pitfalls and hurdles that you encountered on the whim of how the dice fell. The principle was simple; first past the post won the game. *Lotto* was like *Housey Housey,* an early form of *Bingo* played with a scorecard and cardboard counters. Another popular game was *Paper, Scissors and Stones* in which players used their fists; one player shouted out a number as he or she showed the same number of fingers from a clenched fist. The winner was the first player who showed the correspondingly correct number of fingers. If more than one player won, the game was declared a draw.

Like many other kids in Dunbar, we used to make *peeries* [whipping tops in England]. We made them from *pirns* [the wooden reels round which thread was wound]. You begged the *pirn* from your mother, took it into the coal shed and poked a hole in it, then inserted a small stick in the hole with one end sharpened to a point. You then held the stick between thumb and forefinger to start the *peerie* spinning. The trick was to make it spin steadily on one spot, not *skitter* [wander] all over the linoleum - the best surface for the job - and come to a prematurely abrupt end.

The best games of all were those we made up ourselves, something which perhaps distances us from today's children. With his toy 'tooker', Ken conjured up a perfect image of a diminutive chef, fussing over his pots and pans and preparing a full (plasticine) dinner while I fought battles with my lead soldiers. As he rattled his miniature cooking pots on the hob, he'd open the tiny oven door to inspect whatever it was he imagined he was cooking in there.

He muttered endlessly, mildly scolding himself for this or that mistake, or shaking his head when something like toast or potatoes were 'burnt'. I accompanied him in equally low tones, making up dialogue for my soldiers as they marched and fought. I had to promise to stop my wars when Ken's food was cooked, pretending to be a customer. All of a sudden, he would yell at me

'S'READY. TUM AN' DEDDIT 'FORE IT'S TOLD!'

So I had to come and get it before it got cold.

If my mother was nearby, she'd clutch her heart or drop a stitch in her knitting, then tell him off.

'God, laddie, ye near gave me heart failure!'

How Ken knew how to impersonate a chef or cook in those pre-television days is still a mystery; what was even more surprising was that he'd serve up the 'food' with a handkerchief (as napkin) draped over his arm. He would then ask me if I liked the gravy or if the beef was done to my taste. It was a great surprise when he grew up and joined the Civil Service; we were all convinced he would go into the catering business.

Another favourite game was playing buses on the indoor staircase. He and I made the small lobby behind the front door the bus cabin, the upstairs landing being the upper deck of our double-decker. I would sit in a cardboard box in the lobby, acting as driver, while Ken was the conductor. I made appropriate bus-driving noises and we took turns wearing a black peaked cap belonging to one of us from some Christmas outfit. Ken liked being the 'tonductor' because it allowed him to shout a lot, although by nature he was a quiet child in those days. Probably that's what attracted him to the role. He collected used bus tickets which he issued to imaginary passengers from a small square cardboard box which contained the one gas mask we had kept as a souvenir from the war. The box had a string attached to each end so that you could carry it over your shoulder. Ken immediately saw it could have other more useful purpose. He put the string round his neck so that he could wear the receptacle on his chest. Thus suitably equipped, he would call out thus:

'Any more fares PREASE!!!!! Move up the bus now. T'mon, move up the bus! Next stop Summerfield Road!'

Sometimes I'd infuriate him by ringing the imaginary bell for an imaginary passenger to alight and he'd yell at me:

'Too late, dliver! Next stop!'

Then he'd go up the stairs and take his fares on the landing, sometimes pushing another imaginary passenger downstairs, accusing him or her of going beyond the proper fare stage. With his 'tooking' and his bus 'tonducting', at an early age, Ken proved he was already equipped to deal with the wider world. I remained the incurable romantic, at home in the womb-like quality of my personal cardboard box....

# Firelight and Starlight

There were still one or two outdoor chores to perform in autumn but I never regarded these as tedious; they were part of the fun of the season. With autumn reaching its climax, I was given the task of bringing in the last of the garden vegetables - usually potatoes and onions. These were lifted and placed in the coal shed, the onions strung up to dry from the rafters. All that was left in the soil were the leeks, turnips and Brussels sprouts for gathering when we needed them. I also chopped more wood for kindling and soon the coal-shed shelves were filled to capacity, with sticks laid in alternate crosswise layers so they could dry quicker.

Outdoor leisure activity was largely restricted to weekends. No autumn was complete without a visit to the blacksmith's at Beltonford, where we watched the noble Clydesdales stand patiently waiting to be re-shod for the winter ploughing. I loved the smell, the heat, the sparks that spiralled up-wards, marvelling at how the smith fixed the shoes on the horses and worrying that they would feel the heat and the nails being driven in. The smith assured me the great animals felt nothing and were actually happy when they had a new set of horseshoes.

'Jist like yirsel son, when yir Ma buys ye new boots for the school.'

By October, we were well into the school routine and the first class tests were looming on the horizon. The mornings were growing increasingly colder and we kept ourselves warm by brisk walking. When the first frosts appeared, we knew the slow, autumn languor was almost gone and winter was just around the corner. We looked forward to more and more hours of outdoor games round the street lamps. But in the morning, we hurried to school, late as al-ways, clutching battered schoolbags and chewing a syrup roll on the hoof. In those days, my mother took afternoon work in the fields, gathering potatoes or docking turnips. She then came home to make our evening meal and by ten pm, she was already nodding off, chasing us to bed before she herself went to sleep.

On school mornings when Ken and I were really late, Jock the Wild Man would bring his bike screeching to a halt beside us, giving support to Ken and I by dawdling though he didn't have to.

'Three meenits tae the bell. Aye. Ye'll get the belt for shure. So'll Ah. Ye'd better wipe yer mooths. Thir a' covered in syrup.'

Three minutes to nine o' clock, the school bell rang to summon us to class. Usually, we were at the top of Countess Road and almost at Station Road, though sometimes we cut it very fine. Needless to say, Ken and I never got the strap for being late, although Jock did.

## Cinema, Wireless, Comics

Before the days of television, the cinema and the radio, or as we knew it, the *wireless*, for obvious reasons, were the chief source of canned entertain-

123

ment. Cinema was popular with us, possibly because we could afford only one visit per week to the *Playhouse,* now the site of the Beehive Nursery. Youngsters were usually given sixpence [2.5p] pocket money that bought a ticket to the *matinee* on Saturday mornings or afternoons and threepence worth of sweets. Apart from the weekly children's serial which lasted all of fifteen minutes, the main attraction was the same as that shown to adults in the evening, since 'adult-only' and 'x-rated' films were hardly ever shown. The cliffhanger serials were undoubtedly 'B' standard, invariably shot in black-and-white - what wasn't in those austere and gritty post-war years? The serials were corny and predictable; most ended with the hero/heroine suspended over a cliff or in some equally hazardous situation from which it was virtually impossible to escape. The following week, we'd arrive breathless with anticipation only to find some highly unlikely and even ridiculous *denouement* had taken place in the intervening period. Despite our tender years, we knew there was a good deal of cheating going on but the object of the exercise was to bring you back to see the hero/heroine make a miraculous escape. I list some of the characters who appeared in these dreadful serials - *Nyoka, Queen of the Jungle, Flash Gordon, The Scarlet Horseman, The Vigilante, Captain Marvell, Superman, The Cisco Kid, Hopalong Cassidy, Zorro* and not least, *Tarzan,* played by the Olympic swimmer Johnny Weismuller, the best actor ever to play the role. (Recently, I read that *Tarzan's* chimpanzee *Cheetah* was still alive at the ripe old age of 75!). And of course there were the inimitable Roy Rogers and Dale Evans, Trigger the horse and Bullet the Alsatian dog. The manager of the *Playhouse* was Mr Rodgers, a jolly fat man who used to pull my leg and say that if I'd been his son, my life would have been different.

'Aye, laddie. Roy Rogers. If you'd been my son, you'd have been famous!'

We loved the serials on Saturday mornings and afternoons. The *Playhouse* was the place for the matinees (originally afternoon theatrical performances). We would queue at the box office, offering up grubby threepenny bits, receiving the ticket and rushing down to get the best seats at the front. We got to see the serial then the main or 'big' picture. All the while, Tommy Rodgers used to walk up and down the aisles, wielding an incredibly long cane which he used to whack the bare knees of boys and girls who had the audacity to rest their feet on the back of the seat in front of them. Many a sore knee I suffered. Then when the performance was over, the National Anthem was played. God Save the Queen meant nothing to me, for I didn't know who she was. But old Tommy Rodgers would parade up and down the aisles, wielding his wicked cane stick, shouting 'Up on yer feet! Up on yer feet!' And we obeyed him.

Tommy Rodgers' even fatter wife ran Scott's *Empire* at No 42 High Street – it ended its life as a cinema around the mid-1950s, then became a sale room and finally a café run by a very kind and sweet lady called Mrs Chaumiack. Today, it's a gap site called Empire Close. *The Empire* cinema was a less prestigious establishment than the *Playhouse*, less comfortable with its mainly wooden seats. Its sole virtue was that it was cheap.

When we were old enough to go the evening performances, the programme always consisted of the 'Big' picture, the 'Wee' supporting picture, the *Pathe Pictorial News* with its distinctive crowing cockerel flapping its wings; there was usually a cartoon, usually supplemented by a 'trailer' (advertisement) for forthcoming attractions. The *Gaumont British News* was recognisable by its revolving multi-screen camera showing extracts from world events, sport and so on. Its commentator was a laconic newscaster who made feeble jokes that were seriously corny, even to our unsophisticated ears.

We all had our favourite actors, whose films we would beg, borrow and steal to see. Among my favourites was Errol Flynn, who couldn't act for toffee but who kept me spellbound in his invariably historically inaccurate roles which involved swashing his manly buckle. I think I saw every film he ever made; the one which stands out more than any other is *The Adventures of Robin Hood* in which he played the eponymous hero battling against Basil Rathbone as the villainous Sheriff of Nottingham. Who of my generation can forget the epic swordplay between the two shadows etched on the stair of the Hollywood version of Nottingham Castle's Great Hall. They don't make them like that any more....

In those days, the cinema was pure escapism; reality didn't encroach on the screen until much later. Recently, I read that in 1951, Scottish people paid more visits to the cinema than anywhere else in the UK. UK average attendances were 29 per thousand; in Scotland, it was 39. Who said the Scots are dour and unromantic? My mother's personal attendances for that year must have numbered at least 200, not just because she liked the cinema but because you could see five films a week in the two picture houses; it seemed to me she was always there in the winter evenings. I envied her that.

So, the films of that time. Who from my generation can forget George Sanders' assiduously poison-pen theatre critic in *All About Eve* with Bette Davis and a young Marilyn Monroe, a cynical film about theatrical life? I think it won six Oscars. I saw Flynn in the historically inaccurate *Charge of the Light Brigade;* yet another historically inaccurate film was *They Died With Their Boots On,* a highly romanticised account of Custer's Last Stand and many others, memorable though they were. So what were my favourite films during the period 1948-58? Here is a baker's dozen for you:

*King Kong* (1933), despite Fay Wray's continuous, persistent and downright irritating screaming, her virtually only response to the simian *Big Yin*; *Snow White and the Seven Dwarfs* (1936), Walt Disney's beautifully-crafted and immortal classic for children of all ages; Selznick's *Gone with the Wind* (1939), one of the greatest movies ever made, with the vixenish Vivien Leigh as Scarlett o'Hara, the perfect foil to suave, cool Clark Gable's Rhett Butler; *Gunga Din* (1939) with the unforgettable Sam Jaffe as the blacked-up water boy who saves the day in war-torn India, loosely based on Kipling's epic story; *The Stars Look Down* (1939), Carol Reed's classic adaptation of A J Cronin's timeless novel about Welsh miners and pit disasters; *Beau Geste* (1939), with Gary Cooper playing the eponymous hero in P C Wren's tale of three devoted brothers serving in the French Foreign Legion, with Brian Donlevy as the sadistic martinet of a commander; *Wuthering Heights* (1939), Emily Bronte's story of doomed love beautifully acted by Merle Oberon and Laurence Olivier, the latter's *Henry V* (1945) being another triumph; *The Wicked Lady* (1945), with Margaret Lockwood and James Mason as highwaypersons in love, even if the critics slated it as unconvincing stuff; *Treasure Island* (1950), with Robert Newton as the definitive Long John Silver, even if he went over the top with his eyeball-rolling scenes; *High Noon* (1952), Gary Cooper's man alone, almost as good as Alan Ladd's *Shane* the following year; *Love is a Many Splendored* [sic] *Thing* (1955), a classic whose slightly trite love affair is beautifully executed, with Eurasian doctor Jennifer Jones and war correspondent William Holden set against the background of the Korean war; and finally, *Dracula* (1958), Christopher Lee's definitive, smooth, sexy, eponymous anti-hero.

Of these films, I have seen *Gone with the Wind* and *Wuthering Heights* at least six times, the latter perhaps even more than that; I have also seen *King Kong* about the same number of times, but the second remake was a poor substitute, failing to capture the drama and special effects of the original. I have yet to see the third. And of course, Christopher Lee's *Dracula* is a masterpiece which never fails to excite me –maybe you will deduct from that my obsession with what society calls evil....

After the cinema was the wireless - we never called films 'movies' and equally never referred to the wireless as the 'radio'; the wireless was just that, as it had no wires. It played an important role in my childhood, developing my imagination in a way television has never been able to equal, though I listen in rarely nowadays - my sense-buds have been anaesthetised by nearly fifty years of the 'box' I am sad to say. In many ways, the wireless was superior to the cinema for the same reason as books. In Chapter 2, I mentioned some of the programmes we listened to during and immediately after the Second World War; these excited the imagination in the way that books would in my later years.

The wireless was part of the household furniture; it provided us with cheap entertainment and knowledge which TV, for all its attractiveness and presentation has never quite equalled. I watch very little TV other than news broadcasts, films and historical documentaries. Today, much of TV is aimed at the masses, consisting largely of soaps, 'makeovers', 'reality', [oh dear!] gardening programmes and so-called 'comedies'; the comedies leave me cold. My mother used to say that English TV comedies proved that the English can laugh at nothing; she may have been right. I find most modern TV comedy shows banal, predictably streetwise, inane, cheap and forgettable - especially those imported from the USA.

We owned a very attractive 1930s style wireless that was unusual in its design. Most wirelesses were squat, square, heavy blocks that needed a strong table to support them; ours was triangular-shaped, the cabinet made of brightly polished wood rather than the dull brown jobs of many households I visited. I suspect my mother was to blame for our set, probably more expensive and bought on hire purchase. Like all contemporary wirelesses, it ran on an accumulator which had to be re-charged every week at *Stark's Garage* in the High Street, where Old Kirk Close is today. It was my job to lug the heavy battery or accumulator up town and back, taking care not to let the acid splash on my legs, as my mother warned me it would scar me. (The battery was perfectly safe but I was told not to shake it or disturb its equilibrium).

We tuned into all the popular programmes of the day and night - *The Archers, Mrs Dale's Diary, Workers' Playtime, Children's Hour,* the last hosted by Derek McCullough, better known to children as 'Uncle Mac'. We listened to the music programmes broadcast by the BBC's Light Programme, although my mother drew the line at classical music; she said it sounded like a cat having its guts removed; for her, it was too noisy and full of tinny, brash sounds. There was however classical fare of a different kind provided by Valentine Dyall, then Orson Welles, who had us spellbound with their fifteen minute programmes of (respectively) *The Man in Black* and *Tales from the Black Museum* - monologues delivered in heavy, Shakespearean tones with more than a touch of menace. Welles had taken America by surprise in his famously realistic 1930s 'live' broadcast of H G Wells' *War of the Worlds,* delivering the story as a series of news bulletins. (Nazi Germany must have listened in avidly, noting the effects of mass hysteria produced by the broadcast. Lies are formidable weapons....).

In our house, wireless listeners were particularly keen on *Saturday Night Theatre* since kids under thirteen weren't allowed into the cinema in the evenings. Often, Ken and I would tune into that programme which, as the name implies, consisted of a play; it usually lasted about one hour. I vividly recall one production called *Mighty Like a Rose*, the title of a popular song of the time. One of the characters kept singing or whistling this tune throughout the play, which was ostensibly a tragic love story with a ghostly ending. The plot was simple and for we post-war kids, familiar. The heroine is killed in the Blitz in London and her lover visits the house where she lived. Standing in the shell of the building, he hears the sound of an approaching *Doodlebug,* or V1 rocket. He listens to the droning sound that cuts out - a sign that the pilot-less bomb is about to fall - and he waits for the explosion which kills him. He is thus re-united with his dead lover and the play ended with his whistling their tune. It seems trite today, but that long-ago Saturday night, Ken and I were enthralled by the play. (Somehow, I managed to transpose the bomb to a local site - Gala Green, which wasn't very far from where we lived in Lammermuir Crescent. Why I should do that escaped me then, as it does now. Possibly it was because the play was set in a leafy suburban street, which of course Gala Green was in those days).

As youngsters, we were fond of all kinds of comedy. Comedy is anarchy and most kids are anarchic - it's their knee-jerk response to what they see as overbearing, fuddy-duddy adults. One of the most anarchic and funny programmes was *ITMA* ('It's That Man Again') described in Chapter 2. Another memorable wireless show was *In Town Tonight,* with its sharply drawn sound image of London - traffic noises, tugs hooting on (supposedly) the river Thames, the voice of a newsvendor inviting you to 'Read All About It!' and the endearing image conjured up of a little old lady dressed - well she was for me - in the clothes of a Victorian or Edwardian poverty-stricken person who plaintively offered 'Violets, lady, lovely violets' for sale.

We enjoyed even mediocre programmes but no one prepared us for the anarchic bombshell that burst in the BBC in the shape - or more accurately, the sound - of a few men who called themselves *The Goons. The Goon Show* was first broadcast in 1951; it changed the face of comedy forever. The Establishment didn't know - perhaps still doesn't know - that *The Goons* was its greatest enemy. The *dramatis personae* included *Major Denis Bloodknock* (Military idiot, Coward and Bar), *Dan Eccles, Bluebottle, Spotty Minnie Bannister* ('Didn't I pass you on the stairs?'); the latter was a spinster of the parish who had a live-in lover called *Henry Crun* who cracked silly jokes like 'Min, Min, the cat wants to go out? 'How do you know, Henry?' 'Coz he's got his hat and coat on'. Henry Crun never knew who he was. He was the epitome of *dementia praecox* although they didn't call it that then. The other characters included *Neddy Seagoon* (British Idiot and Hero) and the arch-type villain *Grytype-Thynne, Count Toulouse-Moriarty of the House of Rolande.* They were all memorable characters who mercilessly and collectively sent up every arm of the powers-that-were. My favourites were *Eccles* and *Bluebottle,* respectively played by Spike Milligan and Peter Sellers. I loved the latter's 'He's fallen in the - water!' (Note the deliberate pause, which was superbly effective – the best comedy is all about correct timing). Sellers also did the voices of *Blooodknock Min* and *Henry*, while Harry Secombe did Neddy Seagoon. I am told that Sellers got his line for *Bluebottle* when he saw an adult toppling into a swimming pool somewhere in England; the man's small daughter had said the words and Sellers used them to great effect.

Spike Milligan's immortal line was ' Hello', I'm the famous Eccles.' Eccles was all tortured, uncomprehending innocence; he strove never to cause offence and epitomised the trusting simpleton, possibly because of his war time service, of which he wrote brilliantly and comically in a trilogy of four (!) books; his sidekick, the diminutive Bluebottle was a naive, trusting, immature little lad - or so he seemed. Eccles was me to a T. Min and Henry were the

# Firelight and Starlight

prototype British married couple - even if they weren't wed - and they never listened to one another, which is common among many of those who have tied the knot. Harry Secombe was the linkman for every twist and turn of the plot - if that isn't too strong a word for what was on offer. The plot often fell apart halfway through the broadcast; that didn't matter, the dialogue produced laugh after laugh. A brilliant, surrealistic show, I was saddened beyond any consolation when the programme was taken off the air, chiefly because the actors wanted to move on to other things. Later, we grew more 'with it' and began to tune in to *American Forces Network* (AFN) and *Radio Luxembourg* on Sunday nights, as we could listen to the *Top Twenty,* a show that broadcast the leading twenty records of that time. We also tuned in to strange radio stations like the static-distorted Dutch *Radio Hilversum* just for the hell of it.

Another programme we avidly listened to was *Take It from Here* featuring Jimmy Edwards who would earn further fame in the 1960s with the TV comedy series *Whacko!* a weekly half hour skit about a Dickensian Dotheboys' Hall prep school softened by humour. Edwards the headmaster held sway over a bunch of mildly effeminate public schoolboys dressed in caps, blazers and short trousers. His great handlebar moustache was invariably gleaming with beer froth as he strode about in mortarboard and gown, wielding a cane he whacked on desks but never on the bottoms of his charges - well, not on screen at any rate. He bullied his nervous colleague Arthur Howard, the bald-headed brother of the famous film star Leslie Howard who made his name in the role of Ashley Wilkes in *Gone With the Wind.* One of the pupils in *Whacko!* was Richard O'Sullivan who played a snotty English public schoolboy - was he ever anything else, even when he appeared as an adult in a later sit-com called *Man About the House*? But it and *Whacko!* were far into the future. The contemporary *Take It from Here* brought Jimmy Edwards into contact with Richard 'Dick' Bentley, the most successful Australian comedian of the 1950s. The show featured the working-class lives of the Glum family, with Jimmy Edwards as Pa Glum who was forever walking in on courting couple Ethel 'Eth' his daughter played by June Whitfield and her gormless boyfriend Ron (Bentley). The conversations between Ron and Eth were heavily larded with sexual innuendos, an example of which follows:

Ron: 'Take 'em off, Eth.'

Eth: 'No. I don't want to, Ron.'

Ron: ' Garn. Take 'em off.'

Eth: 'Oh Ron, do give over.'

Ron: 'Oh Eth. Please take ' em off for me. Please.'

Eth: ' Oh, Ron, give over, do!'

But eventually she gave in, removing the offending article - her spectacles.

Another show in a class of its own was *Hancock's Half Hour* which was first broadcast in 1954, introduced by a farting trombone which played the distinctive theme music. It featured the famous and sadly late Tony Hancock,

129

the hapless occupant of 23 Railway Cuttings, East Cheam; his cynical wide-boy pal was played by Sid James, who went on to make his name in the *Carry On* films. Television had little impact on our teens as not many people could afford the sets until the mid to late Fifties. However, a few families bought sets to watch the Coronation on 2nd June 1953. The Harkess family next door to us in No 77 were one of the lucky ones; they had a small six-inch screen job which in those days only transmitted for short spells, with several intermissions. Ken and I were among a half dozen other kids who were invited in to sit on the floor and watch the pageant. (Ken was spellbound throughout; he later informed our mother that he'd loved seeing the 'Tween' ). I can't remember the other kids who were in No 77 that momentous day but maybe some of those whom I hope will read this book will remind me.

As the nights grew longer and adults encroached on our free time by staying home, even the wireless couldn't keep us by the fireside. We congregated round the lamp post outside the house, playing games like *Deserters* - a form of hide-and-seek with a 'den' for the leader - and other games I have already described in detail. After conversion from gas to electricity, the standard street lamp was transformed into a straight concrete pillar topped with what resembled a question mark. When we weren't playing street games, we sat at the base, swapping comics and cigarette cards beneath the friendly glare. If you were on your own, the lamppost became your companion; all you needed was a length of rope to tie round the pillar, becoming an unruly horse or whatever else you wanted it to be. Occasionally, after a gang from another street had held a meeting in ours, the gang leader would leave a trademark or calling card in the form of a bicycle tyre festooned round the lamp post; enterprising youngsters who took a pride in their streets soon removed such unsightly objects and in the process, became expert at shinning up these branchless concrete 'trees'.

We were fanatical about swapping comics/cigarette cards/anything. They were vital as a means of currency as well as social contact. Swapping comics was frowned on by my mother, who maintained that paper was a 'harbour of disease'. Needless to say, it didn't put us off and I can't remember anyone ever catching a disease from these tattered, well-thumbed publications. If I learnt rubbish from comics, I amassed considerable knowledge from the ubiquitous cigarette cards. Adam the Signalman gave me duplicates from his collection, some of which I still have to this day. He also gave me a pile of back numbers of the *Meccano Magazine,* which proved a godsend. I soon got rid of these boring (to me) magazines by swapping them; two lead soldiers for one issue, a *Dinky* toy for five. This way, I increased the size of my army and gained army trucks, tanks and field guns to support it.

Comics were the main articles of barter. No one who took the *Beano* or the *Dandy* every week in those days needs to be reminded of their popularity. It is statistically possible that everyone who reads this book will have come across those two famous comics published by D C Thomson and Sons of Dundee. Because of their popularity, they were worth little in the swopping scale of value; the *Dandy* made its debut on 3 December 1937, followed by the *Beano* on 30th July the following year. Today, first editions are valuable collectors' items; in fact any pre-Second World War issues fetch astronomical prices. Priced at twopence [less than one new penny], I have read that issues in good quality sell at £50-100. Recently, a friend reminded me that they were superior publications, having existed on the newsagents' shelves for over sixty years in the face of fierce competition from other children's publications which never quite matched their integrity or imaginative power.

The *Dandy* featured characters like its front page hero *Korky the Cat,* a red-nosed feline with green eyes who possessed more than nine lives. Other famous characters were *Desperate Dan*, the *Cactusville Cowpoke* whose phenomenal strength outstripped that of the Biblical Samson; his stubbly jutting-out chin, hip-hugging six-gun (which he never used) and battered hat were his trademarks, as were the massive cow pies he ate (with the horns left in), lovingly baked by his diminutive *Aunt Aggie,* of whom he was terrified. The *Beano's* front page star was *Eggo the Ostrich,* later supplanted by *Biffo the Bear,* himself later replaced by *Dennis the Menace.* Characters have come and gone. *Keyhole Kate* no longer indulges in her compulsive snooping, *Hungry Horace* seems to have faded away to a shadow of his fat self, *Pansy Potter the Strongman's Daughter* has left for pastures new. No more is *Julius Sneezer the Sneezing Caesar,* or *India-Rubber Ron.* How well I remember *Lord Snooty and His Pals. Snooty* was dressed in an Eton collar, top hat and bow tie, studiously avoiding his thin, turkey-like *Aunt Mat(ilda);* he bossed his gang about -characters which included *Hairpin Huggins, Skinnie Lizzie* and the mischievous twins *Snitch* and *Snatch,* dressed in romper suits with pixie-type hoods attached. Later arrivals were the *Bash Street Kids* featuring *Plug,* a gormless, buck-toothed version of *Goon Dan Eccles* - aided and abetted by an assortment of ugly mugs that plagued the life out of their stereotyped and long-suffering, gown-and-mortar-board-clad headmaster who sported a weedy moustache. In 1951, both comics were anti-Establishment but we didn't know it then; schoolmasters, swots and sneaks received knocks and rough justice. The curious thing is that no matter how naughty or anarchic the characters were, we never imitated their behaviour, which rather destroys the fatuous arguments by modern child psychologists that TV and other media violence encourages anti-social behaviour in children. Either that or today's children are easily led, impressionable and have, as a consequence, lost the plot. Comics provided us with useful safety valves in our daydreaming; we knew they were nothing more than that and the antics the characters got up to had little or nothing to do with real life. Who can say kids (and adults) like me cannot tell the difference between fact and fiction? Let them come forward....

Comics which were less popular but of good quality included *Knock-*

*out,* featuring *Stonehenge Kit the Ancient Brit, Our Ernie(Entwhistle)* whose catchphrase was 'What's for tea, Ma?' to which father Entwhistle would respond on his little lad's latest adventure 'Daft I call it!' I was an avid fan of *Chips,* with its cheery *Casey Court* characters like *Billy Braggs* and *The Nibbs.* I also took *Comic Cuts* with its front cover characters *Weary Willie and Tired Tim,* two jolly tramps. I also bought *Film Fun* on Tuesdays and *Radio Fun* on Thursdays along with the *Dandy* and the *Beano* on the same days. *Radio Fun* featured Arthur Askey ('Aye thenk yew' being his trademark), George Formby, Jimmy Jewel and Ben Warriss and many other personalities from the world of wireless. Its counterpart *Film Fun* was on balance the better of the two in terms of entertainment. The front and back pages were devoted to Laurel and Hardy; other characters were *Old Mother Riley* (the male actor Arthur Lucan) and 'her' pretty, leggy daughter Kitty, Joe E Brown, Frank Randle and Abbott and Costello. Both these comics were a little less rowdy than the *Beano* and the *Dandy,* probably because their characters were caricatures of real people. The two *Funs* featured stereotyped characters like the burglar in striped jersey, cap, domino mask, his loot stuffed in a big sack labelled 'swag'; there were top-hatted, fur-collared-coat-wearing landlords smoking large cigars who squandered their ill-gotten gains on 'slap-up' meals served by snooty waiters in places called the *Hotel de Posh* while lesser mortals like Laurel and Hardy had to survive on huge plates of sausage-and-mash, the sausages sticking out of the mash like rubber truncheons. I still possess a copy of the *Film Fun* annual for 1953; its F-word alliterations confidently advertising its popularity as 'The Film Fan's Favourite - Famous for Fun, Film Features and Fine Fiction'! I especially enjoyed the Christmas editions of *Beano, Dandy, Film Fun* and *Radio Fun,* when the capital letters of the titles were capped with festive snow, the page corners sporting sprigs of holly and New Year Bells. I never read comics like *The Rover* or *The Wizard* as they didn't appeal to me; somehow, they smacked of brutishness, although they were meant to inspire young boys to do Brave Things.

My first comics were the junior ones like *Chick's Own,* with *Ru-pert the Chick*; the text and dialogue were cunningly but annoyingly hy-phen-ated to help the Very Young with their spelling. There was also *Tiger Tim and the Bruin Boys,* later transferred to the *Rainbow,* then to *Jack and Jill.* And of course, there was *Rupert the Bear* in the *Daily Mail,* a comic strip rather than a comic, although there was always a delightfully coloured Christmas annual. *Rupert* was aimed at the discerning child, probably with a middle class background; the art-work was of an extremely high standard. I loved the annual, which featured Rupert's bear Mum and Dad, Bill Badger and Algy the Dog, aided and abetted by an assortment of pixies, fairies, witches and mermaids. I was also a great fan of Enid Blyton's *Sunny Stories.* Ken followed me in reading these comics when I graduated to more adult fare.

There were more prestigious comics like those produced by the Walt

# Firelight and Starlight

Disney Corporation and World Comics Inc(orporated), as well as home-grown ones like *The Eagle* featuring *Dan Dare, Pilot of the Future* and his arch-enemy, the *Mekon*, a little malignant-looking green man who floated about on a kind of hovering pillow. I was fortunate in that my cousin Jim Cockburn had an uncle in Canada who worked as a steward on luxury liners plying the eastern seaboard of America and who regularly sent Jim bundles of American comics left on board by the passengers' no doubt spoilt children. Titles included *Tarzan of the Apes,* all the Walt Disney ones like *Mickey Mouse* and *Donald Duck,* characters from the *Saturday Evening Post* like *Li'l Abner and the Schmoos, Little Orphan Annie and Daddy Warbucks, The Katzenjammer Kids, Blondie and Dagwood* and many others.

As I grew older, my taste for American comics changed from the juvenile to the serious horror comics - *Tales from the Crypt, Eerie Tales, Beyond the Grave* and so on. Bloodthirsty, gory and frightening for the time, they wouldn't cause a mild case of nightmare today, considering what appears on the TV screen. They were eventually banned as tasteless, unhealthy and morbid, unsuitable reading material for impressionable minors because of their scenes of blood-dripping axes, flesh-rotting corpses returning for vengeance from their graves, gory, ghostly figures looming out of the fog and men guilty of some dreadful crime being haunted and tracked down by their deceased victims, great beads of perspiration rolling down their faces to denote their fear. When I think of today's horror films like *Friday the Thirteenth,* these comics were almost in the Walt Disney category. Even Britain managed to publish a more superior horror comic, the monthly *Black Magic,* which distanced itself from the lurid American comics by publishing classic ghost tales from literature. When I look back on the comics we devoured then, I recall the cliches on which their popularity was founded and depended - all well-dressed men and women were 'toffs' and 'swanks', the 'superior' male characters always wore monocles, had toothbrush moustaches and were invariably called Cecil; snobs had sharp-pointed, beaky, upturned noses, protruding teeth and patent leather shiny hair. Christmas puddings were round and large as cannon-balls with the obligatory sprig of holly on top, jellies were fashioned like castles and cakes were crammed with fruit, dripping with icing and always topped with a large cherry. Childish exclamations played a large part in the narrative, the rotters screaming such things as *Aaaargh! Yikes! w*hen they got their deserved come-uppance and were invariably hit with a cake/snowball, it went *Splat!* all over their clean-shaven features.

So on winter nights in the 1950s, groups of kids could be seen scurrying about in all weathers, knocking on doors and enquiring whether you wanted any swaps. If the answer was in the affirmative, a noisy exchange would take place just inside the front door, especially when it rained. Nobody would swap for a wet comic. In deepest winter, the frost-laden air would resound with the condition 'Nae backs!' meaning that once swapped, a comic couldn't be reclaimed.

For my generation, comics were pure escapism, just as they are today. Comics offered a glimpse of another world that didn't exist for us except on the illustrated page but brought laughter and cheer into our gritty, post-war, black-and-white world. There was little colour then except for the cinema. The British tend to regard comics with a mixture of suspicion and scorn, material fit only for the young. I never suffered any psychological harm from my comic-reading years and they encouraged me to seek out more serious stuff. Many people play down the fact that they avidly read juvenile publications they prefer to forget or dismiss as childish trivia. The nonsense read by children inevitably contains a germ of truth. In support of this, I cite Lewis Carroll's *Alice in Wonderland, Through the Looking Glass* and the classic *Wind in the Willows.* I am not ashamed to admit that I sometimes take a peek into the current issues of the *Beano* and the *Dandy.* I am heartened by the fact that comics are still with us, still thriving; they always will so long as there are people who are young in heart.

For me, reading books was a chore imposed on me at school which on principle, I avoided at home. In my home, no one told me what I should or shouldn't read; I was content with my beloved comics. Then gradually, Adam the Signalman exerted his subtle influence; he would point to one of his own books and say this:

'My, laddie, ye're missing a right good yarn. Ye'd love it'.

At last, to his intense and undisguised relief, I put away my comics and turned to the books he had recommended. There was very little intellectual stimulation in our household, so I joined the local library, being unable to afford the kind of books I wanted to read. My first full-length book was *With Lawrence in Arabia*, selected obviously on Adam's advice, he being an avid fan of T E Lawrence. After that, there was no holding me back. By the time I was fifteen, I had read most of Robert Louis Stevenson, Walter Scott, John Buchan and the G A Henty historical novels. At school, I languished over Jane Austen – she is still a lacklustre and boring author to me - struggled with Chaucer, was bored by Thackeray and some of the Brontes. But I loved Emily Bronte's *Wuthering Heights* - even if I stopped at Chapter Seventeen, when the Heathcliff-Cathy saga ended. I liked Charlotte Bronte's *Jane Eyre* and read and enjoyed most of Dickens, especially *A Christmas Carol, Oliver Twist* and *A Tale of Two Cities.* Melville's *Moby Dick* is a perennial favourite, as is Fenimore Cooper's *Last of the Mohicans.* I devoured fiction by the shelf and suffered because of it; I rarely read fiction today, preferring biographies and books on history. The last two fictions I read were Tolkien's *Lord of the Rings* and Lewis Grassic Gibbon's fine and memorable *Scots' Quair,* especially *Sunset Song,* the best of his Scottish trilogy. For me, it is a masterpiece, the definitive book on Scottish farming life and much else.

# Firelight and Starlight

## *Red Letter Days*

In every child's life there are - or should be - red letter or special days, like birthdays, Christmas etc. It goes without saying that most children have their special day marked at least by gifts and if very lucky, a party arranged by their parents. However, this Chapter concentrates on the other days in my childhood special to me.

Hogmanay and New Year's Day are the last and first festivals of every year and as children, we were allowed a few privileges on these occasions. In my household, my brother Ken and I were allowed to stay up late on Hogmanay, until the bells at midnight, when we were treated to a glass of ginger wine, a piece of shortbread and a hunk of Blackcurrant Bun. Then we were shoo'd up to bed, leaving the adults to their mysterious and noisy gatherings. We were allowed to read our Christmas annuals in bed until about one am on New Year's morning. After lights out, Ken and I would settle down, listening to the raucous din that went on for about another hour or two, when our street went strangely quiet almost on a pre-determined signal. Often, we heard bagpipes playing in the distance, people calling out their greetings, wishing each other 'A Happy New Year!' as they collided in the dark streets; in those days, the street lights went out as normal at their usual time, around midnight or so. By three am, my mother would turn out the house lights to deter any late revellers, her view being that by then, men would be drunk and incapable. However, if someone called and wasn't too much the worse for wear, she'd spy out who he was and the state he was in, then gingerly open the front door, *wheeshing* him repeatedly, for if there were any others nearby, they would have made a bee-line for the house. The celebrating might then go on until four am but by then, we were out of it, fast asleep and dreaming of the food we would enjoy later in the day.

In those days, every household hoped for a *first foot* who fitted the bill; he had to be tall, dark-haired, carry a piece of coal for luck and expected to bring a bit of *shortie* [shortbread] or *black* [currant] bun as well as something cheering in a half-bottle. My Uncle Jimmy was a great one for tradition and ritual at Hogmanay and he always first-footed the Harkess family next door. Before that, he would wait for the 'Bells', then pour us all a measure of what we were allowed, himself taking a large dram and toasting the house, wishing all a Guid New Year. Then he would open the front door to let out the Old Year and welcome in the New. After that, he would disappear next door to No 77 Lammermuir Crescent to wish the Harkess family - John, Tommy and Ann - the best. We never understood why when John and Tommy came to first foot us, Uncle Jimmy wasn't with them. It was years before I found out. When I was about twenty, I sneaked out after he'd been gone a few minutes, quietly pushing the half-open front door wide and peeping into the Harkess living room. That year, I saw why he was always late in returning; there he was, standing on a small stool kissing Auntie Ann full on her lips, she blushing and saying 'Oh, Jimmy!' as if she was happy and embarrassed at the same time. (Ann never married; she looked after old Grandma and her two brothers until John married and Grandma and Tommy died. I think Jimmy loved her but he would never have dreamt of asking for her hand because of his disability; his spine bone having been locked in the 1930s so that for the rest of his life, he was bent forward. He was working in Hoylake, England, at a boys' private school, where he worked as 'boots', then went into what was known as 'gentlemen's service' ie he became a butler. He wanted to get engaged to his Mary in Hoylake but after his disability, he broke off the relationship and came home to Dunbar. He said it wouldn't have been fair to the girl, saddling her with a deformed cripple, though he never thought of or called himself that until once when he was very drunk and depressed. He was the kindest, most honest and sincere man I ever knew. When he died in 1963, Ken maintained with justification that our family began to disintegrate after his death. Looking back now, forty years on, I know Ken was right.

The next red letter day fell on 17th February, my birthday. For years, we couldn't afford parties and when she could, my mother refused to have any more after a particularly boisterous one to celebrate Ken's birthday on 20th May. She complained about the noise and the mess the kids made in her house - she was intensely house-proud - and it was a nuisance she said she could well do without. I can't remember having more than one party to which only one girl was invited, Roberta Paxton, on whom I had a crush that year. (Roberta tells me she thoroughly enjoyed herself, being in constant demand for *Postman's Knock*!!!!) My party also ended with the rougher lads being ejected - boys like Willie Tear who had the gall (in my mother's eyes) to complain to her when he wanted to play with my toys and dragged out my toy-box from under the chest of drawers where it usually sat. Out he went on his ear, followed by those who sympathised with him. I was left with Roberta and my mother thanked her for being so well behaved....after all those kisses?

For my birthday, I was invariably given 'sensible' presents like socks and a shirt and maybe a book or a box of lead soldiers. There were usually five cards - one from Mum, one from Norman and Uncle Jimmy, one from the Harkess family and Ken's home-made one which usually consisted of a skinny stick insect with a mop of crayoned hair with an arrow pointing at it saying 'You' and 'Happy Brithday' [sic]; for many years, Ken got his letters out of sequence with words like 'hopsital'). My birthday cake was invariably a homemade sponge with icing and artificial cream but it was nevertheless a treat and I loved blowing out the candles and wishing a wish. Uncle Jimmy usually gave us each a pound as a present and I would run out to the Post Office to change it into eight half crowns [a half-crown was worth 12p then; often referred to as a half-dollar as a USA dollar was worth five shillings or

# Firelight and Starlight

25p in those days]. I am certain I did that to make the pound look more than the slip of paper it represented. Most of the money went into my *Dinah* bank which I'd inherited from Norman. A *Dinah* was a negro head-and-shoulders female with grinning mouth which opened when you pressed a lever at the back; you placed the coin in her open palm, pressed the lever and she swallowed the money. I usually blew one half-crown on sweets and ice cream and to finance extra nights at the pictures, as we called the cinema in those days.

Next came the birthdays of Uncle Jimmy, Norman and my mother, respectively on the 12th, 30th and 31st March; these were hardly personal red-letter days, but they were celebrated with food treats we all shared. A week or two before or after Mum's birthday was Easter - it came late in March one year and mid-April the next, what the Church still prefers to call a moveable feast. (Jesus was only crucified once as far as I am aware, so why isn't Easter celebrated at the same date every year, like Christmas, supposedly his birthday?) Then came Ken's birthday on 20th May, when we sat down to a special tea. Then we counted the days to 30th June, the start of the school summer holidays - eight whole weeks of freedom from schoolbooks and teachers. When we returned to school in late August, we knew the next special day - Hallowe'en - was a whole two months away. I never did well at school in the autumn term; it took me a long time to settle down after summer and besides, autumn was and still is my favourite season, an exciting time when the harvest was brought in and all nature showed her finest colourings as well as her bounty. Autumn came slowly in September, then the pace grew quicker; a time of intense activity on the farms and in the fields, the season enchanted me. All those years ago, were - or at least I was - imbued with a sense of achievement, when we walked the country roads and watched the grain and the potatoes being harvested. The hedges brimmed with brambles and other berries, especially rose hips, which we gathered on Sundays for the church, as the minister said they'd be turned into rose-hip syrup and sent to the poor children in Africa. And of course, the chestnuts were ripening and nearly ready for collecting for our games of conkers. I also went mushrooming, first on the back of Uncle Jimmy's scooter to *Boorhoose*, then on my own, foraging along the country roads at Little Spott and other places renowned for their prolific crop of *mushies* or mushrooms.

Finally, the next important red-letter day arrived on 31st October. Hallowe'en is of course an important festival in the old church calendar - the pre-Reformation one, that is - the day preceding All Saints' Day on 1st November. Of that fact we were blissfully ignorant. For us, Hallowe'en presented an opportunity for kids to make some cash for the next red letter day - or, more accurately, night - which fell on 5th November. We went *guising* for pennies - the word derives from disguising - dressing up in outlandish clothes, *chapping* [knocking] on doors and inviting the occupants to 'help the guisers.' Most of us carried *bagie* lanterns made from the biggest turnips we could find or afford; these were called *bagie lanterns* from the Scots' corruption of the Latin name for the Swedish turnip or Swede - *rata baga*. The idea was to scoop out the flesh, make triangular holes in the front to form eyes and nose and add a square gash for the mouth. A lighted candle was placed inside to enhance the hobgoblin's eerie look, the turnip top serving as a lid to keep out the wind. It was carried by means of a string handle with knotted ends threaded through holes on either side of the turnip. I believe the custom has its origins in early pagan Celtic festivals, when the skulls of enemies were stuck on poles to ward off evil spirits. According to Scottish superstition - celebrated in Robert Burns' poem *Hallowe'en* - it was the time when witches, devils, fairies and other imps of earth and air held their annual holiday. At some point, the Church grafted this ancient pagan festival into its calendar and called it All Hallows-Even - hence the name.

Before we set out on our mission, we were treated to a meal of haggis and *chappit tatties* [mashed potatoes] and *neeps* [turnip], then we *dooked* [ducked] for apples and nuts in a large basin or tin bath filled with water. You were required to bend over the basin or bath you're your hands behind your back to prevent you from cheating; you held a fork clenched between your teeth and tried to spear an apple or suck up a nut, the latter being much easier. Some households also suspended treacle scones - by that I mean ordinary drop scones smeared with the sticky stuff - on strings from the ceiling. Again, you had your hands tied behind your back and you tried to bite into the scones which the lady of the house would swing back and forth. The result was messy with sticky mouths and cheeks but it was great fun. After these preliminaries, boys and girls dressed up in their costumes and went off into the chilly night, carrying tin cans which contained washers so they'd rattle and shame the folks on whose doors they knocked to reach into purse and pocket. Most households gave what they could; some were able to afford only a sweetie or an apple or orange. You had to work for your gift however. You were expected to recite a poem word-perfect, sing a song, tell a joke or perform a dance in the living rooms of people whom you knew intimately but who pretended not to know you. The modern equivalent imported from the USA- *Trick or Treat*- palls in comparison with the former Scottish *guising*; it is bland, self-seeking and materialistic and the kids who practise it here are quite frankly, greedy, deserving nothing, which is what they get from me when they come knocking on my front door.

Once I broke the mould of boys dressing up with their jackets turned back to front and wearing their fathers' hats, rolling up their trouser legs and masking their faces with a grubby handkerchief. I dressed up as a female, with one of my Mum's old frocks, wore high heels and nylons and carried my turnip in one hand with a handbag in the other. I inflicted myself on folk, singing Vera Lynn's *We'll Meet Again* - answered by loud and indignant promises that We Would Certainly Not! Even so, my act went down a bomb and I collected more cash on 31st October 1952 than most of my fellow *guisers*. They ragged me and said I was a big *jessie* but the following year, there was a veritable army of female impersonators!

After a hard and chilly night entertaining difficult-to-please mothers and grumpy fathers parted from their pennies, we ran home to empty our tin cans and count the spoils. I usually made enough to buy a respectable number of fireworks for Guy Fawkes Night; in that year when I imitated female pulchritude, I had enough to buy a five shilling [25p] box of Brock's best pyrotechnics. The few nights after Hallowe'en were given over to really hectic activity as we all raced about cadging waste paper, cardboard boxes, firewood and anything else that would burn; if it wasn't that, it was groups of small boys clamouring for squibs and other fireworks in Knox's paper shop and any other which stocked Brock's best. The waste paper and wood were piled on the site of the street bonfire, unsupervised by adults. After all, who would want men and women to encroach upon what was a kids' festival? In Lammermuir Crescent, we had ideal storage in a building a few doors from our house - the brick-built air-raid shelter in the cul-de-sac named for one of the nearby inhabitants as *Paylor's Corner*.

One memorable Guy Fawkes Night in the early 1950s - or rather the night before that event - our shelter in Lammermuir Crescent was raided by persons unknown. They set alight to our store of paper and wood and the fire was so bad that the local fire brigade had to be called out. The harassed firemen had to fight off hordes of small boys ferrying unlit fuel out of the narrow entrance to deposit it out of harm's way in the Sailors' Park over the wall. It was the reverse of the water bucket-and-chain line but the firemen for some curious reason failed to see the funny side of this. Most of the fuel was saved by removing it through a hole in the roof. The shelter survived the fire - but not for long. Its blackened bricks were finally demolished in 1955, nearly ten years after the end of the war. I have since learnt the identity of the culprits; we always suspected the *Shories* or harbour-cum-Parsonspool gang, retaliating for some attack made by us on their territory. My good friend Bob Cameron confirmed these suspicions about a year ago, when he was doing electrical work in my house.

'Aye, it was us Roy. Your lot had attacked Parsonspool in the summer that year. You threw divots and poked us with long poles. We defended the boundary wall like it was a castle.'

Fair enough. Guy Fawkes' Nights were unsupervised by adults and usually passed without serious injury. All over Dunbar - and once atop Doon Hill - bonfires blazed and flared in the night; the sky was seeded with rockets every few minutes and squibs and bangers were set off with the intensity of a World War artillery barrage. We had firecrackers called *Jumping Jacks* which when lit, did exactly that, chasing and being chased by excited small boys; there were *Catherine Wheels* which you pinned to a post and which whizzed round and round; another favourite was *Mount Vesuvius*, a conical-shaped firework which emitted a stream of coloured sparks then exploded with a violent bang rather than the wimpish versions of today. (Did T S Eliot find his famous line for the *Waste Land* observing some firework which simply fizzled out rather than ending with a bang? It 's entirely possible).

So the night went on, kids whooping like Red Indians round the fire, potatoes baking in the embers, helping the older boys to position rockets in milk bottles to assist their flight path. The scene was one of wild faces lit up by the cascades from sparklers and star fountains and of course, the flames from the fire. About two or three hours on, the smoky sky over Dunbar was still being rent with rocket-fire and it was well into the evening before the bonfire burnt itself out, dampened by some adult male collecting his brood of sooty-faced, tired children. We all went home ready for bed, smelling of wood smoke and triumphant, chewing on our not-quite fully cooked spuds. Little did we know then that the baked potato, with its limitless fillings would become almost as popular as the hamburger in fast food places. To us, a baked spud was simply a by-product of the night we celebrated the execution of Guido or Guy Fawkes, a misguided Catholic who had tried to blow up king James VI of Scotland and I of England.

After Guy Fawkes, we knew we had nearly two months to wait for the next - and best – red-letter day, the Big Day which fell on 25th December. We saved as much as we could from our Saturday sixpences, or ran errands for neighbours, hoping to get a few coppers for our trouble. All my cash went into the voracious belly of my *Dinah* bank.

In Scotland, Christmas Day was a normal working day until well into the 1960s; it was either a Popish festival or as my Uncle Jimmy put it, a time which only the daft English saw fit to celebrate:

'Heathens. Why do they no' celebrate a proper day like Hogmanay?'

Christmas then and now posed a problem with cash flow in many household budgets; even so, it was better then than today's over-indulgent, glutinous and materialistic celebrations. Practically every connection with the Church has disappeared from post-Christian Britain, although those of the Catholic persuasion still pay lip service to its underlying religious significance.

My mother regarded Christmas as a nuisance interrupting the normal routine of the house. We always had paper chains or 'decorations' even if she said they were 'a harbour of dust' and there was a small real Christmas tree which shed its needles and was another source of annoyance to her. Eventually, she hit on a solution; she bought a tiny artificial tree in *Woolworth's*, which until the year of her death (2002) was ceremoniously unpacked from its plastic bag, still bearing ornaments like the fine wire icicles from every Christmas since 1955. I last saw that little tree at Christmas 2001; it was more important to me than all the luxurious fake Christmas trees which proliferate today, for it was the tree of my childhood Three of my mother's shibboleths or taboos were that no holly was allowed in the house, no Christmas cards with pheasants on were put on display and finally, everything remotely connected with Christmas had to be removed and stored away by *Twelfth Night*; failure to observe these were guaranteed to bring bad luck, like breaking a mirror.

We counted the days on the calendar, deleting them one by one. We sent up prayers for snow on the *Day*, or better still, Christmas Eve. My mother grew more anxious as the date drew nearer, counting the coins in her 'savings' purse, her furrowed brow betraying her feelings. Her face always gave her away, little lines of anxiety and worry which she tried to hide with extra make-up. She grizzled and groused when we pestered her to put up the decorations, saying the paper chains were a fire risk, the shed pine needles were absolute murder to sweep up - there were no hoovers in those days, just *Ewebank* sweepers, virtually a brush on four wheels with a box affair to catch the muck. She kept wishing aloud that we were older and no longer needed such childish things. A week before the Big Day, Ken and I would sit conspiratorially before the fire at evening, when Mum was making the tea, speaking in hushed tones:

> 'Loy, you ask. Det her to put um [the decorations] up. You bigger than me.'

I would shake my head, saying this to him:

> 'No, you ask. She'll listen to you.'

> 'Me too wee. You ask.'

And so it went on until I eventually plucked up the courage to speak. I wore her down every day, saying that so-and-so's mother had put up their decorations; this usually worked if it was a woman whom she didn't like and therefore didn't want to be one step ahead of her.

> 'Right' she'd say. 'Up go the buggers the night. It'll stop yir peengin [whining]'

The *peenge* at Christmas usually worked although not until about a week before the *Day*; today, cards, decorations and Christmas trees appear in the shops in September/October and houses are decorated at least four weeks before Christmas.

At last, the living room ceiling was festooned with chains and the huge paper bell which always hung from the centre; it moved in draughts coming down the chimney or when the living room door opened. The real Christmas tree we used to have fascinated me; I loved sitting before the fire with the lights out, watching the leaping, dancing flames reflected in the tinsel and tin decorations which mysteriously moved all on their own. The tree seemed alive, the firelight making it glitter and wink.

School usually broke up on 21st December, the shortest day of the year. There was usually a school concert and party, then a Sunday school party organised by Belhaven Church in West Barns parochial hall, where after a couple of hours of games and dancing, lemonade and *Store (Co-op) baps* [rolls] spread with margarine and jam, *Shipham's* meat and fish paste sandwiches, sticky cakes and jelly, we were wished a happy Christmas by the Reverend Ritchie and his Sunday school teachers. We received an apple and an orange when we left the hall. The Saturday before Christmas, my mother made her annual pilgrimage to Edinburgh alone, returning home late in the evening with bulging shopping bags she immediately took into her bedroom, shoo'ing us away to bed.

The first day of the school holiday, the High Street in Dunbar was thronged with kids doing their Christmas shopping. Norman and I affected to believe in a gentleman with a long white beard and dressed in a long red coat in the style of the Inverness cape (with shoulders) like the one worn by Sherlock Holmes. We did this to please our mother but more to encourage Ken, who was hooked anyway. He said Santa couldn't be his Daddy because he was in the Army and far away. On Christmas Eve, he always insisted on leaving out a clean carrot for 'the 'Laindeer' and a glass of lemonade for 'Father Twistmas'.

One year - in 1951, I think - my mother asked Ken wanted specially from Santa that year. Quick as a flash came the reply:

'A TOOKER!'

My mother looked at Norman and I, then shrugged her shoulders when we couldn't come up with an explanation.

'What's a tooker, then?'

'For tookin' he insisted, not a little irritated 'like we dot.'

'But what is it?'

'Y'know. For tookin'.

My mother was still puzzled.

'No, Ah don't ken what ye mean. Draw a picture o' it.'

Exasperated, he marched through to the scullery and pointed to the gas cooker, at the same time looking at my mother, Norman and I with ill-concealed disgust.

'A tooker! Like we dot. For tookin!'

Ken's problem with the letter c should have been a dead giveaway. He had seen a toy cooker in *Woolies* on one of our rare trips to Edinburgh and he'd set his heart on having it. It also had to have little pots and pans for him to 'took' with. We thought it a strange present for a little lad, but then Ken was a realist from a very early age and he certainly enjoyed his food.

As the *Big Day* drew close, I decided it was time for me to examine the contents of my *Dinah* bank. I unscrewed the iron grill at the bottom and out poured a veritable treasure trove of coins on to my bed. There were too many halfpennies, pennies and threepenny bits, but here and there I could see the reassuring gleam of sixpences, shillings and even a two-bob bit and a half-crown. The latter was one of my birthday half-crowns, the other six having been spent on the squirrel savings stamps and stuck in my Post Office National Savings book in February. I asked my mother if I could cash the stamps for Christmas presents and she nodded in agreement. I was rich! In 1951, I had about thirty shillings [£1.50] to spend on presents for the family, with a shilling or two left over for things I wanted to buy for myself.

The presents I bought for my family were rarely ever practical; my mother warned me that if I wanted to buy her anything, it wasn't to be 'for the house' as that didn't count as a present for her. So she invariably got scent - I once bought her scented bath salts and she screwed up her nose, enquiring whether I was trying to tell her something. The small bottle of scent I could afford took nearly half my savings; Norman and Uncle Jimmy got cigarettes and Ken usually got a *Dinky* toy, or something for his toy farm, of which he was inordinately proud- and some sweets. Bonzo, the little mongrel belonging to the Harkess family next door always got a rubber bone or dog biscuits. I always wrapped my gifts in coloured tissue paper, which my mother said showed the ' English' side of my nature. She thought that was exorbitant, unnecessary expense:

'It just gets ripped apart. Mind you, it'll light the fire.'

Then at long, long last, it was Christmas Eve. It usually rained or at best, there was a hard frost. I can't remember many White Christmases in my childhood. Snow often fell in England but in Scotland, it either rained on Christmas Day or there was a grey, murky sky. I put that down to the fact that the Scots celebrated Christmas with some reluctance. I used to think that the English had a hot line to God. But even without snow, Christmas Eve was a day filled with anticipation and undisguised excitement. I filled it by chopping up more kindling for the fire, hauling in an extra bucket of coal, helping in the scullery and generally making a nuisance of myself.

'Will ye get oot of my road?'

My mother would say this loudly, in exasperation. She threatened to cuff my ear if I didn't leave her alone.

'D'ye want a skelp on the ear on Christmas Eve? No, I thought not.

Weel, away ye go for a walk or play at somethin'.'

I knew it was vital that she was in a good mood on the Big Day or else there was no telling what she might cancel or do at the last minute. Like taking down the decorations.

My mother frowned on the 'English' custom of bringing holly into the house; she said it was unlucky. Another shibboleth was Christmas cards featuring pheasants in the snow - they brought bad luck as well. But she did allow a real Christmas tree – reluctantly, as she never ceased to bemoan the fact that the pine needles were shed after a few days. Carefully, she would unwrap the little glass baubles and ornaments she'd stored in cotton wool from the previous year. I recall the few nights before Christmas, sitting in the dark kitchen with only the light from the fire making the baubles and ornaments wink and glitter on the tree.

After tea on Christmas Eve, we were allowed to play in front of the fire while my mother knitted and listened to the wireless, chewing sweets. Then at

9 o' clock, when her wedding clock present chimed the hour, she'd clap her hands and order us to wash and get into pyjamas while she made us cups of *Ovaltine* to make us sleep on our earlier than usual bedtime.

'Ye'd best get to bed or Santa won't come.'

In those days, we hung pillow cases at the foot of the bed; stockings were silly, as everybody knew you couldn't fit the *Beano* or *Dandy* annual into a sock. Washed and wearing clean pyjamas, hair brushed and combed after our *Ovaltine,* we were chased upstairs to clean our teeth and get to bed. Ken and I lay awake for what seemed like hours, he constantly whispering that he could hear Santa's sledge landing on the roof.

'Loy, listen! It's him! He's on the loof!'

I would dampen his enthusiasm by trying to be adult.

'No, no. It's too early. He'll not come till we're asleep. Mum says he never comes when we're awake. Anyhow, you'd hear his sleigh bells if he was on the roof.'

'Heard 'em! Did, did!'

'Didn't, didn't! Now go to sleep or he'll never come.'

'Did, did hear 'em! '

He wouldn't be put off. He'd lie quiet for a few minutes, then he was at it again. I usually had to tell him a story in the dark and finally, he fell asleep, perhaps a comment on the calibre of the tales I invented for him. Somehow, I too managed to drift into sleep; never once did I hear my mother tiptoe into our room, remove the pillow cases, fill them downstairs, then return them without a sound. Neither could I fathom how I woke up every Christmas morning at about 5 o' clock, when every other day in the year, I had to be hauled out of bed at 8.30am. Ken would waken before me, tugging my pyjama sleeve to waken me, asking if Santa had been.

Without looking, we knew Santa had come. We could smell the presents, hear them shifting ever so slightly at the foot of the bed, making small creaking noises as they settled or moved in the pillow cases. We didn't wait for the grey east coast light to filter through the curtains so we could see the shapes of our Christmas 'stockings'; I was first out of bed, feeling the bulging pillowcases before sorting out which was which, then dragging them onto the bed so we could dip in. There was a small paraffin lamp in our room. I lit it so we could inspect the goodies. The sacks bulged excruciatingly, tantalisingly.

Now follows a few words for today's over-indulged young. The perfect Christmas morning begins early, before daylight. The gift sacks should be lumpy, knobbly and should creak when you lift them, the contents rubbing together. When you open the sack and look inside, your nostrils should be assailed with a variety of smells - fruit, chocolate, cellophane wrapping, tin, paint, the pristine smell of annuals unopened, the lead from a box of soldiers. If you are lucky, you should find inside a selection of Christmas annuals - *Beano, Dandy, Broons* or *Oor Wullie* and in those far-off days of my childhood, the *Film Fun, Radio Fun* and *Daily Mail* annuals. If you are very lucky, you should have a box of lead soldiers, all gleaming and polished and smart in their scarlet uniforms, presenting arms or shooting their guns. A 'must' then was a junior smoker's outfit containing liquorice pipes, shredded coconut for tobacco and a packet of twenty sweetie cigarettes, a *Mars Selection Box,* a net bag of gold or silver paper-wrapped chocolate money, an apple, a tangerine orange and a bag of mixed nuts. (In 1951, Ken got his 'tooker', the *Daily Express Rupert Bear* annual, the *Teddy Tail* annual (it featured its mouse hero from the *Daily Mail*), a box of coloured plasticine, a cowboy outfit complete with cap-gun, a jigsaw puzzle which consisted of blocks rather than cardboard pieces, a colouring book and crayons and of course the same confectionary as I got). Finally, in the ideal Christmas sack, there should be some small object hiding in one of the corners which has escaped your attention and turns out to be a *Dinky* or some other prestigious acquisition like a pocket torch which you hadn't expected to get. You should then sample at least one of the sweet packets to make sure its contents are fresh; in justifying this, you know that breakfast is hours away. And you should read at least half the contents of one of your annuals before it is time to go downstairs in pyjamas and slippers to show your mother and father - assuming you have both - what Santa brought left you.

When you get downstairs, the fire should be blazing merrily away as you hand out the gifts you have bought for your family. A decent breakfast that day should be porridge with sugar, a bacon roll and a good cup of tea. Then you should go back to your room, get dressed and venture out into the street to compare notes with an assortment of midget cowboys, indians, nurses, pirates, policemen and bus conductors already playing there, showing off, whooping and firing their cap-guns. At dinner time (one o' clock in those days), you should eat seasonal food like chicken or turkey, trifle, plum duff covered in custard, quantities of walnuts and brazil nuts, supplemented by sweets from your Selection box. Then you play with your brother's presents while he plays with yours. At three o' clock, you should listen to the Queen's Christmas Message to the British Empire (well, Commonwealth now), then listen to (or watch in those days of TV) your favourite comedy shows which are special Christmas editions. Then after a long day, you should go to bed a whole hour later than usual; you will go without complaint, as you want to lie in a warm bed reading your Christmas annuals, using the small electric torch which was hiding in your Christmas sack and was discovered only at the end.

The above is representative and a fairly accurate account of so many childhood Christmases whose magic I still recall over fifty years on.....

Modern parents delude themselves that their children are more sophisticated than they were and that their needs are greater than their own. Children - especially young children - don't need expensive toys to enjoy themselves. There is of course too much pressure through advertising on television and elsewhere which makes it essential that the modern child isn't 'disadvantaged' on the day. In 1970, in Greenfield Road, my first house in Balerno, I saw a child ignore the expensive toy car his father had bought him for Christmas ('It cost me an arm and a leg') and play with the large cardboard box in which it was packaged. Christmas will continue to decline, to appeal to the inherent greed of children with too much already; it is too commercialised today for society to get back to the basic version. Christmas is meant to be a time of giving, a time of love, laughter and gentle anarchy. I loved every one of my childhood Christmases. Christmas is a time to be enjoyed and celebrated by children of all ages.

I shall never forget my childhood Christmases. I was rarely disappointed as a child and there have been some memorable grown-up Christmases that I treasure; in 1968, I rediscovered Christmas with all its fun and magic when I met a lady in Newcastle that year and who was my wife for a few years. But that is another story, the subject of another book.....

# 7

## Jaunts and Joyrides

With very little money for luxuries like holidays, we were fortunate to live by the seaside, so we never thought ourselves underprivileged. In addition, when my mother was 'flush', she treated us to the occasional 'jaunt', as she called our trips to Edinburgh, or a 'joyride', when we went further a-field to places like the Trossachs. These joyrides were usually by bus, outings organised by one of the women's guilds. We never called these trips excursions or outings – they were either jaunts or joyrides. I use the latter word deliberately and not in the American slang sense which describes something easy, a pushover. For us, a joyride was a major event that lasted most of the day and extended into the evening. Joyrides were organised weeks or months ahead and required a con-siderable degree of forward planning; every eventuality had to be considered, down to the possible need for medical supplies in case of accidents or sickness during the proceedings.

The night before a joyride, my mother would check all her gear with the thoroughness of a soldier embarking on a mission. She laid out the necessaries on her bed, muttering the name of every item as it went into her largest hand-bag - elastoplast for cut or skinned knees, travel sickness pills - for me - head-ache pills, lint and bandages for the more serious mishaps and surgical spirit and cotton wool to soothe the effects of an insect bite. In Scotland, midges are a torment, something you have to put up with; voracious little swine, they're bad enough but a more aggressive insect like a *cleg* or horsefly can inflict a really serious bite. So our mother would ransack the medicine chest for the required items; a separate bag or holdall contained food for the journey - sand-wiches, buns and biscuits - and of course at the last minute, my mother's trusty thermos flask without which she never undertook any joyride. She used to say she was useless without her cup of tea, so that meant packing a small bottle of milk - usually a recycled medicine bottle - and a screw of paper containing sugar. More about a joyride appears later.

The jaunts required less forward planning and usually never lasted more than six hours. The first of these occurred on Easter Sunday, when we went on a picnic to *Osie Dean*. How vividly I recall these expeditions to the pictur-esque valley at the foot of Doon Hill. On Easter Sunday, there was a mass exodus from Dunbar; entire streets emptied as families began the trek up the High Road to Spott for the annual event of rolling the Easter eggs. Doors were locked but the keys were left hanging on strings tied to the inside of the letterbox so that they could be easily retrieved. Today, that custom would be the realisation of a burglar's dream.

The road to Spott was crammed with men, women and children from about noon. Very young children were pushed in prams and go-cars (buggies in modern language) so that the long crocodile resembled a Wild West wagon train winding its way up the High Road, past the water filtering plant until it reached the rough path to the left about a hundred yards on. This path took us to the valley, where the crocodile dispersed into little family groups seeking the choicest spots.

In 1949, Ken was still in his go-car (buggy) on his first jaunt to *Osie Dean*. He wasn't quite three years old; I was eight and Norman was fifteen. Ken's little buggy was a godsend, a convenient vehicle that saved us the bother of lugging our bags and the heavy travelling rugs my mother brought to spread on the grass in case it was damp. She was averse to outdoor cooking or making tea over an open fire, so the undercarriage of the go-car was laden with packets of sandwiches, bottles of *Aitken's* lemonade, a bottle of *Renton Dairy* milk and of course, her thermos. Added to that were half a dozen eggs she'd hard-boiled the night before, using cochineal dye and used tealeaves to colour the eggs; our eggs were either pink or deep brown, with our names written on the shell in pencil. There were two each for Norman and me, one for Ken and one for her. The sandwiches were usually egg and cress, boiled ham from *Miller* the butcher's in the West Port; the same butcher provided the *potted heid* or *hough* for our sandwiches. The *potted heid* ones were usually avoided except in cases of extreme hunger; the spread was a horrible concoction of shreds of meat imprisoned in a jelly-like substance, very salty and not nice to look at. Marginally less unpalatable were the sandwiches made with *Shipham's* meat paste - the beef or ham spread which came in small jars and which my Uncle Jimmy called *penny-a-mile* because a jar of it could make several sandwiches at very low cost. In addition to the sandwiches, we enjoyed *Smith* the baker's best buns, cream cookies and fancy Easter cakes. It was a feast indeed.

On those Saturday nights before the Easter picnic, I was preoccupied with weather watching, scanning the night sky anxiously for the build-up of clouds and possible rain. I became very religious that night, praying to the Almighty to send us a clear, sunny day. I recall some wet Easter Sundays when we were obliged to roll our eggs in the back garden or on the carpet in the living room. I once rolled my eggs down the stairs from the landing, arguing that the linoleum wasn't any good for cracking eggs; I got clouted for cheating. However, there were more dry *Osie Dean* picnics than wet, stay-at-home ones between 1946 and 1958.

The valley is about a mile from Dunbar but it seemed longer in those days, the road to it being mostly uphill. As soon as we arrived, my mother camped out in a sheltered spot near the stunted thorn bushes and gorse that still thrive on the slopes to this day. She spread the rugs, unpacked Ken and the food and poured herself a cup of tea from her trusty flask. The ritual followed by our family was that after we'd eaten the sandwiches, buns and pop, we were allowed to roll our eggs.     Rolling eggs at Easter is of course a Christian custom, symbolizing the rolling away of the stone from Jesus' tomb after the Crucifixion on Golgotha on Easter Friday. On the Sunday after the Crucifixion, the Roman soldiers set to guard the tomb fell asleep and on waking, found the stone moved and the tomb empty. Thus the myth that the crucified one had risen from the grave began. I doubt if any of the picnickers at *Osie Dean* paid much heed to the story behind the custom – even if they knew of its origins. I certainly didn't. For me as for others, Easter Sunday was a day out, a jaunt into the hills. There were precious few of those carefree days in the years immediately following the Second World War.

I can see the valley now, crammed with groups of happy people, mainly women with children content to lie on travelling rugs or clustered round the small fires, the fathers and older children having been sent out to gather firewood. Most of the afternoon was given over to communal games of *tig* [chase], *rounders*, football and Cowboys and Indians. Nearer the end of that tiring, energetic afternoon, many of the children contented themselves by lying beside Spott Burn, *guddling* for small trout and minnows or collecting frogspawn in jam jars. All that afternoon, the valley resounded to cat calls, whistles, war whoops from the boys, the girls screaming and shrieking when they were chased and pelted with *sticky willies* - the hooked bracts or burrs of the burdock plants which grew in profusion there. In late afternoon, when the boys were fishing, the girls and their mothers would wander off in small groups to gather flowers like wood anemones, primroses, celandines, marsh marigolds and buttercups. Buttercups were popular only because of the fact that if you held one under a friend's chin, you could tell if they liked butter. The myth was that if your throat reflected the bright yellow colour - as it always did - you were fond of butter. (Much good did that do as butter was still rationed in 1949). The myth may date from an earlier time, the custom probably giving the sweet little flower its name.

It was usual to see family groups sitting in a circle, like a Wild West wagon train. The reason for this was that there was often a herd of cows in the valley. Cows being curious animals, dangerous only when with calves, they would wander inquisitively towards the picnickers. The women and girls were terrified of these normally docile creatures and would huddle round their fires, begging their men folk to keep the brutes away. All afternoon, the fire-makers had blackened kettles and pots simmering away on their fires, slung gypsy-fashion from tripods of wood. My mother turned up her nose at this behaviour, saying that the women were too lazy to make sandwiches. She would sniff and say this:

> 'I for one am not drinking tea stewed over a bonfire. I'll not eat half-raw bacon sandwiches, half-cooked sausages and burnt beans. That's

not for us. We're better than THAT.'

One day, later in my life, I would cycle into the hills with a tin of beans and a few sausages, a frying pan and a pan for heating water for my tea, all done over an open fire. It was more fun that way.

After the picnic proper was over, Norman and I wandered over to the burn to look for frogspawn and minnows, jam jars clutched in our hands. It was a rare Easter Sunday when I came home empty-handed; Norman kept the minnows in his jar, I used mine for the *taddies* [tadpoles]. Few of my catches survived long enough to become young frogs, even when I used burn water and vegetation to feed the little creatures. At least I had the pleasure of watching what I thought looked like little mobile commas losing their feathery tails and sprouting legs. I think at least one of my tadpoles matured into a frog, for as I write in Chapter 5, I learnt to swim simply by studying the actions of a young frog.

In that enchanted valley, there used to be an old building about halfway along the glen; we assumed it had been a mill as there was evidence of a mill-lade dug out of the ground to divert water from the burn to drive a mill wheel. I have since learnt that the building was known as the Old Broomhouse Mill and that it belonged to Easter Broomhouse farm, which has a Standing Stone in the middle of a field overlooking the valley. Today, the site and the mill's ruined stones have been incorporated into a fine house owned by my good friends Dorothy and Keith Knight. In my day, the mill was a shell, its walls covered with branches of trees that hung over it, the interior being floored with a paste of mud and cowpats. The cows would congregate there in a rainstorm - they aren't stupid creatures - seeking shelter from the weather. I used to pretend it was an ancient castle where I defended the honour of some imaginary princess, usually based on the girl I currently had a crush on at school. It was many years later, when I was researching my book *Swords, Loaves and Fishes* that *Osie Dean* had been the scene of a disastrous Scottish defeat in April 1296, a battle that marked the beginning of the long, dour Wars of Independence. I also found that the same ground - or almost the same - was the site of the defeat of the Covenanter army led by David Leslie against Oliver Cromwell in 1650, a battle which took Scotland on the road to union with England in 1707. So that hallowed ground saw the beginning of the struggle for independence and the end of it. *Osie Dean,* that quiet, beautiful valley or glen of my childhood belies its nature; it was the scene of much bloodshed, lost causes, unfulfilled dreams.

By late afternoon, after we had eaten all the food, the moment came to roll our eggs. My mother clapped her hands.

'Right, you lot. It's time to roll your eggs.'

The ritual was subject to a set of unwritten laws. You were forbidden to break the shell by deliberately aiming the egg at a stone. That was cheating, as was using your boot to help the egg on its way. It had to be done fair and square by rolling it in the grass - bouncing the egg was also frowned upon - which was a great frustration to us. To crack an egg could take an inordinately long time - too long for some wateringly expectant mouths. But eventually, you cracked it - in both senses of the word - and enjoyed the flesh, even if the white was marbled by the cochineal pink of or the tealeaf brown. Very soon, the valley floor was littered with eggshells, scattered through the tussocky grass like coloured confetti.

So that Sunday, the last when Norman came with us, we were happy. Norman was sixteen and felt he was too grown-up to share Easter Sunday with his Mum and kid brothers any more. I recall we tumbled the eggs over the grass, surreptitiously booting them in the long grass, pretending we'd lost them. Many the time I complained to my Mum that we should be allowed to kick the grass; she said that would be cheating. When we finally 'cracked it' - is that the derivation of the modern slang phrase? - we got stuck in. My mother rolled Ken's egg for him; he hated the white of an egg, thinking it was fat - perhaps he still does - and I was given the white coloured part with the cochineal pink or the tealeaf brown. In those days, it was said that a sign of the cheap egg was a thin shell, one that broke easily. I can't say if that is true, not being versed in animal husbandry.

The last hours of our jaunt into the countryside were spent playing *rounders*. The teams were massive. But by then, I wanted to be alone, wandering by the burn, seeking out tadpoles and minnows. We were of course warned not to attempt to climb as it was considered dangerously high. Doon Hill is hardly that by Scottish standards; in 1949, to me it was Everest and I knew that I would climb it one day. I loved and still love that hill. It's one of the least high in the Lammermuirs, none of which exceeds 1,700 feet; I think it's about 900 feet. Doon Hill remains a prominent landmark in my life, having pride of place in my emotional luggage over fifty years on. I believe it was from that hill that the town of Dunbar developed, as I argue in *Swords, Loaves and Fishes;* it also features in a historical novel, *The Hill,* which I hope to publish one day.

As if by a pre-arranged signal at about 6pm, reckoned by the position of the sun's lengthening shadows - very few of us possessed watches in those days - the madding crowd in the valley began to pack their bags. The bags were of course much lighter on the return journey, their contents having been consumed. But this benefit was cancelled out by our tiredness. Children grizzled and *wheenged* [whined], complaining of sore legs and feet. This brought the response from my mother that we should have thought about that before we'd played the last game of *rounders.*. The very young were lucky; they had their prams and go-cars so the little ones including brother Ken could lie back and enjoy being pushed home in the rapidly freshening air, invariably an indication there'd be frost in the evening. Norman and I trotted alongside our mother and the go-car; as most of the road was downhill to Lochend Wood, I hung on to rather than helped to push the go-car. I recall one teenage girl about

# Jaunts and Joyrides

Norman's age who every year without fail would walk home in her ankle socks, her shoes strung round her neck. She was part of the Easter jaunt, a familiar sight whose absence would have spoiled the day. I forget her name today but she was unimaginatively nicknamed *Sair* [sore] *Feet.*

As I said earlier, Norman stopped coming on picnics with us in 1950, preferring to go off on long cycle runs with his friends, their sandwiches and Easter eggs stored in their saddlebags. I went with him one summer's day on the crossbar of his bike to Little Spott, the Halls and the Pleasants, places he knew intimately from his van boy job with Petrie's *Lammermuir Laundry,* housed in Spott Road. Anyway, on that lovely summer day, Norman stopped at the top of a steep hill near the Brunt, where he laughingly pointed out the place where he'd let go of my pram at the top of the hill, watching it crash and throw me out into the road on my head.

'Aye, that's how ye got brains. I dunted [knocked] them into ye that day.'

For other reasons, I shall never forget that day we stood at the crest of *Starvation Brae* which overlooks Spott village. Below us was spread the panoply of an azure blue sea, the familiar landmark of the Parish Kirk, then and now Dunbar's most distinctive landmark. To the west lay a diminutive Bass Rock with a toy ship sailing beyond it. To me, the rock has always looked like a snail, though you get an entirely different perspective from North Berwick, where it looks like a crouching lion. When I was older and owned my own bike, I used to cycle up there on many a Sunday to renew my acquaintance with that breathtakingly beautiful view.

Easter Sunday now behind us, we looked forward in hope that in the not too distant future, Mum would be able to afford a jaunt to Edinburgh, or even further a-field. Usually, our trips to Edinburgh came at the beginning or end of the school summer holidays, when the jaunt was mainly to buy us clothes for the summer or for the school. The trip to Edinburgh usually meant going by train, something Ken and I always enjoyed. Travelling by train in the days of the great steam engines was an adventure not to be missed. Trains to and from Dunbar were more frequent in those pre-Beeching days as there were few cars on the road and the public service buses were slow, smelly and uncomfortable. On the days we went to Edinburgh, breakfast was a hurried affair, my mother eating hers at the kitchen sink while she applied what she called her 'war-paint' or make-up. No matter how early we rose or how organised we were, we always seemed to end up running for the train.

In the 1950s, trains were almost human - they were certainly alive - and like many small boys, Ken and I imagined they had faces, which in a way they had. Even if they were dirtier and noisier than the diesel powered engines which would replace them, they were far more interesting, especially to children. As the train arrived in the station, you took the trouble to note the name on the brass plate on the engine. I remember trains with names like *Mallard,*

# Jaunts and Joyrides

*Kingfisher* and *City of Edinburgh*. Today's youngsters have no conception or appreciation of a journey by steam train unless they have been fortunate enough to visit the Railway Museum at York or nearer home, at Bo'Ness. I visited the latter a few years ago and was fortunate enough to renew my friendship with an old school friend, the late Billy Peddie from Dunbar. Billy worked all his years on the railway and in retirement, spent his leisure time at weekends servicing the old trains at Bo'Ness.

The enjoyment began when we reached Dunbar station. While my mother bought the tickets, Ken and I would inspect the station garden on the north side of the platform. In those days, every station competed for the prize for the best-kept garden and Dunbar won it more than once and was often runner-up. It was - and still is to a certain extent - a beautiful show; a profusion of seasonal flowers laid out in shapes and circles, borders and little plots punctuated by small models of local buildings like the Barns Ness lighthouse. The whole effect was set off by decorations of shells from the beach painted white, the name *Dunbar* picked out in whitewashed limpet shells. At that time, there was a bookstall selling newspapers, magazines, paperbacks sweets and tobacco, where the modern ticket office stands. You could also buy penny packets of seeds you threw out of the window in the hope that they would take root in the embankments. This explains why many stretches of Scottish railway embankments are studded with flowers like the lupin, a popular perennial whose seeds we often bought.

When my mother came on to the platform, she was usually greeted by one of the local porters who seemed to be on duty all the time. We called him *Toothpaste* on account of his permanently fixed I'm-on-duty smile. He was a nosey parker, always enquiring where you were going and why- this done under the guise of concern for your welfare. I suppose he was being friendly in his own way, but we resented his intrusions. He was the inveterate *sweetie wife* and was often also called *The News of the World*. A typical conversation would go like this:

'Aye. It'll be Edinburgh the day, Mistress. With the bairns. Aye. Will ye be shoppin' at the big stores? Aye, I suppose so.'

My mother would answer in the affirmative to both questions, then shoo us along the platform to get away from him. But he invariably followed us, carrying on his interrogation.

'Looks like rain, I'm afraid. Will the laddies be getting sweeties? Or is it new suits and shoes? Aye, I suppose so.'

And so it went on until thankfully, the train arrived, huffing and puffing importantly as befitted their status, stopping at the north bound platform in a great hiss of steam. Usually there were no corridors in these local trains from Berwick - and therefore no toilets - so we had to 'go' in the station before we got on board. The station toilets were awful, like the school toilets, with green slime in evidence but we 'went' nonetheless. These trains were without corridors and were known as Parliamentary trains on account of the fact that Parliament had decreed that a certain percentage of trains were required to stop at every station on the line. The compartments tended to have a musty smell, a cocktail of stale cigarette smoke, dusty upholstery, cheap hair oil and perfume. We didn't care. It was all part of the fun of a day out.

We scrambled inside arguing who should sit nearest the window and on which side, hoping we'd get a compartment to ourselves which we invariably did until we got nearer Edinburgh. The train took on water at Dunbar, exhaling great gouts of steam from the funnel we just *had* to watch from the open carriage window. After considerable snorting, shuffling and puffing, chuntering and wheezing, the steam-enshrouded monster started to inch forward, then it halted again like an animal catching its breath. The false start always perplexed my mother; she would yell at us to haul up the window using the leather strap for that purpose. She would tell us to do it NOW as we were holding up the train's departure and would get sooty marks on our nice clean white shirts. After another few seconds' inexplicable delay – that hasn't changed in fifty years – we watched *Toothpaste* extract his big 'turnip' watch from his waistcoat pocket, consult it, green flag in hand counting the seconds until it was time to go. Then with a blast on his whistle and a flourish of his flag, we were OFF!

Ken and I spent the first few minutes watching the familiar fields and woods drift by, feeling safe and luxurious, pointing out sheep and cows and the odd passer-by on his/her bicycle on the road – usually the postman or some old dear on her way to Dunbar for her shopping. There were few cars and not many tractors on the roads in those days. Then as the train gathered speed, we would turn our attention to the photographs and aquatints hanging on the walls, usually of popular watering holes like Bath, Windermere, Cornwall, Tintern Abbey and the Scottish Highlands. (Now, when I read Philip Larkin's poem *Sunny Prestatyn*, with its graphic and cynical observations on a contemporary poster advertising that holiday town in Wales, I think of those childhood train journeys). We always cheered when there was a photograph of the Scottish Highlands; our exuberance was immediately cut short by my mother's whispered command:

'Wheesht, wheesht! They'll hear you next door! Behave!'

These far-off places might as well have been on the moon, as they were beyond our mother's purse. Some of the place names were familiar from my geography lessons at school; we would kneel on the padded seats and study the prints until my mother would order us to sit properly.

'Sit down. Sit right! You were brought up proper! And not a word out of you until we get to Edinburgh.'

I noticed that she never spoke Scottish dialect when she chided us loudly. She always talked 'proper' in public, especially on trains and buses.

I could never understand why we had to 'sit right'. That confused me.

# Jaunts and Joyrides

You either sat or you stood. What was 'right'? And we also felt we should be allowed to chat as we had the compartment to ourselves. But we were ordered to be quiet during that fifty-five minute journey. To help us, she would rummage in her handbag for the large bag of sweets she always carried on these journeys; we spent the next half hour or so with cheeks bulging like squirrels, jaws clamped together on toffees.

We were mesmerised by the sights we saw as we approached Edinburgh. The train stopped at East Linton, Drem, Longniddry, Prestonpans, Inveresk and Portobello (where my great uncle Tom Cockburn once was stationmaster) until it at long last entered the famous long dark tunnel that leads into Waverley Station. The train chugged along at a steady pace, rocking slightly from side to side. We looked into back gardens of small cottages and council houses; women were hanging out their washing, men were digging their vegetable plots. As we passed, some would wave to us and we waved back politely. Some of the country folk kept chickens and the odd pig in their back gardens and we even saw a garden with goats grazing the extensive lawn.

At that time, I hadn't encountered the poems of Wordsworth, so Earth hadn't anything to show more fair than the scenery between Dunbar and Edinburgh. Rarely were we left alone after we stopped at East Linton. Folk got on at East Linton, then Drem and other stations so the compartment soon filled up and my mother ordered us to 'bunch up' or sit closer together. I was shy in those days; when a man or woman spoke to me in the confines of a railway carriage, I blushed uncontrollably, afraid I would 'let my mother down' when speaking to them. But at last, the train entered the long, dark Waverley tunnel, when the train was plunged into darkness. We blinked as it emerged into the sunlight; I saw a large building I took to be Edinburgh Castle and what in later life turned out to be St Andrew's House, where I spent thirty years of my working life.

When the train stuttered to a halt in Waverley Station, it disgorged its passengers, then was shunted into a siding where it went on to a large turntable to point it for the return journey south. Ken always insisted on waving goodbye to the driver and engineer, muttering to himself. When I asked him what he said, he refused to reply at first, then he looked at me seriously and said this:

> 'Me saying bye-bye to tlain and dliver so they will mind [remember] us and tum back to take us home 'gain.'

I guess he was always worried we'd be stranded; it was a measure of his insecurity in those days, without a father to reassure him.

We struggled up Waverley Steps against the ever-present wind, my mother bringing up the rear and clucking like a broody hen, telling us not to run into Princes Street when we got to the top of the steps. When we got there, I was always mesmerised. Edinburgh was a magical place, a different world with its fine castle and beautiful clean wide streets whose shops were more interesting and individual than those of today which seem to sell the same goods. We walked past the *North British Hotel* – now *The Balmoral* – then crossed over to Leith Walk at the old GPO building. I knew where we were going - *The Brown Derby* otherwise known as *Littlejohn's Restaurant* at the top of the Walk. *Littlejohn's Brown Derby* was an upmarket restaurant a few steps away from Princes Street, on the first floor of what is today a pub. *Littlejohn* was ostensibly a bakery, with its shop on the ground floor, the bakery being behind the edifice in Lower Calton - you can still see the name faintly stencilled on the wall from Waterloo Place. The baker's shop windows were filled with mouth-watering concoctions - cream cakes, iced buns, cream cookies, bread and rolls.

The restaurant was above the shop; it was clean, conservative (with a small c) and was renowned for its excellent service; the food was reasonably priced and of good quality. We always sat at a window table where we could watch the trams in bustling Princes Street. There we could enjoy a three-course lunch of brown Windsor soup, mince and *tatties* or steak pie made on the premises, followed by apple pie and custard or a blob of ice cream. I think the meal cost 2/6 [12.5p], children being charged half price. The friendly wait-resses were dressed in neat uniforms - black dresses, stockings and shoes, the dresses with white lace accessories of pinafores, detachable cuffs and small lace caps with the peaks turned up at the front. The ladies who served you were a mixture of young and old but they were all attractive and jolly; I loved going there not just for the food but because these ladies treated Ken and I as if we were grown-up, making us feel important as well as welcome. My mother always left a small tip, even though she couldn't afford one; she of all people knew how hard these ladies worked for a pittance, for she'd done similar work in Dunbar in Mrs Shearlaw's boarding house in Marine Road, Dunbar in the 1930s. Besides, the ladies in Littlejohn's looked after us well and always tried to get us a window seat.

After filling our faces, the next stop was nearby Woolworth's or Woolies, as we knew it. The store was the first shop in Princes Street next to Leith Walk; after it closed, it became a Menzies bookshop and is now a fast food joint. No trip to Edinburgh would have been complete without a visit to that magical emporium, with its creaking wooden floors, its smells, its sloping counters crammed to overflowing with good things - tin toys, lead soldiers, sweets and books as well as boring commodities like clothes and stationery. It was a veritable Aladdin's Cave. Ken and I always made a beeline to the toy counters to spend our sixpences. Invariably, I bought a couple of lead soldiers, Ken a tin toy on wheels. There was an air of excitement about Woolies then, equalled for me by Grahame the ironmonger's shop at No 99 High Street, Dunbar, espe-cially at Christmas. Woolies was never the same after it was modernised. The wonderfully animated creaking wooden floors were covered with vinyl; the sloping counters were made level counters and shelves were added where you served yourself. The whole effect was lost as the shop fell victim to the curse of the twentieth century - sterile, clinical efficiency. Such is progress. Before it finally closed, it had become a supermarket with only shelves and no counters; the former numerous, friendly and helpful staff was replaced by a small workforce of young girls whose main job was to keep the shelves stocked. Customer contact disappeared overnight. I recall going in there in the 1960s to buy something; when I couldn't find what I wanted on the serried ranks of shelves and asked a passing shop girl, her response was blunt:

'If it's no' oan [not on] the shelves, we've no' goddit [got it].'

Gradually, all the shops and stores would lose their individual character, their facades transformed into brash, modern concrete, glass and plastic; this vandalism destroyed the ambience of what was one of Scotland's - and arguably Europe's - finest streets.

My mother was a lifelong customer of Jenner's, a shop that today still retains vestiges of its unique, if quirky character. Ken and I weren't overjoyed with that store since it had few attractions for us, although today there is a very good toy department in the basement. Maybe there was even then, but the wares were probably priced out of my mother's range. We always liked to visit Binn's at the far end of Princes Street for one reason. We were mesmerised by the way that customers paid for their purchases. This was achieved by means of a really fascinating network of tubes which were attached to the ceilings. The tubes were called baillies - slender, hollow pipes that were attached to the ceilings with brackets. The customer handed over the money, which was then attached to the bill and inserted into the mouth of the pipe; at the push of a button, both were whisked away on the overhead rail to a central accounts department in the top floor. A few minutes later, the tube returned, bearing the exact change and the receipt for the purchase. It was impressive and fascinating to us kids. After that experience, we were taken to the chemist shop *Duncan and Flockhart* which sold blackcurrant jujubes and which Ken and I sucked as sweeties that were of course rationed until 1953. The jujubes were supposed to alleviate colds; with or without colds, we loved them for their juicy, fruity taste.

After we left *Binn's*, the afternoon was wearing on and we were growing weary, struggling through the crowds of shoppers and Hibs and Hearts supporters, returning home from the football games. Our trips to Edinburgh were usually undertaken on a Saturday afternoon, the busiest day of the week. Standing outside *Binn's,* my mother would announce that she'd to visit one more store in Lothian Road. I forget the name of the shop now, but it involved a tram journey. I loved the Edinburgh trams; they travelled at such a sedate pace that you could jump on and off them while they were moving, although my mother never allowed us to do that. On one visit, we were about to board a tram in the West End; my mother wasn't sure about its destination. She asked the conductor if it went near such-and-such a store. He said it did, but she wasn't quick enough to climb on board, much to the annoyance of an old lady in the queue behind her. It had started to drizzle and she was impatient, wanting to get on the tram. She prodded my mother with her umbrella.

'Are you going thither?' she asked in a slightly annoyed tone.

My mother was nervous but plucked up the courage to answer her:

'Yes, all of us are together. These are my sons.'

That had no effect on the old lady who pushed past us. Then I began to snigger and quietly let Ken in on the joke.

'Mum thought she said 'are you thegither [together]'

No Morningsider - for she was undoubtedly that - worth her salt would have used a Scots dialect word like that. Well, not in a public place...

During the brief tram trip, the old lady tried to make conversation. She tickled Ken under the chin and said

'You're not from Edinburgh. Where do you come from?

Ken thought for a minute, then replied

'Me tum flom Bass Lock [Rock], like Loy tumed from. Stork bringed us'

The old lady smiled. My mother was nervous, embarrassed.

'We tell the children that when they're born, the stork brings them from the Bass Rock to Dunbar. That's where we're from'.

The lady smiled, then said this to Ken:

'So, Dunbar, sonny.'

Ken misunderstood her, hesitated for a moment, then replied

'Uh-huh. But lainy, too. We not dot tlam tars there, like Embro. Det wet sometimes.'

He thought she'd asked if Dunbar was sunny. He'd never heard the word 'sonny' before....I am sure my mother was relieved when we got off the tram in Lothian Road, a few stops on. Shepherding us onto the pavement, she warned us not to speak to anybody else that day.

'I was that affontit' [embarrassed]. What did I tell ye? Children should be seen and not heard. Mind now, not another word out of ye.'

Finally, tired-out, hot and sticky, we pleaded with my mother to finish her shopping and take us to the station and home. But it was a whole day out she said; we caught another tram to Leith Walk, when she announced that we would have 'high tea' at *The Brown Derby.* That cheered us up. We alighted from the tram, crossed the street to the restaurant, by then busy with other Saturday shoppers. No matter, the waitresses knew us and steered us to a table set in a discreet corner. We usually had a fish tea - with golden chips- and bread and butter slices that were delicately thin. Scones and 'fancy cakes' were set before us on a cake stand; we could each as much as we liked. Then at last, we left the restaurant to catch the 6.30pm train home. Ken anxiously looked for the driver who'd brought us to the city six or seven hours ago. Our train was often driven by the same man, which reassured Ken. By the time we got to Dunbar at 7.30pm, he was fast asleep and my mother had to carry him while I carried her bags. An hour later, he was in bed, no doubt dreaming of his jaunt to the city, his latest toy lying on the bedside table.

There were several evening jaunts to Edinburgh, usually organised by the *Women's Guild* or the *Women's Rural Institute* (*WRI*). I never enjoyed these trips as they were visits to the theatre for some singing show or the pantomime, both of which I detested for the simple reason that they bore no relation to reality. I hated the community singing, the false emotion, the dancing and the clowning nonsense of the *pantos* that never absorbed me or suspended my belief. Most of my life, I have avoided live entertainment, which I unaccountably find false, although I have seen some plays on the stage which have moved me. The venues chosen by the *WRI* were anathema to me. However, when Norman had to do his National Service, my mother lost her childminder and so we were dragged up to Edinburgh every time she wanted to see a 'show'. 'Show' was a misnomer in my book; had I known the word then, I would have called them caricatures. I have seen *Chu Chin Chow* on stage, on roller skates and even on ice. I have sat through many mawkish, maudlin, excruciatingly sickly-sweet performances of *Rose Marie,* although not as many times that qualified your average Civil Servant who is described as a man who lives with his Mum, doesn't smoke or drink and has seen *The Sound of Music* twenty times. I unashamedly detested that film when it was released and still do today. I am sure Julie Andrews' predecessor Jeanette MacDonald and her trusty *Mountie* Nelson Eddy made a worthy twosome but their imitators who trod the boards and sang to the *Gods* or high galleries in the Lyceum Theatre were poor substitutes. If I ever hear the *Indian Love Call* again, I swear there will be blood on the carpet. Of course, I didn't know words like mawkish or maudlin in my youth but I felt these performances were fake, a sham, not in the least romantic. *Requiescat in pace Rose Marie*; I hope your graveside companion is the singing nun in *The Sound of Music…*

The Edinburgh trips were comprised mainly of women and children who were too old to be left at home; their fathers had to supervise the babies or with luck, were able to hire sitters so they could (wisely) visit the pub while their wives were away. The ladies on the buses that took us from Dunbar to Edinburgh weren't averse to indulging in a little tipple themselves, usually on the way home. In those days, it was considered unseemly for a woman - even a married woman accompanied by her husband - to visit a public house. I can only surmise that the ladies who went to those Saturday evening jaunts to *pantos* and musicals took the opportunity to refresh themselves in secret, drinking from half bottles concealed in their handbags. And yet I can state without fear of contradiction, I never saw any of the ladies who went on these bus trips raise a glass or bottle to their mouths, even if some of them were obviously the worse for wear on the trip back home. My favourite lady on these trips, Ella Ogilvie, sadly died in April 2005; every inch a lady, she made these trips to Edinburgh memorable for me, as she was always game for a song and a dance on the way home.

# Jaunts and Joyrides

After the show, we piled into the waiting charabanc which travelled for about ten minutes, stopping at the *Deep Sea* (then a well known rallying point for ladies of the night) fish and chip shop in Leith Walk - it is still there today but not as colourful as it was then - where the ladies disgorged themselves after taking orders from all and sundry. I usually asked for just chips. The suppers were wrapped in newspapers unlike the modern cardboard boxes I maintain absorb the fragrance and the taste of the fish supper and make them soggy. The suppers stank out the bus, masking alcohol fumes I have to admit I never noticed. Ella, a lifetime teetotaller, had consumed her fish supper long before we reached Musselburgh, when she was ready to begin her act with her favourite number of that time - Guy Mitchell's hit number *She Wears Red Feathers and a Hula Hula Skirt*. Ella belted it out much to our enjoyment, dancing up and down the bus aisle, swinging her hips and an imaginary grass skirt. When she came to the line *She lives off just coconuts and fish from the sea* she used to pat her bosom when she sang the word *coconuts*; in those days *coconuts* was the slang word for breasts. We were treated to her repertoire for the next half hour and it was better than the acts we had seen on the stage of the *Lyceum* or the *Kings* theatres that evening. Well, I thought it was.

After about a half hour in the bus, the entertainment tailed away as the drinkers sunk into their seats. My mother sat opposite Ken and I and frequently put her finger up to her lips to indicate we should be quiet. By the time we reached Haddington, I was fast asleep, oblivious of the singsongs in the bus. Ken was asleep before me. There was nothing to see out of the bus window and at last, I succumbed to counting lampposts in the way that insomniacs count sheep. Then suddenly, my mother would shake us awake as we had arrived at the bus stop at Belhaven Church.

I have to admit I enjoyed two memorable evenings in Edinburgh in the early 1950s. The first was a show featuring the famous cowboy Roy Rogers, his wife Dale Evans, Trigger the horse and Bullet the Alsatian dog. Rogers looked like a Red Indian or at least Oriental, with slit eyes. Maybe he had some Inuit Indian or Eskimo blood in him. For all that, he was one of my childhood heroes and I clearly recall him riding Trigger across the stage of the *Empire* in Edinburgh. Sweating under the arc lights, he put the horse through its paces, ending the act by sitting on the horse rearing into the air. Years later, I read that the horse almost broke its legs in that stunt. Rogers sang a few cowpoke songs I could have done without. Then he launched into his truly awful sentimental song *My Four Legged Friend*. When that was over, he did a few fancy tricks with his six-gun, blasting away into the roof of the theatre. At the finale, he bowed to the audience and bade all his *Li'll Scaats Podners* a fond farewell, inviting the children present to discharge their toy cap pistols. Neither Ken nor I had a pistol so we had to shout 'Bang!' So that was the visit of the famous Roy Rogers.

The other legendary act staged by the *Empire* occurred about a year later, when I saw my heroes Stan Laurel and Oliver Hardy in the flesh. They were at the height of their popularity in Scotland and worth going to see. I can picture them on that Edinburgh stage today, doing much the same routines as they did on the screen. Laurel and Hardy began their career as *Vaudeville* or music hall entertainers, so treading the boards at the *Empire* in Edinburgh must have brought back nostalgic memories. With hindsight and more sophisticated tastes today, their acts were predictable, following a standard pattern; their act was pretty average but at the time, they were the people's favourites, their performances enjoyed by young and old alike. No one would have thought of criticising them because they were of the people and so the people loved them.

Now it is time to describe a joyride in terms of the most momentous trip of the year. The annual all-day bus tour to the Trossachs, which to me was a journey of heroic proportions yet one that for all the excitement and joy it engendered, was spoiled by my bus-sickness. That never put me off but I was a poor traveller by bus until I grew older; even now, I prefer trains to buses. The curious thing about my sickness was that neither trains or boats brought it on. Anyway, these trips were organised by the *WRI* and they were unforgettable. (Today, I would describe them as unforgivable but then cynicism has kicked in since those halcyon days). The scenery alone was worth the hour or so I felt queasy, then voided the contents of my belly at the side of some nameless road. Also, we enjoyed the company of the incomparable and redoubtable Ella belting out her song-and-dance routines; she was always able to take my mind off my predicament.

We started the journey at about ten o' clock, the bus picking up groups at various designated spots, ours being Belhaven Parish Church. The driver liked to make the first stop on the other side of the River Forth, where in those pre Forth Road Bridge days, we had to catch the ferry at South Queensferry. When we got to the other side, the bus stopped at some respectable café so that the women could have tea, the kids fizzy pop, then we would get back on board to enjoy our packed lunches. We drove along scary, narrow roads through breathtakingly beautiful scenery until we arrived at the Trossachs, the famous mountain pass in Perthshire, extending for a mile west of Loch Achray to Loch Katrine, about eight miles west of Callander. The beauty spot was of course immortalised by Sir Walter Scott in *The Lady of the Lake*. Loch Katrine still has its steamer (launched in 1899), named after the great novelist himself, which plies up and down the loch. Next stop was Loch Lomond, the 'Queen of Scottish Lochs' which is deservedly famous for its quiet beauty and one of the saddest and tragically beautiful songs Scotland has inspired; in that song, a young Scot proclaims that after the tragic battle of Flodden, he will take the High Road and his dead friend will take the Low Road to Loch Lomond. In those days, there was far less traffic on the roads and the driver was able to make frequent and unscheduled stops to allow matronly - and sometimes unsteady - ladies to whip out their Box Brownie cameras to take a few snaps for the family album, then disappear into the bushes by the roadside for a 'comfort' stop; small boys like me were shepherded to the other side of the road where we could find a convenient bush behind which to do likewise - or be sick again. We didn't possess a camera at the time, so we'd to store our memories in the mind; sadly, most of the inner vision has gone.

By the time we stopped for afternoon tea, I had been sick enough to feel hungry, although I ate sparingly. As we bowled along through the darkening landscape, my queasiness began to disappear, probably because I was becoming accustomed to the motion of the charabanc, laid on by *Stark's Garage* in Dunbar. There I was nearing the end of the day's joyride, beginning to enjoy myself; I felt cheated. But my problem never stopped me from going back the following year; I always enjoyed my joyride to the Trossachs.

The next memorable joyride was the holiday I spent in the school camp in the summer of 1953, the year of the Queen's coronation. That year, I had suffered the agonies of the Qualifying Test and perhaps my mother agreed to pay the few pounds to compensate for the ordeal I had gone through. I have to admit that going to a school camp was not my idea of fun - I was a loner then and am today - but that year, I wanted to have a holiday without my family. The East Lothian District Council's Education Department organised holiday camps each year at Middleton, a fly blown, muddy site from what I heard at school. But that year, the venue was to be Abingdon, Lanarkshire. I thought it might be fun to go there, for I had never been to Lanarkshire. The beauty of the site was that, instead of the usual leaking tents of Middleton, we would be housed in stout, wooden huts. This appealed to my - admittedly lukewarm - sense of adventure and my mother readily agreed that I could go, for in truth, she wanted me out from under her feet.

When school broke up for the summer holiday that year, we had a week to prepare for this exciting joyride, courtesy of Dr John Meiklejohn, the Director of Education in East Lothian County Council. His was a name to contend with, inspiring a mixture of fear and admiration in parents all over the county. To get a letter with his signature on was either a blessing or a torment. The blessing was usually in the form of a letter granting a bursary to somebody's son or daughter, the torment usually a threat about the truancy of the same. (As I was fortunate enough to receive a bursary two years later, my mother hadn't a bad word to say about the man, even if she feared him).

As the day of our departure neared, we were sent letters with instructions to report to various designated stopping points for the bus that would take us to deepest, darkest Abingdon. If I recall correctly, the bus roamed through the leafy, country lanes of the eastern outer reaches of our world in those days - Cockburnspath, Innerwick and Oldhamstocks before arriving at the GPO building in Dunbar High Street to pick up the Townies. I was among the small contingent that stood clutching small bags/suitcases at Belhaven

# Jaunts and Joyrides

Church. Other stops were West Barns and East Linton, which in those days were frontier villages to me. Our suitcases - many were ex-War Department issued to fathers who served in the war - mainly contained clothes but all the kids seemed to have smaller bags stuffed with bottles of pop, sandwiches and packets of crisps for the journey into uncharted, unknown territory.

So off we were whisked, chattering, farting, singing, making jokes, whistling and pulling the pigtails of the girls who sat in front of us. Not one had the slightest idea where we were bound as no one had taken the trouble to bring an atlas of Scotland. And wonder of wonders, on that long (to me) bus ride, I managed not to be sick.

My travelling companions were a mixed and motley crew. Some were lively and entertaining, some quiet and scared, a few positively morose and resentful. There was one particularly moody lad from East Linton who clearly hated his parents for sending him on the school camp holiday. He announced to all and sundry that he had wanted to stay at home during the holidays but his parents had insisted that he make the trip.

'Feggin' buggers. Well, youse'll see. Ma brother went last year an' it wis like a bluidy prisoner-o'-war camp. Teachers bossin' ye about. Jist like the airmy [army].'

I feared the army partly because my father who was something of an ogre in those days served in it. But curiosity soon dispelled my misgivings as we bowled along through the Lanarkshire countryside which wasn't much different from that around Dunbar. In a sense, our grumbler wasn't wrong entirely but I have to admit that when we arrived in Abingdon, the scenery was idyllic, breathtakingly beautiful. As we descended to the plain of the river Clyde, I felt excited. Above the camp were hills carpeted with green, a few offering the sight of acres of fir trees, more than I had ever seen before.

When the bus dropped us off in the low, wooded area beside the Clyde, I was impressed by the majestic hills that surrounded our encampment. Lanarkshire or Clydesdale - was it the home of those splendidly majestic horses on the farms around Dunbar? - is graced by hills between two and three thousand feet high, dwarfing my beloved Lammermuirs. We stood around, waiting for someone to tell us where we would sleep that night. A man called us together and informed us that the village of Abingdon, which we had just passed through, was out of bounds except when we were chaperoned by an adult. We were promised one visit to the village, maybe two, depending on how we behaved. We were advised to inform our dormitory masters about intended trips to the village as the bus that would take us there seated only a couple of dozen. We were issued with a sort of timetable informing you of the week's activities and which left a blank space for our official visit to Abingdon; it was asterisked 'to be arranged'. We were then allocated team leaders who doubled up as dormitory masters and informed that if we had any requests/complaints, these must routed through the team leader. Our time was rigidly controlled so that everyone in authority could check where you were supposed to be and what you were scheduled to do at any time on any particular day.

We were allocated huts according to an alphabetical list based on the area of East Lothian from whence we came. Thus Cockburnspathians were allocated the letter C, Dunbarovians the letter D, Innerwickians the letter I and so on. Inside our hut, the team leader directed us to our bunks, giving each boy the choice of sleeping on the upper or lower bunk. I begged a bottom bunk for the simple reason that if I had to 'go' during the night, I could do so quietly and not disturb my companions but more importantly not advertise the reason for my nocturnal wanderings which caused me acute embarrassment. To my surprise, the team leader agreed, thus refuting our grumbler's belief that they would 'make it awkward for us.'

That first night, our team leader showed us how to unfold our sheets and blankets neatly piled on our bunks. He showed us how to make our beds and how we should fold them for inspection the following morning. It was as close to National Service in the army that I ever got. Our dormitory master left us to get on with it while he inspected the bunks of the adjacent dormitory. A few minutes later, he returned to inspect our handiwork. He stopped at my bunk and shook his head.

> 'No, no. This is all wrong. It won't do at all. You must tuck the sheets and blankets under the mattress so that they won't trail on the floor. You haven't folded them in properly at the corners as you were told. Do it again. The lot of you. You are ignorant, what are you?'

We responded in Marine-like responses. The dormitory master stormed out in high dudgeon, muttering something about country bumpkins that needed to be taught the 'ropes' when they had to do their National Service. I think he must have spent some time in the Army. After he left, our young grumbler from Block E (East Linton) appeared. He stood in the middle of the hut, picking his nose.

'Did I no' tell youse? This camp is like the bluidy airmy.'

Somebody threw a pillow at him but that didn't deter his moaning for the rest of the week. He criticised the food - which I have to admit was not too bad - the weather, the early morning rise, the cold showers, the lack of amenities, the hill walks. Our grumbler called them route marches - no doubt an expression gleaned from his elder brother's letters complaining about the inconveniences of his National Service barrack block.

The first day did seem to suggest the atmosphere of a military camp. We were treated to an 'early rise and shine' call at 6.30am. The dormitory master kicked the door of our hut open. He stood framed in the doorway, resplendent in striped pyjamas, yelling at the dozy, sleepy-headed kids who stumbled out of their bunks like zombies.

'Wakey, wakey, you dozey lot! '

He gave a fairly accurate impression of the *Billy Cotton Band Show* I used to listen to on the wireless on Sunday afternoons. In short clipped sentences, we were informed that breakfast would be served in fifteen minutes, after our persons were washed, our teeth brushed, our hair combed and our persons dressed. That bloody sadist shouted at us during our showers.

> 'Come on, come on, jump to it, you lazy beggars! If I catch one of you undressed in the next five minutes, look out! I won't have any of my lot on cookhouse duties! Cookhouse Johnnies are failures. I don't have failures in my dormitory.'

As we ran past him, he flicked a wet towel over our bums. Our eyes were still bleary and swollen with sleep. I hated that man, as I hate all those who attempt to impose their will on me. On that first day, I went outside to listen to the blackbirds carolling. Birdsong saved me from becoming embittered as I went sullenly to the washroom, where I was embarrassed to see boys naked as I was. Later, I was informed that any boy found hiding under his bunk after *reveille* was whipped unless he could prove he was sick. I was beginning to think that our East Linton grumbler had been telling the truth

Ablutions over, we got dressed under the eagle eye of the dormitory master who kept looking out of the window to see if our lot could now join the queue for the morning meal. Because of the restricted space in the refectory hut, we ate by numbers, each batch taking their allotted turn. My group was third in line that morning; when we arrived in the mess-hut - the word 'mess' describes it perfectly - the folding tables were already littered with scraps of bread, spilt milk puddles and blobs of congealing porridge. As usual with local authority-run establishments, there wasn't enough staff to serve the food more often than not dished-up lukewarm or even worse on your plate. Cold porridge isn't one of my favourite dishes but hunger forced me to overcome that. Some of us were appointed as table monitors, bestowing the doubtful privilege of filling empty milk jugs etc, then at the end of the session, we were handed smelly string cloths with which we swabbed down the tables.

> Our dorm master hovered over us when we cleaned up after ourselves.
> 'Come on, come on, look lively! It's you monitors' job to make sure everyone returns their crockery to the kitchen hatch. If they don't, you'll have to do it.'

He pointed to the kitchen hatch already crammed with the blue-and-white striped mugs, plates and porridge bowls from the previous intake. As most of the kids at our tables had scarpered, we groaned at the sight of the piled crockery.

> 'Come on, come on! Others are waiting out there for their breakfasts. Now another announcement. I am warning you here and now that any boy or girl who breaks a camp rule will be punished according to the severity of the misdemeanour. The most common reprimand is serving for a minimum of one hour in the kitchen.'

At this, I sneaked a sideways look at the young grumbler who stood nearby. His expression was that of someone about to receive a hundred lashes. One enterprising lad shot up his hand.

'Will we get the belt, sir?'

The dorm master shook his head.

'No, lad. It'll be worse than that. You'll spend time in the cookhouse, the number of hours being determined by the seriousness of the misde meanour. You're not in school, you're in a holiday camp. You're here to enjoy yourselves but rules are rules. Obey them and you'll have nothing to worry about.'

After breakfast, we were marched back to the dormitory and told to amuse ourselves until the rest of the camp had been fed. After that, we would be mustered in the refectory to hear the day's bulletin of planned events and activities. But at least this time, we'd be joined by the girls and some of us like me were anxious to investigate the 'talent' which East Lothian schools had on offer.

Half an hour later, I met the girl of my dreams - dreams shared by several others. She stood out like the lighthouse at Barns Ness did the Lady Gladys. She didn't giggle or fidget like the other girls; she was cool, grown-up and exuded confidence. I was standing between a boy we nicknamed *Blackbird* because he could whistle like one and a lad called John who was very unpopular because he'd pee'd the bed while occupying the top bunk until the poor lad underneath complained to the dorm master.

A stout man with a red face looking ridiculous in long shorts came to speak to the assembled crowd. He informed us he was the Camp Officer - today, an entirely different interpretation would raise more than a passing snigger - he then introduced his staff, including the nurse who had a face like the Store horse and legs like our dinner table at home. (Why was it in those days that the female school employees, including some of the teachers, looked like that? Were they chosen for these attributes? Am I imagining it?) We were informed as to which of those we should consult if we had any problems or wanted more information about the camp activities. Then we were shown the football and cricket pitches, the tennis courts and a rough piece of ground where we could play *rounders*. Then, as the skies began to darken ominously, he hurried through the rest of his speech.

'Now, in the unlikely event of any outdoor activity having to be can celled due to adverse weather' - what was that? - 'you'll be pleased to know that alternative pastimes and indoor games will be laid on in the refectory hut or in your own dormitories. Those that will be held in the refectory hut will include film shows ' - this was greeted by muffled cheers -'or dances' - groans at this -'but in the case of film shows, there will be two houses owing to the restricted space. So please remember to inform your dorm master as to which show you wish to attend in the event of rain.'

He might have added 'Be happy at your work' like some German or Japanese prisoner-of-war commandant.

It was almost as if the weather had been paying attention to his speech. As he delivered the last few sentences, the heavens opened. Down came the rain in chilly, gusting sheets. I guess it was the hills round about; you can't have hills without rain.

For the rest of that day and night and the next day, it poured. We were confined to our dorms all that day, playing snap or some other stupid card game. The following day, we had a film show; my memory is faulty but I seem to recall a Laurel and Hardy short, followed by a full-length film like *Gunga Din* or some B-rated western. In the evening, we had a dance and so I was able to get to grips - literally - with Lady Gladys. She turned out to be not only a good looker but also an accomplished dance-partner, better than me, although even in those days, I wasn't too clumsy on the dance-floor, thanks to my mother. We seemed to hit it off that first night.

On the evening before our final day at the camp, the Camp Officer visited each dormitory to inform us that because the weather forecast was fine for the last day, he was organising a mass hike into the hills at ten am.

'After breakfast, you will assemble on the football pitch, where you will be given coloured armbands. These will be yellow, blue, red, green, white and so on. The teams will start out at regular intervals of five minutes. The winning team will be that which arrives back at camp first. The prize will be a double helping of ice cream. The last team to arrive will clean the refectory after they have had their evening meal. The entire camp will participate. Only those with designated duties or who have reported sick will be excused. You will report to the refectory first, to collect your packed lunches. Then you will receive your arm bands from your dormitory master. Dismissed!'

The young grumbler who had said all along that the camp was no more than a front for impending National Service was heard to groan audibly. Later, he had this to say:

'You guys didnae believe me. It's a route march, just like in the airmy. I wish Ah was seek.'

The *airmy* or Army apart, reporting *seek* [sick] seemed the best bet but not one of us had the resourcefulness to face the horse-faced nurse with the dinner table legs. She would have declared us all fit. Her stern, no-nonsense expression convinced me of that. In our bunks that night, we grumbled and groused, but we knew we would go. Some of my lot managed to wangle themselves cookhouse duties, for when the hike ended, food would be served to the first teams and extra hands would be needed to serve them. By the time Iain Cornes and I got to the cookhouse, all the vacancies had been filled. The next day would be memorable in more ways than one; Iain and I would also cement our friendship.

The next day dawned clear and bright, the cirrus clouds were high in the

# Jaunts and Joyrides

Lanarkshire sky. We assembled on the football pitch; my lot were given red armbands. Red was the colour of blood. The adults who were in charge of us counted us as we marched past them, exhorting some of us to 'pick up your feet' as the crocodiles of kids left the camp. Iain and I had agreed we'd bring up the rear, a fact which didn't go unnoticed by our dorm master.

> 'Come on you two! Speedo, speedo! Pick up your feet! Two young healthy lads like you should be at the front! Never saw the like before. A spell of National Service will cure you of that! Hup-two-three-four! Come on, you lazy pair, put your backs into it!'

That 'hup-two-three-four' stuck in my memory; when I saw Walt Disney's entertaining and colourful cartoon, *Jungle Book*. Thirty or so years later, when I saw the Elephant Patrol scene with its pompous Colonel Hawty at the front, I thought of Abingdon Holiday Camp………………..

Iain Cornes and I shared a mutual dislike of the jolly hockeysticks mentality of those sadists. We detested the communal singing that was meant to inspire the camaraderie of that time. I was young then, inexperienced, naïve, but even then, I always felt uneasy about the songs which were sung to encourage a community spirit. I never felt comfortable with bands of brothers, be they Lifeboys, Boys' Brigaders or Scouts. To me, the falseness of their messages and mottoes was crystal clear. Iain and I were at the tail end of our crocodile because both of us knew the hollow message of enforced camaraderie. He and I were born loners. I still am.

When the pace faltered, the leader of the pack would exhort his charges to sing banal songs. We heard them muted, glad that we didn't have to sing. I recall one of them called *The Happy Wanderer*, an excessively dreary and mundane song with what I considered redolent of Nazi Germany; it went like this:

> *I love to go a-wandering*
> *Along the mountain track;*
> *I love to go a-wandering*
> *With my knapsack on my back.*

This nonsense was followed by the equally banal and silly chorus:

> *Val-de-ree*
> *Val-de-rah*
> *Val-de-ree*
> *Val-de-rah-hah-hah-hah-hah-hah-hah*
> *My knapsack on my back!*

It was dire stuff anywhere on earth, meaningless drivel. In deepest Abingdon on a sweltering summer day, it was even less welcome. We weren't allowed to drink our pop, open our packed lunches until the Dorm leader gave his permission. That day, I wished myself back in Dunbar. Even chopping kindling in our coal shed would have been preferable. And yet, the scenery was memorable, challenging, beautiful.

Iain and I lagged even further behind until we found ourselves alone. We were fascinated by the flora and fauna that abounded in that idyllic landscape. We shared a common interest in the little birds, the animals, stream creatures and flowers. To us, they were more interesting than marching into the uncertain blue yonder. That afternoon, bathing our hot feet in a burn, we saw a water rat, a little vole, a young trout struggling to swim upstream. Then I saw the biggest frog - maybe it was a toad - I had ever encountered. We started to chase it up and down the burn. We could still see the tail end of the happy wanderers who were now singing *The Gipsy Rover,* another ballad of appalling banality. The eponymous hero was given his reward in the chorus:

Aw-dee-doo, aw-dee-dah

Aw dee-doo, aw-dee-doo-dah,

*He whistled and sang till the greenwood rang*

*And he won the heart of a lay-ay-ay-ay-ay-ay-dee.*

Another stupid chorus of a stupid song best ignored. I was far more interested in the frog than the lovesick gypsy who got his woman. Just as we thought we had cornered the big bugger - Iain swore it was the biggest frog he had ever seen - he made an impressive leap on to the dry stone dyke bordering the burn. I jumped the burn to catch him, grabbing the top stones of the dyke. I missed the frog but pulled down several heavy stones on to my left leg- well, my left ankle. The pain was bad and I bled for a while. Iain took out his big handkerchief, wet it in the burn and bound up my ankle.

He said he would run after the singers, get them to come back; at least maybe it would stop them from torturing us with their stupid songs. I said I didn't want them to break off their trip. Iain said that maybe it would be best if after I had rested, he could carry me on his back and return to the camp. I refused his offer, saying that if we followed the others, it might mean a shorter journey. I argued that as it was nearly 2pm, we would get back quicker if we followed the crocodile. After all, it was a circular walk. For half an hour or so, Iain carried me on his back, struggling through tussocky grass, ferns and heather. In the intense heat, he succumbed to exhaustion. As we lay in the grass, he took off the bandage and said my wound had stopped bleeding. I was able to stand but there was still pain and so I had to lean on Iain's shoulder. We hobbled for a mile or so, seeing the grass trampled by the feet of our crocodile. Iain decided to treat it as a game.

'Let's pretend they're a band of renegade Injuns that we're tracking.

Let's pretend we're army scouts on their trail.'

I will never know if Iain Cornes was destined to be a psychologist or a psychiatrist. He and his family emigrated to Australia in 1956. I have no way of knowing his chosen career. (If you are out there Iain, let me tell you this. Thanks buddy. With your juvenile psychology, you got me through a painful time that hot and sticky afternoon in an unfamiliar and slightly hostile place). Iain was enjoying himself, having the time of his life.

'Look Roy! Another clue! They left the moor here. The grass is flat
tened and there's a sweetie paper. There's also a crushed clump of heather.
Yep. I reckon we're on the trail of them Injuns.'

*Corneylugs* - as we would later call him - really spoke like that. His
favourite phrases were straight out of the *Beano* and the *Dandy*. He used expressions like *Jumpin' Crocodiles* and *Cripes* and *Whizzo!* Is it my imagination that when confronted by his poor results in a Latin test set by the late,
great J I W Milne, his response was loud and unequivocal:

'Jeepers creepers! Oh, golly gosh! Mr Milne, I owe you an apology. I
am so ashamed! Maybe next week, I shall be better.'

But let us return to the bosky woods of Abingdon. We finally caught up
with the weary footsore crowd in front of us. We were done in ourselves and
they were about five miles ahead of us. We were met by an anxious team
leader who had done a head count and found that he had two people missing.
He was relieved to see us, covering up his worry by giving us a lecture on
safety.

'Knew you lads would make it. I wasn't worried. I knew you weren't
far behind. You can't keep country lads down. But as you're the last
of my lot,
I'm afraid you'll be on cookhouse detail, washing-up after supper.'

Iain was not one to take that sort of thing meekly, without protest; he
had a strong sense of justice, that lad. He pointed to my bloody ankle and said
in the circumstances, it wasn't fair that we should be punished for being late as
I was wounded. Wounded was a bit much - injured perhaps- but he was making a point. Maybe Iain became a politician. It had the desired effect. Our
leader whipped out a bandage from his bag, smothered it in iodine and wrapped
it round the affected part.. He promised to speak to the Camp Officer on our
behalf and get us excused from cookhouse duties. He was as good as his word.
That night in the dorm, we were cheered by the others.

That night was our last in Abingdon. It was one of unfettered hilarity.
We were healthily boisterous in those days - or nights. The fun began just after
the usual supper of cocoa and biscuits and went on well after midnight. Kids
were getting bolder and cheekier by the minute. Before the pillow fights and
the nocturnal wanderings, some lad had bad-mouthed the cook when his back
was turned. The boy must have learnt what he said from an older brother
doing his National Service because his words were almost identical to those of
my brother Norman who was in the RAF at Royston, England and who recounted a similar tale. A hush fell over the refectory after the lad shouted his
accusation. The Camp Officer was summoned and clearly disgruntled at being
dragged from his end-of-holiday (sherry?) party, he stood before us, arms
akimbo, jaw thrust out like Mr MacKay, the bureaucratic prison warder portrayed by Fulton Mackay in the TV comedy series *Porridge*.

'Right, you horrible shower. Which impudent boy called the cook a B? Come on, own up. If the miscreant doesn't identify himself and take his punishment, I promise you this. You will all be confined to your huts for the rest of the evening. Will the culprit please stand up and identify himself?'

The immediate response was a heavy silence, followed by some sniggering from the back row. In the furthest recess of that darken hall, somebody shouted out this:

'Please sir, who called the bugger a cook?'

The balloon of authority thus pricked, there was a round of applause and we could all breathe again. I am sure I saw the Camp Officer's mouth broaden. All he could say was

'Right, then. You're dismissed.'

It was our last night after all. There had been a dance in the refectory before supper and once more, I had held my glorious Gladys in my arms. I asked her for the last dance, always a prelude to the next phase of asking if the lady wished to be escorted home - or in this case, to her hut. She said yes.

After supper, we met outside Gladys's hut, whispering to each other so that her dorm mistress couldn't hear. I asked her to walk beside the now tamed river Clyde. A romantic film director couldn't have done better with the scenery. I can't remember what we talked about but knowing myself intimately, I probably prattled on about the landscape, the clouds, the shooting stars, the generous moon. We stood holding hands beside the river, listening to it whispering, I pecked her on the cheek, then walked her to her hut. As she quietly opened the door to enter the now dark hut, she turned to me and smiled. Then she vanished inside and was gone. Forever, as it turned out.

The next day, I recall feeling infinitely sad. I had enjoyed my jaunt to Abingdon, Lanarkshire, had met some good friends, but on that bright morning, I believed I was saying goodbye to them and so we would never meet again. That tells you much about my worldliness and my sense of geography. When I got off the bus at Belhaven Church, I stood on the pavement, gawping and waving goodbye. The tears weren't far away. For the rest of that summer, I moped about, missing the boys and girls I had met.

To my surprise, when the school took up for the autumn term, they were all there. Gladys lived at East Pinkerton, John Douglas belonged to East Barns, where his father was headmaster of the village school, Billy Crawford hailed from Crowhill, near Innerwick and Iain Cornes lived at Whittingehame, where his father taught the bad boys from the Borstal. They had all known that after they sat the Qualifying Exam, they would be coming to Dunbar Grammar. Not one of them had bothered to inform me of the fact. Maybe I should have known, maybe some of them thought I knew. As for the Lady Gladys, our paths crossed at the school dance that Christmas; it was a brief encounter for me. She soon moved on to other, better-looking boys than me. After three years at the Grammar School, she left. I have never seen her again since 1956. Recently, I was having a drink with my good friend Peter Combe, who lives in West Barns. Peter was – and is - an accomplished ballroom dancer. (He partnered my mother in 1999 and she complimented him on his proficiency on the floor, a compliment indeed as my mother was fussy about her dancing partners). But that evening, as we reminisced about the old days, Peter asked me if I had ever danced with the Lady Gladys.

'Yes I did. At Abingdon, on a school camp trip, then in the Gymnasium at the school. She was great at the dancing, but I wasn't good enough for her.'

Peter smiled.

'Nobody was good enough for Lady Gladys. She was in a class of her own'.

Maybe he was right.

The next joyride I recollect was organised by the Grammar School. It must have been in my First Year (Class SIL- meaning First Class Latin). In that year, we had John (Jack) I W Milne as our form master. (There are many people in Dunbar who recall the incomparable, unique, highly entertaining Jack Milne. He made fun of his initials; he told many of us that they stood for John Ignatius Winterbottom. A few of his former pupils who still live in Dunbar insist that his name was in fact John Ingram Wallace, which is probably nearer the truth. Jack was an intellectual comedian, not an unusual combination. I loved the man for his anarchy, his intelligent wit, his unforgettable *bon mots*. I miss him today…

So that summer term of 1954, we went on a trip to Rothesay and the Kyles of Bute, shepherded by the incomparable J I W Milne. It was idyllic. We boarded the steamship *Waverley* which sailed the length of the lovely Kyles. That steamer must have played host to thousands of children of all ages. I can imagine the scene on that beautiful June day. A clear, blue, brilliant sea leaping beside our boat, a cloudless sky populated with the ubiquitous seagulls which followed in our wake, expert at catching in their beaks the crisps and bits of bread we threw to them.

The island of Bute grew more beautiful by the minute. At first, it was small, then it grew large as we approached it. We raced about the deck, trying to find our bearings. Some of my classmates began to look a bit more sedate as the ship cleaved the waters, rolling a little. The motion induced sickness in some of my schoolmates. I wasn't affected, which surprised me, given my years of bus sickness. I thought the trip a wonder; I felt confident and enjoyed every minute of it.

But what I recall most of that jaunt was the beginnings of a romance with a sweet, dark-haired little girl called M___. She was the daughter of a shepherd in Springfield, then part of Dunglass Estate. I had seen M___ often in the quadrangle of the school. Her lovely dark, flowing hair and her beautiful black eyes intrigued me. Yes, she was attractive, with slim, neat legs. My mother always said that I should go out with women with slim legs....

M___ was in the Domestic class, I was in Latin and French, so our paths crossed only in the quadrangle as girls had a separate playground (with toilets) to the seaward side of the school. Our friendship came and went over the next few years, but when we were together, we were always happy. I have never forgotten her and was deeply saddened to learn that M___ had died of cancer in 2003. I was devastated, for I had always promised myself we would meet again. But I return to my tale of that time.

We were together most of the afternoon on board the ship. I wanted to cuddle her but I couldn't find a place that was free from kids running up and down the deck. I whispered to her that it would be OK on the train journey home, so I asked her if we could sit together. I reminded her of the long, dark Waverley Tunnel, hinting of a passionate clinch. When we boarded the train, she followed me. I couldn't wait for the darkness to envelop us, so that I could kiss her in the dark. I shall never forget that first, sweet, chaste kiss, not only because it was lovely but also for what she whispered in my ear.

'I think I've got German Measles. I've got this lump on the back of my neck and my Mum says that's a sign.'

I shook my head. I said she was probably imagining it. A few days later, I had a lump as well. We both had a holiday from school, a blessing even though the symptoms were unbearable. As I lay in bed that week, I thought of M___ and how we were falling in love; I couldn't feel bad about her, not for any lump on my neck or the rise in body temperature which accompanied it. When I got back to school, Jock the Wild Man said this when he found out why I'd been off school:

'Kee-rist! Ye should be gled [glad] that she's only got a lump on her neck and no' in her belly. Kee-rist! Ye kissed in the dark! Did ye no' ken they get awfy [awful] passionate in the dark?'

I could only bow to Jock's superior wisdom, but something inside me told me I knew better.

Later that same year, our form master Jack Milne organised a personal trip for our class, this time to Edinburgh. When I describe it as personal, I mean in relation to Jack. Our jaunt coincided with a needle football-match between his hometown of Aberdeen and Hibernian at Easter Road. I think his team won that Saturday, so he was in a great mood. He left us in *Woolies* all afternoon. We ran riot there. Then we had fish suppers. Jack had come back from Easter Road to enjoy a few swallows in his favourite pubs - the *Guildford* and the *Café Royal*. He loved his *Guinness*. Before the match, he took us to Edinburgh Castle - my first but not last visit - and I revelled in the thickness of the castle walls, was amazed by the size of *Mons Meg*, the cannon which James IV had had cast before Flodden. I ran my hands lovingly over her iron flanks and wondered what it would have been like to fire the monster at ships or men.

# Jaunts and Joyrides

The day ended far too soon, but I was glad to get back to Dunbar, because M___ would be at the cinema as usual and I would be able to sit with her during the second showing of whatever film was on offer. She had to leave the cinema at 9.30pm to catch her bus home. We got off the evening train before she went into the first showing, so I was able to see her and kiss her before I went home for my tea. She asked me if we were *wynching* [walking out together] and I said yes. That night, I saw her for only twenty minutes in the darkened cinema but she kissed me stronger than ever before. When she left to catch her bus home, I knew it would be Monday before we saw each other again in the school quadrangle.

But by far, the most epic journey of all in my young life occurred at Easter 1958 - not 1957, as recorded in *From Slate to Disk* which was published in 1997 to mark the centenary year of the Grammar School. I was privileged to appear in it - or rather, I am in one of the photographs taken in 1958. (I am identified as Roy Leigh, not Pugh. Leigh was never one of my several aliases! On reflection, I think I would have rather been called Leigh than Pugh, a name with which the Dunbar kids had a field day, as I mention in Chapter 11). Anyway, in 1958, Dunbar Grammar School organised a trip to Paris, France. Only the Fourth, Fifth and Sixth Years were allowed to participate. That year, I was in the Fifth.

In 1957/58, my father returned to us, prompted by a letter I had written to him, saying that it would be nice to see him again. He replied to me, asking where he could stay in Dunbar. I asked my mother and she supposed he might come to 75 Lammermuir Crescent, as it was technically his 'home'. My father never regarded anywhere as 'home'. Home was where his regiment happened to be stationed. On reflection, I don't think my motive was entirely altruistic or even remotely intended to bring my parents together again. I knew the Paris trip required more money than I could save from my grocer message-boy part-time job with the local branch of *Lipton's*. Although the trip was partially subsidised by the East Lothian Education Authority, as it was partly educational, my slender resources would never have met the shortfall.

My father came home. We met him at the railway station and I looked apprehensively at my mother's face. I think I knew even then that the marriage was stone cold. He'd put on weight, was less attractive than the photographs we had of him. Time had not been kind to him. He looked older than his years. My mother had also changed, had turned her heart away from him. She couldn't forgive him for the years he'd ignored us or written harsh letters to her. I had made a terrible mistake. At least young Ken was pleased to have his Daddy back, especially when he was given an electric train set for his twelfth birthday. My reward was the jaunt to Paris.

It was the most exciting thing that had happened to me up to that time. Paris was an adventure and I was going with my good friend T who was in the Sixth Year. The holiday was arranged for Easter 1958; no holiday ever sped by quicker.

The outward journey was one of almost epic proportions. We were going ABROAD! It was an all day and night journey by train to Newhaven, from where the following morning, we caught the packet steamer for Dieppe. I had expected rough sea in the Channel but the day was calm, with bright sunshine, the sea like a millpond. Like many of my classmates, I had sailed on the *Waverley* to the Kyles of Bute but this was the open sea, with no land visible for twenty miles. I stood in the stern that sunlit morning, watching the famous White Cliffs of Dover recede into the milky haze. I imagined I was going to war and tried to recreate within myself the feelings of the young men from Britain, America, Canada and France who only fourteen years earlier had embarked on troopships for the D-Day invasion, prepared to give their lives to free Europe from the Nazis. But on the day we sailed, the sea was azure, the sky a brilliant, azure blue, the gulls performed their mid-air aerobatics as they on the wing the crisps and leftover sandwiches we threw to them.

My friend T was eccentric, intentionally so. He stood beside me at the ship's rail and musing like me on the Second World War. After a few minutes of this nostalgia, he suddenly announced that he'd solved the problem of travelling light. He had always refused to wear the school uniform on the principle that he hated uniforms, a sign of submission. (That didn't deter him from joining the Lothian and Border Horse a year or so later. But then T was and still is a man of contradictions). Anyway, that day, he wore his usual dog-tooth check sports jacket, black bow tie and - as he proudly informed me - a green drip-dry shirt which he said he could wash every night and wear it the next morning. As he optimistically informed:

'It's more practical than white, which gets dirty after only a day. It's the latest thing from the States.'

We all thought he was joking, including his current girlfriend and my good friend Karen Cheetham. T was renowned for that. We thought the green shirt was one of several he'd brought with him. When we arrived in Paris and made our way to *Hotel de Villas* where we were staying, we registered and were given the keys to our rooms. T bunked in with myself, Derick and another lad; the four Sixth Formers shared the room next door. When we started to unpack, we were amazed at T's lack of clothing. His wardrobe consisted of the clothes he stood up in. All he had packed were spare socks and underwear. The first thing he did that night was to wash his drip-dry shirt.

After our evening meal, we stayed in the hotel, leaning over the outside balcony and staring at the bustling streets of Paris. T's shirt flapped in the breeze as we craned our necks to catch a view - only just - of the famous *Tour Eiffel*. Then we went to bed, tired out after the long journey and a night spent on a train.

The next morning, T went to retrieve his shirt. It was still damp, so he'd to cadge a spare from one of the lads in the next room. Dripped it certainly

had, dry it wasn't. He swore he would sue the shop in Edinburgh where he'd
bought it. Either the manufacturers had failed to take account of capricious
Gallic humidity or they had conveniently omitted to state on the label that the
wearer would have to wait a couple of days before it was fit to wear again.
Drip-dry only meant that the shirt didn't have to be ironed; there was no guarantee that it would dry within less than 24 hours.

For me, Paris was magical, the holiday of my life. We tried out our rough
schoolboy French on the hotel staff and the locals and couldn't understand
why the *Parisiennes* failed to understand their own language. Well, that's not
entirely fair. I recall a Frenchman standing outside our hotel one morning,
who, on discovering we were *Ecossais*, demanded to know why we weren't
wearing *Le Kilt*. He made sure we understood him; he waved his hands over
his knees and fluffed up an imaginary kilt, lifting an imaginary corner to show
that he was wearing nothing underneath by exclaiming in loud tones:

'Oo la la! Pas de *kniquers!'*

Well, I think he used the last word, or perhaps it's my vivid imagination.
The French no doubt remembered their experience of encountering Scottish
soldiers in Paris after Napoleon's defeat at Waterloo and during World War 1.
(In some contemporary cartoons of 1815, Scottish infantrymen are depicted in
a gale, showing their bare bottoms to giggling *Mademoiselles*. The French
continue to be fascinated by the kilt which some of them wear when they come
to Murrayfield for the international rugby matches. I have worn a kilt once
only - with underpants on - and I have no desire to repeat the experience.

We did the lot in Paris, just like American tourists. We visited Notre
Dame. I was fascinated by the gargoyle drainage spouts which certainly worked
when it rained; but I looked in vain for a statue of Quasimodo, Victor Hugo's
hunchbacked, stone-deaf bell-ringer, played by the great Charles Laughton in
the famous film of 1939. We went to Sacre Coeur which dominates the northern aspect of the Paris skyline. (There, I stood on the steps, imitating the
stance of Marlon Brando who played an arrogant Nazi officer in the film *The
Young Lions* which I'd seen in Dunbar only a month before). To the rear of
Sacre Coeur is La Place de Tertre, where the artists of the day displayed their
impressions of the river Seine, the boulevards and Notre Dame, although the
main trade was in charcoal sketches of yourself. How I wish I had bought one
of me! After that, we went to the nearby *Pere Lachaise* cemetery to visit the
graves of Victor Hugo, Oscar Wilde and the novelist Collette.

After lunch, we took transport to Versailles, where I was astonished by
the geometric precision of the palace's beautiful, formal gardens. T's sole
comment was that it was no wonder that the French peasants revolted as they'd
slaved in the gardens for a crust of bread. The palace was built by Louis XIV
and became the seat of his court. It became the symbol of feudal tyranny in the
eyes of the revolutionary *sans-culottes* before the Terror, when hundreds or
perhaps thousands of the nobility were guillotined. For those of us like my-

self, interested in history, the significance of Versailles was the treaty that secured the peace terms at the end of the First World War.

We were taken to view the site of the Bastille, then to the *Hotel des Invalides* and *Le Musee de L'Armee* where we saw Napoleon's massive and it has to be said, *kitsch* porphyry sarcophagus; on reflection, perhaps those who erected it had an eye on the future, realising that the Emperor's remains would become a tourist attraction. The museum itself is a 'must' for anyone interested in arms and militaria, as I was then and am now. The types and range of cannon alone is impressive; I suppose that is not surprising, as Napoleon began his military career in the artillery.

After that, we trudged down to the Champs de Mars and the Eiffel Tower. I unwisely agreed to accompany our party on one of the several lifts that take you to the summit of the tower. I have to admit that I found the vista of Paris breathtaking but it was on that occasion I discovered I suffer from a fear of heights. Well, perhaps the Eiffel Tower confirmed an earlier suspicion. I couldn't get back to *terra firma* quickly enough. I have never forgotten the sinking feeling in the pit of my gut when I looked over the edge and saw people a thousand feet below. Ants came to mind....

Paris then and now - I revisited it again in 1981 on honeymoon - is conjured up through the olfactory sense, the nose. The rich scent of hot, steaming coffee served up milky in wide cups at breakfast; they are more like bowls and you do what the French do, dipping your golden, flaky *croissants* into the coffee, the best way to enjoy them. I recall the hot, foetid blast of air from the *Metro,* or Underground, which isn't unlike the smell in the London Underground. How I remember the rich smell of freshly baked *brioches* and *baguettes* from the *boulangeries,* the roasted coffee beans from the *epiceries*......the heavy, leaden smell of oil paints mixed with turpentine of the pavement artists by the Seine, the greasy exhausts of the *bateaux mouches* which plied the river all day long... ...the *perfumeries* with their bouquets of scent, the *Gaulloise* cigarette smoke which caught your throat and made you cough... ...the heady wines, the fruit and vegetable stalls, the smell of feathers from the caged live chickens and swans, the salty tang of fresh fish laid out on slabs. It all comes back as I am typing this. Paris is a city of scents and smells. If Rome is an old man being read to by a young boy, Paris is a mature woman seeking the love of a young man....

If I recall right, we spent the last day at L'Arc de Triomphe, the tomb of France's unknown warrior of the Great War. It is impressive but it is a monument to man's folly and the irony, the stupidity of war. I have to say that I was moved to tears when I saw the little flame which is never allowed to go out. When I went to Paris with my wife in 1981, it was one of the first places I wanted to see again.

But the afternoon of Easter Sunday was marred by an unfortunate incident, one of an older Dunbar boy bullying a younger one. One of the Fourth

# Jaunts and Joyrides

Year students was having difficulty with his - or rather his father's - camera; he fiddled about with it for a while and finally announced that he couldn't get it to work. A Sixth Former said he could fix it. He snatched the camera from the by now alarmed younger lad. The younger lad attempted to retrieve it from the older; in the struggle, the older boy dashed it to the ground. The camera was irreparably damaged. Nobody spoke to the bully for a while. The younger lad was left with a broken camera, a film spewed out of it, with no photographs of the Unknown Warrior's Grave or anything else. He later told me his father had asked him to take a shot of it for him. The incident struck me to the quick, although I was too young to appreciate the symbolism then.

All good things must come to an end. On that last April night in Paris, we were invited to sample snails cooked in garlic butter. Somehow, I managed to swallow the nauseating rubbery thing. I did what I was told, holding the snail in the special tongs and prising out the meat with a hooked instrument. I didn't want to be a dog in the manger before the lovely Irene - pronounced *Eeraine* - our voluptuous waitress. In the boys' eyes, she was a pocket Venus, a goddess, beautiful and sexy, with ample breasts that cradled our heads as she stood behind us, instructing us in the proper way to eat *l'escargots*. I don't recollect us eating frogs' legs, another Gallic delicacy.

That night, the Sixth Formers asked *Shorty* Muir, our French master in charge of the trip, if we could have a party; the girls asked the same of Ina Donaldson, the Maths teacher who had come along to chaperone them. Both agreed so long as there was no noise, as there were other hotel guests. There was to be no alcohol, which didn't worry me. But it annoyed the Sixth Formers, who had already smuggled in a few bottles of red wine. As far as I was concerned, there was no need for drink. I was intoxicated with Paris, as I confessed to my girlfriend Verna that night. Who needed alcohol as a stimulant in romantic Paris?

That night, I sat in Verna's room - we were both fully clothed, in case you are getting animated. We watched the city lights grow stronger as the nightlife of that great city reached its peak. Then we heard what sounded like a car backfiring. It happened a second, then a third time. Looking down from the exterior balcony, we could see uniformed *gendarmes* on motorcycles chasing a man on a motorbike; we later learnt he was an Algerian terrorist. France was having problems with her colony in Algeria at that time and the backfiring we heard turned out to be gunshots. Reality and the wider, political world were encroaching on our innocent, happy holiday. I think that night I experienced another world, a harsher one of politics and not one I wanted to inhabit. .I suddenly longed to be back in Dunbar and its safe streets.

Verna and I spent that hour discussing the highlights of the week. I was a little in love with her that night, but somehow we both knew that our paths would separate. Verna came from a different background to mine; we were young and didn't know what lay ahead, nor if our holiday romance would survive. (I am happy to say that we have remained friends since then). It was about midnight when I left Verna's room to go back to the bedroom I shared with T, Derick and Ross. I think T had taken some wine, for he snored that last night in Paris.

The return journey was unforgettable but not in the memorably enjoyable sense. We boarded the cross-Channel ferry on a grey, overcast Sunday morning - it must have been Easter Sunday - which promised heavy seas and rain. The English Channel can be vile and on that misty morning, it lived up to its reputation. The moment the ferry cleared the greasy swell of Dieppe Harbour, we were buffeted by strong waves, driving rain and chilling fog. The ship was crammed with English school kids so our small group was lost among them. I think they too were returning from a Paris holiday. Some of the girls in our group were appalled by the behaviour of one bunch of girls in gaudy green blazers trimmed with yellow piping and wearing straw boater hats; they were probably from some top-notch English public school judging by their accents. They were confident and 'facey' as my mother would have said, drinking red wine from the bottles they passed around. They flicked their green-and-yellow striped ties at each other and lent them to the young deck hands, flirting with them, teasing them. They could have been straight out of St Trinians.

Most of us were too sick to care. Everyone had their own remedy for seasickness, including Mr Muir and Miss Donaldson, our teachers. One was to lie flat on your back with a handkerchief over your eyes - not very practical on the wet deck of a heaving ship. Surprisingly, although I felt a little queasy, I didn't lose my breakfast over the side like some of the others. My remedy was to stay on deck in the fresh air and eat nothing. I visited the 'heads' or toilets only once; it was awash with sea- water and much else besides. I recall Derick attempting to pee into the urinal on tiptoe; as the boat lurched from side to side, the water would slosh this way and that, so our shoes were soon soaked. I did what I had to do, then returned to the deck, taking up my place at the rail. Norman, one of the Sixth Formers had insisted that the secret of avoiding seasickness was to have a good meal. He took himself off to the dining room where he blew seven and six [37.5p] on a three course meal which he promptly threw up a little while later. As for the two teachers, they remained below deck, prostrated by seasickness.

For the most part of the four-hour sail, I stood at my position at the bow, scanning the grey misty distance for a sight of the damned White Cliffs of Dover. There seemed to be nothing out there, only grey gloom and wild waves. Then suddenly, there they were, looming out of the murk. Like some demented character out of *Treasure Island,* I yelled out

'Land Ho! On the port bow! It's land!'

Robert Newton, the definitive Long John Silver, had nothing on me in the Walt Disney film. In an instant, figures emerged from their misty refuges or the bowels of the ship, staggering to the rail and staring in the general direction of forward – they were too sick to care about terms like port and starboard. Yes, the idiot Pugh wasn't seeing things. Land was dead ahead. We had survived. The odd thing about seasickness is that the minute you step on to dry land, it goes away. I had made it without puking. As we filed ashore and went through Customs, I suddenly realised I was hungry, ravenous if the truth be known. A crowd of us swarmed round the small shop on the dock, buying packets of crisps and bars of chocolate as if they'd just come off the ration. On the long train journey home, we stuffed ourselves silly.

We arrived in Dunbar railway station on a bright April morning with the experience of a lifetime behind us. T and I walked home together. It was the Tuesday after Easter and by the rising of the sun promised to be a fine day. It was 7am. We didn't care. We had stories to tell. Whistling as usual, T left me at my garden gate, clutching my suitcase which contained my dirty laundry, a *baguette,* a bottle of red wine and 200 duty-free *Senior Service* for my father. I had bought a small bottle of perfume and a miniature brass replica of the Eiffel Tower for my mother. I still have it to this day, a reminder of the year we went to *Gay Paree* ….and I mean 'gay' in the proper sense of the word.

I woke the family at that ungodly hour, giving them a potted version of my adventure, then I went to bed and slept for twelve hours. Travel is all very well but it is tiring. I had learnt much that week and what's more, like the others, I had made a profit on the exchange rate. Before we left Dunbar, we had bought £5 worth of francs; the local bank gave 1200 to the £. In Paris, we'd have received only 992 so we were nearly a whole pound to the good. I still have a franc coin from that holiday and sometimes look at it as though it were some religious icon. It certainly brings back the memories.

Two small memories I have of that exciting trip which, for me, was one of the most important incidents in my rite-of-passage to adulthood. They are about the two teachers. The first is of the overcoat Miss Donaldson wore. It had a strange pattern on the back. Was it a dragon or is that symbolic wishful thinking, as she had the reputation of possessing a temperament similar to that mythical creature? It was certainly an oriental motif, as my good friend Verna Smith (Tennant) recently reminded me. (I can't ask Miss Donaldson now, as she passed away in her Nineties in 2004). The other memory is of the gaudy and voluminous cravat *Shorty* Muir affected to wear, possibly to give him a suitably rakish, Gallic touch. In point of fact, he was a modest, shy man who would rarely if ever draw attention to himself. The moment of our departure to the French shore is frozen in time in a photograph in this book.

Such, then, were the jaunts and joyrides of my childhood. Few and far between, they were nonetheless treasured. Perhaps they didn't instil in me a burning desire to travel but at least I saw something of the wider world. I have visited most of Western Europe in my life, notably to Italy and Pompeii, which I consider the most memorable holiday of all. I also spent a week on Thassos, a small, undeveloped - in terms of tourism - in the northern Aegean, another trip I recall with great pleasure because of the island's unspoilt charm. Today, I believe it has degenerated into the equivalent of Ibiza and other awful Blackpool-ish towns of Spain. Thank god I saw Thassos before it became commercialised.

# 8

## Turnips for Starters

Turnips, *tumshies, baigies, neeps*.  No matter what you call them in your part of the world, the very name of this humble, unpretentious, staple vegetable of farm animal and Scotsman alike evokes a stirring in my heart.  Whenever I eat a sliver of raw turnip or fork a cooked dollop into my mouth, I am reminded of my childhood.  Marcel Proust had his cake which, when he bit into it, evoked vividly his own childhood as he recounts in his famous book *A La Recherche du Temps Perdu* [In search of lost time].  My catalyst is the humble turnip, which Dr Hamilton of Hallhill Farm introduced to Dunbar in the year 1784.  The Swedish turnip, or Swede, is known locally as the *baigie*, which is derived from the vegetable's Latin name *rata baga*.  As children, we didn't know that; *baigies* were *baigies, tumshies* or *neeps*.  Not content with the advantages of an above average fertility in the local soil, East Lothian farmers are celebrated for their progressive farming methods and Dr Hamilton was no slouch when push came to shove.  He quickly followed the other innovators, appreciating the advantages of a root vegetable which would become winter fodder for cattle and sheep, thus ending the wholesale slaughter and salting of beef and mutton at Martinmas every November simply because there was no way of keeping large stocks alive in the lean winter months until the turnip arrived.  The potato has long been king of the vegetables around Dunbar, with its highly productive red soil; the Dunbar 'red soil' is not however a variety of potato, so it is pointless asking for it in any greengrocer's as the term 'red soil' is a qualitative term applied to the loamy sandstone-based earth in which named varieties like *Epicure, King Edward, Pentland Crown* are grown.  The potato may be king but for me, the turnip is queen; it has a special pride of place in my heart for many reasons.  For one thing, it reminds me of autumn, my favourite season; for another, it evokes sharp memories of autumn Sundays and the way we children spent them.  When the crop ripened and lost its yellow flowers, you could spot a turnip field a mile off by the crisp, dark green leaves or shaws.  When the greeny brown skin was revealed as the leaves thinned, you knew the flesh was ripe and yellow-gold inside.  My mouth is watering as I type this....

Turnips were literally the bread-and-butter on which a farmer's wealth was fed.  Not only used for cattle, it became a popular kitchen vegetable and was even served as a dessert in eighteenth century Edinburgh, as we are told by Captain Topham in his *Letters from Edinburgh* (1770).  While generations were brought up on *chappit tatties and neeps* [mashed potatoes and turnips], the turnip assumed a special significance for small boys and some girls on 31st October, as already discussed in Chapter 5.

# Turnips for Starters

For me, the peppery taste of the turnip brings back memories of autumn Sunday walks to *Boorhoose*. Appetite is primitive; it is an essential trigger in our biological makeup that not only keeps us alive but also gives us extremes of pleasure when it is satisfied. When appetite goes, so does life. In modern times, we may succumb to the titivation of advertising to revive our tired and bored taste-buds but basic taste and smell are everything and rarely do we need reminding of these features of our favoured foods; in my childhood days, there wasn't a great deal to advertise anyway - well, we had *Oxo, Bisto, Cadbury's Cocoa* and *Bird's Custard* and we knew what they were without the promptings of advertising.

Autumn Sunday afternoons were special. Arguably, autumn is the most interesting of the four seasons. The landscape is well suited to the mood and temperament of the weather; the colours of the vegetation enhance the scenery, especially in the hills and hill-farms scattered about the Lammermuirs. There are calm, warm days, with brilliant sunshine that the leaves seem to absorb, making them all the more beautiful. Even when it is dull, wet or misty, the trees never seem to be sad. They only become that when the last leaves are gone. For me, the season has nothing to do with the melancholy foisted on it by Romantic poets like Wordsworth, Keats and Shelley; nor does the season reflect the sadness that long-dead writers considered was Scotland's natural mood, with its history of betrayal, broken promises, defeats and the songs of lost causes we were better without. Autumn is the time of sleep and renewal rather than death and corruption. The soft autumn light in this part of Scotland imbues its landscapes with contrasting beauty, a beauty so profound and illuminating that you wonder whether it is indeed the end of the year. You are more aware of the sharp outlines of hill, wood and valley than at any other time of year. For me, it is the definitive Keats' 'season of mists and mellow fruitfulness' when, with breathtaking aerobatic flights and astonishingly beautiful superscriptures writ high above Dunbar High Street, the 'gathering swallows twitter in the skies.'

The autumns of my childhood were slow, peaceful, dreaming interludes that preceded winter. The smell of earth and decaying leaves is acute, inescapable; that of a ripening field of turnips is the perfect Proustian trigger for my own *temps perdu....*

God and my mother had long ago agreed between them that if the Sabbath was fair and sunny, she would do her washing; if not, it was usually Monday. (I suspect it was her way of getting us out from under her feet on Sundays, giving her an afternoon to herself, even if it was a busy one). For her, Sundays were non-days if she couldn't get her laundry done; she made sure we were breakfasted early and bundled off to Sunday school in our best clothes with this warning ringing in our ears:

> 'Mind now, you're not to come home till teatime. And woe betide you if you get your good suits dirty!'

# Turnips for Starters

Imagine sending kids out in their Sunday best with a command to stay away all day and not get into a mess? But we did as we were told, for our generation was nothing if not biddable, even if we muttered under our breaths.

Before I go on to describe our typical autumn Sunday, let me pause to again consider the turnip. It is certainly not an exotic vegetable but I have always associated it with happy times as well as for its sustenance. In our house as in many others, the turnip was used extensively in autumn and winter to make soups and stews or eaten as a vegetable with potatoes and haggis or the piece of boiling beef which provided the stock for our *tattie soup*, the meat being eaten as a main course – with, of course, turnip and potatoes. I loved to eat my portion of boiling beef in the soup plate we'd just used; the meat was slightly sweet and stringy but with salt added, it was a particularly delicious and nourishing meal. The turnip is a homely addition to a winter meal; it's enjoyable eaten raw, especially when just uprooted from a field or kitchen garden. Its place in the treasure trove of my memory is indisputable. Turnips still make me think of autumn and Hallowe'en, both being favourites even today.

Sunday school was fairly innocuous and pleasant, especially when we had a local lady called Molly as our teacher; I was a wee bit in love with her until finally, we graduated to Bible Study class, overseen by the inimitable, incomparable Sandy Hunter of Belhaven Brewery fame. But after the church attendance - whether Sunday school or Bible Study - we usually came out to calm, Indian summer weather in September that often lasted until to mid-October. Thus we were unleashed on the unsuspecting countryside to kill time until we were due home for tea at about 5pm. The season was a hive of activity in field and garden alike and I can smell the beery smell of wet corn, the slightly doggy redolence of damp wool and the musty scent of chrysanthemums decaying in cottage gardens. All these smells contributed to the rich soup that was autumn, an exquisite bouquet at its most acute in the early morning frost.

The fallow field next to our house - known as the *Sailors' Park* - was festooned with myriads of spiders' webs sculpted by the pearly dew in the long grass where we hunted for button mushrooms for our Sunday breakfast. The early morning sun set alight these hoards of pearls as it struggled to penetrate the gauze or cotton wool swathes of mist or *haar* that drifted in from the North Sea during the night. In those days, local lighthouses had foghorns that lowed like sick cows; the one I recall most was Barns Ness. As we walked to church for attendance at 12.15, the robins added to the special effects with their distinctive twit-twittering morse code that signifies to other robins that they have staked out their territory for the winter. (Apparently, only so many square yards can support a single robin, so the morse code grew ever more frantic whenever a rival cock-robin encroached upon territory already spoken-for). So, the sights, sounds and smells were amplified as the season progressed slowly but purposefully through the month of September until it finally came into its

184

The author's grandfather and great-grandfather, both George Cockburn, c1910

Author's mother, Georgina (Jean) Cockburn with her favourite doll, Rosemary, 1920

Author's uncle, James (Jimmy) Cockburn, Hoylake, 1929

Site of future Summerfield Road and Lammermuir Crescent pre-1933 Knockenhair on the hill in the background (photo Mark Beattie)

Grandmother,
Margaret Cockburn,
Castle Place, c1931

Norman's father,
Norman Hall,
c1932

Author's half-brother,
Norman Cockburn
aged one, 1934

Right: The four generations 1934, (seated) Grandmother
Cockburn with baby Norman, Lizzie Wood, (standing)
Margaret Henderson, cousin of author and daughter of Lizzie

187

Family group 1934, (probably same day). As previous photo plus; (back row) Uncle George (Doddie) Cockburn and Pony Moore, (seated) cousin Emily Wood with Norman, cousin Dennis Wood (small boy), Aunt Margaret (Maggie) Cockburn, (front) Jimmy Cockburn

Jean Cockburn with friend and Norman c1937

James Herkes and his mother Jenny; James, a Royal Marine, was lost when the battleship *HMS Repulse* was sunk off Singapore in 1941.

Author and half-brother Norman in 1943, note the blond curls!

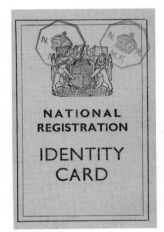
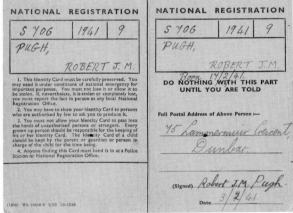

The author's World War II Identity Card, very advanced for his age, he signed it himself!!

Left: The author's father, Robert William Pugh, c1947

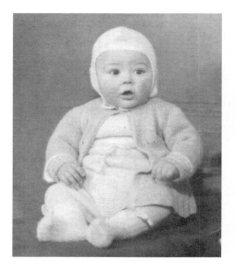

Kenneth Burns Pugh
aged nine months, 1947

Above: Norman aged 14 in 1947
(Isobel Marr in the background)

Primary School Class, 1948, author back row 5th from right and inset

Anne Fawcett, the author and tall friend, c1949

The Lunam sisters with friend, May left, Norah right.

Younger brother, Kenneth, 2nd from right front row and inset

Above: Norman aged 18,
1951

Right: Jimmy Cockburn with 'Gadabout Swallow' scooter presented
by Messrs George Wimpey and Son for loyal service, 1956

Author's father (also inset), Armistice Day Parade, Warrington, 1956

Left: Georgina (Jean) Pugh, 1960

Below: EastBeach, Dunbar, summer 1954

Bottom: The High St in 1976, but showing many older shop fronts (Crown Copyright: RCAHMS)

Teaching Staff at Dunbar Grammar School c 1957: (back row) William Scott, David Paterson, David Drever, Frank Bonar, George Hutchinson, William Christie, (second row) John Muir, John (Jack) Milne, Douglas Dudgeon, A Roxburghe, ?____, Donald Ross, Carnegie Brown, James (?) Fyfe (third row) Miss McNaughton, Miss Margaret McDonald, Miss Jean Myles, Miss Lena Mackay (Glass), Miss Cunningham, Miss Duncanson, Miss Temina Tinning, Miss Margaret Darling, Mrs S McLeod, Miss Jean Campbell, Miss Joyce Maxwell, Miss Ishbel Peebles, Miss Christina Donaldson, Miss Jessie Gunn, Miss Mary Hastie, (front row seated) Miss Ismay Johnstone, Miss Rhona McPherson (?), Miss Ena Murray, Donald MacVicar, Hugh Cowan (headmaster), Miss M Reid, Miss Mai Intin, Miss Betty Pride, ?____, Mrs Nicholson, Miss Elisabeth Fraser,

194

Third year class of 1956: (back row from left) Bill Brunton, George Robertson, Derick Souness, (seated) David Barry, Sheila Denholm, Deanna Combe, Catherine Fallon, Susan Hogg, Jean MacKenzie, Helen Cox, Roseanne Pearson and author (in those wretched short trousers)

Trip to Paris 1958: (back row from left) Derick Souness, George Gray, Sandy Cowan, Norman Macaulay, (middle row) Christina Donaldson, Bobby Craig, author, Tom Johnston (wearing bow tie), Ross Blakemore, (front row) Katherine or Kit Willens, Emily Kerr, Moira Young, Dorothy Purves, Karen Cheetham, Esther Bruce, Elizabeth Grey, Anna Bruce, Verna Smith, Isobel Taylor, John Muir

Empire Saleroom, High St, as it appeared in 1996
(Crown Copyright: RCAHMS)

No 3 High St, 1968, now a front yard next to the Dentist's and Logans Close
(Crown Copyright: RCAHMS)

Woodbush, where St Catherine's Hall, the school dinner hall,
was situated (1976 Crown Copyright: RCAHMS)

Former Beach House Hotel as it is now, 2006. The entrance to the
Cosmo Ballroom was on the far side of the building towards the rear

Dunbar Railway Station 1989 (Crown Copyright: RCAHMS)

Playhouse Cinema, Abbey Road, 1984

Dunbar open-air swimming pool in the 1950s

Scooter Parade, High St, 1956

The castle and harbour entrance from the SW, 2006

The shingle beach below the castle.

own in October. Suddenly, it spilled a rich, syrupy sweetness, a ripeness and an *El Dorado* of colour over the countryside; gradually, the rich brocade or tapestry of trees and hedges unfolded before our eyes, a kaleidoscope which changed as the days changed, the repertoire of nature lasting only a brief few weeks before the high winds came and stripped the branches down to the bare bones of winter. Somehow, despite the doleful 1950s, with their threadbare look of a country bankrupted by the Second World War, we were confident there would always be food on the table and a cheerful fire in the hearth. I tried to pretend the worried look on my mother's face wasn't there; either that, or I got accustomed to it because it was always there. I noticed that her tongue was sharper as winter approached, a time she feared because of its threat of coal shortages, lack of paid work and horror of horror, frozen or burst pipes.

Attending Sunday school in autumn always irked me and my concentration easily strayed, despite the delightfully beautiful Molly who taught us seasonal hymns we sang about everything being safely 'garnered in'. What did *garner* mean? I would have used the word 'gather' but then I was a simple schoolboy. It was rather presumptuous to celebrate the harvest home in September, a month that still saw more than half the outlying fields under corn, waiting to be cut. Sunday school was bad enough but when we were kept at home because of bad weather - which didn't improve my mother's temper - it was torture. All children and particularly those who live in the countryside have little concept of time except when they are forced to do something they don't like, whether it is domestic chores or homework. On these occasions, the clock seemed to stand still. Fortunately for us, most of our autumn Sundays were spent out of doors and while it may be a trick of memory, I can recall few days of rain in that glorious of seasons. When Sunday school came out at 1pm, we would slink past the watchful eye of the man with the club-foot who distributed and collected the tattered red leather-bound hymn books at the start and close of the services; I'm sure he counted them out and back in. I cannot remotely imagine any kid wanting to filch anything as boring as a church hymnal, not even for prestige points. The limping man took his duties seriously however, attending to his task with military precision like a quartermaster sergeant accounting for his stores. His face was a study of ill-concealed joy when the figures tallied but he wasn't averse to delivering the odd cuff on the ear of any kid who handed back a book he considered was in a more dilapidated state than when he'd issued it earlier. It was his way of showing how much he cared.

Out we would pour under the benevolent avuncular eye of the kindly Reverend J C Ritchie, the only minister I cared about in my entire life (I have since met one or two whom I respect, although I don't share their faith). We stood blinking in the misty autumn sunlight, shading our eyes from the sun. Ahead of us was an afternoon entirely free from the eyes of adults, the schoolbooks, the chores at home. As mentioned earlier, we wore our Sunday best which somewhat restricted our activities but at least the ubiquitous grey stockings could be pushed down to your ankles without fear of reproach. Those who wore *tacketty* boots amused themselves making sparks by scuffing their heels on the pavement; a couple of lads from West Barns followed two girls (one of whom, Brigid Aitchison I was destined to marry in 1981) throwing stones at them for their timidity. Ken and I were envious of the stone-throwers; on the one hand, we were forced - privileged - to wear shoes and on the other, my mother belted us if she heard of us throwing stones at girls.

The only drawback to these fabled autumn Sundays was that we had nothing to eat after breakfast and wouldn't get anything until 5pm so we knew we had to live off the land, making do with what was available in hedgerow and field. We knew where to find brambles, wild or 'crab' apples, beech mast, thistle cheese and of course chestnuts, although we never found the Spanish chestnut which could be eaten and which it was rumoured existed on several country estates. The horse chestnuts we sought were strictly for playing games of *chessies* - we never used the English word *conkers*. And finally, when all else failed, we knew where the best turnip fields were.

Delirious with anticipation of the day's promise of turnip, Ken and quickly devoured the afternoon's rations which consisted of a tube of *Rowntree*'s gums. Off we swaggered into the nut-strewn country roads, meeting the winds from the Lammermuir Hills head-on. Coatless and hatless, we were afraid of nothing, least of all the weather - unless it rained. In October, our cheeks were scorched red and blue, our eyes streamed with tears brought on by the cold. But we were happy.

Most Sundays, a crowd of us would head for the chestnut wood at *Boorhoose*. Going on Sunday expeditions for *chessies* gave us no cause for concern because the chestnut wood was by the side of the road at *Boorhoose* and the gamekeeper or *gamie* couldn't chase us as he did in spring, when we raided the gardens there for daffodils and hid them under our *burberries*. Chestnuts were the magnet, the season's currency without which no self-respecting boy would appear at school on an autumn Monday morning. We coveted our favourite *chessie*-laden trees, their thick leaves having the rough consistency of cats' tongues, their nuts encased in spiky lime-green casings which hung tantalisingly in clumps from the topmost branches. When we got to the site, the first thing we did was to hunt the floor of the wood for any nuts which had fallen since our last visit, then gather short, stout sticks to throw at the tree. The thicker and shorter the stick, the more chance you had of retrieving it as longer missiles were prone to snagging in the branches. Many a time I have heard a kid mourning the loss of his favourite throwing stick to a stubborn chestnut tree. Perhaps one throw in every five would bring a small cascade of nuts bouncing into the road and bursting free from their casings. I loved their shiny brown look; with their buff-coloured centre, they looked to me like miniature boxing gloves. (Years later, I would describe them in a poem, comparing them with the rolling brown eyes of horses, an image which must date from those horse-dominated farming years). We threw none of the nuts away, no matter how small they were; I used the small ones as imitation boulders in carpet war games with my lead soldiers.

Sometimes when we grew tired of hunting chestnuts, we varied our routine by playing by the small burn at the foot of the steep bank ending in a field famous for horse mushrooms. When I was fifteen, my Uncle Jimmy used to wake me up early on Sunday mornings - about 6am - and seat me behind him on the *Gadabout Swallow* scooter he'd been presented with from *Wimpey's*, his employer in 1956. He used to ride down the rough path and lean the bike against a tree, then we'd gather the huge plate-sized mushrooms he loved fried with bacon and eggs for the Sunday breakfast.

Often, we were disturbed by bigger, older boys who were out on the same ploy as ourselves and we'd run and hide in the thicket at the bottom of the wooded slope where we found a natural bower of wild roses and thorn stretching across the burn and providing an ideal hide-out. We would lie there till the danger passed, storing our bags of chestnuts until the coast was clear, the bigger lads moving on to other trees further along the road. Occasionally, we were disturbed by a strange girl we called *Pluto*; poor lass, she walked the country roads day and night. Somehow, we knew she wasn't well. She never spoke to us. She had a round, white moon-face that reminded me of one of the *Bisto Kids* in the famous advert for that gravy sauce; her nose seemed to be permanently turned up to the sky, as if she were sniffing it for traces of the lovely gravy illustrated by wavy lines on the *Bisto* poster. She looked at us with the disdain of one who knows more than he or she is letting-on; unkind souls said she was *touched*, which is the Scottish word for madness but I am sure she wasn't that, although I felt then that she thought we were. Why would little lads throw sticks into the air at trees? Her buxom figure was always masked by the clothes she'd been given - invariably a man's sport's jacket which she incongruously wore over a feminine floral dress, her ensemble completed by down-at-heel shoes but with spotlessly white ankle socks.

So, ensconced in the fastness of our secret hideout in the green gloom beside the trickle of water that hardly qualified as a burn, we withstood attacks from marauding English or Indians. We took turns at being Errol Flynn, buckling a few swashes beneath the great spread of the chestnut trees sighing in the wind. I used to stand still, bidding Ken to be quiet so that we could listen to their prodigious breathing. I have always believed trees are not only living things, they have personalities as well. I don't consider that in the least a ridiculous comment.

These dreamy afternoons wore on, punctuated by reckless charges through the undergrowth, then we had another go at the chestnut trees, then another battle when victor and vanquished lay down together in the soft lush grass, mindful of the cowpats which stained your clothes and couldn't be erased by burn water and leaves. Often, Ken and I would lie for ages, listening to the hum of the flies, staring at the copper blue sky, saying nothing to each other as we listened to the occasional booming of the pheasants in the bracken, or the sudden crack of a frightened pigeon's wings. The day seemed endless. Time didn't matter then; when you are young, time isn't your enemy.

But eventually, though imperceptibly, the sun began to disengage itself from the sky, spreading out over the west, a red-gold egg yoke that grew runny and diffused itself through the white clouds as the air began to stiffen with falling frost. Then we knew it was time to head homewards. Famished, growing colder by the minute, we packed up our treasured chestnuts and tightened our belts. As we walked towards Eweford Farm, Ken and I looked at each other and simultaneously said the magic word:

'Tumshies!'

We started to run as if the turnip field might somehow uproot itself and escape from us. There, before the crossroads on the left was the field of turnips, the broad leaves shaking in the early evening wind, catching the last rays of the sun so that the green was tinged with gold. Usually Ken acted as lookout while I jumped the dry stone dyke, crouching near the edge of the field and hopefully shielded from any hostile eyes. I was always selective, taking time to choose the right size of turnip. When I found a couple to my liking, I would whisper to Ken over the wall:

'Come in! I've got two good yins [ones].'

Scrabbling among the leaves, we were stung by the small and therefore hidden nettles but we didn't care. We uprooted the desired pair, twisted off the shaw and broke off the roots, rubbing the skin with the shaw leaves to remove the earth that clung to the bottom half; when that didn't work effectively, we used our hands as there was no nearby burn or puddle to wash away the dirt. We never managed to wipe it all off but even if the dirt got into your teeth as you tore away the thick skin, you didn't care. All you needed to do was expose enough of the sweetish, yellow flesh to allow you bite deeply. Conscious of the sun going down fast and the cold getting worse, we got out of the field quickly, hiding our turnips behind our backs - no polythene bags in those days - until we were past Eweford Farm road end and into the Lochend Estate road to Hallhill. As I write this, I can picture a diminutive Ken, sitting at the side of the rough path that ran past the *Kennels*, the two houses west of *Lochend Cottage,* both of which are occupied to this day. I can see him holding a turnip bigger than his head, chewing away to his heart's content. Theft it certainly was but not vandalism. After all, we only took what we needed to assuage our hunger and we always ate the lot; we didn't uproot half a dozen only to throw them away, as invariably happens nowadays.

About half an hour later, we threw away the runts, then attacked the bramble bushes beside the path, chasing away blackbirds snatching a last meal before total darkness came down. By the time we reached *Lochend Cottage*, it was fully dark and we shivered in the cold as we walked along *Lovers' Lane* and past the ghostly silhouette of the old *Wishing Tree*, watching the gulls scavenging the potato field to the left, a field cropped only a week before. The outlines of the fir wood began to take on menacing shapes as they slowly merged into the October night. By the time we reached the railway tunnel at *Underedge*, we met up with other groups of kids clutching their own spoils. I looked behind me and watched the space we'd walked through fill with darkness and the night. As we entered Lammermuir Crescent near the football ground, I urged Ken to walk faster or else we'd get *tokyo* - our word for a row - when we got home. I knew that my mother took in her laundry before dark and that she would be making our tea. We still had about half a mile to get to the house and Ken was moaning about sore legs.

At last, the battered wooden gate of 75 Lammermuir Crescent hove in sight. My mother never stood there looking anxiously for us; she knew we'd come home when we were hungry. And despite the turnip repast, we were. On Sunday night, we knew the meal would be ham and eggs with an apple tart, Eve's pudding or apple dumpling to follow, apples being in season, plentiful and cheap. Before tea, my mother would inspect our clothes for dirty stains, then we were told to wash up and change into ordinary gear for after tea, we were allowed to play in the street for an hour or so.

Usually, we were out again by six pm; our friend Anna White from Summerfield Road was usually there, directing the kids and organising the games we would play. She was the self-appointed question master - should it be question mistress in today's correct political climate? - who made our games those which involved answering her questions. Anna prided herself about her knowledge of film stars, so that was usually the game we played. She said she knew more than us because she was older than any of us and had seen more films than we had. I gave her a hard time. After all, I had seen the famous Douglas Fairbanks Junior photograph in my mother's wallet, a snap taken when he stayed at the *Craig-en-Gelt Hotel*; I had also seen every Laurel and Hardy short ever made and I was a fair bet for answering questions about Robin Hood, Superman, Tarzan etc. I regularly answered more questions correctly than the others, making me something of a swot.

No matter, Anna was queen-pin, the self-styled connoisseur of the Big Screen. She also fancied herself as something of a singer. Many years later, in 1987, I was attending a wedding in the *Navarre House Hotel*, Penicuik - owned by my ex-wife's sister - and Anna and her husband were among the guests. After the meal and the toasts, there was a band and dancing; Anna couldn't resist getting up on the dais and belting out some of the favourite hits of her time, pop songs she would entertain us with underneath the lamp post in Lammermuir Crescent. I seem to recollect that night she did Connie Francis' *Lipstick on Your Collar* - a ditty she was ably suited to render and which had the entire company in thrall. In the distance, I watched her husband being quietly, unobtrusively - in his mind - sick in a flowerbed. I tiptoed away from the bandstand. Anna was frozen in time. She didn't recognise me and I was too shy to approach her with a rather wimpish 'Guess who I am and do you remember when we played Film Stars in Lammermuir Crescent?' I simply slipped away to the bar, hoping that we wouldn't meet. We didn't. Some memories are best left undisturbed.

In those far-off days, we were rarely disturbed at our games on Sunday nights because we didn't make much noise. Weeknights were different, when we rampaged everywhere, running through gardens and generally making a nuisance of ourselves. We were particularly wont to dare each other to enter the garden of an old man who lived with his family near our house. He was a grumpy old individual whom as I said in an earlier chapter looked like Paw Broon in *The Sunday Post* and rarely smiled. By nature a moaner and com-plainer, his threats and curses were always met with impudent, anonymous catcalls out of the darkness until we overstepped the line and had to hide after being seen in his back garden; we would slink home then, awaiting the inevita-ble knock on the door and our subsequent clout on the ear. Another character whose feathers we regularly ruffled was a small, bird-like woman we nick-named *Tinto* and disliked because she was in cahoots with Paw Broon. Be-tween them, they mounted guard at the window, betraying their surveillance by occasionally twitching the net curtains. They did their level best to ruin our autumn and winter street games.

On Sunday nights, we were never out later than 7.30pm, not simply because of a curfew imposed by my mother. Sunday night was favoured be-cause as mentioned in Chapter 4, we listened to the wireless programme we waited for every week, *The Man in Black* featuring Valentine Dyall, replaced by Orson Welles' *Tales from the Black Museum*. After fifteen minutes of Mr Welles' rich and resonant tones, we were relieved when the next programme came on, light classical pieces courtesy of Mr Albert Sandler and his Palm Court Orchestra. We had visions of Mr Sandler and his ensemble ensconsed in a forest of potted palms of the kind you used to see in the tearoom of *Patrick Thomson*'s prestigious shop in the North Bridge, Edinburgh, a site now occu-pied by *Argos*. After Albert's stalwarts had sawed their way through several pieces, we were chased into the scullery to get washed and don our pyjamas. I never understood why my mother insisted on us combing our hair carefully on Sunday nights; it was all over the place the next morning, tousled and un-kempt. Perhaps it had something to do with the fact that it was the Lord's Day....

After our wash, we donned our freshly ironed pyjamas still warm from the flat iron my mother heated over the fire. We were given steaming mugs of *Ovaltine* along with a rich tea or digestive biscuit. There was always a bit of nonsense at the dinner table on Sunday night, probably because we were eking out the last minutes of freedom before school the next day. On one occasion,

# Turnips for Starters

Ken grabbed me by the neck from behind as I was sipping my drink and it went all over my front, burning as well as wetting me. He was scolded and sent to bed while I had to sit by the fire until another pair of '*jamas*' was ironed.

Most of these Sunday evenings, we tried to spin out the time before bed but eventually, my mother would lose patience with our delaying tactics and excuses; she would lift her index finger for silence, then order us upstairs with instructions to read for a half hour, when she would come upstairs and blow out the paraffin lamp. True to her word and punctual to a fault, up she would come and plunge the room into darkness despite our moans that we only needed another minute to finish our comics. After she closed the bedroom door, we would lie quiet until we heard the living room door close behind her downstairs, then the fun would start again.

In the darkness, I would entertain Ken with stories I made up about a fictitious gang I had joined; he was particularly fond of a character I invented called *Daw* because that was his catchword when faced with some insurmountable puzzle or situation. I would have him saying such things as
'Daw! Ah got the belt at the school the day!'
I am certain I based *Daw* on Dan Eccles of *Goon Show* fame.
For years, Ken believed these creations were real people and he would beg me to tell him a tale by singing out
'Daw-Daw-de-Daw!'
I don't think he ever forgave me when years later he discovered my famous gang existed only in my imagination.

As we lay in the darkness punctuated by the intermittent flashes from Barns Ness Lighthouse, we would grow sleepier and sleepier as we listened to the wind in the telephone wires strung along the not too distant railway line. The low moaning sound made us burrow deeper into the bedclothes. Another eerie sound was the creaking of the staircase or that of the furniture downstairs as the wood contracted when the fire died down. But most spooky of all was when the embers fell in the grate, a weird sound which was sudden and unexpected. After midnight on Sunday, the railway workers would start their night shift and goods traffic shuffled past, clanking and jolting in the still of the night. Sometimes we were treated to the eerie sound of an owl hooting in Lochend Wood and in our drowsy state, we imagined it was sitting at the foot of the bed.

We didn't appreciate then the significance of these simple Sundays because they were part of a routine which it seemed would never end, a world which would be permanent. We inhabited autumn - or perhaps I should say it happened to us. It was a bountiful season and a familiar friend. I wish I had written down all the sights, smells and sounds that went into the making of that so vivid time of year. How could I have known then what it would come to represent in my mind in later life? How can words possibly do justice to the feelings I experienced during that hectic, lovely time? I can't do other than try to describe Belhaven Bay on a late October afternoon, with a smoky blue autumnal haze descending from the hills and gathering in the distance below clouds tinted with pink in a western sky kindled by deep red, scarlet, blue and gold flames.  In deference to those Romantic poets I mildly rebuked earlier on for the quiet, hushed reflections which autumn drew from them, a little sadness creeps in when I think of the voices from a time that is gone forever.

# 9

## The Many Splendoured Thing

Whoever it was that said a woman's most powerful weapon is a man's imagination knew what he - or more likely, she - was talking about. I am living proof of that profound aphorism. Before I enter the tender, sensitive minefield of human love, the adolescent love of this account which is part of the title of this chapter, I admit unashamedly that it is pinched from the American film made in 1955 by D Henry King; the film featured Jennifer Jones and William Holden and was set at the time of the Korean War, when the individuals of two cultures mix and find love together. The third word in the title of the film was spelt the American way; splendored may be acceptable across the Pond, but I wish to remain true to the English poet Ernest Dowson, who spelt it properly, as in this chapter's title.

In my adolescence, I inhabited a fairly self-contained personal world in which glamour was exclusively provided by the cinema. The post-war society in which I grew up had precious little in the way of colour and light; it was a dusty, gritty, black-and-white world, which the newly emerging medium of television confirmed. The cinema and the wireless played a major role in the lives of a tired, jaded population still oppressed by wartime rationing. Film-makers then ignored reality - or else they studiously avoided it by offering films portraying life as a whimsical, Technicolor dream. Perhaps many of them had read T S Eliot's famous poem *The Fire Sermon* in his *Waste Land* collection of poems, taking to heart his contention that human kind cannot stand much reality. Perhaps I am crediting these men with an intellectual level they didn't actually possess; however, in fairness to them, they knew how grey and drab our world was, so they dished up the frothy fare which we of that generation of war and its aftermath craved.

The cinema influenced my thinking in a way not possible today. I looked to it for a sense of morality, duty, honour, respectability - and a bit of excitement, which I didn't realise then would be called titillation in a few years, then sexy when the cinema - and the young cineastes of the 1960s - came of age. But in 1952, I emulated my screen heroes. One day, I would be the strong, silent Alan Ladd; the next, I imitated romantic, physical swashbuckling heroes portrayed by Errol Flynn and Robert Taylor (Robin Hood and Ivanhoe respectively). Taylor was a particular favourite in our house. My mother was romantic too. She was so much taken by him that I was named after him - not as Robert, my 'real' name, but as Roy, the name he had in a film she saw when she was pregnant with me. She almost fainted over his performance in the

209

sentimental *Waterloo Bridge* released in 1940, the year before I was born. In the film, Taylor played a First World War British Army officer, Roy Cronin who falls in love with Vivien Leigh, a ballet dancer. It was a story of doomed love and while outrageously sentimental, was extremely well acted; in the course of the film, Taylor loses his memory during the war and so he forgets his Vivien and their assignation on Waterloo Bridge. She descends into prostitution and they never meet again. Along with many other cinemagoers, my mother wept buckets. She promised herself that if I were a boy, she would call me Roy. When I was born, my father insisted on his name -Robert - which by lucky coincidence was Taylor's first name - very convenient for my mother. So while I was christened Robert, she always called me Roy and Roy I have been stuck with ever since- very inconvenient for bureaucrats, my bank manager and people who write cheques in my favour. I have to use Robert in my deal-ings with officialdom and in doctors' surgeries; I am happiest with Roy, for to my mind, it is sums me up - short and sweet!

When acting out my fantasies inspired by the cinema, I imagined - not without a grain of truth - that I was battling against the dull, insipid, boring and hostile world and suffering in splendid isolation and silence. I played my selected role for all it was worth in my teens. I knew then that no one under-stood me or wanted to; not much has changed in this unromantic, materialistic world. Then as now, I preferred to walk windswept, empty beaches in autumn and winter, brooding like Heathcliff and talking to myself, wishing for a Cathy to love my Heathcliff. I smiled rarely, affected a stoical outlook and showed very little emotion. This behaviour didn't go unnoticed among my contempo-raries at school. They thought me morose, bad mannered, slightly cracked or ill. And above all else, I was still wearing short trousers when other maturing contemporaries were in long pants. Maybe that more than anything was the cause of my preferred isolation. How short were my trousers; that sounds like the title of a novel.

From an early age, I somehow sensed that saying you loved someone didn't mean you were a sissy or, as they say in Dunbar, a *jessie*. Not to be able to say it to that special person meant - for me and surely many others - that something vital was missing from your life. Of course, in those days, I wasn't mature enough or sufficiently well read to put it so succinctly. However, I knew by instinct that professing love for someone else was - is- proof that you know you are lonely and that you need other people. I am now about to clum-sily re-enter that clumsier world of adolescent love in the forlorn hope that I will be able to honestly recall my feelings in that so bewildering time.

No matter how young or old you are, you are aware of the Other within you, the *alter ego* or whatever else modern psychologists and philosophers call the essential *you*. My Other manifested itself in a firm belief that I should try to be an obedient son and help my mother as much as was in my power to do so; perhaps that wasn't my own idea, because to her dying day, my mother assured me that a man who was good to his mother would receive his reward. Even though I believed her, I also possessed the natural anarchy and rebelliousness of youth; I was a romantic rebel who spoke to that Other self which had to remain hidden because to reveal its existence would have attracted scorn and mockery from my schoolmates. My big mistake was that I believed I was the only person who had an Other. I had to fight hard to hide my real self and I waited for the day when I would meet the One with whom I could share my secret self. She would be chosen because of her special gift which was of course, recognising and sympathising with the *real* me, the Other.

I affected to sulk during adolescence; that happened nearly every day, finding release only when I was alone. My romantic disguises were hung on an imaginary clothes' line in the open air or delivered to some long-suffering and conveniently mute swans at Belhaven Beach. Had I been a bit brighter and more intelligent, I might have put down my feelings on paper but I hadn't found that ideal solution then. I longed to share these feelings with a kindred spirit - preferably a female one - but I couldn't find her. I looked hard without success; this surely explains why I had more than my fair share of casual girlfriends which made me look something of a *Lothario* - a *jessie* in Dunbar-speak - which I hope isn't too strong a description for my innocent affairs. All I craved was the Right One, the One whom.....it would take another decade before I found someone reasonably close to my unquiet heart. It was the American novelist Grace Metallious, in her best-selling novel *Peyton Place,* who prophetically wrote that 'it is a pity that youth is wasted on the young'. I knew exactly what she meant when I read her book between leaving school and the time I met a special lady called Alice in 1966. And yet even then, I believed that youth wasn't wasted if you learnt its bitter lessons; however, no one warned me that learning these lessons cannot guarantee you won't make the same mistake twice.

I pause in a moment of self-indulgence to record a few aphorisms which to me seem to describe what love essentially is.

*Love is building your first snowman and helplessly watching it melt in the sun*

*Love is not finding enough courage to say the important words to that special someone*

*Love is that kind of loneliness which enters you the first time you are infatuated*

*Love is drowning just when you have mastered the art of swimming*

Trite though they may be, in their own way, they sum up my backward-looking glances to that time.

Adolescence has two things in its favour. The first is innocence. The other is freedom - well, up to the point of bearing a degree of responsibility not to interfere or threaten the freedom of other people. Young people are expected to fall in and out of love as much as they need to; they should have crushes on each other that should be short-lived. They have a duty to moon, swoon and act the buffoon - all in the name of love. Adolescent love affairs are probably the best we ever experience for they are - or in my day were - pure, causing only temporary hurt that is absorbed as we grow to maturity. I have forgotten none of the girls on whom I had a 'crush' or more serious relationship; each was special in their own way. But another lesson I learnt very quickly was that the world doesn't love a lover; in fact, the world is invariably hostile, if only in the shape and form of worried parents. However, when you love, the world is a kinder, more worthwhile place and life is sweet. If our adolescent affairs contain an element of self-discipline and self-training, they also teach us the need to make contact with others and with our own feelings. There is no handbook or guide; youth will find its own way, even if it is blind and in the dark.

One of love's paradoxes is that its tears are not only an expression of sadness but of joy. Being by nature a solitary, I shed mine on lonely walks. But at least I could indulge that secret self, the Other that existed in me. What I took a little longer to learn is that the greatest gift you can bestow on another human being is to put her or his happiness above your own. That was something I would slowly and painfully assimilate as I went along the road of adolescence.

To those who dismiss their early love affairs as immature and embarrassing, I have only this to say; ignore them at your peril. I believe they set us on the road to maturity and stability in adult relationships. I am the first to acknowledge that what we learn from our early experiences will not necessarily ensure we will meet the Right One, but at least they may give us some idea of that person. Of course you can't expect your partners to conform to your idea of them; the harder you try, the more likely you are to fail. I didn't always appreciate that -and still don't - so now I am about to apologise to many of the girls I knew and loved and who despite my promptings, remained supremely themselves. Better late than never, I say to all the girls I met and knew through Dunbar is this. Sorry girls; we knew it wouldn't have worked....

As I said earlier, I was possessed of a rich imagination fuelled at first by the cinema, then by books. I knew that my heroines didn't exist in life, being the stuff of celluloid or paper, so I admired the actual ones who came closest to my standards. Many of my girlfriends must have thought me weird or a bit light in the head when I took them to remote places, spouting some deathless lines from a film or book which had entered me instead of getting to grips with what they feared most but secretly hankered after - adolescent sex. What was that I hear you ask? It was touching each other, holding hands and kissing. Nothing erotic I'm afraid - well, almost nothing; there were a few who were more adventurous and kind. In those days, there was no touching below the Mason-Dixon Line, the line that divided the Northern and Southern states before the American Civil War.

# The Many Splendoured Thing

Looking back on those early 'crushes', I have to say that while most boys had a girlfriend, they were kept in the background, firmly in their place. After all, girls played meaningless ball games, skipped as they chanted meaningless rhymes and jingles. They also cried a lot for no apparent reason. Some of the bolder spirits readily joined in the rough-and-tumble of the boys' street games and were considered good sports. Most were supremely themselves, wearing their mothers' or older sisters' clothes. They congregated in small groups, whispering and giggling as boys passed by. I tried to treat them as equals, a mistake in the eyes of Jock the Wild Man.

The onset of puberty, that post-infant, pre-adult intermission brought about alarming changes in the body as well as in the mind. Inside, you experience uncontrollable fluctuations in your heartbeat, usually accompanied by inexplicable flutterings in your stomach. These were aided and abetted by disturbing physical changes; you had no idea that such things were caused by the internal secretions that invade the blood, stimulating your organs. The revolt of the hormones - for that is the scientific name for such secretions – and the production of testosterone brought pimples, sproutings, stiffenings and inexlocable nocturnal emissions. I felt I was losing control of my body – or rather that my body was taking me over. Your palms were sweaty, your mouth got dry - all because of the close proximity of girls. I never descended to the physical comparisons other young lads made with each other, nor did I want to know how they felt and what they got up to with girls. I felt embarrassed, even ashamed and certainly different; I never resorted to drawing the naughty bits of the human body on the school toilet walls. Somehow, I sensed that was an insult to and a degradation of the human shape. I was, in short, a Puritan.

My earliest recollection of an 'experience' with the opposite sex occurred when I was about four years old. Betty Jeffrey lived a few doors away in Lammermuir Crescent. She was - still is - a tomboy, about the same age as me but wild as they come. She wasn't much given over to wearing her sister's or mother's clothes and high-heeled shoes; one day, she surprised both of us by wearing the lot, wanting to do a bit of spooning, which was totally out of character. She came clip-clopping - dragging the high heels would be more appropriate - along the street, dressed to the nines and wearing badly smudged lipstick. Her mouth was a bloody wound. She looked through the spars of the garden gate, watching me playing in the dirt roads I'd made in the border for my Dinky toys. After a while and because I was studiously ignoring her, she lifted the latch and came in.

'Gie's a kiss, Roy. Goan, gie's yin.'

The only response to That Kind of Thing was to ignore it. I kept on playing, making motorcar noises in the dirt road. She stood with her hands on her hips which meant she had to let go of the hem of the (for her) long dress she was wearing so that it covered her feet. She moved to the side of the gate, catching the hem of her dress on the hedge. With entirely honourable intentions, I got up to free her. I was at her feet, the first and only time that would happen. She was soon undone and I stood up beside her. I too would shortly find myself undone.

'Ta. Kin Ah see it? Oh goan.'

I hadn't the ghost of a clue what she was talking about. The next minute, she'd unhooked the snake clasp of my belt and my short trousers plummeted to my ankles, leaving me in the standard white underpants with the slit (for peeing). She made a grab for them as well, pulling them down to my ankles. At that crucial moment, my mother appeared at the front door. The Mason-Dixon Line was being crossed in front of her very eyes!

'Betty! You wicked, wicked girl! Away home with you! I'll tell your Ma on you!'

Then she turned on me.

'And as for you, you wee fool! Away inside!'

I was unceremoniously pushed in front of her, clutching my knickers and trousers, not even given the time to 'adjust my dress' as they used to say coyly in tabloids like *The News of the World* in those days. In the house, I was treated to a right barracking, was told I was a stupid boy, letting silly wee lassies do that to me. I wondered why not. It was exciting. Today, I often meet Betty in Dunbar High Street; she remains unreconstructed, unreformed, her laughter as loud as ever it was, loud and hoarse and rumbustious, a laugh which stays with you long after she's gone. (She tells me she was wild because when she was wee, she didn't have a bike! Betty, are you having me on after nearly sixty years?)

In those early years of fumbling love, the most daring game we played with girls was *Postman's Knock*. Playing with girls marked you down as a *jessie,* so games with them had to be rough-and-tumble. Hulking big lads who wanted to snog would readily join in a game of *Postie's Knock* because it didn't compromise their masculinity. I vaguely recall only one of my birthday parties - maybe I only had the one - when a local lass called Roberta was the only female my mother allowed me to invite, perhaps because she liked her, not because her sweet lips were made for the *Postie Knock* game. (My mother didn't care much for girls, especially those that came to our front door; she said they were a 'nuisance' and put on 'airs' as they were always combing their hair and their ribbons got undone so she had to fix them. She also said they made the boys 'create' which was her word for becoming unruly, unmanageable. Over these last fifty years, I have often thought about undoing Roberta's hair ribbons....)

Another game we played at parties was *Truth, Dare or Promise (TDOP)*. Often, there was dirty work involved in *Postman's Knock* as some lads would engineer it so that they got the object of their desire. But *TDOP* couldn't be manipulated; you had no chance of escaping the girl possessed of lips like the inner tubes of bike tires and making cow's eyes at you the moment you entered the room. It was a guessing game in which the questioner asked the victim to tell the truth, make a dare or offer a promise to the girl behind the door. At my party, there was only Roberta so I told the truth and made the dare because I knew what she looked like. I can't remember her keeping the promise. I suppose the game was an early form of Cilla Black's *Blind Date*.

Another game was one that could predict whether you would get married, a kind of casting the runes - only it was done with prunes. You counted the prune stones on your plate - prunes were very popular in those days, being available freely even during the war. You counted with your spoon to the rhyme *Tinker, Tailor, Soldier, Sailor, Rich Man, Poor Man, Beggar Man, Thief.* If you had all eight stones that completed the rhyme, you were certain to get spliced. If not, the number of stones told you what you'd become in life. I always asked for five stones, for that would mean I would be a rich man....

We used to also recite another rhyme when we counted our prune stones; *One's a Wish, Two's a Kiss, Three's a Letter, Four's Something Better.* At home we had a novelty measuring tape with homilies on the reverse; you measured your chest and when you got the reading, you consulted the reverse to see what would happen to you in later life. My vital statistics rarely changed so the tape measure always predicted that I would father many children. It was one hundred per cent wrong - thank god. Maybe the memory of the tape measure's predictions encouraged me to take up weightlifting when I was eighteen....

Some of the bolder spirits went through the voyeuristic and exhibitionist stage, sometimes showing each other their private 'bits'. I once pretended to do that in the *Bleachfield*, challenging three girls called S___, A___ and J___ to show me 'theirs' in exchange for me showing 'mine'. I declared J___ the winner; the others probably thought her 'fast', although nothing untoward had happened. My choice of J___ was, I am now ashamed to admit, not without an ulterior motive; she was about to celebrate her tenth birthday and her parents always gave her a good spread. I wanted an invite to her party and I succeeded by a devious ploy. J___ and I never showed each other our 'bits'. That birthday was one of the most enjoyable and memorable but sad days in my young life. After tiring of the crowd of us making a noise in his Summerfield Road cottage, J___'s Dad took us in his car to see a school of whales - which were being destroyed on the beach we knew as *Silver Sands*, near Thorntonloch. These lovely creatures from the deep had come in too close to the shore for some reason - possibly because one or more had been injured or were sick. Whales are extremely loyal to each other and a school will protect the ailing members, even to the extent of sacrificing themselves. Although driven out to sea on several occasions, they kept returning to the stricken one. We watched the extermination of these splendid creatures take place - a kind of Auchswitz of whales. Every single one was shot by police marksmen and the carcasses were later dragged away to manure the fields. That day, I learnt a very poignant lesson about love.

# The Many Splendoured Thing

Not long after this tragic incident, I allowed myself to be coached by a serious researcher into the mysteries of the human body. Or, to be more precise, SEX. Jock the Wild Man was the researcher and he knew absolutely everything there was to know about IT. He could talk for all of thirty seconds - maybe even a full minute - on the subject. He was a great expert on where babies came from. He solemnly announced that they came about when women's belly buttons were excited; he was roughly in the right direction. He knew about the *Mun-thlee Pee-ry-ud* and claimed to know when you could have 'safe' sex with a woman - meaning sex that wouldn't result in a pregnancy. God knows where he got it all from.

Jock almost put me off for life with his graphic descriptions of the female anatomy. It was years before I could use the proper words, referring to women's interesting 'bits' as 'down there'. Jock would end his sexual lecture by reciting his favourite poem about women and sex. Its origins remain a mystery - unless he made it up himself; I can't ask him now, as he is no longer with us. He may well have been the author of a single stanza poem, which went thus:

> *The long and thin*
> *Go too far in*
> *And do not please the ladies;*
> *The short and thick*
> *Do the trick*
> *And manufacture babies.*

As we grew older, boys and girls used to send each other Notes in class, carried in envelopes that were sealed with mysterious acronyms written across them - maybe I have forgotten some but the ones I remember were SWALK (Sealed With A Loving Kiss), BOLTOP (Better On Lips Than On Paper), HOLLAND (Hope Our Love Lasts And Never Dies), ITALY (I Trust And Love You) and - the ultimate in raciness - BURMA (Be Undressed Ready My Angel). The last was reserved for the one you really fancied....

On St Valentine's Day, we knew how successful we'd been in our attempts at conquest by the number of envelopes that landed on the mat, courtesy of Mr Postman. It was a poor year when I didn't get three. One card I recall in particular came from M___, the shepherd's daughter; it contained the following verses:

> *My heart is like a cabbage*
> *divided into two,*
> *the leaves I give to others,*
> *the heart I give to you.*

This was followed by

> *Roses are red,*
> *violets are blue*
> *sugar is sweet*

*and just like you.*

And finally, the suggestive one, which made my mother laugh when she read it (she always read our Valentine cards if we didn't hide them before we went to school):

*Oh goodness, oh gracious, oh Lord god almighty,*
*I wish your pyjamas were next to my nightie,*
*But don't be mistaken, don't be misled,*
*I mean on the clothes' line and not in the bed.*

I showed M___'s Valentine Card to my mother that year. She thought it was cheeky and brilliant. She also said maybe I should marry her. Sometimes I wish I had.

We were never given sex lessons at home or in school, not like today. Sex was taboo, a closed book. In our house, we were simply told not to go 'too far' with a girl. One day, I disobeyed my mother. I liked going for long walks on Sundays and often took a girl with me; in this case, I was walking out with M___ from Springfield. I never felt embarrassed when my mother slyly enquired whether I'd 'gone too far' with any girl, especially when I came home later than usual and - worryingly to her - more tired than normal. That particular Sunday, my response was flung at her, not without some degree of indignation.

'We went to Co'path [Cockburnspath]. It's not too far to go with a girl. It's only fourteen miles there and back and besides, she likes walking and she lives near Oldhamstocks. It wasn't too far for her.'

Yes, we were naive in them days.........

By the time I reached First Year in the Grammar School, I was growing more aware of sex. I was still preoccupied with my fantasies, my 'secret ladies' and heroines from the silver screen. Looking back over the last century with its obsession with sex and the exploitation of women, perhaps our parents were right to insist that chastity, as well as charity, begins in the home. For my generation it certainly did; we always felt sorry for a lad and a lass who'd gotten 'into trouble'. All the moralising and proselytising failed to prevent several 'shotgun' weddings and pregnancies which came perilously close to the legal definition of under-age sexual congress. Not surprisingly, few of these forced marriages lasted.

My fantasies were fuelled by newspapers and magazines like the *News of the World, Titbits* and *Blighty.* Usually, we encountered the last two in *Law's* barbershop, where we took sly quick peeps at the scantily dressed and occasionally topless models. They were nothing like today's *Page Three* ladies however, not by any yardstick. The best fantasy I ever had didn't involve any degree of nudity - I lived on that fantasy for nearly a year - involved the actress Ann Blyth; she played the lead female role in the film *The Golden Horde,* a 1951 spectacular about 13th century Arabia, with Blyth using her brains to outwit the invaders of her peoples' city. Brains? I think not. Miss Blyth wore a costume which encased her breasts in armour which of course accentuated her cleavage. She stuck out like the proverbial *headlamps* or *knockers* or *coconuts* - contemporary popular nicknames for female mammalian splendour. (Does my fascination with that part of female anatomy have its roots in the fact that my mother had been unable to breast-feed me as a baby?) Madonna wasn't even born but if she'd been around, she undoubtedly would have approved of Ann Blyth's gear. Jock the Wild Man saw the film and had the last word; he swore he saw her nipples, how I never fathomed.

'Thir stickin' oot like chaipel [chapel] hatpegs'.

His graphically crude description couldn't put me off my dream lady.

Now it is time for me to describe some of the girls who at one time or another meant something to me.

There was of course Gladys, Lady Gladys of the school holiday camp mentioned in chapter 7. About as unobtrusive as a lighthouse on a benighted seacoast, she was a real stunner, to put it mildly; she was beautiful and stood out among the pale-faced, humdrum, straight-haired lasses in her class. They either hung around her, hoping to catch the crumbs from her table or they ostracised her in the playground. She was what they called 'fast' in those days. The irony in this is that she wasn't; she was just a very pretty girl who grew into an even more attractive woman. Gladys was a country lass through and through but she couldn't afford to let us know that, for it would have ruined her image. She knew as women do that all the lads 'fancied' her, that she was a prize much sought after. If you were favoured, she would allow you to dance with her at school dances and Christmas specials. A goddess to me and to countless others, we panted and tried all the wiles in what was an extremely limited repertoire - today, they'd call it foreplay - to snare her but she wasn't buying. After she left school, she went to London, where I think she still lives. I was only one of a crowd who 'lusted' after her; she probably thought us all pretty moronic, but few who knew her in those innocent days and talk about her now cannot hide the misty look that comes into their eyes when her name is mentioned.

I had a passion for a girl called Margaret who lived in Doon Avenue; cool as the proverbial cucumber and I never managed to win her over. She still lives in Dunbar today; I met her recently, an attractive lady with a fine figure who keeps men like me in their place.

Then there was the tomboy with natural good looks, a fresh, ruddy complexion, dark hair and winning smile. I wrestled with her along the West Promenade after many Christmas dances. She usually won. She hailed from West Barns and I never heard her surname again until a certain President of the USA was impeached for spying on his colleagues in 1968.

Then came M___ who will always be special to me.

I must confess to a preference for flamboyant girls. I was enraptured by one - besotted would be nearer the truth - who wore a red taffeta skirt and a white satiny blouse and tap-danced her way across the Corn Exchange stage one idyllic summer evening. She was Scots-Italian, a lethal mix - and she was one of the Forte family. She was the most beautiful and exciting girl I'd ever seen out of captivity on the silver screen. Alas, Tilda (presumably short for Matilda), I had to love you from the depths of that darkened hall. If you are still out there, you might be interested to know you had a timid stage door Johnnie waiting for you out in the High Street. I missed you and never saw you again.

There were at least three girls called Ann in the 1940s and 1950s. The first was Ann Fawcett, a shy blonde who was probably the first love of my life. The second was a local fruiterer's daughter whose deep, velvet voice combined with a strong Geordie twang sent me into paroxysms. The third Ann was a tomboy who recently told me that what she most recalls of me is that I showed her a shooting star round the Promenade, the first she'd ever seen.

There was of course a succession of holiday girls from Edinburgh and Glasgow, cities that took their 'Fair' fortnights and either rented places or took 'digs.' The east coast girls were more difficult to please, more sophisticated than their west coast counterparts. However, we country boys learnt much in the way of social etiquette from the Edinburgh girls. The Glaswegian lasses were more boisterous, tomboyish and daring. One I recall with fondness was Martha from Springburn, a rough area of the city. She was physical and liked to wrestle on the beach, outsmarting me easily and even some of the bolder spirits like Jock the Wild Man. ('Kee-rist Awmighty! She's bloody lethal!'). Martha had no sense of shame and often popped out of her swimming dress, much to my excited embarrassment. When she caught me looking at her small but well-shaped breasts, I ventured to say that I liked them. Typically, she stuffed them back inside her costume and said this:

'Och, they're a damned nuisance. They get in the wey [way].'
One Saturday night, she let me put my hand on her nylon-clad leg in the cinema. I stroked it in my uncertain self conscious, reluctant way, as I vaguely knew I was doing something 'not quite nice'. She didn't seem to care, for she drew my quivering hand further up. Shy and excruciatingly embarrassed, I didn't know what to do next. Then suddenly, she closed her legs together, trapping my hand in between them. In the cinema's darkness, she whispered this to me:

'That's yir lot. Ye've jist reached the giggle band.'
When I asked her later what she meant by the 'giggle-band', she didn't hesitate in her reply:

'Och, weel. Once yir past the giggle-band, yir laffin'.'
We wrote to each other several times that winter. I was having fantasies again. I wanted us to walk in the woods and lie down in the bracken and kiss and cuddle - and maybe get past the 'giggle-band.' The following summer, she

went to Saltcoats for her holiday and wrote to say I was too young for her - she was fifteen and I was fourteen - and anyway, she was walking out with a Glasgow boy who was sixteen, an apprentice joiner who made 'pots of money.' I never saw Martha again.

I was growing dreamier, more romantic than ever. I began to seek out girls who wanted soulful love. One of these holiday girls was a bird of passage in 1956. She was called Maureen and her family had taken a flat in Lamer Street, near the East Beach. She looked like the actress Muriel Pavlow, maybe even a young Angela Rippon. Each evening, after I'd finished work at Oxwellmains Farm, I'd rush to meet her. She was always walking the East Beach alone and I imagined she was waiting for me, her lover. We swore undying love one dark July night at the breakwater at the end of the beach; she was sitting on one rung and I was standing beside her. I put my arm round her and kissed her forehead and she sighed. She said this:

'Oh, Roy, I shall never forget this beach because we met here.'

My heart leapt, soared even. We swore undying love and then she went home a few days later. I wrote to her. There was no reply. I wrote to her younger sister Joan, begging her to convince Maureen that I wanted her to be my pen pal. Joan wrote back saying Maureen wouldn't be writing to me again because she had met someone else. These 'holiday' girls could be fickle, even in romantic settings. Maybe they realised that the settings were unreal for them, just the scenery of a holiday romance. I was bitter about 'my' Maureen, swearing I would never go out with anyone with name ever again. I also resolved that next time, I would try a more fleshy type. That didn't happen until1958....

Maureen was followed by Kay, a Glasgow lass who was attractive but zany like the actress Goldie Hawn. A pawky, perky little thing, she never stayed in one place too long. And Kay went about singing all the time, she just didn't want to moon and spoon, like me. That summer of 1956, she sang her favourite song every day, all day. She drove me to distraction. The song was Doris Day's *Moonlight Bay* and she sang it at the most crucial moments - like when I was trying to kiss her. She sang it morning, noon and night and it went like this:

*I was sailing along*
*On moonlight bay*
*When I met a boy I wanted*
*On moonlight bay.*

The chorus went like this:

*On moonlight bay on moonlight bay....*

She and her song drove me insane, so I'd go off in a huff and leave her to her singing. When she wasn't singing it, she enthused about Doris Day's voice. I never cared for Doris Day or her squeaky-clean, tomboyish image. Kay said that when she got married, she would live in a house like the one in

# The Many Splendoured Thing

Moonlight Bay. (A few years later, she and her family came back to Dunbar and she and I walked along the beach, where she admitted she'd deliberately set out to infuriate me, take my mind off Other Things. She didn't say she'd missed me or loved me, so that was that).

After these experiences, there was a hiatus - or so it seemed to me. I worked on the farms at East Barns and Oxwellmains, courtesy of the brothers James and Robert Hope; I was dog-tired when I got home at night. I mooned around the local cafes - Togneri's and Johnny Jennetta's - on Saturdays, went to the *flicks* [pictures] alone, bought sixpence worth of chips from Togneri's and went home. Sunday mornings were spent in bed, reading *The News of the World* and *The Sunday Post,* followed by a long walk, evening meal, then bed, for in the morning I was destined for another week of singling turnip shoots, weeding beetroot and thinning carrots - all done on my hands and knees.

During the period 1953 to 1958, I worked a great deal on my internal emotions. I still saw girls but I was living increasingly in my imagination, which wasn't healthy. I began to think there was something wrong inside my head. For example, I had this irresistible urge to tell someone - preferably female - how a wood smelt in high summer and early autumn, how the sea was different in winter, why the positions of the star constellations changed in different seasons. I wanted to talk about the leaves falling in autumn and how the wind felt on my face; I eulogised over the soft hush of falling snow. I tried my hand at a few lines of furtively written poetry that I would be embarrassed to show to anyone today. It was a wise thing to do. (I have kept a few of the less banal pieces from that lost, confusing time, chiefly to remind me how bad I was then). The only poem I wrote prior to 1960 is a short piece which survives; it was published in the school magazine for 1955, a few verses about Black Agnes who successfully defended Dunbar Castle against the English for 22 weeks in 1338. (*Tall, gaunt and black the castle stands against the leaden sky...* .....Oh dear.)

When the summer birds of passage migrated to their hometowns, the boys reverted to the local girls who were just as well pleased, having had their own 'flings' with summer boys. It was a practical arrangement that suited everybody. As a result, we boys never grew tired of the local girlfriends. We went to supper dances and socials right up to Christmas and New Year, then the long winter ground us down, honed us to a sharp edge but to no avail. We had few diversions until Easter. It was rare indeed for summer visitors to return to Dunbar for the festive season - well, New Year at any rate. But once in 1960, a whole crowd of Glasgow lasses came back and my friends and I had the best New Year ever.

But usually, the summer girls came and went with the swallows. There were promises made at the railway station, firm promises to write during the winter months - I did, but got few replies. Most pen pal correspondence had fizzled out by Christmas, although I was fortunate with one or two girls continuing to exchange letters until the following summer, when we met again.

Then, all of a sudden, sex, or to put it more scientifically, the free flow of testosterone which was fuelling all this longing unrecognised by me - and countless others - crept to the surface. I can't say it erupted - that would be too dramatic a word, though the pimples that went with it certainly flared. It was innocent but it was THERE. The condition which young people of every generation are afflicted with was manifested in moist palms, dry mouth and a strange nervous sensation in the pit of the stomach - and of course, the obligatory pimples. To be perfectly candid, the nervous sensation was a bit like fear. The knowledgeable among the lads who 'knew better' referred to these assaults on the nervous system as 'knee-tremblers'. My first pre-adult fumblings were imposed on a girl who had severely parted hair and wore glasses. I forget her name but she wasn't local. It was her delicious protuberances around the region where I imagined the heart was which brought on a knee-tremble. She was having none of my sly attempts to brush my fingers over her chest. Nice girls didn't DO THAT SORT OF THING. Next I fell for a local girl who was the proud possessor of a well-padded heart area. I took her up to Spott Glen one summer Sunday evening, without in the least entertaining any evil intentions. She was wearing a most fetching electric blue sun-top and matching skirt. To my surprise, she explained that her sun-top was detachable from the skirt and gave me a demonstration, revealing all her beauty and charms quite unselfconsciously. She was a nice girl, a bit wild but completely innocent. I have never forgotten that golden, sun-kissed August evening redolent with the heavy beery smell of wet grain when, leaning against a dry-stone dyke, she showed me her mammalian splendour. After that, there was no holding me back.

But animal attraction - and co-operation - essential in the pursuit of the Many Splendoured Thing - were in extremely short supply among the local girls. It was only the few 'fast' ones that allowed you to sample their nice bits. The problem with heavy petting and fondling was that it usually resulted in frustration for the participants. Most of us - boys and girls alike - were afraid to go 'too far', which I suppose says something about the influence our parents exerted in those far-off, halcyon - who am I kidding? - days. Halcyon they may have been on the surface, outwardly calm displays like the ducks on the pond at Seafield; but we knew that underneath, the ducks were paddling like mad, as were boys like me in that confusing time known as adolescence.

It was many years later that I plucked up the courage to use the D H Lawrence words responsibly and accurately, words which would land Penguin Books in court in 1960 and my being sent to Coventry by the local girls I tried to convince; at least Sir Allen Lane upheld Lady Chatterley's undoubted honour against the tides of an overly nervous prurient Establishment of the day. This victory would be lost on the modern generation, who start experimenting with sex about a decade earlier than my generation did. My use of the f-word in the context that Lawrence intended attracted the disgust of many of the girls I knew. I agreed with Lawrence that phrases like 'making love' came nowhere close to describing that beautiful, sensual and satisfying experience with someone of the opposite sex. The accepted, popular words were, I insisted, poor substitutes for the real thing, the Anglo-Saxon thing. I also agreed with Lawrence's view that an explosive act like sex needed an explosive verb to describe it. Expressions like 'spooning' or 'having it off' were to me either juvenile or crude. As for the clinical or medical terminology, the words in use were a real turn-off.

I know I was ahead of my time, trying to use the word 'f\*\*\*' in its proper context. It did me no favours. Girls were scandalised by my use of it and avoided me like the plague. They thought my mind had rotted, that I was sick. Somehow, I knew that Lawrence was right; I also knew that he was a poet and a puritan - often, they are comfortable soul mates, if not always bed mates....

Suddenly, schooldays came to an end. That late summer of 1958, I met a lad who figured significantly in my life for the next six years. (I hasten to add that our friendship was in no way sexual!) He lived in London but had been resident in West Barns, where his Italian father and Scottish mother ran a small chip shop; he went to the parochial school but by the time he was due to start secondary education, his parents moved south. We met on the beach at Belhaven one evening in August, a few days before I was due to leave Dunbar for my Civil Service job in Dundee. We were swimming under Seafield Bridge and struck up a conversation. Although he had a cut-glass English accent, he mimicked the Dunbar dialect so accurately that I could have taken him for a local. We became firm friends. He was about four or five years younger than me but was older than his years - and more experienced with girls. More of him follows. A week later, I left Dunbar for Dundee, which was the end of the earth as far as I was concerned.

I was lonely in Dundee but became a regular letter-writer to JP, my new friend, mimic and swimming companion. And of course, I wrote home to my mother and to Betty with whom I had worked in *Lipton's*- more of Betty appears later, (in the purely literary sense, in case some of you are getting excited) in Chapter 12. A few weeks in Dundee brought a welcome adventure; I was scheduled to attend an induction course for new entrants to the Civil Service in London. London? God, was I scared, a wee boy from the sticks being sent with all expenses paid to the great metropolis. In terror, I wrote to JP, asking that he meet me at King's Cross Station the Sunday night I was due to arrive. He kindly did so, even to the extent of taking me by Tube to my digs in Brixton. That night, I fell asleep in a strange bed, stranger city, wishing I were somewhere else - like Dunbar.

The course was to put it mildly both boring and confusing. The evenings were enlivened by JP's conducted tours of the West End, Soho and other raunchy places he wanted to show me. One night he suggested we go to Hyde

Park, the haunt of prostitutes before the Street Act was passed by Parliament not long afterwards, the idea being to get the poor creatures off the street so they wouldn't frighten the horses; many of their clients were members of the Upper House of Parliament, which I am sure may have had something to do with the passing of the Act. These sad, benighted ladies plied their sadder trade in the park bushes. JP said he had tried one once - at age fourteen! - but hadn't enjoyed the experience because he said it wasn't the same, paying for sex;. He said there was no tenderness.

'And besides, I blew all my birthday money on the bitch.'
However, despite his pessimism, he suggested I might like to try a lady.
'Nobody in Dunbar will know. It'll be our secret.'
He knew I was a virgin. I went with him to Hyde Park on my last night in London, apprehensive and incredulous. Did women really crawl among the shrubbery and take off their clothes? The oldest profession in the world fascinated and repelled me at the same time. It still does. It had nothing to do with being Scottish, paying for your ten minutes. Moral and health considerations apart, sex for money degrades both parties to the bargain. I argued that if women like that enjoyed what they were doing, why did they want to charge money for it? The naivety of callow youth…I walked about the park that night with JP, watching sad balding men emerge from the bushes. To me, they should have been ashamed of themselves but there is the Puritan again. But perhaps they were when they got home to their wives. I have never gone down that road and I never will, no matter how lonely I am.

My first adult love affair - meaning I suppose, one in which I touched a girl intimately - occurred in 1959, the year I said goodbye to my last adolescent summer. She was blond, beautiful and hailed from Glasgow. To me, she was a goddess disguised as a Glaswegian. A friend of a close friend, it was love at first sight when she stepped into the *Craig-en-Gelt Hotel* that Saturday night. I called her *Bernadine,* the title of a hit song by Pat Boone that year. JP agreed with my choice when he came to Dunbar with his family for the August holiday. She was fair from the outset; she said I was far too young for her but she would be my friend. She said she was having her last holiday alone, for next year, she would marry her boyfriend in Glasgow. Until the very last night of her holiday, it was innocent and nothing remotely fleshly passed between us. We had gone everywhere together but always in a crowd or gang. She was special; her body was sacred and I for one would never sully it, for it was a temple I couldn't and wouldn't violate. Sometimes we lagged behind the others, touching each other but never holding hands; she said our friendship was platonic and there couldn't be anything else in it, for she was faithful to her Glasgow lad.

I spent two weeks of unmitigated bliss - and agony - in her delightful company. We were never alone. This made the agony more poignant, frustrating and ultimately sad. We went swimming, dancing, walking and haunting the cafes. But I knew it had to end and end it did. The last night of my goddess' holiday, there was a big dance at the *Craig-en-Gelt*; afterwards, we went a walk round the West Promenade, where I showed her the brilliant starscape, describing the various star constellations I knew. We sat on the bench in the small shelter at the end; we seemed to be there for ages. I swore undying love for her. She said I should and must forget her. I was too young, she'd be accused of cradle snatching, she was going to be married the following year. I was devastated. She was three years older than I was and so I thought she was wiser than me. We sat in silence for a while, then she asked me if I had ever 'petted' a girl. I was unfamiliar with the term until she explained what 'heavy petting' meant. She showed me and I have to confess I felt bad about it afterwards. But she said it was quite normal and that I shouldn't worry about it. By the time I walked her home - she was staying with an old lady in my street - I felt better. We kissed goodnight, said our farewells because as she said, the next day the crowd would be at the railway station to see her off.

Part of me died that balmy, August night; another part went off to Glasgow with her the following day. What was left of me wasn't worth a candle. A few days later, I would be returning to my office in Dundee, a place I detested. JP was sympathetic; he had been seeing E's friend P; although she was several years older than he was she was fascinated by his worldly charm which was impressive by the standards of the time, even if he was only sixteen. Their affair didn't survive that golden summer, so JP and I commiserated with one another at the end, when he was leaving for London. I said I never expected to see E again and that I would never fall in love with any other girl. My heart was shattered; JP was sympathetic but said I would get over her, as he would get over P. He was much more experienced than me; I made myself a promise that I would never let myself fall in love again.

After that heady summer romance, I began a relaxed and gentle friendship with a local girl who was fourteen to my eighteen years. We both liked dancing and her mother and mine had been good friends until her mother died, when she was barely months old. When I got home for the occasional weekend in the autumn and winter of 1959, we went off on long walks together. We even got to the stage of planning a future together. We walked to Spott Village, saw a small cottage with diamond-shaped windowpanes; I said I would try to get a transfer to Edinburgh so that we could be together every weekend and sometimes in the evenings. We were too young. We went out for about six months, then JP came back for his Easter holiday. JP being Scots-Italian as A was, I assumed they'd be friends. A hated him on sight, said his parties were just excuses for getting drunk and that there were orgies in the bedrooms. She refused to come to the party he threw that Saturday night, A and I fell out and that was the end of our attachment, though I am happy to say, not our long friendship, which survives albeit at a distance to this day.

# The Many Splendoured Thing

JP's family owned *Dunollie* on the beach, east of the Coastguard or East Beach. For five summers, it was my spiritual home, where in the spacious lounge overlooking the sea, Mrs P would recite poetry to me and I to her - chiefly R M Rilke, the German poet of whom she was particularly fond. Often we sat, JP, his mother and I listening to classical music to the enchanting and beautiful background music of the sea. It was in that house that I began to appreciate classical music. I often walk along the beach and look up to the lounge where so many summer nights were spent in the company of people I loved and who encouraged me to write.

That summer, which I reckon was the end of my childhood, I met a girl who had a profound effect on me; I say profound because it outlasted the season. It was a long time before I got her out of my system. Mina hailed from Kilwinning, Ayrshire; she was slim with short, dark hair and she had a wistful, waif-like smile. She wore an unusual ring which she proudly informed me was made from Celtic silver; this was announced under the street light outside her parents' rented summer cottage at the West End. Needless to say, my fumbling attempts and monumental awkwardness were met with a decidedly bemused and somewhat patronising smile which I think said 'you'll have to do better than that.' But perhaps her mother's wise warning was echoing in her shell-like ears. Boys were after only One Thing, especially holiday romance ones. At seventeen, all I wanted from a girl was a kiss or three and perhaps be allowed to touch her breasts - through her blouse of course. Mina and I had been on a cycle run that afternoon and I'd shown her my secret place in the hills, where as a child I'd gone to gather frogspawn and catch minnows. In her company, I thought that the valley of *Osie Dean* offered possibilities for more intriguing pursuits.

We sat in that sun-kissed, drowsy valley, shyly holding hands and marvelling at the shimmering bluish haze of the damselflies that hovered and darted over the burn which whispered to itself all that insect-orchestrated afternoon. I think I may have been her first love, she was my second. But on that evening when moths fluttered round the street light, she refused to let me kiss her, perhaps with a certain amount of ambiguous fascination. She said she didn't do THAT with boys. In my naive logic, I thought she would have realised that my intentions were honourable as I hadn't 'tried' anything at *Osie Dean,* where I could have done considerable damage that afternoon.

Now, looking back, I know that it is most women's unenviable and unsolvable problem whatever their age - how to refuse a man's advances, especially those from the one she loves. I know Mina loved me in the immature way adolescents think is grown-up; undoubtedly, she cared for me. I noted in my diary that when she left Dunbar the following day, I travelled all the way to Edinburgh with her to see her off on the Glasgow train. I had never done that before, which was an indication of how strongly I felt about her. But we parted, exchanged a few letters, then they stopped. I still remember the *Girl with the*

# The Many Splendoured Thing

*Celtic Silver*, as I called her then; I am sure she forgot me before the year was over.

I took up with M___ again, the shepherd's daughter; she came back from her new home in Lanarkshire to visit relatives. That October, we had a day in Edinburgh and climbed the Scott Monument in Princes Street; my diary reminds me of that so memorable day.

There is however a sense of uneasiness coursing through me as I write these words. I have this to say to the girls who are still here in Dunbar whom I loved– or with whom I was infatuated – in that far-off, magical time. Please believe me when I say I cared about you, that I meant what I said at the time. I was hardly a hunter in the predatory sense but even then, I knew that the heart is a lonely hunter......

Not long ago, a year or so after I returned to Dunbar in 2000 to take up permanent residence, I saw a couple of former girlfriends - now women - in a hotel bar; they nodded to me and turned away. I wondered if I had hurt them. When buying a round of drinks for the two friends I was with, I overheard one of the women whisper:

'Mind him? Roy Pugh? Yes, he was a good dancer. But the stories he used to tell.'

Her companion was less kind - or perhaps more truthful, which is the  s a m e thing.

'Yes,I remember him. I knew his brothers better but I only went out with him. He was OK but too backward in coming forward. Far too slow.'

So much for the so-called obsession of men after only one thing.............

Sleepy Dunbar turns in her bed at night, unaware that her charms, attractions, her starscapes and seascapes had anything to do with my romanticism. She can't really be held responsible for she exists for herself. Many nights now I have walked by the shore, watching the cleavings of the sea, mesmerised now as I was then by the soft sh! of the waves that will go on forever. Recently, rummaging among some old papers, I came across a poem I wrote in 1960. It has no literary merit whatsoever but it commemorates an unsuccessful love affair, clumsily as perhaps I pursued the object of my desire over 40 years ago:

*Suppose*

*Suppose she entered the room*
*where we met so long ago;*
*words wouldn't matter*
*for we would both know*
*that silence speaks volumes*
*over many lost years.*

*Why should this emerge*

# The Many Splendoured Thing

*to unhinge a secure, closed heart?*
*We move on in our lives,*
*finding new places, new loves*
*even though we crave the old*
*on nights such as this, in the cold.*

As I said, not immortal lines but they meant something then.

So to sum up. One thing I have learnt in life. Love should never be taken for granted. It may not be around tomorrow, so we should live each day as though it were the last, knowing the joy and letting it flow through us. Love isn't eternal; that is the prerogative of the sea and only the rocks remain.

In my time, I have whispered one or two names into a glass of whisky. That isn't an admission of fickleness; it is simply that I believe a man can love many women genuinely, without being sexually involved. In my life, I saw different things in different women and I hope they saw these in me. A lady I loved nearly a decade ago, who died before her time once told me this:

'It is a far better and kinder thing to give love than receive it. You should always give love and not expect that love to be returned. You'll find it'll be returned twofold.'

Think about it. She was right. For if we all followed her homily, the world would undoubtedly be a more loving and kinder place. I had hoped to marry that lady one day but it wasn't to be. I still love her, still thank her for the kind and tender way she opened my eyes and made me see what has sadly gone from the light of this modern world, for when she died, she took it with her.

I know that unselfishness is the best part of love, immortalised by the poet who described it as the Many Splendoured Thing....

# 10

## Lions and Donkeys
## (Part 1)

Whoever it was that said schooldays were the best days of your life probably misspent his youth in billiard rooms or else was at best a sentimentalist, at worst a pathological liar. I wonder if, during his time at school, he actually believed that, or whether like most of us, he was looking back, his vision distorted by a patina of nostalgia. In my own case, there were certainly highlights and good memories but for the most part, I was happy in infants' school, less so in primary and periodically indifferent to the secondary or grammar school in Dunbar. In the lower school, I resented the unremitting, petty discipline and the method of teaching by rote; I suspect I wasn't alone in failing to understand what exactly was being dinned into us. I was acutely afraid of making a fool of myself in front of my classmates in those days, being easily embarrassed then and now. What particularly annoyed me was that we were expected to look up to our teachers whether they deserved our respect or not. Most were dedicated, a few were sadists, some were useless and a sizeable number were well past their sell-by date. No matter, they all demanded respect; what is worse, they got it.

There was always the possibility of physical punishment in infant and primary school, a deterrent that worked for most of us. I am a great believer in the old adage that sparing the rod spoils the child, not a view with which modern educational psychologists would concur. All I can say to them is this – to what do they attribute the small minority of ill-disciplined, rude and bad mannered kids of today who influence others? And how can they be encouraged to change their anti-social outlook? The politically correct answer is that you must offer these rotten eggs rewards to control them. The rotten eggs will always be prominent; it's just that nowadays, there seems to be more of them, kids that don't have a better nature to appeal to. Some modern children simply fail to make the distinction between freedom and licence and sadly, the pendulum in school discipline has swung too far in the opposite direction. The strap, *tawse* [belt] never did me any lasting psychological damage; I was more ashamed than physically or mentally affected, although one or two teachers were overfond of physical punishment and did some kids physical and possibly psychological harm. For obvious reasons, we were never informed officially of disciplinary action taken against such sadists, although the grapevine was effective. Usually, we worked it out for ourselves when a teacher fond of using the belt over-zealously suddenly began to use it sparingly

# Lions and Donkeys (part 1)

As adults, most of us can look back and smile at things which happened to us - and better still, to our classmates. The occasional bad experience was traumatic for a while but children are remarkably resilient and eventually shrug off their anxiety over time. Well, almost. One or two incidents involving myself still rankle today and I have never forgotten - or forgiven - those who inflicted physical and mental punishment without justification.

I suppose our schooldays in Dunbar were happy-ish. I left Dunbar Grammar School with mixed feelings; on the one hand, I was exchanging a cosy, familiar and ordered world for a strange and daunting one of work among strangers. The question I asked myself so many times in that last year at school was - would I make it in the adult world? Would I be able to hold down a job? And worst nightmare of all - would I be found out? Getting your feet off the ground and putting them on the first rung of the employment ladder is possibly the greatest step anyone ever makes - contrary to the oft-quoted American astronaut's self-congratulatory remark when he set foot on the surface of the Moon.

Looking back now, I am surprised I managed to learn anything. Like my contemporaries, I certainly absorbed a great deal, probably because knowledge was drilled into us. And I would be less than honest if I didn't admit that some of it has stood me in good stead during my working life. A lot of it ended up like driftwood on some uninhabited beach however. Perhaps the mark of sound education is that it creeps up on you; you are subconsciously being taught to develop a desire to gain knowledge and education is the beginning of that long *drouth* [thirst]. Education also has a way of entering you insidiously whatever your limitations; before you know where you are, you are educated. A friend once said to me that the only reason young people go to university is because they are aware that they know nothing; he may have been perilously close to the truth. However, university is optional; in my day, no one could escape primary and secondary education until the age of fourteen until I think 1948, then fifteen afterwards.

I think the education my contemporaries and I were given was excellent in some respects, poor in others. We were required to study subjects determined by the level of our achievement in the famous - or infamous - Qualifying Test, taken at age eleven or twelve. Your pass level - A, B or C - set you off on the then standard course of study. We had to study subjects for which we had little or no aptitude which meant there was less time to devote to subjects which we liked and therefore might become good at. I know that I could have used my time more advantageously had I enjoyed more English and History periods, less Science and Mathematics, although the former had its enlightening moments. In those days, I had neither the staying power nor the inclination to go to university; in any case, my parents couldn't have afforded it. I regret that now, although I have continued to work at my two favourite subjects. One major criticism of the educational system of that time was that it failed to make

# Lions and Donkeys (part 1)

allowances for the individual, a fault hopefully corrected in modern education. My generation was to a great extent hindered by our naivety. We lacked sophistication - or to put it in its modern context - we were less street-wise than today's kids. We rarely questioned authority of any kind, though we resented its intrusions and punishments. But at least we were allowed to be young and grow up slowly. Today's children are acting like teenagers by the time they reach the age of nine; and even before that bewildering stage, they consider themselves grown up years before their time. They think that by imitating their older peers, they are demonstrating to the world that they have shrugged off adolescence – ample proof that they don't appreciate that they haven't grown up. And they are aggressively materialistic, expecting as of right weekly pocket money of several pounds. By contrast, whatever little we received, we usually worked for it and treasured the few coppers, because we knew material things didn't come easily. There was little to go round. The materialistic, acquisitive society hadn't arrived. Also, we were taught to value our possessions, so we took better care of them. On balance, I think our childhood was more fulfilling, less self-centred than the present generation's.

Before digging deeper into my personal experiences of school, it is appropriate here to pause and ask the vital question. What is education? It is the passing on of knowledge and information by past generations to the contemporary generation. Primitive societies had teachers and scholars but no books; learning from books - literacy - was the form of education introduced in Scotland by the early Christian Church - hence the close relationship between religion and education. The poet who referred to Scottish education as nothing more than 'I telt ye, I telt ye' has to be of my generation, for that was basically how the educational system operated. Maybe the course of many fine minds was altered by formal education; when working in HM Inspectorate of Schools in 1990, I recall a poster in one of the younger Inspectors' rooms on whose wall was pinned the realistic (if cynical) legend that 'Many a fine mind is ruined by education'. Be that as it may, remarkable people will always come to the fore whatever the level and extent of their education. There is no better example of that than Dunbar's most famous son John Muir, known throughout the world as the father of conservation. Muir had the standard, rudimentary Scottish education up to the age of eleven, when he emigrated to America and attended university - without the intention of obtaining a degree. He only wanted to harvest the knowledge of others so that he could develop as an individual, not simply to receive a piece of paper proving he'd attended Wisconsin University. Many of the best Scottish brains nurtured by a canny, basic Scots' education left the country because of lack of opportunity in the land of their birth. It was Walter Page, US ambassador to Britain during World War 1 who said the Scots were 'the most capable race in the world - except at home.' Think about it.

Education blossomed in eighteenth century Scotland, building on what

# Lions and Donkeys (part 1)

had begun in the sixteenth century, with the advent of the Reformation. In Dunbar as elsewhere, schools were pressing ahead and new ideas were coming on stream at the same time as agriculture - the main source of employment - was developing at an impressive rate. How far the so-called 'Agricultural Revolution' was attributable to formal education would be difficult to assess. Progress comes about because a few visionary individuals see beyond their noses; progress cannot be taught; it comes about because of individual effort and commitment and great individuals will make their mark whatever the extent of their formal education. (The John Muirs of this world will emerge and achieve their ambitions despite rather because of formal education). In the small community of Dunbar, at least three schoolmasters or *dominies* made a significant contribution to formal learning in the country as a whole. The first was Andrew Simson who produced a Latin primer or grammar in 1564; the second was Andrew Home whose Latin grammar was adopted throughout Scotland in 1612 by order of the Privy Council, the governing body of peers which ran Scotland after James VI went to London to rule both Scotland and England as James I. The third schoolmaster who furthered education in the country was James Kirkwood of Dunbar, whose *Grammatica Facilis* was adopted as the blueprint for teaching Latin. The Dunbar authorities were among the first in Scotland to recognise that there should be a balance in work and play. Had we known such things at the time, we might have been even more proud of the rural school we attended at Woodbush.

My first recollection of school was being told by my mother that I had to go there or else she would be put in prison. In 1946, when I reached the statutory age for attending school, the infant, primary and secondary schools were all housed at Woodbush, a site beside the sea and now occupied by a modern housing estate. For little toddling, stumbling infants, many of whom had to walk a mile to school clinging to older brothers and sisters, the first weeks were a nightmare. I can't recall being afraid of infant school but I certainly remember being nervous and confused. On the first day, my mother took me to the school gate at Woodbush; she waved goodbye and said she'd collect me at 3.30pm. It was the only time she took me there and back. As she said that afternoon:

'You'll have to go yourself son. But Norman will take ye there.'
My brother Norman hated school and couldn't wait to get away from it. But he looked after me on the mile-long walks —four times a day - from our house to Woodbush, even if he teased the life out of me.

'Aye, wait till ye get Miss Tinning. She'll sort ye oot.'
I was glad that I was able to find my own way home after infant school, which closed at 3.30pm, Norman being incarcerated until 3.55pm.
So, flickering images from the past. Imagine two schoolchildren, sticky-eyed with sleep, sticky-mouthed from syrup rolls devoured on the hoof - Norman and I were always late in the morning - making our way to Woodbush. We

approached this massive grey forbidding building with its bell-tower, sunken quadrangle with flower trough and memorial plate commemorating the former pupils who had given their lives in two World Wars. We had our entire lives ahead of us and despite the apprehension and confusion, we were as jaunty as two small bubbles in a chuckling burn or stream. I loved my picture books; Norman hated books of any kind and for him reading was a form of torture. I never understood his aversion to the printed word; clearly, education by literacy worked on me.

That first year of infant school was spent in a wooden hut that was set apart from the main building and which later housed the Special Class of pupils who were disabled in many ways. You climbed the few wooden steps and were greeted by a kindly maternal teacher, Jean Myles, who led you by the hand into an anteroom and helped you remove your coat and show you where to hang it. The classroom seemed large but of course it wasn't. The windows were greasy and dirty and there were strange things like radiators, rumbling and burping and emitting other strange noises though they kept us warm. We spent a year in splendid isolation - at school but not in it. That lady teacher should have been called Miss Smiles; maybe a lot of the diddleys believed that was her name. We certainly pronounced it that way and she rewarded us with so many lovely smiles.

Shown to our desks, we were told to sit while Miss Myles brought out a large book from her desk. She asked each of us our names and wrote them down. She said that every day, she would call out our names so she would know who was present and who was absent. I was confused. Wouldn't she know who was there and who wasn't? How could I say 'absent' if I wasn't there? To my tiny mind, adults were weird.

In that first year of infant school, Miss Myles acted as a communal surrogate mother; we were always falling down or losing our schoolbags/coats/gloves/hankies. A good deal of the time was spent in play or resting sleepy heads on arms. I can still smell the heavy, dusty wood, damp paper and sick that emanated from the insides of the desks. Our attention span was short; the entire class was easily diverted when a little diddley stood up, yawned, scratched himself/herself and drifted to the window in a hazy, dreamlike trance until he/she was led back gently to his/her desk by the kind, gentle Miss Myles.

Our wooden hut overlooked the gymnasium in the 'big' school. The gym was separated from the Hut by a trench several feet deep, fenced off to prevent infants falling into it. We would often crowd round the fence, peer through the gym windows, trying to spot elder brothers and sisters at gym. All I recall seeing were vague, leaping shapes in gym shorts and vests. Once I recognised Norman and I called out to him and waved. I never understood why he didn't wave back.

The schoolwork we were given in that first year consisted of chanting after the teacher, usually intoning the alphabet - A is for Apple and so on. The bee-like

# Lions and Donkeys (part 1)

hum of small voices was soporific, especially on warm days. Several of us nodded off. I hadn't a clue what the lessons were for, just as I would blindly join in any line that was formed, following equally confused little ones. We played a lot with toys, plasticine and bits of paper from which we cut out vague shapes - usually in my case, something I thought resembled a circle. We 'read' picture books, one of which I recall was called *Janet and Jim*. The extroverts among us wandered about the room, showing their efforts to other children, giggling and chuckling - often at no one - bubbling with what I suppose was enthusiasm or wearing furrowed frowns when they were shepherded back to their seats. Like many children, my favourite pastime was drawing stick men - a round O for the head, straight lines for body, arms and legs, the face given expression by using two dots for eyes and a gash for a mouth and jagged lines for hair that screeched upwards in bold strokes of crayon. The interior of the Hut was a place of strange smells; unbeknownst to me then, the smells were a combination of damp wool, ammonia-smelling cotton underwear and the occasional *poomp* which was our word for a fart. Occasionally, kids messed themselves seriously and had to be led away quickly, the stench of something nasty lingering in their wake. Wet coats, damp woollen gloves and scarves added to this rich and heady brew in winter, so that season was a particularly memorable time, in the olfactory sense.

We chattered like magpies - to each other, to our toys, to the teacher, to the walls. Even to thin air. The stream of consciousness which the famous Irish novelist James Joyce perfected so well must surely have its origins in the ceaseless, meaningless babble that passed as dialogue in Irish infant classes. One day, shortly after we joined the school, Miss Myles announced she was going to tell a Story. Not about fairies or elves or pixies or gnomes, she said. 'This is a Real Story. Put away your toys, boys and girls. I am going to tell you about Baby Jesus, who is always with us.'

A few heads turned round to look at the room, wondering where the baby was and how it had gotten into our classroom. The more distracted and enquiring spirits were gently coaxed to face the front. Miss Myles said she was going to tell us about a little baby called Jesus who had been born in a stable. Did we know what a stable was? A hand shot up.

'Aye. Where the moo-cows bide.'

'Yes, that's right. But in this stable, there were other animals. Oxen for example.'

The same hand went skywards again.

'Whit's a oxen?'

'A kind of cow, but the word is ox. More than one ox are called oxen. Not oxes. Oxen.'

Common sense should have informed her that a frown was all she could expect by way of response.

I recall being slightly alarmed at the thought of a little baby lying in a stable amongst cows and the other animals with the strange name. They might have stood on Baby Jesus. But it turned out that he was safe in a crib or cradle and his mother was there to look after him. We were told he was born on Christmas Day. At this, the bovine expert's hand was up again, enquiring if he got any presents in his stocking. No. There wasn't a stocking like we had but three wise men from afar brought the baby presents. The animal specialist persisted.

'Did he get a wee Dinky caur [car]? I got yin at Christmas.'

No, nothing like that. The gifts were money and scent. The inquisitive child screwed up his face. He was about to ask another question when he was stopped short; Miss Myles took him into the anteroom where we hung our coats. A few minutes later, she brought him back; he was white-faced and looked as if he'd been crying.

That afternoon, I couldn't wait to run home and tell my mother about the Baby Jesus who was so poor he'd been born in a stable and only got scent from Santa Claus. Laying a plate of the inevitable *tattie soup* before me, she said I would learn all about Jesus when I went to Sunday school later in the year. Another school? I was puzzled. Was my life to be nothing but going to schools? Apart from this episode, most of infant school - well the first year of it - is a blur. I do remember playing a lot of the time with plasticine which is marvellous stuff. For some reason, I used to push a lot of spent matchsticks into the dollops I rolled and pounded on a special board we were given for the purpose. We learnt to sing songs and recite rhymes but now I can't recall any of them. In the second year of school, we exchanged the warm security, comforting female bosom and splendid isolation of the Hut for the 'Big School' Infants' Department. We entered our new part of the school at the lower, seaward end which was guarded by two stout pillars and a heavy iron gate beside *Woodbush House*, a gate which had to be opened by the friendly and kind janitor, Mr Blair. We were summoned to our lines by a hand-bell rung by the duty teacher, usually Miss Tinning who had a face straight out of the *Beano* comic. We formed up in parallel lines - boys to the left, girls to the right. Once indoors, we were welcomed by the head of the Infants' Department, whom I think was a Miss Duncanson, known to elder brothers and sister as *Doaly*, perhaps a corruption of 'Dolly'. (Recently, I learnt that she had retired in 1945, a year before I started school. Yet I remember her vividly on account of her wispy, white hair, so perhaps she was brought back to work as a supply teacher, or perhaps to train Miss Tinning as her successor. I certainly recall Miss Tinning inspecting our lines, dressing them to a degree of perfection that would have met with the approval of even the fussiest British Army Regimental Sergeant Major. When Miss Tinning was satisfied we were 'in order', she would frog march us into the cloakroom, making us keep time with a clap-clap, one-two beat of hands. When I first saw her, I didn't like the look of her at all. She had a raw, lean face, a beaky nose and an extremely shrill and cold voice. Not like

# Lions and Donkeys (part 1)

Miss Myles, who had a lovely soft voice and often whispered to us. Miss Tinning barked out commands; she was strict with both boys and girls, so she was fair, I suppose. For me, it was getting worse by the minute.

After Miss Myles, a lady called Miss Sinclair, became our teacher. She was cheerful, stout and wore green tweedy suits - jacket and skirt in case you think Dunbar was so advanced that it allowed its lady teachers to wear slacks - heaven forbid! Miss Sinclair looked like an owl, peering intently at us from behind owlish glasses. There was something odd about her, something Not Quite Right; even at that tender age, most of us sensed it and we would shortly discover the reason. One day, a couple of weeks into the autumn term, in the midst of writing down times' tables on the blackboard, she suddenly paused, stared at the chalk stick in her hand, then she wrote a word in large letters. Beside it, she drew a man in a tall hat with a beard that looked as if it had been stuck on his chin, then a funny, pointed shape and finally what looked like an animal lying down like a lion, except that it had wings and a human face. She spoke to the blackboard that September afternoon of grey, chill mist. Her words came out slow, deliberate; she wanted to make sure we understood her. 'Now, children. As a change from your tables, I want to give you a treat this afternoon. You may not have seen what I have drawn on the blackboard before but I shall tell you. Hands up any children who have heard of a country called Egypt? Have any of you heard of the Sfinx?'

That was how I imagined the word was spelt. Blank stares greeted her. Her back was turned to the class while she scribbled the words *Pharaoh, Pyramid* and *Sphinx* on the blackboard, then she suddenly whirled round to face us. Her usually stodgy face was transformed. There was a calm, almost gentle look on that owl-like woman; she positively beamed at us but somehow, her smile wasn't reassuring. One or two little ones began to whimper, as she looked so strange. She held her pointer like a spear, then proceeded to tell us about Egypt, a strange, faraway country. Hers was an animated and fascinating tale. 'Do you know why I know so much about Egypt? It is simple. I lived there many thousands of years ago. I wasn't a teacher then. I was an Egyptian princess. My father was the Pharaoh, a kind of king. He built the thing you see before you on the blackboard. It is called a pyramid. I went to sleep in it many hundreds of years ago and now I have come back to tell you about my life in that lovely country which my father ruled.'

One or two children giggled nervously, myself included. But I felt uncomfortable. Miss Sinclair went on to inform us about her life beside a great river called the Nile, how she was dressed in the finest silks and wore jewels and had slaves to bathe her and feed her. She told us she had watched her father's slaves build the pyramid she'd drawn. We were being treated to a whiff of something older than time itself that day, a thing called history; the scent was so different from the lavender water she always trailed behind her as she walked up and down our rows of desks, chanting times' tables along with

# Lions and Donkeys (part 1)

us, beating time on the floor with her pointer.

Then she stopped and started the times' tables again. It was as if she had switched off, becoming herself again, the self we recognised and slightly feared. But the next afternoon, she was back in Egypt with tales of her former life coming fast and furious. One day, we came to school and were shown into Miss Nisbet's class. Of Miss Sinclair there was no trace. As far as I recall, she never returned to the school. A few days later at playtime - leavetime or *leafy* as we called it - I was eating my roll and syrup when a bigger boy came up to me and said Miss Sinclair had been taken to the *nuthoose* [asylum]. I had a vision of Miss Sinclair sitting in a room counting nuts and beating time with her pointer on the floor. Poor soul, she was harmless but her belief in reincarnation was apparently well known to the school authorities. Maybe things had gotten too much for her that year and she'd snapped. We never saw her again. Miss Nisbet was yet another dedicated and kind lady, her face lined by the effects of years of controlled patience. I remember her looking tanned, or swarthy-skinned. Like Miss Myles, she was infinitely patient with her young charges, although she was firm when the occasion demanded. She was a great believer in tidiness and order; she was forever commanding us to 'sit up straight' with arms folded. (I could never understand why teachers always exhorted us to sit 'up' straight - why not 'down'?). After all, we were already sitting down and the command always confused me. She got cross if we looked out of the window at the school quadrangle, especially when some class of bigger boys and girls were passing by. 'How many times do I have to tell you not to look out of the window Roy Pugh' was a common and frequent complaint. In her charge, I experienced a sense of injustice and mistrust which was never far away in all my dealings with even the nicest teachers - except for Miss Myles, then many years later, Miss Mackay or Glass, my history teacher.

Miss Nisbet's classroom was situated on the ground floor. We sat at different levels, the room being structured on the lines of broad step-like levels or tiers that rose to the back and nearest the windows. Our desks were bulky and clumsy iron-framed affairs not designed for comfort, probably deliberately so to stop you falling asleep. Cumbersome and riveted to the wooden floor, the desks had sloping lids, like something out of Ebeneezer Scrooge's bleak counting house in Dickens' *A Christmas Carol*. At least the heating was adequate, provided by the bulky and rumbling radiators found in most schools of that time.

The desk was yours until you gave it up or were ordered to another one when closer supervision of the less attentive was needed. In the right hand corner was an inkwell, although as infants, we never wrote with the scratchy ink pens used by older children. We were given slate boards to write on in those days. The sound of several slate pencils squealing and screeching over the surface of these boards set your teeth on edge. Noisy and noisome things, their only advantage was that you could hide your mistakes by spitting on your handkerchief and erasing an offending word or incorrect additions of sums. At the end of every writing lesson, a damp rag was passed from child to child to wipe the slate clean. Could that be the origin of the old saying which means 'to start again, ignoring past mistakes'?

Even in that second year of infant school, many pairs of glazed eyes and worried faces stared at teacher, hoping to find answers there. When we were told to sit quiet for five minutes, it seemed an impossible task. Five minutes? That was an eternity for kids brimming over with an excess of energy and adrenalin. After two minutes, there was invariably an outbreak of coughing, squeaking, giggling, whispering - and *poomping*. As I said earlier, *poomping* was our word for farting. The class seemed to be perpetually engrossed by absent-minded, unselfconscious nose-picking or the careful removal of scabs from skinned knees, fidgeting, hair-pulling and ribbon-undoing - the last two perpetrated by boys on girls. Finally, even Miss Nisbet's exceptionally long fuse burnt out and she would explode in anger, tweaking the ear of some wretched, sniggering boy. She told the class she wanted Silence and that she would have it. Often, an uncontrollable loud *poomp* erupted, raising parox-ysms of laughter which brought Miss Tinning from the adjacent room. The noise would then end abruptly, for Miss Tinning was feared by all. We were given a final warning from Miss Nisbet, the rest period was abruptly termi-nated and we were back at our books, chanting rhymes or times' tables. I remember chanting 'A is for Apple which we love to eat' or 'two times two is four' etc. These mantras were drummed into us and we chanted them back as good as any Harikrishnas, without the need for accompanying finger bells.

Our bad behaviour was gentle enough anarchy and we usually settled down quickly to the routine work. But bodily functions still preoccupied boys and girls alike. Some wet themselves and very occasionally, a boy would mess his trousers. The *poomping* was endemic, probably as a result of the healthy post-war diet of the Brussels sprouts and cabbage on which so many of my generation were reared. Sometimes, a boy would fart time and time again until Miss Tinning was called in because his neighbour had shouted that his desk mate was smelly. The wind instrument and his accuser were both removed - usually by their ears - to Miss Tinning's room. She was convinced they were in league. As she led the troublemakers out, she turned to the rest of us, in-forming us she had 'ways of dealing with troublemakers.' The miscreants returned a few minutes later, white-faced, snivelling and blowing on their hands for some reason that escaped me. I would shortly find out what caused the hand-blowing performances.

I was a talker - still am - not because I am confident or like the sound of my own voice but for the simple reason that I am nervous. Nervous people either clam up or they talk the hind legs off the proverbial donkey. As a child, I talked at every opportunity, chattering to anyone within a twenty-foot radius; when there was no one handy or listening, I talked to my toys and as a last resort, myself. The stream of consciousness fairly spewed out of me when I was alone. I talked to stones, to flowers, bushes and trees. In those early days, my best monologues were reserved for my plasticine models, then my lead soldiers - all of the soldiers had personal names which only I knew and of course I gave them different voices, which may explain why today, I can sometimes mimic other people. My favourite game with plasticine models was to make a little bridge rather like that at Belhaven beach, the 'bridge to nowhere'; there I would place a little man with a rod fishing from it. Underneath was another little man in a tiny rowing boat, also fishing. My plasticine men story went something like this:

> ' So the wee man goes up the bridge like this [marching him up the steps] and he takes his fishin' rod like this and drops the line in the water like this, see, then the other wee man comes along in his wee rowin' boat and he's fishin' too and he says to the wee man on the bridge 'Hae ye caught anythin' yet?' and the wee man on the bridge sez 'No, they're no bitin' the day hows aboot you? And the wee man in the boat sez 'Nah, nae luck at a'' and he rows up and doon an' in an' oot and catches nuthin' then they eat their pieces, jam for the man on the bridge and cheese for the man in the rowin' boat and sometimes they change the pieces for they dinnae like whit their mothers hae put on their pieces an' want a change. '

And so it went on, day in, day out. I was happy playing the roles of the wee men and happiest when no one interfered with or bothered to listen to me. One dark early autumn afternoon, I was in full flow. It must have been September because I was still wearing a short-sleeved summer shirt - how I can recall that point of detail will be revealed presently. Miss Nisbet told me to keep quiet, then she told me a second time; then she came up the tiers or steps where I sat and moved me further back because I was a 'chatterbox' and was disturbing the other children. I didn't know what a chatterbox was and imagined it as tin with a lid that flapped up and down. But I wouldn't - couldn't - shut that lid, so Miss Nisbet said I had run out of warnings and she was going to get Miss Tinning. That stopped me but by then, it was too late. Once summonsed, Miss Tinning came striding into the classroom like a valkyrie. She was unstoppable, mowing down anything that got in her way. Miss Nisbet and Miss Tinning were whispering. Miss Tinning didn't look in my direction but I knew they were talking about me. Then she looked at me. Feeling isolated, I started to say I was sorry and that I promised I wouldn't talk any more. My weak pleas fell on stone-deaf ears. Miss Tinning held up a bony forefinger and ordered me to hush. Her ruined, crumpled face was unforgettably horrible. Her red nose positively glowed; as I said earlier, she was like a character of authority in the *Beano* comic which I'd begun to read by then. I looked down at her from my back-of-the-class loftiness. She strode towards me, taking the steps two at a time. I knew I was in trouble.

# Lions and Donkeys (part 1)

'So, we have a chatterbox, do we. Who won't take a telling. Which one is it Miss Nisbet?'

I knew she knew perfectly well but Miss Nisbet pointed to me.

'So this is it, the talker, Roypugh.'

She said my name as one word. Despite my innocence, that didn't make me feel any better. I felt my face burn. I shrank in my seat. By now, Miss Tinning was at my side. She laid the big, cold iron key she held in her hand on my bare forearm - that's how I remember I was wearing a short-sleeved shirt. I said it was awful cold. Miss Tinning smiled bitterly at me.

'Oh, we are cold, are we? Well, I have something that will warm you up. Something that is good for talkers like Roypugh. Come and meet my Tommy.'

That sounded quite nice, a bit reassuring. Maybe Tommy would be friendly. Obediently naive, I followed her as she beckoned me to follow her with her skeletal forefinger. When we went into her classroom, a sea of up-turned shiny faces greeted me. A ripple of whispering broke out, instantly silenced by Miss Tinning. Fingers were pointed at me; I waved back and smiled as Miss Tinning went to her desk, unlocked it with her big iron key and from it, drew out a large leather thong, like a belt.

'This is Tommy' she said. ' Tommy, this is Roypugh. A talker. Shall we show him how we deal with talkers in the classroom?'

She ordered me to hold out my hand with the palm uppermost. She drew a deep breath and raised the strap, then brought it down with full force on my unsuspecting palm. She did it twice. I was six years old. I felt the initial sting, then the throbbing as my fingers turned into fat sausages. Blinking back my tears, I was ordered back to Miss Nisbet's class. The shiny faces didn't look at me; they had their faces fixed on their desk lids. Miss Tinning prodded me, frog-marching me back to my seat. She said this in a loud voice so that all my chums in the class could hear:

'He'll not talk any more.'

I sat and sniffled, wanting my Mum. I hid my face by resting my head on my arms. My innocence was shattered forever. Iron entered my soul. A child's hatred is more intense than an adult's because it is uninformed, confused. Miss Nisbet ignored me for a time, then she ordered me to sit up straight. I never trusted her or any other teacher in the primary school again. The belt didn't cure me of chattering; it only drove me underground. I never have lost that feeling of shame and resentment. I felt I had been violated and the feeling has never left me. Maybe this vindicates the psychologists who recommended the abolishment of the strap. I disagree with them. Punishment for wrongdoing is justified; being chastised for being innocent is inexcusable.

Most of the rest of infant school is shadowy. Like the others, I was bewildered most of the time. Two other memories persist however. One is of my mother putting waves in my hair for the first school photograph in 1947; I

# Lions and Donkeys (part 1)

still have the photo but the waves aren't obvious. My mother used to buy this white, sticky liquid from Willie Law the barber in the High Street; it must have cost something like 10p the gallon. She plastered it on my and Ken's hair so that it dried to a hard crust which highlighted your 'shed' or parting on the left of your head. She made the waves with vicious, steel-hinged hair combs that looked like the mouths of alligators and could have taken off your fingertips. We always had waves in for special occasions but they rarely lasted for long. The other memory is disgustingly, acutely embarrassing. I believed my mother when she said that after mastering my potty and graduating to the toilet, I could control my 'movements' and therefore could 'wait.' How much damage in later years was done to the innocent, anal retentives of that time? I refused to use the disgusting school lavatories in the playground; they had long ago lost their wooden seats, the toilet bowls were permanently and irretrievably stained with a slimy green stuff and the cubicles often had no doors. Most were defaced by holes made by penknives so that the bigger boys could gob at you as you sat in there. I never actually saw any boy being chased, caught and put into these disgusting receptacles head first but I believe it happened. The urinals were smelly and bad but they had nothing on the cold, filthy cubicles. I was - and still am - fussy about where I attend the necessary calls of nature.

A word about the girls' toilets; although I never entered them, I listened to stories which the girls told us lads. Their loos were to the rear of the school, set against the sea wall; this meant that the poor lassies were constantly soaked by waves breaking over the wall in winter. It was a silly place to site them but then girls in those days were considered less important I am sad to say. ('They're going to be shop assistants or hairdressers so why waste time on their education.' This has been confirmed by teachers still around in Dunbar who taught them in those days).

One day, I misjudged my capacity to 'wait'. After we were let out of school at about 3.30pm, I struggled to contain myself; about nearly three-quarters way home, I could hold out no longer. I shat myself. Filling my *wellies* is no exaggeration. Within sight of my house, I clung desperately to a convenient lamppost but couldn't hold on any longer. A sympathetic neighbour heard my distressed cries and led me home. Despite her pleas, my mother hauled me inside and belted me for being a dirty boy. I was then pushed upstairs to the bathroom where I was divested of soiled clothing and plunged into a bath. Later, when Norman came home and learnt of my wee accident, he came upstairs and chanted at me in the bath:

' 'Oo messed his troosers, 'oo messed his troosers!'

These distressing episodes never leave us. I have never felt confident again as far as bodily functions of that kind are concerned.

I ashamedly but freely confess I cannot recall all my infant teachers' names after Miss Nisbet, whose name conjures up a day of infamy for me, though in later years, I mellowed towards her. I do recall a little old lady called

# Lions and Donkeys (part 1)

Miss Duncanson, who died a couple of years ago. The transition from infant to primary was relatively painless but is also an almost closed book 55 years on. Just as I was becoming acclimatised to the warm, comforting bosom of some ageless lady who smiled a lot, tied your shoelaces and helped you on with your coat, you were abruptly denied such comforts, thrust into an entirely new - and terrifying world of times' tables and the other tortures that made up the three 'Rs' of Reading, 'Riting and Rithmetic. Discipline was strict and public. If you managed to escape the belt, you were made to stand out in front of the entire class, hanging your head with your back to the others by the blackboard. You knew your classmates were sniggering at your shrunken, cowed back every time teacher turned *hers* to write sums on the blackboard. Later, we were treated to the less painful but no less embarrassing knuckles assailed by a thick ruler, tweaked ears, pulled hair. Occasionally, you were kept in at playtime or even worse, after school; you were ordered to copy out poems like Tennyson's *Hiawatha* and other marathon literary works. Gone forever were the comforting arms, warm bosoms; in autumn and winter, the afternoons were wet, cold and darkness fell before you left the building.

The primary classes were tiered like those in the infants, the 'achievers' seated at the front, the rubbish consigned to the back; some teachers reversed this arrangement so that the back-sliders could be closely monitored so they could be 'found wanting'. As I progressed through the primary classes, I found myself usually occupying the middle ground so I never knew whether I was getting better or worse.

In those days, teachers exuded an air of unquestionable authority, they Who Must Be Obeyed which included many who didn't deserve to be obeyed, let alone respected. Little had changed since John Muir's day in the mid-nineteenth century; Muir gives us a graphic account of the way he was taught by floggings and beatings which he said had a remarkable effect on his ability to absorb knowledge, albeit learnt parrot-fashion. His unfinished autobiography *The Story of My Boyhood and Youth* containing graphic descriptions of school discipline will be familiar to my generation as it was endured by his own. His impressions would not have been out of place in Dunbar about 50 years ago; for example, he relates how

'Old fashioned Scotch [sic] teachers spent no time in seeking short roads to knowledge, or in trying any of the new-fangled psychological methods so much in vogue nowadays....we were simply driven point blank against our books like soldiers against the enemy, and sternly ordered, 'Up and at 'em'. Commit your lessons to memory!' If we failed in any part, however slight, we were whipped, for the grand, simple, all-suffering Scotch discovery had been made that there was a close connection between the skin and memory, and that irritating the skin excited the memory to any required degree.'

Perhaps ours were not quite so bad as Muir's educational experiences but the fundamentals continued well into the twentieth century, certainly until

# Lions and Donkeys (part 1)

1954. A gentle, nostalgic account of school life between 1897 and 1997 appears in *From Slate to Disk,* edited by Mrs Lena Glass, a History teacher I adored in Secondary School and still adore today. However, I have to say that the reality of school life in Dunbar was somewhat different from the sanitised version contained in *Slate to Disk*, as Mrs Glass has admitted to me in recently. Teachers were strict disciplinarians and in my time, some of them believed their writ went beyond the school gates; they thought nothing of reporting erring schoolboys to the headmaster and the police, even when these juvenile transgressions were committed after school hours. Examples which come to mind are using bad language in the streets, riding bicycles without lights or hands on the handlebars.

The upper school primary teachers were demoniac about correct spelling, proper grammar and proficiency in mental arithmetic, although many were poor on specialised subjects like history, geography and literature.

Primary school - and to a lesser extent - secondary - were populated by 'female' teachers of both sexes. Some were unashamedly austere and even sadistic. Most dripped with sarcasm. I can recall teachers in primary school like Miss Caldwell, a young woman whose name matched her chilly temperament; Miss Intin, a pretty lady who could be extremely kind one minute and a raging virago the next. After Mai Intin, we had Miss Gunn, known for obvious reasons as 'Tommy'; she was quiet and firm, her jaw set determinedly in her efforts to prepare us for the final primary school class, the year of the Qualifying Exam, which was a terrifying year of preparation, hope and fear. The *Qualy* results determined the future course of your education in the upper school, so it was a kind of 'rites of passage' year, capably handled by Miss Ena Murray, a great lady in everyone's book. Miss Murray gave you the belt only after you'd spelt a word wrongly three times in a row, fair treatment for that time I suppose. It meant you were wasting hers.

The intention in those days was to break your spirit, control you and get you to knuckle down to hard work. In Mai Intin, I found yet another of my hopeless crushes which I took to incredible flights of fantasy. I imagined myself her champion. I was her slave until the day she destroyed that love by her unfair judgement on me in a spelling test. But that occurred after she'd shown us her very human and kind side. At Christmas, she distributed homemade treacle toffee to us all - remember that sweets were still on ration after the war until 1953 - and we thought her splendid. But she could lose her temper with frightening suddenness. Her delightfully slim frame shook, her sensitive nose became flared nostrils and her lips went white and quivered. She often treated Jock the Wild Man to one of her withering and chilly stares followed by a loud tirade which could end with her belting him soundly for his dumb insolence. But you cannot wither the Jocks of this world with stares or flagellation; Jock accepted the belt with resignation and took it like the man he was. However, as long as I wasn't the object of her anger, I continued to defend her honour against imaginary thugs, assailants and pickpockets. To me, she was the epitome of beauty, even in her wrathful moments. She wore the three-quarter- length white 'swagger' coat very fashionable at the time; it offset her lovely dark eyes and dark hair. I was besotted with her. Of pale, porcelain-thin complexion, she makes me think now of those fragile Elizabethan portraits - I mean Elizabeth 1 of England of course. In my febrile and testosterone-fuelled imagination, she was always being set upon by ugly thugs in my daydreams, wearing nothing under her swagger coat except - promoted in the melodramatic films of that time - a string of pearls. I never actually envisaged her naked; in my fantasy, nakedness meant vulnerability and not sexuality; it also meant that when I saved her from indescribable imaginative violations, she was more grateful. Mai Intin taught me a very valuable lesson, unbeknown to her; you should never argue with a woman, no matter how beautiful she may be, if she has power and authority over you. Such women are deadly and more infinitely dangerous than the compliant or even unattractive but sexy ones....

Where she failed me, destroyed my faith in her was in the aforementioned spelling test. The test consisted of her standing before us, pronouncing a word we had to write down correctly. About halfway trough the test, she uttered the word *further* - except that she deliberately said *farther.* Not unnaturally, I spelt it with an 'a'. She deducted a point from me even though I had the guts to tell her I'd seen it spelt that way. I even took the trouble to consult the *The Concise Oxford Dictionary* which allows both spellings. She would hear none of it. I lost that vital point which I think cost me a place in the first three correct answers so that I came third instead of second. She accused me of bad grace. My illusion of her as a fair and lovely lady was shattered for all time.

When I encountered her again in secondary school, Miss Intin had been appointed Music teacher in place of Miss Boyd, a kindly, genteel soul. Music as a school subject was one I detested and thought an utter waste of time. The relationship between Mai Intin and myself did not recover and eventually, during the time of the Higher exams, she ordered myself and several others from her class. We were 'high' on account of those so important exams and one day, during her Friday afternoon period, several of us behaved even more badly than usual. She told us to remove ourselves from her class. We thanked her, took her at her word and said we could spend our time more beneficially studying in the school library.

'Go. Get out of my sight. Let those who are interested in and appreciate music enjoy this class.'

We slipped away quietly and went to the library; engrossed in our books, we were surprised when Hugh Cowan, the headmaster walked in. He ordered us to his study, where he interviewed us individually that bleak February afternoon. When it came to my turn, I was ordered into a chair and studied closely. A month earlier, I had sat the Civil Service Clerical Officer Exam and was waiting for the results. Hugh Cowan eyed me with disdain. He told me I was too old to be belted but that he was disappointed in me, for I had proved my worth, passing the Civil Service exam. He said Miss Intin had previously reported me as a born troublemaker, which came as a great surprise. The only boy she seemed to favour was TJ, my friend of later years. He had this knack of manipulating people - still has it - and women fell under his spell. She once persuaded him - he'd already planted the idea in her head - to sing the popular Paul Anka song '*Diana*'; I have this lasting image of TJ dressed in dog-tooth check sports coat, bow tie and thick-soled brothel-creeper shoes living a separate life of their own as he danced, like someone not entirely in control of his faculties, before us, his long hair cascading over his eyes. I am convinced his performance was less than genuine. It was TJ's way of thwarting authority and it worked. He was damned good at it - he still is.

After Miss Intin, we had Maggie Darling whose Primary 5 classroom was located in the Parish Church Hall annexe, a poky little room to the rear of Abbeylands, with a small square of tarmacadamed playground. Officially she was located there because the Woodbush school was overflowing; I don't doubt that but there might have been an underlying reason, for she was an embarrassment to the school complement with her unkempt hair, warts and slatternly mode of dress, her fat body imprisoned and threatening to burst out of her greasy cardigans. The classroom was ill-lit and heated by a pitifully ineffective coal fire which required the boys to shovel coal into a scuttle every day from the pile of fuel from a corner of the small playground - usually some poor little sod who'd transgressed one of old Maggie's fussy rules.

Miss Darling was the epitome of my idea of a witch, much more so than Miss Tinning, except that she was lazy and had cultivated a couldn't-care-less attitude; either that or maybe she was just naturally that way inclined. She had stringy, straggling hair that kept escaping from the bun she tried to maintain. The warts were obtrusive and wandered all over her cheeks and chin. I have since learnt that some admirer - possibly a Warrender *roue* - built *The Retreat* for her at Lochend Wood for services rendered but unstipulated; one wonders what these could have possibly been, given the way she looked. But maybe she hadn't always been the hag she'd become in 1951.

So Maggie Darling channelled the energies of the more unruly spirits in her class by ordering them to cart coal into the classroom. Her decidedly laid-back attitude meant that were left to our own devices most afternoons, her favourite ploy being to order us to write 'compositions', as essays were called then, thus allowing her to enjoy her customary afternoon forty winks. She hogged the fire by placing her desk in front of it so that in winter, we froze. The cold rather than her discipline kept us awake. I have this enduring memory of her sitting at her desk, head supported by her hands, daydreaming or sleeping, scratching her crotch which she thought we couldn't see under her heavy deal desk. I was affronted to watch her absent-mindedly picking her bulbous nose until she was jerked into consciousness by our sniggering laughter.

# Lions and Donkeys (part 1)

My only real memory of Maggie Darling's class was my single attempt to whip up support amongst my schoolmates for closer attention to their lessons. I guess somehow I knew that we had to do it because Maggie Darling couldn't inspire us. It was my first excursion into public speaking and I failed miserably then as I usually do now. Maybe it was a cry for help; maybe I realised I was only a couple of years away from the dreaded Qualifying Year and I somehow sensed that Maggie's class was going to be a waste of a whole year. Be that as it may, one winter afternoon during playtime, I got up on a window ledge, called the others to me and gave them a lecture on why we should work harder at our lessons. I held the attention of those 30 or so girls and boys for all of 23 seconds. They drifted away to their games with balls and skipping ropes, leaving me with one loyal supporter called Anne, a local greengrocer's daughter whose family hailed from Newcastle. I was in love with Anne at the time and I wanted to impress her. She listened to my impassioned pleas that day, then she called me a useless article. At least she smiled after she said it.

At this time, the newly formed NHS was beginning to kick-in, a specific section of the National Health Service (Scotland) Act 1947 imposing a long-overdue duty on local authorities to provide a school health service. The provision came just in time to save many of us from extinction from virulent epidemics like influenza, rickets, whooping cough, scarlet fever, diphtheria, polio, measles and chickenpox. The school health service was staffed by nurses with bodies built like outdoor brick toilets and with legs like dinner tables, doctors who were sadistic and uncommunicative, saying things like 'Hm' when they investigated your ailments. They frowned a lot. As for the dentists, they were butchers to a man. Many of these people were ex-army and navy practitioners who took great delight in their bloody work; if we'd known it then, some of these cruel and unsympathetic practitioners learned their trade in Japanese prisoner-of-war camps in the Second World War. 'It's got to come out' was the inevitable diagnosis for milk teeth that stubbornly failed to fall out of our mouths naturally. Perfectly serviceable teeth were yanked out to make way for second teeth as I recall. You got this injection - itself a traumatic experience - then the forceps would be applied, the dentist holding you with his arm round your neck as you stood listening to the horrendous crunch and crackle of a perfectly healthy molar being excised. Note that I say 'stood'; I can't recall any tooth extracted at school with the victims seated on a chair. Finally, you spat blood into an enamel basin, a dental assistant wiped away the blood and ordered you into the corridor to make way for the next victim. If it was winter, you were advised to wear a thick wool scarf over your mouth so the cold wouldn't get in. I had a gap in my lower left jaw for several years as a result of this unnecessary butchery and wondered whether anything would ever sprout in the space; It was fully eight years before my second molar appeared, thirteen before I again visited a dentist of my own free will. Jock the

# Lions and Donkeys (part 1)

Wild Man christened these sadists *Knights of the Bushido* - whatever they were.

The doctors weren't much better. They gave you inoculations to protect you from diphtheria and polio, diseases that could kill or maim you for life. Most of us were disgustingly healthy, possibly because of the stringent war rationing and a better balanced diet than any generation before or since has enjoyed, even if it was boring. We never had enough food but what we got was healthy. Dieticians and doctors today are agreed on the efficacy of the healthy eating habits imposed on us, courtesy of Herr Hitler.

The District Nurse was another dreaded figure. Ours was stout and cycled about her territory until she was finally given a motorcar. Visits from her were universally feared because everyone knew their purpose. She was either coming to your house because you had nits or scabies, impetigo and scrofula - or something infinitely worse and life diminishing. Our District Nurse made it her personal crusade to find out if we had *Beasties* in our hair. We suffered her scouring of our scalps with a cruelly hard and dreaded bone comb, already apprehensive and imagining our scalps were crawling with foreign bodies. Child after child came out of her clinic, sighing with relief; but some children were kept in longer and we exchanged knowing looks until somebody said the awful words:

'They've got Nits.'

'They' were usually children of poor families; today, I find that a strange qualification, for in those days, we were all poor.

The nit-free went Scot-free, skipping and whooping into the sunset. The be-nitted souls had to stay behind to receive a letter they'd to give to their parents. The cure was fairly simple - regular hair washing and a robust application of liquid paraffin on the scalp. The nit carriers were stigmatised and sent to Coventry as the wee beasties were highly contagious, those of us who were nitless avoided them like the plague. I couldn't understand why my mother expressly forbade me to play with Jim along the Crescent after one of the District Nurse's visits. Jim was a good lad and we regularly exchanged comics at the front door. After his diagnosis, he wasn't welcome at our front door any more. My mother ordered us to give him a wide berth.

'Keep to the other side of the street when you meet him. He's that dirty that if he stood against a wall, he'd stick to it.'

One lasting memory of the school health service giving a rare moment of pleasure occurred in the late 1950s, when there was an outbreak of impetigo, an acute inflammation of the skin, heralded by dramatic pustular eruptions. A form of scabies, it was noticeable because of yellow crusts that formed about the mouth. We were warned - ordered - to keep away from sufferers who were cured by a mild antiseptic ointment. Anyway, the entire school was warned about this ailment; we were all examined and thankfully, only a few were handed the Dreaded Letter. My own memory was that of a small boy who lived in our

247

# Lions and Donkeys (part 1)

street and who'd been diagnosed with impetigo; I recall him ring-a-rosying round a lamppost clutching a brown envelope and singing this:

'Impetigo, impetigo, I love you!'

He was overjoyed simply because he'd been ordered home and told not to return to school for several weeks or until the yellow crusts had vanished. He knew that he would miss the term exams - hence his jubilation.

Another figure of authority not connected with the school health service but working in tandem with it was the School Attendance Officer, a post set up by the Education (Scotland) Act 1872. He was feared by all and sundry, avoided at all costs. Of course, the best way to keep out of his clutches was not by *kipping off* as playing truant was then known - I believe the modern equivalent is *bunking off*. The School Attendance Officer was known to us kids as the Truant Catcher, who was called Mr Thom. Mr Thom was a thin, gaunt man who wouldn't have been out of place in a Charles Dickens novel or in one of the westerns featuring Clint Eastwood. We had no Eastwood to sort him out however; he had an aura of authority and standing that equated with the Poor Inspector and the local policemen or 'bobbies'. Mr Thom drove a strange little machine called a *Nira*, a motorcycle with three wheels, then he was equipped with a box-like Morris Minor which we christened the *Boneshaker*. We used to watch the *Boneshaker* cruising in the streets, not necessarily hunting down a truant but his or her parents to whom he would deliver a lecture and a *Brown Envelope* which contained a letter warning them that truancy was a breach of the law and as parents, they could be fined or end up in court. We used to wait till his car was leaving Lammermuir Crescent and the home of some terrified parent, shouting this rhyme:

*Thom, Thom, the truant man*
*Caught a kid when away he ran*

In 1951, I left Maggie Darling's class none the wiser than I had been at the beginning of that year but glad to be back in the bosom of the main school building at Woodbush. We renewed our acquaintance with its familiar smells - the fusty smell of damp books, pungent chalk dust, greasy wooden desks, rusty ink, damp wool and wet knickers, sweat, smelly feet and the inevitable consequences of random *poompings*. In the summer term, chalk dust got up your nose - literally - its peppery powder made us sneeze when the teacher beat it on the board. I used to while away fair chunks of summer afternoons watching the dust motes endlessly falling through sunbeams slanting across Miss Gunn's stuffy room until she caught me out and warned me I'd be severely punished for daydreaming. The windows were high, too high to look out of, so watching the dust motes was a popular diversion. Windows were there to let in light but they weren't supposed to be a source of distraction or entertainment. They were rarely opened even in swelteringly hot weather; it was difficult to keep awake on soporific summer days and many of us were belted because we lost concentration. Looking back, I am sure the seats attached to our desks were deliberately designed to be hard and uncomfortable so that they would keep us awake.

Miss Gunn was Maggie Darling's infinitely better-looking successor, though I found her distant. Jessie Gunn was quiet, retiring with dark eyes and good looks, a woman who kept herself to herself. I was fascinated by her but not in the way I'd had a 'crush' on Mai Intin of swagger coat fame. She was probably quite innocent, yet when I study old school photographs of our teachers, Jessie Gunn looks at the camera with a hint of devilry behind her demure gaze. She apparently led a quiet, ordinary life but somehow, even today, she makes me think of Shakespeare's Dark Lady. As I said earlier, she had been christened by the preceding generations of pupils, our elder brothers and sisters as 'Tommy'. She was yet another disciplinarian but she kept order in her class, rarely resorting to the use of the *tawse* ; she never belted me and no teacher had since Miss Tinning in 1947.

Miss Gunn's task - though we didn't know it then - was to prepare us for the final hurdle of the Qualifying year, when all the primary school teachers through whose hands we had passed would discover whether their individual contribution to our education had brought forth the desired fruits. It was left to Dowager Duchess Murray - I am not being sarcastic here, as Miss Murray was a great and kind lady - to take us over the last fence, exhorting us to Do Our Best. She was my favourite primary school teacher, even if she belted me six times for some misdemeanour I've forgotten. She was the second - and last - teacher to resort to use physical punishment on me, but I never held it against her.

I detested most of the subjects taught in primary school, especially written arithmetic and to a greater extent, mental arithmetic, although I must confess that today, I can work out percentages and add up faster than the check-out girls in the supermarkets. But written arithmetic was a mystery to me; I contracted gut-ache from trying to understand why anyone would want to find out how long it would take two men to fill two baths of equal capacity running the water at different volumes. Who cared? And who would want to know the difference in arrival times between a train travelling at 50 miles an hour between London and Glasgow and another travelling at 60 miles an hour between London and Edinburgh? Maybe one day, this will give my life some meaning but so far it hasn't.

Another refinement of this kind of torture was to calculate how many telegraph poles existed within a mile of rail track, given the distance between each pole. There was also a classic sum - that of two men digging a hole in eight hours and the time taken by three men to dig the same hole. The logical answer is that the second lot of three men were wasting their time; looked at in another way however, the answer would have concentrated the time-and-motion staff of organisations like the Gas Board or the Electricity Board. It should have been easy, since three men should be able to dig the hole in less time than two. But you never know.  I would ask myself pointless questions about the other obvious consideration ie that two industrious men can work faster than three lazy ones.  That wasn't relevant to the test however; the person who devised such fiendish challenges to young minds - obviously a Socialist  - had assumed that all men digging holes are equal, working at equal capacity.

I was poor at such sums because they bored and irked me.  I wasn't interested in train journeys, telegraph poles or holes.  Even History was a bore. It seemed to be all about somebody called Harold who got something nasty in his eye at Hastings, the size of William Wallace's sword and how many times Bruce's spider launched itself between the walls of a cave to make its web. There was also a story about a king called Canute who got his feet wet trying to stop the tide coming in - a stupid exercise, as any Dunbar boy or girl could have told him. As for Geography, it was little more than a cracked old map coloured in pink or red to show the British - English - Empire on which the Sun Never Set, which incidentally was run by Scotsmen.  In winter, that dilapidated map hanging on the wall reflected many sunsets on its greasy surface.  I struggled to understand baffling terms like *Mercator's Projection.*( A modern child would ask who was Mercator and what did he project?  The streetwise minds of today would automatically turn towards thoughts of a sexual nature...............).

At the tender age of ten, I was bewildered by the following:
*My chains fell off; my heart was free.*
*I rose, went forth and followed Thee*
It sounded like the desperate chant of those wishing to leave school at the earliest opportunity, like my brother Norman who reached the age of fourteen on 30th March 1947, just before they raised the school leaving age to fifteen.

At about this time - 1952 - we were subjected to the less than illuminating experience of graduating from slate boards and slate pencils to lead pencils, then the ultimate - the school pen.  This should have been a major breakthrough after the awful slates but we hadn't been warned of the pitfalls.  In one of the primary school classes, we'd moved from slate to lead pencils, with which I felt relatively comfortable.  Now we were told that slate pencils were for babies and lead pencils for juveniles; the real test of character and progress was to write with a *Pen*. A school pen with a nib.  These consisted of wooden holders with a metal sleeve into which the nib was inserted.  The nibs were cheap, of poor quality and they invariably split when any undue pressure was exerted, the parts going in different directions if you were heavy-handed, like me. The result was a Blot.  I once thought that it would be easier with a seagull's feather and I tried that.  It was a vast improvement and for a time, I thought I was Shakespeare, engravings of whom always showed him with a bird's feather. The only problem was that a seagull feather only lasted for a few hours.  I thought that Shakespeare was a genius, with an endless supply of gull feathers though he lived inland.  When we wrote with our school pens, blots occurred and marks were deducted for untidiness.

The day began with the filling of the porcelain inkwells fitted into our desk lids. The ink came from a large bottle kept in the teacher's cupboard. Some toady was selected for this daily task. The ink was watery and smelt of rust. I used to wonder if the school authorities were in contract with *Mattie Bile* - Matthew Boyle - the local chimney sweep. Did he meet the headmaster at night with a bag of soot from chimneys he'd swept? Did money change hands? Did the headmaster add water and some other ingredient to the sooty powder to transform it into ink? This may not be entire fantasy.

At any rate, first thing in the morning, we examined our nibs and if they were broken or damaged we would ask for a new one - at least that was something recognised by our teachers for they must have known how inferior the nibs were. However, if you asked for more than one a week, you were disciplined for being profligate with School Property. The steel pen was meant to encourage you to develop a neat hand and therefore strength of character. I never mastered the art of using the steel pen because you had to write slowly and I couldn't wait to get it all down on the blank pages we were given. The result was that then and now, no one was able to read my handwriting; it wasn't helped in secondary school where I took German in 1957, the German script being Gothic then and making my handwriting shrink to beetle size to avoid the censure of my teacher who said I didn't write fast enough. I have to admit that my exercise books suffered from inky deletions, blots and smears and so I was given low marks for writing. I earned them. My work was neither neat nor legible; the inventor of the Biro would make things worse in my working life. With a biro, I could write faster without the consequential blots, so my illegible hand increased in direct proportion to the speed with which I wrote. Now *that's* a practical example of applied arithmetic. (Incidentally, in my whole life, I have survived without the need of Napier's Logarithms, nor have I found the isosceles triangle, with its two equal sides, particularly vital to my career, nor indeed has the parallelogram, a quadrilateral whose opposite sides are parallel enlightened me. And as for algebraic equations, who needs them?

Teaching by intimidation was the favoured method employed by most of our teachers. I hated the misery of Arithmetic and Mathematics, the confusion of biology that became science - I still don't know what turns litmus paper blue, but then I don't really care. I hated the boredom of Geography and didn't feel in the least challenged that I had no idea what the average or mean rainfall of Outer Mongolia happened to be then - or today. There was never any danger of my becoming practical and that has persisted until today. Thank god.

In some ways, primary school was worse than secondary. I think the philosophy was that primary school was meant to train your mind to think and react in certain ways. To master the art of mental arithmetic was prized above all else. Some of the primary teachers were sadists by nature, others through experience, still more in the interests of survival. Many a hulking *Shorie* from the Harbour or farm lad was reduced to humbled submission, if not to tears. These teachers harassed generations of children with meaningless tasks and tests aimed at breaking the spirit and introducing into formative minds a measure of self-discipline. Now there is nothing wrong with that - the modern generation could benefit greatly from a good dose of it, but in looking back now, what was absent from those formative years was simply that we weren't taught to think for ourselves. Everything was pre-ordained, innovation wasn't tolerated. As John Muir famously put it, we were driven at our books and taught to parrot-learn their contents. All very well if your ambition is to be a parrot in life.

Robert Macaulay, our headmaster until the arrival of Hugh Cowan in 1953, was a great believer in patriots and polished shoes. A First World War veteran who had been badly gassed, he didn't enjoy good health but he was a stickler for discipline. His infrequent appearances at primary school classes invariably meant a lecture on boot and shoe polishing; he impressed upon us the need to have shining footwear, which surely had its roots in his military training. There was more than a dash of a testy, Victorian schoolmaster in Robert Macaulay.

In those days, all paths led not to Rome but to the Qualifying Exam or *Qualie*. The level of attainment and success in that crucial examination determined the type of higher school education you would embark on for at least three years, five if your parents agreed to let you 'stay on'. Going to school the first day of the *Qualie* Exam - it went on for two days - like so many others, I was apprehensive and nervous. I was scared stiff, afraid I'd make a botch of it and end up in the C stream - woodwork and technical drawing, subjects for which I had absolutely no aptitude for or interest in. I had hopes of the B or A categories; an A meant you would take Latin and French, French only in the B stream. That soft, spring morning, I dragged myself wearily along the roads, avoiding the cracks in the paving stones in the same way that Dr Samuel Johnson, equally apprehensive about something or other, would walk along Fleet Street, touching every post he encountered for luck. Miss Murray, our teacher gave no impression of anxiety or complacency. Well, she wouldn't would she? *She* wasn't taking the bloody exam. That fateful day, she smiled at each of us as we trooped into the classroom. Time and time again, she'd warned us that the Big Day was nigh. She was an excellent teacher, hand-picked I am sure for the task. She never let up until the very last minute, gave us plenty of warning when she thought some of us were slipping back. She never let up or gave up on a single child, not even the hopeless cases.

That dreaded morning, the exam papers were brought in at about 9.15am. We had used the first fifteen minutes to check our pens, make sure our inkwells were full. We had a short talk from Mr Macaulay, who blessed the venture almost in the manner of a Roman Catholic priest and urged us TO GIVE OF YOUR BEST.

# Lions and Donkeys (part 1)

Then at precisely 9.30am, the invigilator gave the command.

' Turn your papers over.'

The rest of that day and the next remain blurred in my memory. At first, I stared in panic at the questions, then suddenly I saw one I could answer. I felt a bit better. Silence reigned, broken only by the ticking of the large clock on the wall and the occasional nervous cough. All you could hear was the scratch of about 35 pens, the dipping of them into porcelain inkwells, an occasional groan and even the odd fart or two. Nerves. I was amazed to see my pen race over the blank pages where I wrote down my answers. To my surprise and relief, I was able to answer most of the questions, even those that had to be answered in a specified space of time.

Then incredibly and suddenly, the ordeal was over. When the last paper and our answers were collected, we leant back at our desks. All of us I am sure felt emotionally drained. Dog-tired from the strain, I slept long and late the night afterwards. We had to wait until June for the results that would determine our future education.

Before the results, we had the pleasant distraction of a day's holiday for the Queen's Coronation on the second day of June 1953. A few days before this event, I recall a large crate appearing in the classroom; it was prised open by Mr Blair, our kindly janitor who withdrew from the straw padding several Coronation Mugs, which were duly distributed to us. On the day itself, we had sports for which prizes were awarded for first, second and third places. These were vouchers to be exchanged for sweets - still on ration after the war. I won two third prizes for the sack race and the three-legged race; the vouchers were worth sixpence each, so as I mentioned earlier, I squandered the shilling [5p] on a quarter pound of *soor plooms,* rhubarb rock and brandy balls. The girl prizewinners invariably went for what were called *conversation lozenges,* these were of different sizes and shapes, with various flavours. They were popular with the lassies because they bore little inscriptions on them saying 'I love you' or 'You are my sweetheart.' (I seem to remember getting one once from my good friend Betty Jeffrey; I can't remember what the message was but I do remember it tasted of cinnamon, which I liked). The sports were held in the morning, so we were free to spend the afternoon as we pleased.

There were few TVs around in Britain, let alone in Scotland, in those days. My mother provided digs for two of the engineers who installed the booster pylon at Black Castle, one called Rab Foote whom I think she loved, the other with the bizarre (to me) name of Jimmy Truelove. (If you are out there lads, thanks for the memories). I think Lammermuir Crescent contained fewer than six TV sets - miniscule boxes like wirelesses but with a small screen. I was lucky to live next door to the Harkess family who had bought a set. Along with about a dozen other kids from the neighbourhood, I was treated to a view of the Coronation as it took place in Westminster Abbey, with all the pomp and splendour which 50 years ago, was simply awe-inspiring. I couldn't

# Lions and Donkeys (part 1)

believe they'd invented a machine which showed you pictures in your own living room. Not quite as grand as the cinema, but wonderful all the same. The kids sat cross-legged and mesmerised in the Harkess' small living room, glued to the miniscule screen encased in a heavy, overlarge wooden cabinet which seemed to me to have little steps or stairs leading to the screen. I think the screen was about eight inches wide - possibly less - but that didn't matter. Auntie Ann and Uncle John were attentive hosts, feeding us buns from John's shop at Belhaven. We were seeing our first pictures on TV which is nowadays taken for granted in every household. It was a memorable and lovely day with only one cloud on our young horizons. The results of the *Qualie*.

I have to pause here and make a confession. It was in summer 1953 that I 'got' religion. Not the orthodox variety. It was never that simple for me, nor could I take in the bits that clearly were questionable, if not downright silly in my eyes. The Church never managed to obscure my inner landscape with its sombre, heavy shadow. Nor did it shake my belief that the world does not owe its existence to what for me is an imaginary being. Put simply, I couldn't accept the incomprehensible spiritual algebra. And as for an after-life, well, human experience adequately illustrates proof that there isn't one. If I had any religion, I should call it pantheism today - a belief in the force of nature which of course lacks - or needs - any human attributes to make it work. Accepting these conclusions meant I saw no point in prayer or hymn since they were addressed to nobody. The stern, stuffy and faintly ridiculous Scottish god had - and never will have - any appeal for me. At funerals, I switch off when the commercial comes on; I attend these occasions to pay my respect to the recently departed, to honour their memory and the happiness they brought me. I cannot abide ministers who barely touch on the human personality and his or her achievements and character, simply regurgitating the Auld Sang from the Bible and 'praising the Lord'. Has no one had the courage to tell them that we don't want to hear about some mythical creature that may never have existed, or was at best an ordinary man; we want to hear about our friend?

I joined the short-lived Covenanters, then the Lifeboys. These were my first and only attempts at what today would be called bonding; I had hoped to find my inner light from them but I left both organisations because the light just wasn't there. The light I craved for was in myself. That may sound arrogant but I knew I had strong feelings, emotions and I was trying hard to find some way of expressing them. Naturally, I had first looked to the church to enlighten me. I hoped I would find what I was looking for there but I didn't. The Scottish Church became a symbol of oppression. I was made to go to Sunday school because my mother said I should; next, I went to the Young Communicants or Bible Class, stolidly supervised by the muscular Christianity of Sandy Dudgeon of Belhaven Brewery fame. He didn't convince me of anything except that he was there to teach us the rudiments of Christianity which I couldn't relate to my own life. Not his fault, mine. When we were being prepared for membership of Belhaven Church, I found I couldn't recite the Creed. You had to say you believed in the Father, the Son and the Holy Ghost, the Trinity of three-in-one. I couldn't get my head round that. What is worse is that I told the minister, the Reverend John Stein McMartin.

'You are a wilful, stubborn boy' was all he said on the first occasion. At the next confrontation, he came out with this:

'Why can't you accept the Athenian Creed like the other boys and girls? They don't have a problem. Do you think you are special, different from them? If you do, you are a wilful, arrogant young man.'

How could I accept something I just didn't understand, let alone believe in? I had problems with the Lord's Prayer too. Why should we ask him not to lead us into temptation? Why would he do such a thing? I think the biggest influence on my life at that time was my Uncle Jimmy, who often lectured me on sin; he used to say that we were punished *by* our sins, not for them. Church was also an acutely embarrassing place for me; with my surname, there was always some kid who would comment on my being a church seat. The kid would invariably pronounce the word scornfully. I was often called 'Church seat' in the playground - yet another boring example of what passed as humour in those days.

I was mildly anarchic even in Sunday school, which I was forced to attend and therefore hated. I used to sing different words to the hymns - usually derogative words. The famous one was 'Jesus' bits [boots instead of bids] are shining with a pure, clear light/like a little candle in the night'; another favourite ploy was to slip in the Lord's Prayer the bit about 'Hallo' instead of 'hallowed' being his name. I liked Molly Gray, my teacher, a gentle, nervous soul. One Sunday, she told us about the Firmament and the constellations of stars and how they got their names; the fishermen's children were particularly knowledgeable about these for obvious reasons. We knew about the Seven Sisters, the Plough and the Pole Star; one day, Molly asked us if we'd heard of the Aurora Borealis and what it was. Silence. Then a small lad shot up his hand:

Pleemiss, pleemiss, Ah ken. It's they lights in the sky ye can see frae Abirdeen'.

When I graduated to the Bible Class, I had terrible problems with the Athenian Creed as I mentioned earlier; this meant extra tuition on Wednesday nights at the Manse. The long-suffering minister tried to drum it all into me. I still couldn't accept the words. In exasperation, his temper broke and he ordered me to say the words like any other normal boy or girl.

'Are you going to shame your poor mother on the night? For that's what you will be doing. You do realise that if you can't say the words, you will be denied the right and comfort of taking Communion - not to mention eternal damnation as you will be refused entry into Heaven? You can only gain that by becoming a member of the true Church of God.'

# Lions and Donkeys (part 1)

It didn't work on me, that kind of blackmail. It only made me more stubborn. I think at that point, the church finally failed me. I saw it for what it was - an institution which demanded blind acceptance, blinder obedience. To be fair to John Stein McMartin, I think he considered me too immature - or stupid - to realise the importance of the ritual, believing what he did. He saw me as a young boy putting my soul in jeopardy and he wasn't going to let that happen. Little did he know I was wrestling with a strong impulse and belief - or lack of it - which would develop later. I believed in the soul then and do now, I just didn't believe in the phoney, preposterous propaganda that passes as religion. In later life, I would agree with the Scottish philosopher David Hume who said that those who followed a religion were only indulging the dreams of sick men.

On the night, I said the words, much to McMartin's relief and my mother's, although I stumbled when it came to the bit about the Holy Trinity. It may have seemed that I was being defiant, deliberately trying to upset minister and parent but I was - still am - genuinely and honestly atheistic. To me, the church and the school were hand-in-glove and the school confused me at times. My logic being what it was then, I decided I should beat them at their own game. I became a Sunday school teacher, which earned me praise from the very man I seemed to be trying to thwart. It was a big mistake on my part - and his.

The year 1955 saw the advent of a film which was very popular - Walt Disney's *Davy Crockett, King of the Wild Frontier,* Fess Parker playing the eponymous hero. Crockett hats - racoon-skins with tails that hung down your back were all the rage that year. One Sunday, I was telling my five-year-old charges that God was everywhere and in everyone. One little chap ventured to ask if that included his hero, Davy Crockett. I said of course it did. The next Sunday, the entire class came to Sunday school wearing their Crockett hats. I was asked to stay behind by the minister.

'Please do not tell them such things. They are young and impression able. Your job is to teach them about Christ, not Davy Crockett.'
I weakly argued my case. I said they might understand the difficult personality of Jesus better if they could focus on a figure they loved and worshipped.

'I warn you. I won't tolerate your crack-brained theories in my church. It shall end. Now.'

A few Sundays later, a small boy came to me sniffling. When I asked what was the matter, he said his budgie had just died. I tried to console him by saying wee Joey was in Heaven and so he was happy.

'So Joey's wi' Jesus?'
I said of course he was. Where else? I reminded him of the vets' hymn about all creatures great and small. This brought a rash of questions about deceased dogs, cats, goldfish and even a pet frog. I gave every child the same reassurance. Then one little lad said this:

'I saw a deid robin in the road. Has he gone tae Heaven as well ?'

# Lions and Donkeys (part 1)

Of course he had. A robin was one of God's creatures too, even if he wasn't anybody's pet. The following Sunday, I was asked to stay behind by the minister.

'I hear you've been telling your class that their dead pets are in Heaven. You clearly have no knowledge of the Bible. The birds of the air, the beasts of the field, the fish in the seas were put here for man's use and pleasure. They do not have souls. They live their lives, then they die and are put into the earth. They serve man, who is God's creation, made in His image. If you persist in telling the children such things, filling their heads with such nonsense, I'm afraid I must terminate your posi tion as a Sunday school teacher. You are a heretic and I cannot have you in God's house'

A heretic? I had to look up the word in my dictionary. To my horror, I discovered that a heretic who practised heresy meant devil worship. I was shocked. The following Sunday, I attended the kirk only to inform the minister I was leaving it. I told that benighted man I didn't want to go to a Heaven where there was no birdsong, no animals to brighten my afterlife. I turned my back on the church that day and have remained an atheist ever since.

To my mind, religion is debased poetry. Poetry is vision, expressed in a unique way, straight from the heart - or soul. Poetry attempts to express what the heart knows isn't illusion. The best poetry achieves that. It doesn't moral-ise, it doesn't enforce religious teaching, though often it is religious in its es-sence and may even inspired by religion. What is wanting in religion is best expressed through poetry, which doesn't preach at us. It has always consoled me more than religious belief or propaganda. Jock the Wild Man - a Catholic by birth if not persuasion - summed it up for me. He once said that his lot in Rome and in Scotland were 'a bunch of feggin eejits'. I am constantly irritated and even annoyed by some churchmen of whatever denomination who insist they have the Answer. Those who officiate at funerals are invariably disap-pointing propagandists; few of them are honest enough to admit they didn't know the deceased. I pray and hope that the person who says the last words over me will be a friend who knew and loved me in my life. When the talk turns to religion and the after-life, I have learnt to say 'Pass'. I think in retro-spect the Reverend McMartin was a better historian than 'sky pilot' as my Uncle Jimmy called him to his face. At least J S McMartin had the guts to say to my mother near the end of his life that maybe I was right, for he had asked about me, had remembered the dilemma I was in all those years ago. Perhaps his own faith had been tested and found wanting.

In 1953, a New Zealand beekeeper called Edmund Hillary and a Nepa-lese Sherpa called Tensing were the first to conquer Mount Everest, thus giv-ing the Queen an added gift at her Coronation. (A year later, Roger Bannister, a medical practitioner from Oxford University ran a mile in under four min-utes. I can't be certain but the *Goons* probably made good copy out of his

# Lions and Donkeys (part 1)

name through Eccles

'Spotty Minnie Bannister did a four minute mile! No wonder I didn't see her on the stairs!'

Coronation Day, 2nd June 1953 was an almost feudal ceremonial event with a touch of Hollywood thrown in. In that year, about two million people in Britain owned TV sets although ten times that number watched the spectacle, courtesy of kind and sharing neighbours; in my case it was the Harkess family next door. The BBC gave it lavish coverage and the national anthem was sung, bringing TV-owning people and their guests to their feet in their own living rooms; well, we did in No 77 Lammermuir Crescent. TV was here to stay. In 1955, the Conservative Prime Minister Winston Churchill - a grand old man as far as my household was concerned - retired from political life; he was replaced by Anthony Eden, handsome, gentlemanly and moderate. In that year, 17 million watched the General Election on TV although about only 5 million people had licensed TV sets. That election was the first to be televised, a fact which went unnoticed in our house as we didn't get a set until 1957. Far more people saw the Queen on TV at Christmas 1957, when she delivered the first of her Christmas messages from Sandringham.

The summer of 1953 was the longest ever - well, at least the month of June was, waiting for the results of the Qualifying Exam. To relieve our restless anxiety, Miss Murray took us on what would today be called a field trip. She knew the tension was reaching breaking point and perhaps discipline was beginning to crumble. One day - a Friday - she announced she was taking us out that afternoon on a nature study walk in Lochend Wood. She must have arranged the walk with the gamekeeper who was known as Wullie - hence his woods being called *Wullie's Wud* [wood]. It was an area where signs informed us it was Strictly Private and that Trespassers Would Be Prosecuted, notices we obeyed to the letter as we vaguely knew a great and powerful family owned the property. Hardly an adventurous or remotely epic trek, at least it took us away from our desks for an afternoon.

Miss Murray announced that she would award a prize of a bag of sweets to the pupil who named the most flowers. I will never forget that misty, June day. As we struggled through the dense undergrowth, we suddenly came across a ruined house in a clearing. Miss Murray said it had been once a prestigious place, home of Sir George Warrender and his forebears until it had been burnt to the ground two centuries before.

'It was a gypsy curse, children. The Warrender family built a second house but it also burnt down. The curse warned the Warrenders that three of their houses at Lochend would be burnt, so the family took no chances after the second fire. They moved back to Edinburgh, from whence they had come.'

Since that day, I have researched the site, spoken with David Lunam who lived in *Lochend Cottage* with his father and grandfather who worked the

# Lions and Donkeys (part 1)

estate; David told me about the fires. I swear that on that misty June day in 1953, I could smell burnt wood in the ruin, but that may have been a recent fire, or my fertile imagination. I called it the *Burnt Hoose* but couldn't go back to see it until a few years ago, when the estate was developed and given over to private housing. After that school trip, I went to *Penney* the Newsagents - now the Bank of Scotland - to buy a comic I was fond of in those far off days - *Black Magic* - which was filled with tales of the unusual and ghost stories. That night, I read it in bed, looking out of my bedroom window to Doon Hill, from where a thick mist was descending on Dunbar. It was an appropriate setting, atmospheric, spooky.

At last, the exam results came. I got an A and was over the moon because not only had I achieved what I'd yearned for, it meant I'd only have to endure one period of woodwork a week. I was proud of my achievement, as was my mother. She took me to Greco's *Ice Cream Parlour*, where I was treated to a *Knickerbocker Glory, la creme de les cremes glacees* in those days. It was a concoction of the famous Greco ice cream and tinned fruit, layered and served in a schooner glass, the pile topped with a cherry. It was the most expensive item on the menu, costing about two shillings and sixpence [about 13p today]. But in the midst of all this enjoyment and the school holidays, I knew that the serious schoolwork would begin in earnest only two months later. But two months is a long time in a child's life....

An additional reward was the school camp at Abingdon, which I described in Chapter 7. I met several co-scholars there, boys and girls who miraculously turned up in August 1953 - kids I had thought I'd never see again. Wasn't bureaucracy marvellous? Of course, they came from places like Innerwick, Cockburnspath, Oldhamstocks, parts of the world of which I knew nothing, even if I knew of their existence.

I note from the publication *From Slate to Disk,* the centenary of Dunbar Schools from 1897 to 1997, there is an item which celebrates the end of the summer term of 1953 in the form of a physical education display in which I played a part. The item appeared on the programme as *Health Through Joy,* a gymnastic display staged by Primary 7; I was press-ganged into the team. For about ten minutes in the Parish Church Hall, six boys and six girls cart-wheeled and cavorted across the stage in criss-cross patterns which required accurate timing but was decidedly amateur fare. Then we did handstands and leapt over the wooden horse, finishing with a flourish of something or other - all this executed by twelve youngsters kitted out in white shirts/blouses and navy blue gym shorts. I recall only one team member, my good friend Deanna Combe, who joined the Civil Service in 1958; I never met Deanna again until 1994, when we had a school reunion. I was sad to learn that she died in October 2003.

Years later, I was slightly nervous about the title of that display when I recalled it. *Health Through Joy* is somewhat sinister; since those innocent

# Lions and Donkeys (part 1)

days, I have read much about the Nazi concentration camps at Belsen, Auchswitz, Sobibor and Buchenwald, camps whose gates bore the motto *Arbeit Macht Frei* - Work Makes You Free.  Of course I didn't think anything of that sort at the time, but now....

# 11

## Lions and Donkeys

## (Part 2)

When we resumed school – the upper school - in August 1953, I was amazed to see my friends from the summer camp - Iain Cornes from Whittingehame, John Douglas from East Barns - and the lovely, Blessed Damozel from Pinkerton, Lady Gladys. I couldn't get near her, she was so much in demand. But John Douglas, a sombre, serious lad who was too old for his young years became a fairly firm friend while he was at Dunbar, which wasn't for long. I recall going to visit him at East Barns school, where his father was headmaster. It must have been a Saturday afternoon because the classrooms were empty. Walking through one, John saw something lying in a corner of the room. He bent down, picked it up and showed it to me without the least hint of shame, holding it between finger and thumb of his right hand. This is what he said to me:
'Oh dear. Here's a contraceptive. I had better put it into the waste basket or else the cleaner will get upset.'

I hadn't much of a clue as to what contraceptives actually *were*. They were a mystery to me. They were things you found at the tide's edge, on the beach. They contained a milky fluid and somehow, I knew they were evidence that Something Not Quite Right had been going on. Schoolboys better informed than I was called them *French Letters* or FLs. Some boys used to fill them with seawater and use them as bombs or hand grenades - remember, in those days the Second World War wasn't yet a folk memory. More than one innocent young lad tried to blow them up, thinking they were some kind of balloon....

My first year in secondary school coincided with the retirement of our doughty headmaster, Robert Macaulay who, despite rapidly failing health, managed to make Coronation Day Sports before he faded into the sunset. Not all of us were sorry to see him leave Dunbar Grammar. A fair but firm believer in discipline, he made little differences between teachers and pupils. If a teacher stepped out of line, he - or more usually she - was severely reprimanded. Excessive use of the *tawse* was frowned upon, although he laid it on with the best of them. Being of the old school and a veteran of the Great War, he clung to the old ways, believing that discipline and the Three Rs – 'Riting, 'Rithmetic and Reading were what education was all about. Perhaps in many ways he was right.

# Lions and Donkeys ( part 2)

One thing that sticks in my memory was the order to cover our schoolbooks with brown wrapping paper to keep them clean, which was a bit like shutting the gate after the proverbial horse had bolted. No matter, we were biddable in those days. I and my co-students complied; some of the really poor kids couldn't run to brown paper - unbelievable today - and came to school with their precious books wrapped - if at all - in cheap, garish wallpaper. The kids today will find that hard to swallow, but in 1953, there still wasn't much money around for luxuries and goods were still on the ration after the war.

Mr Macaulay's replacement, Hugh Cowan, was also a military man with a strong sense of justice heavily larded with discipline. They sometimes sit well together. Grammar schools were then considered elitist, with the emphasis being on academic subjects. Hughie Cowan believed in developing his scholars' skills - social as well as academic. He it was who introduced the wearing of gowns among the teaching staff although I think he was alone in the adoption of the mortar board s headgear, making him appear to us as the hard-pressed teacher in *The Bash Street Kids* of the *Beano*. Being a Borderer, he also introduced rugby football to a school that had been staunchly soccer-oriented for generations. After some initial resistance to playing with a funny shaped ball, the local sports' enthusiasts gave in to his weird ways. At the same time, it was suggested that the secondary school should adopt its formal title of Dunbar Grammar School by which name it had been known as early as the sixteenth century. Dunbar schools go back to the Reformation and, as we have already seen, several local *dominies* or schoolmasters compiled Latin grammars adopted throughout Scotland in the seventeenth century.

Hugh Cowan also insisted that the upper school wore uniforms. The school uniform was similar in design to that of Daniel Stewart's in Edinburgh - smart black blazers edged with red piping for both sexes, red and black striped ties worn with white blouses (girls) and grey shirts (boys); the girls were also expected to wear grey skirts, the boys long grey flannel trousers. After initial grumbling and mutterings from impecunious parents on the grounds of cost, the uniform was introduced and worn by most students. But T, my friend of those days, affected to wear unorthodox gear, as I did. By Fourth Year, T favoured a dog-tooth sports jacket and thick-soled shoes known as brothel-creepers, while I wore ex-Army gear provided by my father - long yellow gauntlet gloves issued to despatch riders, black jeans and a windproof despatch rider jacket with a fur collar. We were ostracised for that. Neither of us cared; the clothes we wore were a badge of individuality, of freedom..

Hugh Cowan also gave John (Jack) Milne, our colourful Latin teacher the task of devising a school motto. Jack came up with a beauty. From 1953, the school motto was inscribed in Latin; it was a stroke of genius. *Non Sine Pulvere Palma* was freely translated to mean 'No prize can be won without effort'. Changes were in the air and we all knew they were here to stay. Hughie Cowan made sure of it.

# Lions and Donkeys (part 2)

Even without these innovations, progression from primary to secondary school was a major shock to the system. For me, in one respect, it was a happy transition if only because I encountered J I W Milne who was a friend until his death. Jack Milne could have taught in one of the Merchant schools in Edinburgh; he chose Dunbar, which was fortunate for several generations of pupils. However, that apart, the most noticeable change was that instead of having one teacher for all subjects, we had a different teacher for individual subjects. That was an immediate and major improvement for me, because you were fairly certain that at least some of your teachers might even like you. Teachers in upper school became 'them' and we remained - smugly - 'us'.

On the first day of the autumn term of 1953, First Year boys were 'dumped' by the older boys - much in the same way as 'dumps' or thumps on the back were doled out on birthdays. On that unforgettable day, all of us from the Qualifying class were graded like eggs into the various streams - A, B, C and D. My class, S1L contained only sixteen scholars; the number never went higher than seventeen and by the time we reached Third Year, or S3L, our class had reduced to eleven. As a consequence, we were an easily managed class.

The A stream was taught Latin and French in addition to English, History, Geography, Maths, Science and Music - all of which were tested every term. The B stream took French with another compensating subject like technical drawing to make up for their lack of Latin. The C and D streams were exclusive to boys and girls respectively, the boys being taught practical skills like woodwork, metalwork and technical drawing, the girls having Domestic Science. The theory of this was that the A stream would become academics or administrators - Civil Servants, Bank clerks and insurance agents; the B scholars were destined for engineering and the C and D scholars would adopt work as tradesmen and shop assistants. Well, that was the theory. My great friend Graeme Cunningham was a C pupil who went on to become director of several large companies and who had his own chauffeur-driven car and private jet until his death in 2003. At Dunbar Grammar, serious attempts were made to sharpen the dullest wits, passions were kindled, humour (in acceptable doses) inspired; the last was important because it counterbalanced the sombre, Presbyterian shadow that was never far away, even if officially, it didn't exist. I instantly took to Jack Milne in my First Year because in addition to teaching us Latin, he was our Form Master and responsible for our welfare and moral rectitude, which obliged him to teach us Religious Instruction. At the first RI period, he formally announced to the sixteen of us that he'd no intention of doing the Church's work for it and that he'd teach us Roman History or read us ghost stories, the latter being particularly entertaining on dark, winter Friday afternoons.

Johnnie, or as he was better known to me, Jack - and *Penguin* to all of us because of his curious walk which resembled that of the comical little bird - had a highly developed and intelligent sense of humour. There were some who

# Lions and Donkeys ( part 2)

turned up their noses at him - the girls especially - because he was fond of the blessed Guinness and smoked Woodbine cigarettes at break times. I never found him anything other than congenial, only occasionally out of sorts when some dim idiot tried to best him, or when some thought he was suffering from a hangover or at least excessive indulgence. From the outset, he made us - and me in particular - feel more grown-up; he treated us as individuals and not snotty-nosed little kids. He set the pattern that first day by informing us that his initials stood for John Ignatius Winterbottom, which I know was a bit of leg-pulling. (Some today think that the initials stood for John Irvine Wallace, which has a ring of truth about it). We called him *Penguin* because he walked slowly, purposefully, with his arms stiff and slightly apart from his sides. Looking back with the hindsight and knowledge I didn't have then, he reminds me of the brilliant poet Philip Larkin, whose poetry I am sure Jack Milne would have enjoyed. ('They f*** you up, your Mum and Dad').

One of my earliest and fondest memories of J I W Milne was his obvious eccentricity; in what was a lacklustre class at first, he ended a lesson in First Year by throwing a blackboard duster - his favourite weapon against lesser spirits whose attention flagged - by saying this:

'If I can keep awake during your lessons, will you at least attempt
to repay the compliment?'

Jack Milne's poky little classroom was situated to the right of the school entrance in the quadrangle, next door to the headmaster's study. This didn't in the least deter him from moments of buffoonery, when the entire class would be convulsed with laughter at his antics and his wittily erudite observations. I am sure he was ahead of his time, knowing full well that all work and no play makes us dull people. He didn't care about the stuffy aspects of life and I am sure he must have had many run-ins with the conservative and distant Hugh Cowan.

On that confusing first day in secondary school, he distributed our timetables that identified the subjects and the periods of study, showing the teachers we would have for Maths, English, History and the rest. Some of these produced audible groans. Jack would beam at us and say we would love so-and-so but that we should be careful of this one or that, although we'd already been warned by older brothers and sisters of those they called buggers - which meant they were disciplinarians who used the belt. That day, Jack left us in no doubt that he was a happy atheist. There was more than a little of the actor in him which he indulged by encouraging us to take part in one-act plays he staged in the Corn Exchange during the winter; I was one of his enthusiastic young thespians and I have never forgotten the joy that a successful play brought to him. His eyes really did twinkle behind his spectacles and he would purposefully and deliberately ruffle the hair which only grew on the sides of his head as he yelled out ' Waaaaaaaah!' when a play had been well attended and applauded at the end.

# Lions and Donkeys (part 2)

I make no apologies for this accolade. I loved the man. He was a great and demonstrative *raconteur* who enlivened many a gloomy winter afternoon with his ghost stories and tales of horror. As to his approach to religion - or his lack of it - his favourite story was that of a bishop visiting his young niece. The little girl sat on her uncle's knee as he read an illustrated children's bible to her. One picture showed the early Christians being thrown to the lions in Nero's Colosseum. The child began to sniffle, then she burst into tears. Touched by her concern, the bishop asked if she were crying because of the fate of the poor Christians. Between sobs, she pointed to a lion and replied thus:

'No. There's a poor lion that hasn't got a Christian!'

I like to think the story has a ring of truth. It was typical of Jack Milne's extensive and varied repertoire. Years later, when my friend TJ and I had opened *The Doone Art Gallery* in Lauderdale House, we invited local dignitaries, councillors, ministers and schoolteachers to a private showing at Christmas 1965; naturally, Jack Milne was at the head of our list. That cold night, he came in, congratulated us on our efforts and watched the ministers and Catholic priest walking round in a group, admiring - or making a pretence of doing so - some of the paintings, especially the one or two nude studies on display. He drew back, caught my arm and whispered in my ear:

'Black crows. I detest them and their mumbo-jumbo.'

I think like me, in some way he'd been soured by the church in some way in his native Aberdeen. Perhaps we had more in common than I knew then. I shall never forget the gentle, intelligent anarchy of that lovely man....

After dishing out the timetables, he sent us of to our first class. We moved from one classroom and teacher to the next; the pile of textbooks grew and grew as the day wore on. We were advised - ordered really - to cover our books with stout brown paper and to write our names in the flyleaf, identifying our class. We added to the names of our illustrious antecedents; I still possess a copy of *A Common History of Britain From 1714 to 1939* by Robert M Rayner (first printed in 1916 and obviously revised). In the fly-leaf are legendary names like John Edmonds (Session 1947-48), Gordon Good (Session 1948-49) and other locals like Barbara Callow, George Tait, John Huggan- did he become the controversial golf pro at Dunbar Golf Club?- and Alan Purves. I seem to have defied authority even then, as my name was never entered into the flyleaf of my copy, possibly because I intended to make my mark by drawing a cartoon in it. And so I did. In the flyleaf is a silly cartoon creature I invented called a *Trephontis,* a character remarkably like a later creation called a *Smurf.* An earlier hand had decorated the subsequent page of the same book with a caricature of the boxer Joe Louis for some reason best known to himself.

One of the few lasting memories I have of the old school is its labyrinthine corridors with their stone floors containing mica schist, making them sparkle like frost even in high summer. There was also a romanticised print of

265

# Lions and Donkeys ( part 2)

John Travers Cornwall hanging outside the English room occupied by Miss MacDonald, or Maggie Meeks. Cornwall was a young man who died at his ship's gun during the battle of Jutland in May 1916. He was a boy seaman who refused to desert his post. He wasn't a former pupil at Dunbar; the engraving was pure propaganda, intended to instil in us that to Do Your Duty was the highest achievement. I never once passed that print without feeling a mixture of pride and guilt. Of course, that's what the school authorities wanted to nurture in the kids of that generation.

After receiving our timetables and textbooks, we were allocated to our Houses. There were three in Dunbar, started I believe in 1936. *Victoria* was identified by the colour blue and was named for the new harbour; it seemed to contain all the best athletes. Yellow *Cromwell* was named for the Old Harbour; *Cromwellians* seemed to contain a mixture of athletes and academics. *Castle*, which needs no explanation, was a red badge (of courage?) and consisted largely of bookworms like me, with very few sporting types. At least what *Castle* lacked in sporting prowess and gamesmanship, it made up for in exams. *Cromwell* seemed to come a poor second to Victoria, which excelled in games and sport but had few brilliant scholars. I know I am going to be challenged on this but that was how it seemed in those days.

One of the most daunting tasks given us in the first few weeks of upper school education was to be sent to an unfamiliar classroom with a note for the teacher. I recall having to do this at least once, relaying a handwritten note from the English class to the Science block which you could only reach by crossing an open verandah which revealed a dizzying drop into the girls' playground, about 30 feet below. Returning was easier but I could have done with the ball of string Ariadne gave to Theseus when he was negotiating the Labyrinth in order to slay the Minotaur. Over the ensuing years, we became familiar with that open walkway, crossing it in every kind of weather. When it rained or snowed, there was a mad and noisy dash to gain the shelter of the other side. Some days, we dawdled and even paused to look at the wild winter seas whose waves broke over the boundary wall, crashing into and flooding the girls' toilets. Many a girl who is now a grown woman reminds me of those inhospitable loos where they got drenched whenever there was a high sea running when they were trying to spend a penny.

The first week was devoted to acclimatising ourselves. Not much was actually taught. We were treated to the encouraging lecture from Hugh Cowan, welcoming us to the upper school and reminding us in the immortal lines of the late Muriel Spark's brilliant novel *The Prime of Miss Jean Brodie* that we were joining *la creme de la creme* and that he expected Great Things of us.

The teachers were a fearsome bunch, especially the lady Maths teachers. *Granny* Reid and Christina or *Eenie* Donaldson could have made first class drill sergeants had they chosen a career in the army. We'd been warned about them by older brothers and sisters. My first memory of Miss Donaldson was when she was recording the attendance register. She bawled out my name.

'Are you related to Norman Pugh?

Why did she need to ask? It was such an uncommon surname in Dunbar.

'Yesmiss!'

She ticked off my name on her clipboard, then looked up and wearily sighed:

'Well I hope you make a better job of Maths than he did. He was useless. You'll not have to try really hard to beat him.'

Miss Donaldson had a face hewn from the same rock that had provided her heart. Well, that's what it seemed like then. Both she and Miss Reid were experts at sarcasm intended to make us push ourselves to obtain better results. Neither of them smiled much, though Miss Donaldson would occasionally betray her real feelings when she allowed a faint smile to flicker across her lips. (Today, when I watch Ann Robinson decimate the contestants in *The Weakest Link*, I always think of Ina Donaldson).

Today, I know grown men who still live in mortal terror of her; at a school reunion in 1999 to which she was invited, she asked me - ordered me in fact - to pass her coat to her when she was about to leave:

'Roy, would you please hand me my coat?'

Without thinking, I answered

'Yesmiss!'

and did as I was told. Responses like that are ingested at an early age... before that, I met her at the new school in Summerfield Road when they were launching the nostalgic book *From Slate to Disk* and she appeared on the platform of dignitaries. I was amazed at her lack of stature; she was so small but she had lost neither her presence nor her commanding personality. She gave a short lecture which contained many humorous incidents - but she rebuked the kids who were serving up wine and dips in the corner, ordering them to shut up while she was talking. She had a heart of gold but she kept it secure in the bank vaults. She had presence. I promised myself that on the day she died, I would dance on her grave. Sadly, that happened in October 2004; I went to her grave and reverently said goodbye to her, even restoring one of the two wreaths that had blown on to an adjacent grave.

Miss Reid, whom we all knew as *Granny* on account of her white mane of hair was a formidable figure who peered at you out of gimlet eyes. Her mouth harboured the most sardonic expressions I have ever known; it contained all her in-gathered knowledge of years of spotting the waywardness of unruly boys and intimidated girls. When she was angry, she grew cold and calculating, her glasses winking menacingly in the light. She would express her distaste by visibly hitching up a nuisance bra that lurked behind her starched white blouse. If she caught you running in the corridor, she would pull you by the ears and order you to walk. This is what she would say to her victims:

Running, eh? We don't run in this school unless we are late. Are you late and if so, why?'

If you walked casually or lackadaisically, she would say this:

'How slow you walk.  Do you think this establishment belongs to you, that it is here for your convenience?'

You couldn't win with Miss Reid.  At least she was fair; she belted boys and girls impartially.  She was called up before Hugh Cowan on at least one occasion after she'd badly bruised a girl's wrist.  She never belted me but the most frequent question she asked me was this:

'Pugh, what will become of you?  Don't answer. I shudder at the thought.'

That damning, discouraging lament echoes in my mind to this day.

These two lady Maths teachers *taught* us. You never forgot what they drummed into you. Or if you did, it was at your peril....

By way of contrast, the male Maths teacher, *Dadda* or *Daddy* Drever made me think of Mr Pickwick without the humour; he certainly resembled that famous Dickensian character in stature, if not humour.  His classes were periods of unrelieved gloom as he intoned the lesson in a sombre, plodding way, hugely successful in making an exceedingly dreary subject even more so. His dull, droning voice often sent my head nodding deskwards.  He had this habit of illustrating something on the blackboard, chatting away to himself as he wrote down lines of algebraic equations, working them out as he went along, then drawing a line - no, *two* lines under the answer, then turning to us in triumph to announce that he had squared the circle, or whatever other silly, meaningless (to me) phrase came into his head.  *QED* was the abbreviation he underlined on the blackboard at the end of every geometrical lesson or alge-braic equation; it means 'thus I have proved it.'  Well there you go; I was usually underwhelmed.

Then there was the handsome, debonair English teacher *Dougie* Dudg-eon who made all the girls go weak at the knees - and rightly so.  He once singled me out for praise for an essay I wrote and which I called *The Time Machine*.  I recall him standing beside my desk that afternoon, stroking his usually *seven o' clock* shadow chin and staring at my exercise book, balancing it in his hand as if he suspected something untoward was written it.  Then:

'Tell me, Pugh.  Have you ever heard of an author called H G Wells?'

I truthfully admitted I hadn't.

'Well, well.  When I first read this, I thought you'd pinched the title.  Then I read on'

I have to say that your effort is worthy of Mr Wells - except for the level of spelling which is about normal for you.  I've given you a high mark and I'm going to read your essay to the class.'

I was mortified, embarrassed, flushed and assailed by all the things that afflict spotty youths.  I felt like a *sook* or teacher's pet.  I hadn't cheated by

# Lions and Donkeys (part 2)

using Wells' book but I did get the idea from one of my American horror comics. The difference between Wells and me was that my time travellers went backwards and ended up in the Prehistoric period, which allowed me to introduce dinosaurs and other hulking creatures which fascinate children today.

After Mr Dudgeon came Charlie *Chid* Mungall who sported a Poirot-type moustache and like Poirot, had black, patent-leather hair plastered down with *Brylcreem* and parted in the middle. He was yet another of those lugubrious teachers and I remember him for one incident. As Christmas 1954 approached, he came out with what he considered a terribly funny joke which no one in the class shared. He was reading from some classic or other - perhaps Dickens' *A Christmas Carol* - when he paused, looked out of the window at the sea and intoned the following:

'A coffin at Christmas. A Christmas Box.'

Nobody laughed, which I think upset him, for he turned back to his sea view, scratching his bum as he absent-mindedly did on many occasions. He left Dunbar to join the English Department at Falkirk High School. Years later, I sat opposite him in a train going to Falkirk High, when I was spending the weekend with a girlfriend who lived in Cumbernauld. He got into the carriage at Falkirk Low station and sat down, staring out of the window. He hadn't changed in the least and of course, he didn't recognise me - not just because of the beard I'd grown but because like most of his pupils, I was anonymous. I should have spoken to him, tried to jog his memory but somehow, I couldn't. It didn't seem important then and isn't now.

After Charlie Mungall came Frank *Boney* Bonar, a skeletally thin and bleak man. He had piercing cold eyes and a dry sense of humour. My sole memory of him is that in the autumn term of the Second Year, my mother was in sore need of extra cash and asked me if I would be prepared to go to the *tattie howkin'* that October. Schoolchildren were granted three weeks' leave of absence from school in those austere post-war days; the money was good, so myself and Sheila, one of my classmates, applied for the exemption. Bonar had no idea of the financial straits our families were in and I for one wasn't going to tell him about mine. He announced to the entire class that Sheila and I were interrupting our important studies but worse than that, we would be holding back the rest of the class. Sheila and I said we'd keep up with our studies at night during the period. He sneered at us both that afternoon.

'You most certainly will. I'm not going to have you two dragging down the rest of the class by your selfish interests. You will be required to read three Home Readers and you will be tested on them when you come back. You *are* coming back, aren't you?'

That was uncalled for but we were too young and naive to protest then. Of course Sheila and I were coming back; we wanted to take our Scottish Leaving Certificate. My report card for that term shows my marks for English at 51 - well below the class average of 62. It was the worst mark I had between

# Lions and Donkeys ( part 2)

1953 and 1956, which may tell you as much about Frank Bonar as myself. My History mark was also low but above the class average. My friend Sheila recently told me her report card showed a red cross - I think she meant an 'x' which signified a poorer than usual mark for her subjects. We had only one thing in common that bonded us - we'd both been at the *tattie howkin'*. Yes, they knew how to punish you in those days....

I never forgot or forgave Frank Bonar for his stringent marking. His successor Jean Campbell made up for him. Jean was a jolly hockeysticks lady, vibrant and sexy with a ready sense of humour. What was even better, she smiled a lot and thus put us at ease. Why did so many of that generation of teachers fail to see that there was a direct co-relation between excessive and overbearing discipline and the poor results achieved by their pupils? I recall in later life working for a younger man than me in St Andrews House who challenged me when I said a happy ship was an efficient ship. He said I'd got it wrong:

'No. An efficient ship is a happy ship.'

His ship wasn't happy and it was woefully inefficient.... ...In the opinion of many of his contemporaries, he'd been over-promoted; he was a bully and an egotist with little between his ears. He had this annoying habit of snapping his fingers when he asked you to do something - even if he snapped them at his sides rather than at you. I wasn't impressed or intimidated by this display which I am sure earned me a poor annual assessment that year. People like him could get back at you in the Civil Service, at annual report time. In some respects, he reminded me of the bullying teachers at Dunbar

The most memorable and epic of our English teachers was Miss MacDonald. Nobody who went to Dunbar Grammar School can forget *Maggie Meeks*, a legendary character. Perhaps her nickname derived from Miss Miggs, the shrewish lady in Dickens' novel *Barnaby Rudge*. She it was who prepared Fourth, Fifth and Sixth years for Higher English. Noted for her eccentricity, she also had an unfortunate habit of spraying the two front rows of her classes when she spouted forth - I almost typed *froth* there - surely a Freudian slip. She was spectacularly and blissfully unaware of her absurdities. She never understood why at Friday morning Assembly, when Hugh Cowan said 'Letuspray', his words never failed to evoke giggles and looks in her direction; she was blissfully unaware of the reason, I am sure. She was prejudiced and unfair - impartially it must be said. She was the only English teacher besides Frank Bonar who gave me an undeserved below average class mark for English. She didn't like me because my father was a soldier. It was rumoured that she lost a sweetheart in the Great War, a young man in the Royal Flying Corps; she was forever comparing our generation with that which had perished in or above the trenches. She maintained - with a considerable degree of justification - that the best brains, the finest manhood had been destroyed on the Somme in 1916, which was why Britain was in such a parlous state in the 1950s. She

# Lions and Donkeys (part 2)

used to throw my essay jotter at my head, saying I had written yet another imaginative piece - this was spat out patronisingly as the book whizzed on to my desk as she passed by.

'I'm sure I don't know where you get it from, Pugh' was all she said, the closest she ever got to praise. I resented her for her unjustified refusal to enter me for Higher English. She responded to my protests by saying I was a borderline case and that she couldn't take a chance with me. Clearly, she wanted to preserve her quota of passes. She further upset me by putting up another borderline case who only just scraped through his Higher. Years later, I discovered the real reason why she had refused to enter me for the Higher. Meeting my mother in a Dunbar shop long after she'd retired, she learnt that I was in the Civil Service and had recently done well in an internal exam which brought me promotion. *Maggie Meeks* responded with ill-concealed amazement:

'But you left Dunbar ages ago! You were an army family living in the Barracks!
I didn't bother with your son for that very reason. Your husband was a soldier and probably your son would also join the army. You were constantly on the move so what was the point of my wasting time on an itinerant? Anyway, someone told me your son did go into the army, as I thought he would.'

Taken aback, my mother angrily rounded on her; she said we'd lived in Dunbar all our lives and that the Barracks had ceased housing families for more than ten years and certainly when I was in Fourth and Fifth Years. When I heard this sorry tale, it seemed to vindicate the belief that *Maggie Meeks* hated the army and all it stood for. I loved English and books, which made her ostracism all the more hurtful.

Yet it wasn't all sadness. Two endearing memories of *Maggie Meeks* are worth mentioning. The funnier of the two occurred in the final weeks after the *Highers*, when we were waiting for the results. On a late spring morning, she announced that as we'd completed our formal studies, she was going to give us a treat in the summer term:

'You may choose between D H Lawrence's Sons and Lovers or Shakespeare's Hamlet. Hands up for Lawrence.'
Most of the boys voted for D H. But there was a draw - there were only thirteen students in our class which was comprised of Fifth and Sixth Years and I one of us was absent that morning, so the vote was equal, the girls going for Shakespeare. *Maggie* announced that she wouldn't cast a vote but the decision would be settled on the throw of a coin. She rummaged in her purse for a [pre-decimal] penny she tossed in the air behind her. The coin landed on the top of her stationery cupboard. She looked up at it, towering over her modest five feet.

'Right. It's Shakespeare then.'
Her decision was final.

# Lions and Donkeys ( part 2)

The second incident occurred two years earlier, known as The Valentine Day Card Mystery. She got one on 14th February 1956. Somehow, it caused a flutter in her bleak bosom. We thought some bold or disgruntled spirit in the class was the perpetrator. That morning, during a Latin lesson with Jack Milne, the door burst open and in the little dwarf bounced and staggered, shouting to our amused disbelief:

'Oh, Mr Mill, Mr Mill [correctly pronounced] you naughty man!

What a devil you are!'

Then she left as abruptly as she'd come. I recall Jack Milne's twinkling eyes, his throaty laugh. He usually drew his thin hair over his forehead on such occasions and yelled out

''Waaaaah! She'll never get over the shock!'

He never told us how she knew he'd sent it; knowing Jack Milne, I am sure he gave her a clue - it certainly wouldn't have been his signature, so perhaps he'd used a Latin quotation.

Miss MacDonald was like an evergreen shrub or plant - always the same, always predictable, though rarely boring. She had unsatisfactory relations with this world and probably experienced the same in the next. (At least she would have the company of John Milton, the blind poet and Geoffrey Chaucer, both of whose work she admired). We had a grudging respect for her tantrums and shrewish rages; she would scowl and twist her face in a range of grotesque, lip-chewing shapes. For our part, we sensed they were genuine, somehow knowing that without her accompanying facial expressions, she would never have been able to teach us anything - or at least teach something that would register in our thick skulls. Maybe her method was effective but she lacked insight into her ridiculous behaviour. Her paroxysms of temper, anger and plain impatience rather than psychological teaching skills probably kept our attention; we certainly responded to her shrill, bird-like cries, delivered in tones in which scorn and ridicule were never far away.

Our first French teacher was a pretty, fresh-faced lady called Miss Florence Morrison, known as *Fanny*; she was very attractive and a delightful teacher and sadly left us too soon. In First Year French class, we sang *Frere Jacques* and *Sur le Pont d'Avignon ad lib ad nauseam*. No one after her quite came up to her calibre; she had dark hair and lovely eyes and even when she was displeased with us, she looked beautiful to me, especially when she reinforced her ire with her hands, the French words spilling out as she rebuked us:

'Ca suffit!' [that's enough] she would shout at us.

I am sure many in her class felt they'd let her down when they misbehaved or were more than usually unresponsive. *Fanny* Morrison's classes were taken over for a time by John N Muir, Principal Teacher of Modern Languages until a replacement could be appointed; *Shorty* Muir was elevated to headmaster in 1961. He it was who was instrumental in organising trips abroad - particularly to France, Belgium, Luxemburg and Germany. *Shorty* took us for a few weeks until we were taught by a supply teacher, Sandy Glass, whose brother Jimmy married our History teacher, Miss Lena Mackay.

Sandy Glass gave us one memorable but unintentional afternoon's entertainment when he read in his immaculately perfect French enunciation a short story entitled *La Maison Hanter.* He pronounced the third word in the title as ONG-TAY, which is of course the correct Gallic pronunciation. Little did the poor man know that he'd just awarded himself a nickname. Thereafter, he was known as ONG-TAY Glass, soon corrupted to *Auntie*; perhaps it was fortuitous that he soon left for fresh pastures. His replacement was a thin, shrewish woman who took an instant dislike to me, particularly after she had only two of us for German, which meant both of us were under close scrutiny. I once committed the unpardonable sin of telling her the truth about my failure to complete some homework. There had been an historical film on at the local cinema - I think it was Laurence Olivier's *Henry V* - so by way of excusing myself for not doing my homework, I said I had gone to see the film. She launched into a tirade about the selfishness of some people and thereafter, she treated me with unbridled and undisguised sarcasm whenever I failed to come up to scratch.

'Maybe we were at the pictures again'
was her usual comment. I think when I failed my German Lower, she secretly rejoiced - if you will pardon that unhappy but intentional pun on her first name. At least *Shorty* Muir had faith in me and as head of the Modern Language Department, he took the trouble to write to the Scottish Examination Board to request a reassessment - I think I was awarded 49% in the exam and he considered me a borderline case. The Board refused to change their decision so I was marked down as a fail.

But in compensation, there was History. When we joined the First year, we were expecting to have *Jessie* James, bestowed by some opportunist wag whose spotted the potential for an appropriate nickname. For those of us who were about to enter First year, he seemed a flamboyant but intimidating man. To carry the comparison with the Wild West outlaw to its conclusion, the posse came to the rescue in August 1953, when Mr James left Dunbar to become Rector of Dalkeith Academy, much to our relief. In his place came Miss Lena Mackay. Not only did she make History come alive for me, she was young, fresh and very, very pretty. I fell in love with her at first sight. She was the last teacher for whom I would hold a torch, as they used to say in those days. I carried the torch for a long, long time; it has burned brightly, unwaveringly, for over fifty years....

Geography was never a favourite subject of mine but it was enlivened by a very attractive - and I have to say - curvaceous young lady by the name of Rhona MacPherson. She seemed out of place in the dusty, poky little room that overlooked the sea near the teachers' rest room. Perhaps her room was the Headmaster's deliberate choice; no doubt he anticipated trouble from the all-

# Lions and Donkeys ( part 2)

male and therefore unruly classes of testosterone-fuelled hulks whom he feared would - and did - make her life a misery. These lads teased her without mercy. Once when she was telling a class about the mean rainfall of Poland, she was greeted with hoots and catcalls. Po-land... ...it had endless attraction for these juvenile delinquents. The hulks reckoned she was fair game for this kind of nonsense and they were right. The rain in Spain falls mainly on the plain but in Po-land, it falls into the po.... So it went on

That was one of the milder incidents. I recall another that was tantamount to theft and could have had serious consequences had she not been such a good sport. Somehow, one of the Technical class lads had got hold of a photo of the delectable Rhona in her swimsuit - it might have even been a bikini, which left little to the imagination, executing in profile her well-rounded, ample charms. Every lad in that class had a copy of her holiday snap pinned to the inside of his desk lid. Inevitably, she spotted one and turned a bright red. She demanded he hand it over to her at once. He refused to comply unless the other 29 guys in the class handed over theirs. Poor Rhona was greeted with a chorus of catcalls and the lifting of desk lids while the one of the bolder spirits asked her if she would like

'A photy of me, Miss? That's only fair.'
Poor girl. She fled to the sanctuary of the nearby teachers' rest room, where she was comforted by Jack Milne. Jack descended on that class like an avenging angel; by all accounts, he gave them all he had from both barrels. He demanded and retrieved every photograph of Rhona, admonishing each lad who handed his copy over. It was one of the few times I ever saw or heard of him quivering with unfettered rage, perhaps even hatred. Years later, when we were having a drink in the St George Hotel, he told me he had never been closer to strangling a few of 'the bloody louts.'

We were taught - or were driven to - art by Bill Scott and Carnegie Brown, both fairly quiet and unassuming men. Carnegie Brown was something straight out of *The Prime of Miss Jean Brodie* - well, his name was and there the comparison with his counterpart in the novel ended. I was average at art - no, on reflection, I was bloody awful. Mr Scott was not averse to using the strap but I cannot recollect Mr Brown ever thrashing anyone.

For Science, another subject in which I was an under-achiever, we had *Pop* Fyfe in the First year, then *Davie* Patterson (spelt with two t's) in Second and Third years, then *Ghandi* MacVicar - so-called because he was a white version of that bald Indian politician and statesman. Mr MacVicar was a gentleman in all senses of the word; he was mild-mannered and I cannot ever recall him raising his voice or disciplining any of us. By contrast *Pop* Fyfe was a small, Chaplinesque figure, a man we teased unmercifully by placing an index finger in one cheek and making a popping sound as he came into the classroom. I can recall only one lesson with him - the life cycle of the frog, I think we dissected the frog, which makes me feel squeamish even today. *Davie*

# Lions and Donkeys (part 2)

Patterson was fond of the girls, especially Sheila, a very pretty but shy girl, my co-conspirator in Second year who like me, defied Frank Bonar to go to the *tattie howkin'*. *Davie* contrived to have Sheila seated beside him at every opportunity, as I think he had a soft spot for her. He had heavy jowls, so the more imaginative among us called him 'lantern jaws'. Even so, he was a kind man, as was *Ghandi* MacVicar. Mr MacVicar was one of the most sincere, gentle men I ever encountered in school. Because he was averse to giving the strap, he was considered a soft touch by some of the unworthier spirits among us. Those who respected him never gave him a hard time, although on one memorable occasion, someone who shall remain nameless removed the wire mesh cover from the large glass tank containing a shoal - a spawn? - of maturing tadpoles one Friday afternoon at the end of our lesson. By Monday morning, the little creatures had transformed into mini frogs, hopping about the science room, much to Mr MacVicar's ill-concealed, good-natured surprise.

For Music, a compulsory subject which inexplicably carried only 50 marks in the curriculum, we had Miss Boyd, then Mai Intin, my Lady of Shallott, the teacher I had never forgiven for failing me in a spelling test in Primary, yet whom I still loved - well, a bit.

For Gymnastics, the boys had *Charlie* Flaherty, an Errol Flynn lookalike; the girls had bouncy Miss Bain for their callisthenics. She had a formidable bust and looked sexy in her shorts, but she had a doughy, dumpling face and complexion, sad though I am to admit it.

I hated music from an academic point of view, for I love so many aspects of music - classical, jazz, rhythm and blues and 'black' rock today. I also had an ingrained loathing of woodwork and metalwork, having no aptitude for these subjects. Music wasn't too bad but unfortunately, we - or rather, I - had to endure a weekly period of woodwork or metalwork. Ostensibly for diversion and perhaps to round off the swots, I suppose the thinking behind it was to give us a brief respite from our studies. Forgive my hollow laughter. It couldn't have been further from the truth. Donald Ross, one of our two Technical teachers, had neither time for nor patience with the cack-handed among us; he had a sarcastic tongue and a vicious temper which he vented on anyone in general and me in particular. I am not making this up, nor am I wallowing in self-pity. He expressed his feelings by hurling chisels in the general direction of the hopeless, handless cases like me. He ranted and raved; he said I was thick and that I'd never amount to anything. I kipped off school so many of those weekly Friday afternoons that the headmaster had to write to my mother to ascertain the reason for my repeated absences. I begged her not to tell him the truth because I knew it would make a bad situation worse. But tell him she did, so things quietened down a bit after that, although Mr Ross got his own back in other, subtler ways.

Then we had Mr Christie, a patient and gentle man, although even he couldn't improve my lamentable attempts at woodwork and metalwork. The only article I ever produced was a metal toothbrush rack which my mother - not me you will note - fixed in the bathroom for a time until it could be decently and quietly junked. That small wooden hut near the Girls' Playground still survives and still evokes bad memories whenever I pass it. Later in adult life, when I was working in HM Schools Inspectorate for Scotland, one of the Inspectors - a former woodwork teacher - said men of his profession were no more than failed joiners. Perhaps that explained Mr Ross's violent outbursts; there was certainly something flawed in him. He had three lovely daughters, so he was the only male in the house. He may have resented the lack of career opportunities or perhaps he was a man disappointed in love. Now, being a tad more mature, I could sympathise - or empathise - with him. Well, perhaps not. So these were the lions and donkeys who led us through the educational minefield during the years 1953 to 1958. I think I have covered most of those I encountered. Perhaps in view of the nicknames with which we labelled them, it's appropriate here to mention the names we gave to each other, which is only fair. The lads usually had the letter O added to their surnames - hence Main-O, Kneave-O, Wragg-O [Jim Main, Tommy Kneave, Eddie Wragg]. Girls usually had the letters -EY tacked on to their surnames, thus giving Bell-EY, Smith-EY, King-EY[Christine Bell, Mary Smith and Irene King]. But there were a few poets amongst our confraternity, boys who are lost in time. How on earth did the name-givers arrive at classic and colourful names like *Jonah, Fanny* (a boy!), *Peem* or *Pim*, *Ping, Tossle* and *Yumin* - the last being a corruption of William.

Sometimes, whole families of boys carried the same nickname like *Buttons* from East Linton; there was a *Big Buttons* and a *Wee Buttons* to distinguish the two brothers. Particularly colourful were *Hammy, Cheesy, Spud* - some connection with diet surely – *Beastie, Doaley* and *Louie* - the last named after Louie Dumbrowski, the small soda-shop owner in the American comedy series *The Dead End Kids,* later known as *The Bowery Boys.* We had an Eek and Deek (Eric and Derick), an *Ashes* and *Pishes*, brothers who again had to be distinguished from one another; there was *Hunch,Snakey Hips, Soapy, Fatty* and *Skinny*, there being two of that epithet, one being Robin Mellors who lived in my street, the other, James Hammond, son of a local Coastguard - the connection with physical appearance is obvious. Then there was the ever fresh and evocative *Bluebell,* a corruption of the poor lad's surname of Blakebell, a lad whose physique resembled that fragile flower which perishes when it is picked, a perfect epithet which described his quiet, shy nature. We also had an *Eli*, a *Dishie, Dumbo* and a Flood; in later years, after I had left school, there was a *Scabby*, an unfortunate patronymic which though cruel, was inspired by his physiognomy. We also had a set of identical twins, Caroline and Evelyn Thomas who lived in Summerfield Road; because nobody could tell them apart, they were always described as the Twinny Thomases. I think they left Dunbar in the mid-1950s; in later years, I would occasionally meet them in Edinburgh where I worked and still couldn't tell them apart. (This summer, they visited the Dunbar Town House Museum, when at last I could distinguish one from the other!)

Youth is cruel. I am living proof of that. My surname brought forth several nicknames, some of which were positively awful, draining me of what little confidence I possessed then and now. My names ranged from *Spew, Spewy*, Pugh-EY (I suffered added mortification from the last, as the EY suffix was usually added to girls' surnames), *Speugh* [the Scots' word for sparrow]; more friendly chums called me *Puggy* [the Scots' word for a hole scooped in the ground for playing marbles] and the more affectionate *Pugsy* or *Pugs*, coined by my late and sadly missed friend Graeme *Creamo* Cunningham, a fine man who left this world too soon....

My friend in the last two years of the Secondary School was called *Sook*, a name he hated intensely for obvious reasons; he was eccentric, interested mainly in science but to this day he insists that his nickname was unwarranted, as he never sucked up to any teacher, not even the ones he respected like Ghandi MacVicar, the much-loved and gentle-natured Science teacher. I certainly never saw any evidence of his alleged *sookin'* except perhaps in the case of Mai Intin, the Music teacher, who thought he had a good singing voice, which he had. (As I said earlier, she once brought to school a tape-recorder to record him giving his (in)famous impersonation of Paul Anka's *Diana*; he strode confidently to the front of the class, held the microphone like the professionals, did his usual *St Vitus* dance which entailed bending one of his legs and dragging it across an imaginary stage, his lank, thick hair cascading over his forehead as he did a Quasimodo-like stagger in his thick-soled suede shoes, known then as brothel-creepers and favoured by the Teddy Boys of the day. This part of his ensemble was out of character with the rest and in no way resembled the ridiculous long black frock-coats worn by the Teds; as I wrote earlier, he affected to wear a dog-tooth check tweed sports-coat, black trousers, a green shirt and a black bow-tie. He was, to put it mildly, eccentric. As I was.

There was for a brief time my friend Iain Cornes, known as *Corneylugs* on account of his protruding auricle physiognomy. As I wrote earlier in Chapter 7, he was a bit unreal in that he used *Beano-ish* expressions like 'jumpin' crocodiles, jeepers creepers, cripes' and so forth. Then there was Patrone [Italian for Boss or leader] a name given to a local Scots-Italian boy whose nickname matched his Mediterranean temperament and energy. Names given to some of the girls were less poetic but we had a *Minnie the Moose* (to rhyme with her surname?), *Biffo* (my good friend Valerie Brown) and *Peerie-hole* from Innerwick. And of course all girls called Maureen were called *Mo, Big Mo, Little Mo* and so on. Another good friend with whom I have recently resumed contact was William Jackson who acquired the nickname *Jake* for perhaps obvious reasons.

# Lions and Donkeys ( part 2)

Many of our teachers were small in stature but what they lacked in feet and inches, they made up for in courage and intimidation. Imagine a small man or woman like *Pop* Fyfe or *Maggie Meeks* standing before a class of *Shories* - the collective name given to boys from the harbour area and Parsons' Pool. They were invariably big strapping lads who put the fear of God into you in the playground but underneath it all, were quite gentle - as long as their peers weren't around. I remember a Mathematics teacher saying this:

'What's the point of teaching them? They'll go to the fishing and
forget anything they were taught at school. And the girls will work
in shops, farms or at best, the hairdressers.'

That was a short -sighted view; many of that dismissed generation have achieved great things and gained impressive bank balances.

So there I was with a small, congenial class of youngsters, most of whom I remain friends with today - those that are left. In session 1953-54, our number was never greater than seventeen; by the third term of Session 1954-55, the class size had reduced to thirteen, reducing to twelve in the summer term of 1955-56. In the Fourth and Fifth years, our original class had been swollen by two or three from Sixth year and a couple who were repeating Fifth. But our numbers were never higher than seventeen.

I was a modest scholar by any standards and certainly not in the top bracket, although I developed a penchant for writing English and History essays, two subjects I still pursue today. I wasn't popular and couldn't expect to be - among the boys at least, being poor at games and other pursuits boys were supposed to enjoy – like constructions and airplane modelling. Among those in our Fifth year class of 1957-58 was Sandy Cowan, the headmaster's son who referred to his father as *The Boss*; to his credit, he never *clyped* [informed] on any of us. To me, he was a character straight out of *The Magnet,* a comic popular at the time which featured the boys of Greyfriars School, a private establishment whose famous members were known as *Wharton and Co,* middle-class boys of the Fifth Remove who made Billy Bunter's life a misery. It was an upper-class comic that pandered to an early form of political correctness, having an Indian student in the class. Sandy was fanatical about modern jazz, a form of music I cannot appreciate even today; his followers shared the view that Rock n' Roll was for the plebs and the Teds. I loved it, especially the music of Bill Haley and the Comets, the machine-gun staccato of Jerry Lee Lewis' piano-playing and black singers like Fats Domino, Chuck Berry and later, Sonny Boy Williamson, Howlin' Wolf, John Lee Hooker and many others. I could relate to Rock n' Roll, a wild and exciting new form of dancing - well, jiving, to give its proper generic. Jazz was 'correct' and respectable. I went my own way, had robust arguments defending my kind of music; I also secretly continued to pursue my interest in lead soldiers which by Fourth year would have been considered juvenile. (I recently learnt from my friend William Jackson that Sandy is now living in Fife and attends church regularly as a choir

# Lions and Donkeys (part 2)

member – how things have changed!)

The young have a uniquely refreshing and insatiable appetite for life rather than for that which the powers that be consider will transmute them into worthwhile citizens. Jack Milne, the Latin teacher fed that appetite in me, although he was careful to point out that we all have to grow up - a bit. I revelled in his humour, it being intelligently anarchic. A rebuke from him in class lay heavy on my heart. He treated us like embryonic adults - which I suppose we were - encouraging us to make choices and think for ourselves. His teaching methods were therefore successful - well, at least for me. Some mean spirits said he couldn't teach for toffee, that he failed to maintain discipline; I disagree with both criticisms. He had his own way of making you feel small if you stepped over his line. He was a marvellous *raconteur* and clever - if quirky - poet, his verses often being obscure or heavily larded with private classically-inspired jokes. He took me seriously and like Miss Mackay, my lovely History teacher, rescued my confidence from the pit of despair. We remained firm friends until the end of his life; I loved him and am fortunate that Mrs Glass, the former Miss Mackay is still a dearly loved and valued friend. Between them, they eased me through the painfully awkward time that is called youth.

While I was consistently getting high marks for Latin - an impressive (to me) 83% in the Second term of Session 1953-54 and 80% in the Third term of Session 1955-56, it was a subject that exercised my thoughts as to the likelihood of its usefulness in a modern world. The mastering of declensions and verbs and cases were a veritable minefield. How on earth had the Romans - an efficient and effective world power and military race - managed with the complexities of that ancient language? For example, *mensa* (Latin for table) with a capital M meant O Table!; the same word with a small m meant 'by, with or from' a table; accusatives were a mystery and the vocative - how one would address a table – seemed silly. I shared that view with the young Winston Churchill who pointed out to his stern headmaster that he wasn't in the habit of speaking to tables. Once, Jack Milne asked Derick - a classmate - to 'compare' *mensa*. His pawky reply remains as fresh as the day he said it:

'What with, sir?'

This produced peals of laughter and the fag-end of a piece of chalk that Jack whizzed past his ear, bouncing off the wall behind him. Jack Milne was a good shot and rarely missed; it was his way of paying Derick a compliment for his intelligent humour.

In Latin, female nouns end in -*a;* male nouns end in -*us* and neuter nouns end in -*um*. Thus Brittania (for Britain) was female; not even the erudite J I W Milne could explain that satisfactorily to me. The irregular verbs were a nightmare. I could go on for hours bemoaning the misery of Latin and its intricacies but I shall spare you that. Dunbar had a long love affair with the great classical language in its history; Latin is the foundation of French, Italian, Spanish and other romantic languages and contributed largely to the development of English. It became the official language of the Christian Church and was used in education, botany and science. Three Dunbar schoolmasters or *dominies* in the sixteenth and seventeenth centuries considered it important enough to construct Latin Grammars for the use of scholars in every Scottish school, one remaining in use until the nineteenth century. But why oh why couldn't the Romans have devised a less complex language? Be that as it may, we sweated over our grammars and Latin primers, stumbling amongst the dead of three Punic Wars waged by Rome against Carthage between 264 and 146BC - Rome finally emerging victorious. The subject was relieved by Jack Milne's natural good humour and gentle prodding. He made it all sound so simple. He taught Greek to one or two Sixth year boys, notably Douglas Vickers who mastered classical languages with disgusting ease and went on to become a University Don.

My career in the upper school went undetected - well almost. I preferred it that way, for it came naturally. I was occasionally blessed with success which may be a comment on the variations in my powers of concentration, if not determination. I usually ended up about seventh in a class that averaged twelve members. Once I was third equal in a class of seventeen; I was also bottom on one occasion. I always did poorly in the autumn term, for it took a long time for me to settle down after the long summer holiday. I usually did well in the winter term, falling back in the summer term when that lovely season was *icumin-in*. I was there, I was present in class but much of the time, I was semi-detached; then as the splendid month of May gave way to an even better June, I was fully detached. I felt alone and hid my shyness behind the garrulous nonsense I affected to talk in those days. I was a parasite, drawing from the anarchic humour of the *Goons* - Spike Milligan, Harry Secombe, Peter Sellers and Michael Bentine. As I said earlier, I drew strange outlandish creatures on my jotter covers, weird little things I called *Trephontises,* then *Mirkins* whose images were resurrected many years later as *Smurfs*. My juvenile humour was an escape from reality, like all humour. I never played the 'japes' or 'wheezes' of Iain Cornes who once stuck a pencil into the buttock of Mr Scott, one of our teachers. These properly belong in *The Beano*, an anarchic comic I read but whose characters I never felt the urge to emulate. I looked up to the older boys, especially the clean-limbed and self-assured heroes of the Fifth and Sixth years who complained that the junior classes following them were full of scrawny runts who were getting progressively smaller. I wonder if any of those Golden Wonders ever stopped to ponder whether we were getting smaller because we weren't benefiting any more from the free orange juice, milk and the rest of the healthy dietary items on offer when they were children; after all, my lot were in the middle of the post-war years and money was scarce. And yet I looked up to them, equally ignorant of why I was small and they were large - larger in fact than life itself. They had inspired

# Lions and Donkeys (part 2)

names like Gordon Good and James Dishington and they appeared to me to have their roots in *The Magnet* comic. But they were a tad unreal. Once passing the Fifth and Sixth Years Prep or Common Room in 1954, I overheard a fragment of the conversation between two of these Olympians. The door was open, so I can't be accused of snooping; I distinctly heard one Sixth Former say to another:

> 'I say, Jimmy. Who was that I saw you with at the tennis courts
> the other evening? She's a stunner.'
> 'She's my new girl. She's called Bunny. Were you spying on me,
> you rotter?'

I swear I heard this conversation. I have often wondered whether they were rehearsing a school play but looking back, there actually was a blond 'stunner' called Bunny in Dunbar at that time.

Another confusing moment occurred when I was delivering a note to the form mistress of the Fifth year, three whole years older than I was. I overheard one of the senior girls complain to another that she was having problems with her periods; I assumed that she was confused by her school timetable. Yes, we were - or I was - naive to a fault in those far off days.

My young brother Ken and I had a brief encounter with the dreaded School Dinners in *St Catherine's Hall* at Woodbush. In those days, they were truly awful, the dishes consisting largely of gristly, greasy grey mince and dried potato powder - possibly ex-army rations - called *pomme*. This particular muck was served in a district famous for its potatoes. Another delicacy was cubed cheese salad, which was a non-starter for me as most cheeses were - and still are - a problem for me. The kids that were forced to eat there said the salads were particularly vile as they contained caterpillars - so it was rumoured. There were other culinary delights like ham curled at the edges; the soggy puddings were no more imaginative, the mainstays being semolina with a teaspoonful of runny jam or tapioca which was ubiquitously referred to as *frogspawn*. Sometimes there was a stodgy pudding like apple dumpling, the apples being tart and invariably shoved to the side of the plate, while the stodge filled you up.

In those days, every schoolchild was entitled to one third of a pint of milk each day; the milk was fine in winter, when it was cold and occasionally even frozen but in summer, I refused my bottle as it was invariably 'off' by the time we got it. Even today, I take milk in small doses, mainly to colour my coffee. The only really good thing about the milk was that it was delivered to the lower entrance to the school; if you were on milk monitor duties with another lad, the pair of you could waste time dawdling there and back, one lad on either side of the metal crate.

But to return to the dreaded school dinners. Originally, they were provided at low cost for poorer children, then the scheme was extended to include children whose mothers had to work and could afford to pay for their children's meals; the service was also available to children from the surrounding villages who couldn't get home during the dinner hour. Each day at about 12.40pm, classes were marched to *St Catherine's Hall* in Woodbush. Let me remind my contemporaries of the range of fare offered in addition to the above. There was weak, watery *tattie soup,* then a main course which usually included the lumpy, unsalted dollop of *pomme.* Another gastric torture was boiled fish curled up at the edges with the consistency of a product sold by *Michelin.* The meat day occurred once a week; if it wasn't the horrible mince, the fare was either *Spam* or corned beef, the latter held together with flecks and dots of yellow fat. In addition to the *frogspawn* - which incidentally made great ammunition when stuck to a dessert spoon and held like a catapult, the stem of the spoon in one hand and the spoon end bent back so the contents could be fired at a victim - the sago and the apple dumpling, there was baked rice which looked like sick, spotted dick, apple tart served up with a ladleful of lumpy, unsweetened custard; often it was only sour stewed apples and the aforementioned custard. We were served by ladies with forearms like pink hams in the regulation uniform of head-turban and grimy, off-white crossover *pinnies* [pinafores]. We spent much of the time in the hall pretending to eat or trying to offload a disgusting portion onto someone else's plate. Some kids were so hungry they unashamedly asked if they could have what you didn't want. A few of the rougher lads would shake their heads, then empty the contents of their plates into the pigswill bin in front of some poor little Oliver Twist, then scowl at him. Many boys amused themselves carving chunks out of the long trestle tables, eschewing the food altogether. You had to stay in that hall until the regulation thirty minutes for eating was over; teachers acting as dinner monitors rigidly adhered to this rule, eating with us perhaps in sympathy rather than by choice. I think we pitied the Oliver Twists most of all; poor souls, they were invariably emaciated and desperate enough to swallow every mouthful of that veritably god-awful mess of pottage.

After three weeks of this hell, Ken and I begged our mother to let us go to *The Central Cafe,* better known as Togneri's fish and chip shop in the West Port. The restaurant was above the fish and chip shop in those days and the fare dished up was miles better. And extremely cheap. For one shilling and one penny [slightly more than 5p], you could have two courses; the main course was invariably the excellent locally-baked Scotch pie served with real mashed potatoes (minus the lumps) and either beans or peas or meat – usually corned beef or *Spam* accompanied by a portion of the famous Togneri chips. The sweet was invariably apple pie and custard, well presented and appetising. Sometimes there was sweetened semolina and jam or apple dumpling which was perhaps not exactly nutritional but filled you up. Among the half dozen of us who managed to escape from the horrors of *St Catherine's Hall* to eat at Togneri's was my friend Bing Turner and his younger sister Cath. They lived on the same fare for the three years they attended the upper school - pie, mash

# Lions and Donkeys (part 2)

and peas/beans and apple tart and custard; it cost 5/5 [27p] each week. The restricted diet from 1953 to 1956 doesn't seem to have done Bing, Cath or my brother and I any evident harm; we are still alive and thriving today.

Another subject - well, not a subject but part of the curriculum of the school for which I had no aptitude was sport. I detested football, played rugby with less than half a heart and was afraid of the damage cricket balls might inflict on vital - and tender - bits of my body. I also thought many of the gymnastic exercises we were forced to perform were pointless and stupid. I was something of a runner, which a modern day psychologist might understand, as when faced with trouble, was to run away. To me, that is natural; dogs like whippets who can run fast react in the same way in the same way as birds that fly off when threatened. Animals and birds are sensible creatures.

As I said earlier, we had a likeable, if cynical PT instructor called *Charlie* Flaherty; he was a realist, laid back and didn't extract revenge on the weaker vessels like me, TJ and sundry other forlorn hopes who hung about shivering in November mists every Friday afternoon at the touch lines of the rugby pitch, first at Winterfield, then at the *Sailors' Park*, the field behind our house. The only good thing about these sessions was that when they ended, all I had to do was leap over our garden wall to be home before many of the 'hearties' who, masochists to a boy, got out of their sports gear sweating - no showers and changing rooms in those Spartan days - and cycled/bussed/strolled home after these muddy and occasionally bloody encounters. Fortunately, with rugby teams numbering fifteen a side, I could hide my ineptitude by running in all directions, shouting encouragement to the seagulls if not my team mates. I was never more than a makeweight, or a lad that made up the number. Like my friend William Jackson or *Jake* as he was better known, I ran up and down the park, waving my arms, calling for the ball, terrified that it might come my way, which it usually didn't. I wouldn't have known what to do with a rugby ball in my hands - well I did as a matter of fact. Get rid of it. Quickly. For his part, *Jake* couldn't see very well without his spectacles; a stocky lad, he was known to run alongside whoever had the ball and ask him if he was on his side. On being informed that he wasn't, *Jake* would jump on him gently, apologising for his conduct. I loved that in him.

Gymnastics were different. There was no hiding place. And to add to my misery, I didn't possess attractive gear. In those days, boys did gym in vests, shorts and black sandshoes that squeaked on the wooden floor as you stumbled - in my case - about the hall trying to look energetic and co-ordinated, throwing great heavy medicine balls that had the all the charm of medieval cannonballs, doing cartwheels, vaulting the wooden horse by launching yourself off a springboard that to me didn't possess any springs, a particularly cruel form of torture - climbing knotted ropes suspended from the ceiling, scaling and hanging from wall-bars and running in a circle which of course went nowhere; the Oxford Dictionary accurately defines 'circle' people as those

# Lions and Donkeys ( part 2)

who are 'fussily busy with no results'. In later life, I would encounter many of the same breed in the Civil Service.

My gym shorts had a life of their own. Unlike schoolmates George Robertson and Bill Brunton who were members of the Episcopalian Church, I never wore a surplice; I wore ex-army *surplus*. I inherited a voluminous pair of shorts from my brother Norman who was probably given them by my father, a Battery Quartermaster Sergeant in the Royal Artillery. They may have fitted somebody at one time but never in all creation were they meant to fit someone with a spare frame like mine. Several sizes too big, to call them shorts would have contravened the Trades Description Act. They were long, baggy and so droopy on me that they came well past my knees so that I'd to roll the waist-band over several times over to keep them 'short'. I could - and did - hide my acute embarrassment behind humour and their fortuitous length. I could pull my 'shorts' up to my chin and cover my shoulders with them. I wore the same shorts to rugby matches. They came in handy when it rained and when it was windy; they provided me with much needed shelter. I usually encased my arms in them, which would bring Mr Flaherty to my side as I ran about the field, studiously avoiding the rugby ball, like any good 'circle' person. His words were usually in this vein:

'Pugh. How on earth do you expect to catch the ball, let alone run with it? Get your arms out of there, you useless article!'

I would respond by removing my arms as fast as I could extricate them, whereupon the shorts would descend perilously close to my feet, thus expos-ing my naughty bits. Another gag I perfected was to hold out the waistband and pretend I was about to trap the ball in the gap. I was sent off for dumb insolence several times. That suited me. Frankly, I didn't give a damn and I don't think Mr Flaherty did either. I was a hopeless case and we both knew it. I used to pray that the weather would get so wet and cold that the Friday after-noon game at *Sailors' Park* would be cancelled, thus allowing me to climb the wall into my back garden and let me sit by the fire. At least I ventured on to the pitch; weaker spirits like TJ and his companion Bluebell spent the entire after-noon examining the touchline.

I looked with envy on these individualistic weaker – really, bolder - spirits. Defiant and demonstrably inept, my friend TJ refused to join in what he called stupid games, although he would occasionally and half-heartedly scoop up the muddy ball when it skittered close to him. These two were often joined by a Fat Boy who couldn't run - except for toffee. Often, I would go over the top, wanting to join that trio but scared to leave the field; I did all my party pieces with the long shorts, larking about and dancing in the rain until Mr Flaherty caught me enjoying myself and ordered me back into the muddy fray. I ignored the girls playing hockey on the adjoining pitch, although I am sure they must have watched me clawing at the shapeless mass that was my shorts, pulling them this way and that and I say, exposing bits that the law of the land declared should be covered in the interests of decency and thus unlikely to frighten the few horses that still plied our roads.

The dreaded shorts were related to the equally dreaded knitted swimming costume, described earlier. Two terrible memories remain of them, or rather two occasions when I wore them. The first wasn't as bad as the second but both were occasions for digging a hole and removing yourself from view. As the Christmas school dance approached, the gym period was devoted to dancing lessons. We were ordered to *paddy-bar* and reel and step-we-gaily-on-we-go for the country dances, which I detested, for I thought them fit only for country bumpkins. These sessions were tolerable until we had to learn to do the waltz and foxtrot - the latter in quick and slow - with other boys for partners. The sessions were the veritable pits. The poor lad who had to act as the female invariably learnt to dance that way, which lead to utter confusion on the night of the Christmas Dance. I am ashamed to say that in the course of *Charlie* Flaherty's barked instructions, interspersed with comments which gave new meaning to the taunt about Roman Catholics - he shouted out that he'd never seen so many left-footed idiots outside the Vatican or Ireland - he suddenly went all smiles and said I was the best, the lightest of foot and the most accomplished dancer he would see this side of Christmas 1954. This was received by hisses and calls of *sookie* from my classmates. Then to add insult to injury, he announced that he would call in Miss Bain, the buxom, large-breasted gym mistress to partner me. I cringed a bit though I relished being clutched to her ample bosoms. The downside to this was that I would have to dance before all present in my outsize, baggy shorts. I was anything but graceful, though during the ordeal, Miss Bain was kindness itself. At the end of our demonstration waltz, somebody called out this:

'Ach, g'wan ye wee sook. Curtsey tae her!'

But the worst day of my life was when we had the School Photograph taken in the third term of Third Year, the summer term of 1956. We were enduring gym when *Charlie* Flaherty came into the gymnasium to order us to dress immediately as our class's school photograph was about to be taken. That year, I was still in short trousers, only marginally better than my gym shorts; they were flared and embarrassingly similar to the dreaded blue shorts. I had tried to coax my mother to buy me longs that were worn by the other boys in the Third Year. My mother wouldn't be swayed. She snorted and had this to say to me:

'They're old men cut doon. Ye'll be old yourself before long. Let the air get round your legs. It's far healthier and you'll get nice and brown in the summer. They'll have peely-wally [white] legs for the rest of their lives. Yours'll be tanned a nice healthy brown.'

True but not especially reassuring at the tender age of fifteen. And today, my legs *are* peely-wally.

I was placed at the front of the class to counterbalance David Barry as bookend to a row of girls. The photograph shows a confidant David in his longs at one end and me with a nervous smile at the other. In short trousers. But there was an acutely embarrassing prelude off camera. The photographer began making *sotte voce* noises in my direction. I frowned as I realised he was directing his comments to me. He hissed that I should do up my buttons. I ran my fingers quickly over my shirt and jacket.

'No, no. Not these buttons. The others.'
Still in a daze, I began the business all over again. Then in front of a thirty-strong Domestic class of girls waiting for their turn before the camera, he shouted loudly to me this:

'Your breeks' buttons. Your medals are showing. Och, laddie, it's
your ballop buttons. Do them up!'

'Medals' was the slang for the buttons that did up the front of your trousers, before zip flies became popular, courtesy of Lord Mountbatten. There was I, sitting with my legs wide open, displaying the offending articles. There was a rustle of whispering among the Domestic class; it grew to a crescendo and culminated in uncontrollable laughter. I have never lived down that awful afternoon. I still get ragged about the short trousers with the open buttons to this day when I meet former pupils who were there that day. What is worse, several other people in that photograph still possess copies. O *mea miserum*!

When I entered Fourth Year, my father returned to the matrimonial home, still serving in the army but apprehensive about his future. By 1957, he'd served with the Colours for nearly thirty years and refused to believe a Tory government would reduce the size of the British Army. The police and the army were upholders of the law and the peace and the Tories were traditionally strong on both. For the moment, my Dad was safe; but as Rudyard Kipling famously put it in his poem *Tommy Atkins,* his hymn to the common soldier, no one cares about the soldiers when there are no wars to fight. At any rate, there were side-benefits for me when he came back; he kitted me out with more army surplus clothing, but this time, the items were more attractive (to me). I stopped wearing school uniform after Third Year and the idea of wearing articles of clothing that civilians couldn't buy before the advent of the Army and Navy Surplus Stores appealed to my sense of the dramatic, the romantic and let's face it, the eccentric. Some of the gear was positively flamboyant.

The first items were a pair of canary yellow despatch rider's gauntlets which I wore when I cycled to school; it didn't matter to me that they were stamped WD (War Department). These and a dark blue windcheater with a squirrel-grey collar and black despatch rider's trousers tucked into my *wellies* completed my new uniform. I would arrive at the school on my bike, dressed like a World War Two RAF pilot scrambling for a sortie against the vicious Hun high in the clouds. Unfortunately, the clouds existed only in my head. By then, any residual attempts at cajoling me into wearing the official school uniform tapered off; my mother was secretly pleased as it meant she didn't have to

# Lions and Donkeys (part 2)

spend money on a new uniform; by 1957, I'd grown out of the uniform she'd struggled to buy in 1953. My equally eccentric friend T wore his dog-tooth sports jacket and black bow tie, riding his bike; but on the handlebars, he'd fixed a car wireless aerial topped with a small swastika - bad move, given that many kids had lost fathers in the war. We were both regarded as eccentric and silly, best left to ourselves. However, when we went to Paris with the school in Easter 1958 - a trip I describe in Chapter 7 - I temporarily reverted to my ill-fitting school uniform. As for T, he refused to compromise; he wore the same gear that he usually wore to school, with the addition of the green, drip-dry shirt which offset his black bow tie.

I make no bones about the fact that I was neither popular or unpopular in the upper school years, although I came under fire on account of my friendship with T who was in Sixth Year but attached to our Fifth Year, there being only a handful of Sixth Year students. T went out of his way to be different, affecting a stance his contemporaries either affected to ignore or twitted him about. He deliberately invented a character behind which he hid his true self so that he could lead a fairly comfortable and secure existence. Like me, he was bullied by a boy called Donald who took great pleasure in torturing and beating up boys weaker and smaller than himself. Donald's idea of fun was to inflict damage by pushing his victims into a hedge, holding them there with one hand while he punched them with the other. He regarded this as a kind of honour-able thumping, arguing that if he held his victim upright against a hedge, the object of his attention couldn't fall to the ground and thus stave off further blows. Let me be fair to Donald; he would never hit you when you were down, unlike today's bullies who have never heard of the Queensberry Rules and take a malignant delight in administering the boot when their opponents are on the ground. My Uncle Jimmy always said that it was unforgivable to hit your adversary when he was on the deck; fortunately, Donald shared his view. I say fortunately but I don't really mean it; he took great delight in boasting to his equally obnoxious friends that he would never hit a man when he was down.

On balance, T suffered more than I did but it only spurred him on to outlandish behaviour. I have seen him riding through the school gates on many a morning, his swastika-topped aerial waving in the wind as he skidded to a halt by the bike shed, surrounded by catcalling, jeering boys. It was the swas-tika rather than T that attracted offence. It wasn't the best prop with which to taunt your schoolmates for the obvious reason that many had lost fathers in the Second World War, less than two decades ago.

By Fourth Year, I had retreated even more into myself, creating an inner world from which I have never managed to escape. I was pig-headed and resentful, with a degree of justification. I muttered defiantly to myself that if this was the way they - 'they' included both teachers and classmates - wanted to play, then so be it. I developed - and still have - a deep distrust of those in positions of authority and who run clubs and societies. That distrust has to some extent been justified. I was brought up to be honest but I can't say the same for many men I know who lead 'public' lives today and who regard themselves as pillars of the community. I resolved that no matter how lonely my life would be, I would nurture what was inside me, never compromising myself or what I call my integrity, if that isn't too strong or chauvinistic. A long time ago, I decided I would go it alone. That remains my philosophy today.

There was no cultural stimulus at home, so I created my own. I was not unnaturally attracted to people who were unusual, particularly in the last two years of school and in my early working life. I was fascinated by the discovery of a poet called T S Eliot; he was exciting and new and he expressed himself in ways that I felt were more appropriate to my century than that of Keats, Wordsworth and Shelley - although the Romantics were the 'bloods' of their time. Eliot led me to more exploratory forays into modern literature and I decided that what I wanted most in life was to become a writer. But how? Nothing that had happened to me up to age seventeen was worthy of other people's interest. However, if you want to achieve something vital to your existence, you know you have to persevere; today, I endorse the quotation that writing is 99% perspiration and 1% inspiration. I also think that no writer has a right to publish books before the age of forty, when life has kicked in. Recently, I read that a certain 22 -year-old footballer has been paid a substantial advance to write his autobiography! Autobiography of what? I imagine he will produce all of two foolscap pages – if he tries really hard and is able to spell. In that far off year of 1957, I vowed that I would write and hopefully publish some books before I shuffled off this mortal coil. I didn't start seriously until 1989. Since then, I have published two books and two plays; this book is my third. I have two novels, two other books and a biography ready for publication, with a further two novels in progress.

With this attitude, it was no surprise that I worked spasmodically at school. I had decided my role would that of mild maverick, a poet in embryo, wanting to have little or nothing to do with the accepted values of the day. I think that was what made me comfortable in Jack Milne's classes; in him, I saw a desperately needed kindred spirit who demonstrably offered the things that I craved.

The school years of 1957 and 1958 ground on, with highlights coming in their cyclical time. Summer and other term holidays became more precious, when I could escape to the Lammermuir Hills on my bike, my saddlebag stuffed with sandwiches or a small tin of beans and a quarter pound of sausages I cooked on an open fire beside some nameless little stream in the hills.

And I loved the red letter days of school; Sports Day, though I was no sportsman, Prize-giving Day and Armistice Day. Certain red letter days were celebrated by the whole school assembling in the sunken quadrangle at Woodbush, when flags were hung over the balcony and prayers were said. I was always moved by Armistice Day in the quad because it stirred my patriotic

# Lions and Donkeys (part 2)

soul; also, I'd lost an uncle in the First World War and my grandmother had died on 10th November 1937, the day before the Armistice parade that year. Granny Cockburn's photograph was always decked with the Haig poppies we always wore at school on 11th November. When the service was held in the quad and we observed the two-minute silence at 11am, my thoughts were with Uncle George Henderson who was killed on 25th October 1918 and Granny Cockburn. Perhaps it may strike some people as odd that I felt - and still feel - close to two people I never met. The young choose icons and heroes for their own reasons; I still have an acute sense of my own loss on every Armistice Day morning.

But time's winged chariot was racing towards the finish line. We began to take our teachers' urgings to 'do better' or else we wouldn't 'get on' in the world. To be honest, I was desperately trying to figure out how to get off. Checking my report card for the years 1953-56, I note that I was best at Latin, then History, English and to my surprise, music. I never consistently scaled the heights. There were spectacular comets and shooting stars - I once got 80% for Latin - but these attainments were rare, never sustained and always occurred in the winter term, when I was at my best because I didn't venture out into the fields and the hills, my beloved distractions of that time.

One thing that worried me in 1958 was my future. I had absolutely no idea of what I was going to do after I left school; it worried my parents too. I had to fight my mother to stay on to do a Fifth Year; she'd wanted me to leave in Third Year and take work and earn my keep. I asked her what I could do.

'Get a trade.'

My Uncle Jimmy said that the only trade for somebody like me would be plumbing because it didn't require much brains or scientific knowledge:

'Everybody kens that water runs doonhill, not uphill. Aye, he'll manage the plumbing.'

The arguments went on. I protested that one day, I would go to the university in Edinburgh. My mother was shocked:

'Will you never leave the school? What use is the university to the likes of you? Laddie, are you always going to have your nose stuck in a book when others have to work hard for their living?'

I made a deal with my mother in 1956. I said I would work all summer and at the weekends all year to make up for her expected income. I promised to take a job at *Lipton's,* the grocers in Dunbar and she reluctantly agreed. I worked behind the counter, serving the people of Dunbar for two summers, wearing an apron that reached down to my feet and a white pea-jacket coat that attracted the nickname 'short arse'. It was there that I met Betty Leslie from Grantshouse, whom I loved from the minute I saw her. I still care for her fifty years on. In those summer weeks, I earned £3.18 [£3.90]. It was almost the same as the earnings of an apprentice plumber. After the summer holidays, I reverted to the role of messenger boy, earning £1 a week for working two

289

# Lions and Donkeys ( part 2)

hours on Thursday and Friday evenings and eight hours on Saturdays. This satisfied my mother and allowed me to escape the noxious trade of plumber.

Having to work on Thursday and Friday evenings and all day Saturday meant lagging behind with my homework, a tremendous amount of which we were given, especially in the Fifth Year. As a result, I developed a life-long habit of reading into the wee small hours. I studied until 1am on these nights with the result that I was tired the following day. We also acquired a TV set in 1957 which diverted me on Friday and Saturday nights when we were treated to Errol Flynn movies with titles like *The Charge of the Light Brigade* and *They Died With Their Boots On* - a particular favourite because it was about General George Armstrong Custer - what an appropriate middle name for the sword-wielding maniac he was.

In the year 1958, I was still unsure about my career; I had discarded the thought of banking and insurance, jobs which involved the handling of money and which gave me nightmares. Then Elma Miller, who was in Sixth Year and lived with her gamekeeper father in Broxmouth Estate applied to sit the Home Civil Service Exam for Clerical Officers. She was successful and was posted to the Ministry of Pensions and National Insurance in Dumfries, where her father had secured a new position. Elma recommended the Civil Service to me in 1958 as the pay was reasonable and the job carried a free pension at retirement - rare in those days. There was also a good chance I could work in Scotland. Elma knew how fortunate she'd been as most successful candidates in the Civil Service Exam were posted to London, a place I had no desire to work, let alone live. In those days, Civil Servants posted to London endured hostel accommodation; the thought of living in a dormitory - all that reeking, strange humanity - filled me with horror. Even so, I decided to give the Civil Service a try.

I had to work even harder to catch up at school and to study for the Civil Service examination. At times, I was so tired and perplexed by subjects like algebra and trigonometry that I could hear the mental locks in my head snapping shut. And by the time that the *Higher* and *Lower* exams loomed, my classmates Derick and Deanna and I were subjected to an additional exam. How we did it, I will never know. The three of us sat the exam in Edinburgh's Adam House in Chamber Street one bitter January day. We passed. I think Derick was 69th in the UK, Deanna was 177th and I as usual was in between, attaining 127th position. About 2000 boys and girls sat the exam so our performance was laudable for a small rural Scottish town. The results were read out by Hugh Cowan at the Friday morning assembly and the three of us were congratulated.

In December 1965, I sat the Limited Competition for Executive Officers; by then, I had moved from the Ministry of Pensions and National Insurance from Dundee to the GPO, Edinburgh. It was the best I ever did in an exam. My English pass was incredibly high – *Maggie Meeks,* I hope you are reading this from wherever you are. My essay gave me marks that would ensure my pass. I wrote screeds on the subject which was entitled 'Does the Modern Novel Have to Have a Plot to Qualify as a Novel?' It was right up my street. I couldn't have asked for a more relevant topic for my essay.

At the subsequent interview by a team from the Civil Service Commissioners, held in the Botanic Gardens in Edinburgh, among other questions I was asked was to recite the last two lines of D H Lawrence's poem *The Snake*. I quoted them, answering what I thought Lawrence meant. My answer pleased her. That literary lady from the Commission beamed a lovely smile when I quoted the words. Heavy stuff it was; I wondered how this would equip me to serve my country better as an Executive Officer. I see from my copy of the exam results that I came 12th in Britain, 1st in Scotland; I was assured a posting in St Andrew's House, Edinburgh, where I worked until I took early voluntary retirement in 1996. Apart from a year temporarily promoted to Senior Executive Officer, the last 24 years of my career were spent in the middle management grade of Higher Executive Officer, a grade Derick also reached in the Ministry of Defence – not too bad for two laddies from Dunbar.

Of the three headmasters I knew, on reflection, I think Hugh Cowan was the best. That didn't stop us chanting the infamous song about Robert Macaulay which we adapted to fit in Mr Cowan, then his successor *Shorty* Muir when his time came:

> *There is a happy land*
> *Far, far away*
> *Where Hughie Cowan stands*
> *Far, far away.*
> *Big feet, hairy jaws*
> *He could fairly lay the tawse.*

It was a paean to Cowan's sense of pride in a school that he undoubtedly loved.

Tension mounted as the *Highers* approached. And not just among the scholars. Teachers grew ever more irritable, piling on the homework, coaching us in last minute, frantic exercises. Many teachers managed to hide their true feelings but the air was full of nervous, infectious excitement. One day, a male teacher under whom I wasn't studying unleashed his exasperation with me for some misdemeanour I robustly denied was mine. He took me aside in the corridor and hissed this in my ear:

> 'I was in the Home Guard when you were in your cradle, so don't
> you try to dictate terms to me, boy. I was shot at on Dunoon pier
> for the likes of you in 1940.'

Dunoon pier? The Germans must have been desperate - or hopelessly lost.

Despite having abandoned Latin and Jack Milne, he kept in touch and offered help and comfort when he saw how worried I was about the exams. He used to smile and made no secret of what he thought about the German language studies I'd taken instead of Latin. He bore me no grudge and we remained friends until his death. I shall never forget his mocking of the genders in German:

'The thunder he roars, the rain she pours and the girl it shelters under the tree.'

I remember Jack saying that German was a useful language for disciplining errant horses and disobedient dogs. Maybe he was right. And maybe I should have stayed in his class for he assured me I would pass in Lower Latin. I didn't get Lower German. If there is a special place in heaven for teachers, J I W Milne deserves to be there, on the right hand of the Almighty. Well maybe not. He will be too mischievous, entertaining his fellow angels with ghost stories like *The Beast with Five Fingers, The Monkey's Paw, Monsieur Bourdette* and *The Signalman*. When he isn't doing that, he will play his violin and recite some of his so humorous poems, a special favourite being *To a Very Small Boy,* his muted adoration of the male appendage. He was a lovely man and a good teacher who should have taught in a more prestigious school than Dunbar.

And then suddenly, the exams were over and our fates were sealed in brown envelopes. The results were a mixture of success and failure, just as they are today. We knew - or thought we knew - our strengths and weaknesses. There were some surprises in the hat from which Hugh Cowan drew our results like a benign magician - and some disappointments. I mourned my failure to achieve a Lower pass in German. But the disappointment was mitigated by the fact that I'd gained a pass in Maths. (I have never used Maths during my life; I might have usefully used the German language in my career but as it turned out, I didn't have to).

And so that school year dragged on to its end. It was playtime for the rest of the summer term of 1958. The School Magazine was published, bringing with it a host of memories I treasure to this day. I have lost my copy of that year but I possess the previous year's copy; it is typical example of the usual content. Here are some of the lovely entries from the infants' school:

*I have a cat colled corki it cums to school with me. Corki sits on the rubij dump*

*I went to musselburu with Mummi and Daddi. I went to the beach and I got swets{sweets]. I went to woolis [Woolworth's]*

*My birthday is to-day. I have a big doll her name is Alis. I got a cardegen and wun and six [one shilling and sixpence] and 5 cards. I had a cac [cake] to[o].*

*My daddy sees the world from his ship, he saw pepl from his ship. I think they are black. He brings me dolls sweets and telefons and lots of things. His ship is an noil tanker* [oil tanker]

# Lions and Donkeys (part 2)

*My pet budgie did a notie*[naughty] *thing. He spilt the seed and
the water and Mother said 'Notie Jackie' and Jackie sed 'Notie
Jackie'. My budgie lives and sleeps in the cage. Then he says
'Prety Jackie.'*

School howlers (they really said it).

> *A smock is a skelp [smack]*
> *'Peril' means dimand*
> *A 'tabernacle' is a beast that sticks on the bottom of boats*
> *'Pedlars' are people on bicycles*
> *A word for 'conclusion' is bang*
> *A word for 'hard work' is slavery*
> *The Middle Ages is a district in England*
> *Columbus searched for India under Queen Isabella of Spain*

Perhaps our true feelings about teachers were most succinctly summed-up by
the late Arthur Jenkins:

> *What a Pity*
> *How well I plan to kill that man*
> *Who glares and girns* [complains] *and groans;*
> *But miserable creature, if I did kill teacher*
> *Where would I hide his bones?*
> *The inkwells are a small lot, and the desks here would all rot*
> *And my schooling is much too clean.*
> *Yes, I think I had better stop thinking of slaughter*
> *And work like a well-oiled machine.*

*Requiescat in Pace* Arthur - for I know you aren't here any more. Had I written
that poem, I would have substituted ' better ' with 'oughter' in the penultimate
line. Full marks for resisting the temptation. I couldn't have.

Before the prize-giving ceremony, Sports Day dawned disappointingly
clear and bright, with the House Cup destined for Victoria again. My house
was *Castle*; it was stuffed with swots but somehow, we had to find enough
people to enter every field event. Being I think the oldest in *Castle* House, the
House deputy captain *Patrone* Togneri invited me to enlist. I was annoyed.

'I'm afraid you are going to have to be one of our entries for every
event. Nobody else's come forward.'

That 'nobody else' hurt me to the quick. I was the forlorn hope. I have
always felt alone but the aloneness that day would be public, which devastated
me. I could already hear the contestants from the other two Houses saying 'Is
that the best *Castle* House can offer?' I was beaten before the games started;
there was only one guy – the House captain, Ronnie Gillan, whose father owned
the *Castle Hotel* - who tried to boost my morale

293

# Lions and Donkeys ( part 2)

Like *Patrone,* Ronnie was sorry but adamant. They couldn't get anyone else to make up the number of contestants, themselves being committed in other events. They knew perfectly well that *Castle* - I - wouldn't win anything. To a certain extent, I was the sacrificial lamb. I was entered for the seven-a-side rugby team – I wonder how they managed to get that number of players - in which my lot were slaughtered 57-0 by *Victoria* and 49-0 by *Cromwell*. I think I earned a point for Castle by turning up on the day. Then I was entered for the mile, the half-mile, the quarter mile and the 100 yards dash, the long and high jumps and putting the shot.

*The Boss* (Hugh Cowan) stared at me without a trace of a smirk on his face. But I knew he was struggling to keep a straight face

'Of course, Roy, you can't expect to aggregate all the points you gain because you'd win the top athlete's cup if you were first in every event. However, we will allow you to be credited with every point you achieve for your House.'

Who was he kidding? By the time I ran the mile and the half-mile in the forenoon, I was a blown horse. When I ran the half- mile race in the afternoon, Hughie Cowan paced me for the final 20 yards, cheering me. I came in last. No matter, everybody loves a loser. Well, that's what they say. I thought differently at the time.

In the eight events I had entered, I had gained the astonishing (to me and to others) total of six points. Needless to say, Victoria kept the House Cup, the star attraction being Pat Barnett, a born athlete. I think I gained five or six points. *Patrone* Togneri sidled up to me after the tug-o'-war which *Castle* lost; at least he had the good grace to wait until till I got back my breath, then he spoke to me in his usual laid-back, languid way:

'Well, Roy, we did better than I thought we would.'
We? Who was we? It was me.

A few days later, the final curtain was being hung in the Parish Church Hall, the dais decked out with fresh flowers for the prize-giving day. Prize giving is all very well - if you have won something. Otherwise, it's a big yawn tinged with disappointment and a personal sense of failure. That afternoon, the hall filled up quickly with self-congratulatory parents and their nervous offspring who would have to mount the stage to collect their glittering prizes. In my entire school life, I won a single prize - *Alice in Wonderland and Through the Looking Glass* - a book which was perhaps appropriate to one who has always spotted the ridiculous in human nature, who has seen through the hypocrisy of people, informed by the heart of an eternal child. *Alice* was awarded when I was in Primary 6A in 1952 for what Robert Macaulay decided was deserved for my 'Diligence'. (I had to look up the word in the dictionary, where I learnt that diligence was persistent effort or work, the mark of an industrious character. My subsequent career in the Home Civil Service reflected that, although I got few prizes there for persistent effort or work).

# Lions and Donkeys (part 2)

The ceremony began with a hymn, then a prayer; these were followed by a speech from Hugh Cowan. I think they awarded the prizes in reverse order, although the School *Dux* - best student. To me, the term reeked of *Il Duce*, that pompous Italian ass Mussolini who so embarrassed his countrymen - and his reluctant ally, Adolf Hitler - during the Second World War. Then came awards to the *Head Boy* and *Head Girl*, followed by individual prizes for specific subjects - English prize, History prize and so on. After all the handshaking and the smiling faces came another hymn, another prayer, then we were dismissed for the last time. There was a party in Marine Road that night, at Esther Bruce's house.

The party was a fairly innocent affair, given today's lavish and excessively bucolic celebrations. We had a few cans of *McEwan's Export*, some of us (including me) got tiddly on two cans and the bolder of us necked in dark corners. Then someone suggested a midnight swim in the municipal swimming pool. Protests about lack of swimming gear were met with drunken scorn. I went along with the crowd to the pool but I didn't attempt the cold, dark water, which was just as well. Within minutes of the first naked body sluicing the surface after a crazy dive, the police were on the Glebe, shining their torches and calling on the swimmers to 'give themselves up' as they were trespassing on Town Council property. This was greeted by shrieks and screams, then a daft scramble for shed clothing. I was off like a rabbit, making my escape via the low walkway that led from the Swimming Pool to the *Old Men's Bathe* and thence to Marine Road, where I scouted the street to make sure the coast was clear. We all got back safe and sound and the party went on for another hour or so. I went home dry outside, wet inside and giggled uncontrollably when I fell into the bed I shared with brother Ken who fortunately slept through my drunken snoring.

Then it was really all over. I started work in *Lipton's* the next morning - I am sure it was a Saturday - and I worked all summer long as a counter assistant until 17th August, when I got my reporting instructions to join the Ministry of Pensions and National Insurance in Dundee. I had a week's holiday before joining the Dundee office on 26th August 1958. My world, innocent, kind and comforting came to an end, replaced by one which while not quite a jungle, contained predatory beasts I had never encountered at school. Isn't that the lot of all who are suddenly thrown into the arena of adult life?

Woodbush or Dunbar Grammar School is no more today. Gone is the old, grey, mock Gothic building with its bell-tower and lattice windows, the Quadrangle where we attended the annual ceremony to honour the dead former pupils in two World Wars. I loved the Quad, with its trough containing flowers, poppies on Armistice Day, its hard edges and paving stones softened by snow in winter. It was never happier than when it echoed with young, shrill voices, never more sad when I saw it for the last time before demolition, its paving stones fringed by weeds, an empty, sad courtyard, echoing with the scuttering of autumn leaves. At least they rescued the War Memorial with its alphabetic dead; it now graces the entrance to Summerfield School in the *Sailors' Park* today. Long gone are the huts in the playground, the Special Hut for retarded children, the *duffies* [toilets] and the bike shed. Today, the boundary walls survive here and there, the landward walls still possessed of their sloping concrete buttresses which if there was space enough would no doubt be attempted by skateboarders. We used to try to reach the summit of the wall by running up these sloping buttresses in sandshoes. Few of us ever succeeded.

Though the site is now contained in a modern housing estate, ghosts from the past undoubtedly lurk in the odd corner, those of both pupils and teachers. On a quiet day, when the gulls call plaintively over the sea, I imagine I can hear the sharp, bird-like voices of those children of long ago, calling to each other in the playground. I like to think of John Irving Wallace Milne - was that his real name? - looking down from distant Elysian or Bacchanalian Fields, remembering his time here.

There will be some who attended Dunbar Grammar School in my time who will take issue with this chapter and what it describes. I hope there will be many who will agree with my account and take a fonder, gentler view than I have about many of the teachers. The critics who disagree with me will consider me unfair to the school. That is their prerogative. I wrote this chapter based on my own experiences of the school; my impressions are subjective but they are honest, as close as I can get to the feelings I experienced during that time. I was proud and still am proud of my old school but I see no reason to ignore its deficiencies, portraying it as I knew it, warts and all. If I have offended anyone, I hope that I will be forgiven the occasional uncharitable comment.

The celebration of hundredth anniversary of the opening of the modern grammar school at Summerfield will fall due in 2061, by which time I shall be long gone. I hope it is still standing then. There will be few scholars crammed into its rooms, for by then, they will work from their homes, logging into the centenary celebrations on their personal computers. By then, I predict the school will not be known as Dunbar Grammar; the government of that far off time will have devised another title for it. It may have some name like SEAC/TU/61 (South-east Education Area Consortium/Teaching Unit Year 2061). None of its sophomores - we will by then have adopted the American High School terminology - will understand that in the previous century SIL meant First Year Latin class. They will not even be taught Latin, a dead language which isn't taught at Dunbar today. The sophomores will listen politely to the speech made by the SEAC Director and his four members of staff. They will wear white PVC uniforms in the style worn in *Startrek;* at least two of them will be coloured, maybe one of the two a practising Muslim, wearing what looks like a tea towel on his/her head. Another one will have to be a Catholic. If we are still politically correct, the fourth will be English. There will be no Scottish-born teacher. Some of the sophomores may be curious enough to log into Channel 315 to watch the historic if primitive landing on the Moon. That will probably be the extent of their history lesson.

I think cynically of the sophomores of Dunbar Grammar School in those far-off years: I can sum up my feelings. We were what they never will be. Today, the students are unable to translate J I W Milne's excellent school motto; they require the help of one of their teachers who took Latin many years ago.

*Non sine pulvere palma*

It appears on the school stationery. I wonder how many students know that it means this:

*No prize can be won without effort*

I can only say this to my dear friend Jack Milne:

*Reqiescat in pace, dignus magister* [Rest in peace worthy teacher].

# 12

## Papers, Peas, Potatoes and Pan Loaves

During my parents' twelve years' separation, we lived on a fixed income set by the War Office - £4:12:6 [£4.62] a week, this being the amount compulsorily deducted from a married serving soldier's pay. My mother therefore relied on Norman, then me to contribute to the household expenses. Norman left school at the age of fourteen in 1947, just before the leaving age was increased to age fifteen; he first worked as a telegram boy in the local GPO with his friend Arthur *Ping* Hendy, then when he refused to take an exam there, he left the Post Office to work first as a baker's boy with Mr Hurry, a High Street baker whose shop is now occupied by David Smith's *Tasty Bite,* then as a laundry delivery boy with the *Lammermuir Laundry* owned by Mr Petrie and situated in Spott Road. Norman worked for the laundry until he was eighteen, when he was called up for National Service in the RAF. During his three years - he did an extra year because he was happy in the service - he sent home £1, half of his weekly pay. When he decided to stay on for a further year, his pay was increased, so he sent home half of that. Ken was too young to contribute, so I was the man about the house, expected to help in whatever way I could. As the employment law then didn't allow children to work until age thirteen, I could only contribute in kind rather than in money.

At first, my contribution was restricted to chores at home that allowed my mother to go out to work for much-needed cash. She took several seasonal jobs to massage the family budget. She worked as a cleaner in boarding houses and part-time in the fields of surrounding farms; she hoed, weeded, picked potatoes, docked turnips, lifted cabbages - all back-breaking jobs, as I would soon learn. But her main money making scheme was to let the two upstairs bedrooms to summer visitors during the months of July and August. In the days before the ubiquitous caravan, Dunbar Burgh Council allowed council house tenants to let one or more of their bedrooms without incurring additional rent. A list of approved accommodation addresses was drawn up by the Council and advertised in the Edinburgh and Glasgow newspapers. My mother must have been among the first to put her name down on the 'visitor' list. In retrospect, I suppose the arrangement suited many Edinburgh and Glasgow people, as few families could afford the prestigious boarding houses, let alone expensive hotels like the *Hotel Bellevue* and the *Roxburghe, St George, Bayswell* and *Craig-en-Gelt* hotels. It suited the Burgh Council as the arrangement attracted more holidaymakers to the town; the local traders also benefited from increased business. Cafes like *Greco's,* the *Lido,* the *Bingo* and Togneri's fish and chip shop never had it so good.

For its part, the Burgh Council was able to fund improvements and facilities it otherwise couldn't have afforded and so the scheme was a godsend to the community at large as well as the summer visitors - we were way ahead of *VisitScotland*, calling them visitors rather than holidaymakers or tourists. In its heyday, Dunbar had several putting greens, a public tennis court and of course, the jewel in the crown, the open-air swimming pool, all of which brought in much-needed revenue. Between the two World Wars and until the late 1960s, Dunbar was a boomtown.

The terms offered by council house tenants to holiday visitors were simple: *full board*, which needs no explanation, as the guests were fed and given the run of the house just as if they were in an hotel. The more popular and less expensive arrangement was *with attendance*, a restricted service; the residents bought and cooked their own food, eating it in their own rooms that were cleaned for them every day. Either arrangement disrupted the household to a certain degree. In the case of full board, our family meals were served after the visitors had been fed; the living room was also at the disposal of the guests, who expected - and got - supper in the evenings. Whatever the terms, Ken and I slept in a sofa bed in the living room; it was great fun going to bed late at night, not so much fun in the mornings, when we had to rise early and make way for full board visitors having their breakfasts or the other ones getting access through the living room to the kitchen to make their own early morning meal. I am convinced that my mother made more profit out of the *with attendance* guests as she constantly worried she wasn't providing enough food for those who opted for *full board*. To her, that meant four meals a day; cooked breakfast in the morning, a salad lunch at 1pm, a three-course Tea at 5pm. Even her suppers were sumptuous, consisting of ham sandwiches, teacakes and biscuits. She went over the top because she was afraid somebody would complain she wasn't treating her guests right. My mother always gave value for money, more than she needed to, which meant that her profit margin was low. She never felt she did enough for our summer visitors. That was a measure of the lady she undoubtedly was.

The people who preferred boarding to limited service were predominantly from Glasgow. The Edinburgh families opted for *with attendance,* possibly on grounds of cost as well as allowing them the freedom to choose their own food. Glaswegian holidaymakers are famous the world over for their carefree, unbridled spending on holiday. They believe in spending the lot when they are on holiday, coming home broke but happy. We had several lovely Glasgow families who stayed with us during the Glasgow Trades fortnight, which usually occurred in the third and fourth weeks of July. I recall one Glasgow family of four who were from Giffnock; they were Orthodox Jews who, apart from Solly or Solo Winston who lived in Dunbar, were the only Jews I have ever met. Being orthodox, this meant no pork or bacon on the menu but a lot of liver, fish and chicken. The fish and liver posed no problem but chicken was expensive in those days. They also perplexed my mother (and me) by insisting that an extra place had to be set at table for every meal. Years later, I discovered that this was a Jewish custom; the Messiah might arrive unexpectedly to break bread with them. I found this very weird and said so in a loud voice to my mother.

'Wheesht! They'll hear you! They're paying me good money and if
that's what they want, they'll get it. But -'
- here she reverted to her Scottish nature without any trace of humour or self consciousness -
' - if this Mess-what's-his-name comes to the door for his tea, they'll
have to pay extra.'

Full boarders increased the degree of chores I was expected to do. Whether we had boarders or not, in the summer months, I peeled potatoes, cleaned other vegetables, washed dishes and swept floors which in those days were covered with Kirkcaldy lino and a few scattered rugs. I was never allowed to play until after lunch, which usually meant taking young Ken to the beach.

The Edinburgh visitors vexed my mother - and Ken and I - since, preferring to do their own cooking, they also felt they should have the run of the house; when it rained, they'd lounge about our living room, writing postcards or reading newspapers. They were awfully posh, talked very proper and so Ken and I were given strict instructions to watch our Ps and Qs. I remember one childless couple - maybe that explained why they were friendlier than the other families with offspring. They were nice to me, chatting away, treating me as an adult in embryo; being shy and nervous, I tried to avoid them in case I got my Ps mixed up with my Qs. Inevitably one day, I did.

That day, they came out to the back green and commented on the healthy and prolific crop in my vegetable garden while I was stolidly beating eight bells out of a carpet my mother had hung on the wash line. They praised me for the garden and the carpet beating and asked whether I wouldn't rather be out playing with my little brother. I lied and said no, that I enjoyed my work.

'Oh come now, do you really like what you're doing? Wouldn't you
rather be at the beach or the swimming pool?'

I was in a quandary. Yes, I would have rather been on the beach/swimming pool. But I couldn't say that, as my mother was glowering at me from her bedroom window at the time. She signalled to me to say I was happy at my work.

'Aye. I mean yes. Och, I like this fine.'

I avoided saying it was OK because that was an Americanism and considered *de rigeur*. But I'd said *Och,* which made my mother grimace out of the window. I should have quit while I was ahead, but my nervousness got the better of me. (When I am nervous, I always say too much). This is what I said to the couple:

'Oh mai work is quaite naice but -'

- here I panicked, then recovered my equilibrium -

'- the stower gets into my eyes. It's a nuisance.'

I had remembered my mother's words; I hadn't called the dust *stoor* as we would normally do. My mother heard me at her open bedroom window and made a throat-slitting motion with her hand. She called out to the young couple, smiled sweetly and said she was sorry but she needed me in the house. When I got indoors, she grabbed my arm.

> 'You wee fool. You're not to cry it stower or stoor. It's DUST. They're
> from Morningside in Edinburgh. What did I tell you about speaking
> proper. Now go you out there and apologise to them for being ignorant.
> Let them see we're better than that.'

The argument was lost on me; I thought by avoiding the word *stoor* I had been proper. The Edinburgh couple were amused when I went back into the garden. I had just had my first lesson in pretension. The experience gave me a complex and an aversion to Rabbie Burns and other Scottish writers; for many years, I thought them 'common' for using Scots' dialect. This has been - and to a lesser extent still is - the curse of the Scottish working class. I was relieved when the Edinburgh couple went home, although on the Saturday morning they left, the husband shook my hand as he set down the suitcases and shut our garden gate. There was a stiff breeze blowing that day and as he was about to get into the waiting taxi, he shook my hand. When he let go, I was surprised to find a whole, bright shilling [5p] in the palm of my hand. As the taxi driver picked up the suitcases, the Morningsider leant over the gate and whispered to me:

'My, isn't it windy today, laddie? There's a lot of stoor blowing about.' Edinburgh folk are funny. I swear I saw a twinkle in his eye as I thanked him, then ran into the house to proudly show my mother the shilling.

In her less stressed evenings, my mother loved to sit and knit in the makeshift seat I'd made for her in the back garden. Ken and I would play at her feet while she regaled us with tales of local characters, men and women who even then were fading into legend. For instance, she told us about a pawnbroker who lived in what is now 30 Castle Street, not far from where I live today. You can see the bricked-up front door to this day. The pawnbroker's name escapes me now but my mother told me that queues of fishermen's wives would form outside the shop on Saturday mornings to redeem their husbands' suits so they could cut a dash in the pub on Saturday night and then in church on Sunday morning.

> 'Aye. Then on Monday morning, the queues formed again, as long as on
> Saturday. The suits were pawned until the following Saturday. We were
> right poor in those days.'

Then there was a woman who kept a small shop in the High Street, near the entrance of what is called Castle Wynd today. She sold everything from bundles of kindling wood, paraffin, firelighters, candles to pots and pans, needles and thread. And her specialty – the homemade toffee she laid on a tray and displayed in the front of her shop window. As this was her tabby cat's favourite snoozing place, the toffee was, to put it mildly, a dubious purchase. My mother told us that when she was a little girl, her mother used to send her to the shop to get some kindling for the fire and other things; she would count her change and knew there were a couple of pennies that her mother said she could have for doing the errand. She said this to the shopkeeper:

> 'May I have tuppenceworth o' the toffee in the windae. As it's hairy
> toffee, will I get a wee bit extra?'

The shopkeeper was insulted, indignant.

> 'Away ye go! Ah dinnae sell hairy toffee!'

My mother wasn't put off:

> 'Ma mither said I could spend my tuppence here for ye get mair for the
> pennies than in the real sweetie shop. Ah dinnae mind the hairs fae
> [from] yir pussycat. Ma mither picks them off.'

She was chased out of the shop by the owner brandishing a *besom* or broom.

A postscript to this incident concerns the aforementioned cat. The shop owner had a son called Albert who lived with her above the shop. He couldn't have been very bright because my mother said he always referred to himself as All-but. Be that as it may, the boy was sunning himself at the open window of his mother's flat one day, the toffee moggie lying on the stone windowsill. The said cat panicked, jumped off the window sill and was followed by poor Albert, who'd been told to look after the creature; Albert landed in the High Street, triumphantly clutching the cat, though he'd broken both elbows and fractured his knees when he hit the pavement. My mother said the ungrateful cat walked away from him unscathed!

Cats are like that, self-contained and independent creatures, characters every one; they don't need human beings for anything other than food.

Before they could work legally for wages at the statutory age of thirteen, most Dunbar children were expected to undertake some light domestic chores as soon as they were competent and could be trusted. Pocket money was minimal, maybe a sixpence [2.5p] a week and it had to be earned - unlike today, when kids expect it as of right. Nothing less than a few pounds will satisfy the average teenager of today; even allowing for inflation, I think ten pounds - apparently the norm - is excessive.

In addition to the chores I've already mentioned, I had to chop firewood for kindling the fire, haul in buckets of coal, lug the heavy wireless accumulator to *Stark's Garage* every week to have it recharged, a particularly unpleasant job if you weren't careful; whether it's true or not, my mother used to warn me not to let it touch my skin as it would burn me.

As I wrote earlier in Chapter 4, another weekly task was collecting cinders and *briquettes* from the local gasworks, to the rear of Doon Avenue; the latter fascinated me if only for their symmetrical shape. When I asked my mother how they were made, she couldn't answer at first, then she said

'Your Uncle Jimmy says they're made of coal coom.'

It was many years later that I learnt that *coom* was a Dunbar corruption of culm or coal dust.

As well as my cinder and *briquette* routine, I was put in charge of the garden - vegetable and ornamental. I was also expected to lend a hand with the spring-cleaning, that annual madness which still seizes Scottish housewives. Spinsters, mothers and their daughters succumbed to this fever over the two weeks preceding Easter. The routine of the house was disrupted as blankets and curtains were washed, wrung through the ringer, pounded, hung out to dry and then ironed with a flat iron heated on the fire. Daily mealtimes were disrupted, the quality dropped alarmingly; we were given what my mother called *patch ups* or *pushovers* - an early form of what today would be described as junk food. We ate tinned meals, pies, fish suppers and on really bad days, *potted heid* sandwiches. As I mentioned chapter 7, *potted heid* or *hough* came in small circular glass jars filled by the butcher; it was (to me) a disgusting mess of shreds of cheap meat encased in solid jelly. I am sure it was nourishing, like tripe - another dish I avoided whenever I could - but to Ken and I, *potted heid* was the pits.

The whole town suffered from this madness. Vans that called round the streets did a roaring trade as female washers and scrubbers - I use the latter term in its esoteric sense - downed their irons, unrolled their sleeves, removed their *pinnies* [aprons] and ran to the van men like flies round a jam pot, jostling for their place in the queue and demanding something cheap and easily made for their 'man's' tea in their hoarse, *Woodbine* - roughened voices.

Of all my chores, gardening was the most satisfactory; to see my crops growing and contributing to the household budget gave me a sense of real achievement. I felt I was a natural gardener, possibly inheriting my skills - as my mother used to maintain - from Granny Cockburn. In autumn, I dug up wild daffodil bulbs and primrose roots to plant in the front garden; today, that would be against the law. In spring, I sowed seeds - nasturtium (golden gleams), lupin, nigella, sweet pea, arabis, virginia stock and viscaria.

'They'll not grow, son' my mother said gloomily. 'The soil's too poorly for wee seeds.'

But most of my packets of seeds did, in profusion. She was delighted and proud of me. Why me? It was only Nature lending a helping hand.

My main interest was the vegetable garden. When I took it over, the plot was usually given over to potatoes, year in, year out. The soil had grown tired and the crop was poor the first year I was put in charge of it, so I informed my mother that I'd plant next year's potato crop in hitherto unused parts of the garden. There were two areas that lay fallow every year; one was a narrow strip running down the shaded side of the house, the other was under my mother's bedroom window. I tried to explain to her the benefits of crop rotation.

'I expect you read that nonsense in one of your books' she sniffed. 'Well, we'll not get potatoes this year, that's for sure. I love the new tatties that much.'

She said the soil was poor, the patches didn't get enough sun, slugs and snails lived there, that only weeds would grow there. I argued that if weeds could grow, so could spuds. I tried to explain to her that a potato crop was ideal for 'cleaning' dead ground. She sniffed again.

'OK clever Dick. There might be tatties but they'll be bulls' eyes.'
By this, she meant they'd be so small that they'd not be worth lifting.

So in 1953 - Coronation year - I was given free rein over the entire garden. I manured the uncultivated plots and the one we usually cultivated with a mixture of grass and sheep's droppings I cadged from Dunbar Golf Club; I steeped this mixture in an old oil drum I'd found on Belhaven beach. This noxious mixture was allowed to simmer and ferment; I drained it through an old sack and put the residual mess back into the drum so that it could further ferment in the spring rain that quickly refilled the drum. I poured the liquid over the ground and let nature take its course. I planned to use this soup to water the young seedlings in the growing season. When I dug the potato drills, I drained off the fluid and used the residue as manure, mixed in with a bag of horse manure I'd begged from Boyd's Stables at West Barns. The liquid was kept in lemonade bottles, jars and anything else I could get from the kitchen. In the main plot, I planted various seeds - turnip, carrot, lettuce, beetroot, peas, spring onions and onion sets, leaving enough space for two rows of cabbage plants I cadged from Adam, my mother's signalman friend. Then I sat back and waited to see the little shoots emerge in the spring; every few days, I watered them from my lemonade bottles.

It was a bumper crop that year. Even the potatoes surprised my mother. Every crop was successful except the carrots, which didn't thrive despite my mixing in sand off the beach, reputedly essential in carrot cultivation. I rubbed out their rows and planted Brussels sprouts and leek plants in their place. That winter, we would have onions, turnips, leeks and Brussels sprouts in profusion; all summer long, we feasted on salads made from my lettuce, *syboes* [spring onions] and beetroot. There was no stopping me after that. Even my mother was impressed.

'God, laddie, you've got your Granny's green fingers. I never thought we'd get such lovely tatties.'

In season, kids gathered wild brambles and blackcurrants from the gardens of long-ago demolished cottages or from the roadside. Many - myself included - thought nothing of raiding the orchards of the better off, especially in Gala Green or the West End. The apples in these gardens were often left to lie on the grass and rot away, which I thought was a sinful waste. On many

# Papers, Peas, Potatoes and Pan Loaves

October nights, I would don my black clothes, wear a balaclava and raid the gardens at Gala Green. Unlike modern kids, I didn't trash the gardens; I would come back at nine pm, my pockets and jersey stuffed with apples and pears. I went there to collect the fruit which could either be eaten or made into pies or other sweets like apple crumble, apple dumpling, Eve's pudding and so on.

And in these far off, smoky autumn mornings, I hunted the Sailors' Park on the other side of our garden wall for button mushrooms that grew in profusion during September and October. I loved - and still love - wild mushrooms.

When my Uncle Jimmy was presented with a scooter from his employer, *George Wimpey,* he and I would go off early on Sunday mornings to collect the great horse mushrooms at *Boorhoose.* They were the size of dinner plates. After Jimmy died, I would go up there or to Little Spott on Saturday and Sunday mornings on my bike to gather the mushrooms in the field or by the roadside. To me, mushrooms are works of art; apart from the clean, white heads, their undersides of dark chocolate or blush pink fins look as if they have been created with precision instruments. You have to be up early to gather them however; as the day goes by, they get wormed or disappear as mysteriously and quickly as they come out of the earth. Even years later, I spent many a misty autumn morning searching through the dew-soaked grass for an hour or so, seeking out these strange earth-tasting *fungi.* By then, I was observing the world about me, becoming aware of the poetry in simple things, pausing to look at the delicate tracery my footprints left in the dark, wet grass, marks that reminded me of a snake that had slithered across the fields.

As I wrote earlier, the task I found mightily onerous and time-consuming was the splitting of wood for kindling for the open fire. I seemed to be forever chopping up small logs, wooden crates and boxes - anything that came our way. As a consequence, there was always at least a year's supply of firewood in the coal shed; I used to lay it criss-cross fashion, layer by layer so that it could dry on the shelves. I calculated that as we only lit the fire for eight months of the year, we didn't need as much and that we would never run out. (In point of fact, when my mother did away with the open fire and installed an electric one, I burnt most of the kindling in the back garden one Guy Fawkes' Night).

But my mother insisted and her word was law:

'Ye cannae have enough kindling' she used to say to the neighbours 'and anyway, Roy enjoys the work.'

If only she'd known....

I did have one job that paid a shilling or two in the summer months. Occasionally, the milkman's lad would bunk off or feign sick, so I used to help out; Jackie Fairish, the milkman paid me a couple of shillings from his own pocket for delivering milk in our street and Summerfield Road. That didn't happen very often; I longed to be thirteen and get a job that paid real money so that I could contribute to the family budget and allow me some pocket money.

# Papers, Peas Potatoes and Pan Loaves

I found the law that forbade kids to work until they reached the age of thirteen irksome; it was enacted due to the efforts of well-intentioned Victorian liberals like Anthony Ashley Cooper, 7th Earl of Shaftesbury, the great reformer and friend of the labouring class and particularly young chimney sweeps - children sent up chimneys to clear away the soot - and the women and children who were forced to work in the coalmines for a pittance.

Unemployment came to Dunbar as elsewhere with a vengeance after the Second World War. The post-war kids of my generation saw it in the crumpled faces and hunched shoulders of men lounging at street corners, men who wanted to work but couldn't find any. Emigration increased as families struggled on the *Dole*, or unemployment benefit. Many fine local tradesmen took their families to Australia and New Zealand in the 1950s because they couldn't take the poverty any longer. Most jobs in and around Dunbar were seasonal - the fields in spring and autumn, the boarding houses in summertime - usually employing women and children who had reached the magic age of thirteen. Shop jobs rarely went vacant, the incumbents working most of their lives until retirement. The women who worked on the farms were, with exceptions like my mother and the wives and daughters of the farm workers - they would have been called *bondagers* in the previous century – could be coarse, forward and a bit overwhelming. They grew old before their time; they spoke the same bad language as the men, they smoked and drank and were best avoided on a Saturday night. I would soon discover for myself how hard they were - and how bawdy. Two of the respectable ones lived in our street. Little Jenny Punton and Bella Bisset were still working in the fields when I was in my twenties; they still wore the traditional *bondager* headgear known as the *ugly,* distinctive and eminently serviceable, giving protection against sun, wind and rain.

However, by 1954, the money situation was improving. Norman completed his National Service and took work at the Belhaven Brewery, where he earned reasonable wages and was able to contribute to the household budget. And for my part, on 17th February 1954, I reached the ripe - and magical - old age of thirteen and so could begin work. Almost immediately, I managed to get a paper round with *Penney's,* a local newsagent whose premises were incorporated into the modern Bank of Scotland, where the hole-in-the-wall cash dispenser is now located. Mine was the largest paper round in Dunbar at the time. I delivered 60 papers in the morning and 45 every evening. In addition, I had to take my turn with the two other paper lads in the shop, working one Saturday night in three delivering the *Lates* - the Green *Dispatch* and Pink *News*, sports' results papers printed late on Saturday afternoons hence their collective name. For this, I was paid the princely sum of thirteen shillings [65p] a week, a shilling for every year of my life. I handed over ten shillings [50p] to my mother and kept the remaining three shillings [15p] as pocket money. In those days, ten shillings could feed a family of four for two days. If my memory serves me right, our weekly household income doubled that year, with Norman contributing a few pounds, my mother earning a couple of pounds in the afternoons in the fields and my few shillings to the pot. I think by that year, our household income was £10 a week; out of that had to come the rent, the rates, the electricity bill, insurance, food and clothes; there wasn't much left for luxuries like sweets, visits to the cinema (the 'pictures' as we called the cinema then). But undoubtedly, life had improved; my mother's forehead seemed to lose its worried frown that year.

So, my first job was delivering newspapers. I loved working for the proprietors of *Penney's*. The shop was run by Ada and John Charleton, sister and brother; Ada and I shared the same birthday (as I do with a former school-mate, Aveline Blair, now Ainslie). They were kindness itself, even if at times they didn't quite get the addresses right. They relied on the stalwart support of Peggy Ramage who was quick to deal with cheeky paper lads. I got on very well with Ada, John and Peggy; Ada was a chirpy little woman, her brother John was quiet and shy. They were thoughtful when one of their paperboys went sick; out would come a bundle of comics for the patient with good wishes for a speedy recovery. It was inconvenient when a paperboy went off sick as a replacement had to be found at short notice; often, old John Charleton did the round himself, donning the Hessian sack and mounting the old shop boneshaker which I used as I'd no bike of my own then. If he had to use it, I did my round on foot, which meant an earlier rise than normal. I have always hated early morning rises - I still do - for I am not a morning person, being by nature a creature of the night.

Those of you who have been paying attention will recall that I had abandoned the idea of learning to ride a bike when I was six years old. I swore then that I would never ride a bike again but here was a quandary. At first, I informed the Charletons that I would deliver my round on foot; they said it would be impossible and that I'd be late for school. They were right. With a heavy heart, I wheeled the old bike out of the shop and took it to *Pettigrew's,* the cycle shop next to the Royal Bank of Scotland, today occupied by a beer and wine shop. The friendly Mr Jordan looked at it, shook his head, stroked his chin but said he thought he could make it serviceable. He overhauled it completely, shortening the sagging bike chain in the process. I wheeled it home and left it in the coal shed that Friday night; I didn't use it on the Saturday morning because there was no school and I could take my time. I delivered the papers on foot the next morning but in my heart of hearts, I knew that couldn't last. Somehow, I would have to grapple with the inevitable.

That Saturday afternoon, I parked the bike at the kerb outside our house, taunted by my brother Norman, lately demobbed from the RAF. Nervously, I slung my leg over the crossbar and sat on the worn leather saddle. I was terrified to push myself off the kerb with my foot. After a few seconds and Norman's taunts of being a *feartie* [coward], I did the deed. Off I went, pedalling like mad along Lammermuir Crescent with Norman running behind me shouting that it was all a question of balance. In the seven intervening years since my first encounter with the bicycle, I had somehow lost my fear and gained a sense of balance. So in truth, I never 'learnt' to ride a bike, I simply waited till the time was right. Perhaps there is a salutary lesson in this; if in doubt, do nothing until you are ready!

There was no stopping me after that. I went for long cycle runs, whizzing all over the Lammermuir Hills roads and byways, discovering places hitherto only names. A whole new world was opening up for me and I was enthralled by small communities like Monynut, Elmscleugh, Aikengall, Woodhall and many other poetically-named places in the hills.

In those days, morning and evening papers came by train; the morning papers were collected by the shop owners. The evening ones were the responsibility of the paperboys. Crowds of young lads – Dunbar High Street had six paper shops in those days - congregated at the railway station about 5pm to collect the bundles thrown by the guards off the goods van on to the platform. There was always a mad scramble to see who would get away first with his shop's bundle. The bundle was dumped on the counter, the string cut (and saved, a legacy from the war years) and then the Charletons and anyone else on duty would mark the street numbers on the front page. This was unnecessary except in the case of new employees, as the regular boys knew the routes and their customers by heart. Off we would cycle into the gloom of a November night or the sparkling evenings of summer, knowing that when we were finished, we had the rest of the evening to ourselves.

The paper job had its perks. We got free comics, mostly ones that were damaged.and therefore not marketable. We got a Christmas bonus but even more lucrative was the tips we received from customers. That first Christmas of 1954, I couldn't believe my eyes; I was amazed at the generosity of my customers, many of them with low incomes, especially the Old Age Pensioners. During the week before Christmas, I came home every day with pocketfuls of money; when I counted my tips on Christmas Eve morning, I was astonished to find I had made £5 and a few coppers. My mother was proud of me. And for my part, I was able to hand over £4 to her to help with the Christmas shopping that first year of work. As for me, to be given a whole pound was a fortune, which my mother said I had earned. I think I blew most of it on presents for Mum, Uncle Jimmy, Norman and Ken but I was still able to buy five shillings' worth of savings stamps for my nest egg. How simply we lived in those days - and how grateful we were. But I guess we were fortunate in that there were little jobs like that for youngsters who as a consequence, were rarely bored because they never had too much time on their hands.

As well as its perks, delivering papers had hidden perils, even in the days before the roads were congested with motorcars. In fact, the relative absence of cars made boys like me careless; I thought roads were for walking or cycling and the occasional car was a passing wonder, or a nuisance. One wet October morning, I was about a quarter way through my round, cycling slowly along the Edinburgh road against a stiff wind. Coming towards me on the wrong side of the road was an old man on a bike. He sat on it but had to propel himself along using his foot on the kerb as his bike chain was broken. As we approached one another, he made no attempt to alter course, which I suppose was understandable. I had to swing out from the kerb to let him pass and I did this at the precise moment a small Morris Minor whizzed past me, the door handle of the passenger side catching the strap of my Hessian sack. The car hauled me off the bike, I went up in the air and my papers were spilled onto the road. I landed heavily on the tarmac and was dazed. Further ahead, I saw Mrs Morrison, the Gas Manager's wife who had been waiting for her paper; she ran towards me, not bothering to look at the driver of the car. The car passed her, stopped, then the door opened; when the driver saw me getting up from the road, he sped off. I have never found out who he was.

Mrs Morrison was the soul of kindness. She helped me to my feet and gathered up the sodden newspapers. She shook her fist at the fast disappearing car and enquired if I was all right. I said I had a sore back but other than that, there seemed to be no damage except to my right sock which had somehow gotten torn. She asked me into her house and wanted to give me a cup of tea but I said I had to get on, worried that customers would complain about the late delivery of their wet *Daily Express*. I limped back to where my bike lay and cycled off, thanking the good lady for her help. When I look back on it now, I suppose I was partly to blame as I hadn't indicated I was going to go to the crown of the road. Also, because I mounted my bike from the right, I carried my Hessian sack of papers on my right side, whereas other paperboys carried theirs on the left. It wasn't some eccentricity of mine, I just found it easier that way.

By the end of the week, the pain in my back had grown worse and I went to see Dr Cordin, the local GP. He diagnosed a bruised spine but to be on the safe side, he arranged for me to have an X-ray at the Roodlands Hospital in Haddington. The X-ray confirmed nothing was broken and that I hadn't suffered a slipped disc; even so, I was off school and the paper round for three weeks, during which time I had to use a walking stick to get about. The Roodlands doctor who examined me said that I might contract rheumatism in later life but - touch wood - I haven't had any long-term effects, though I do suffer occasionally from back pain today.

Delivering newspapers has one serious drawback - the weather. Rarely is it in your favour. The roads weren't kind to old boneshakers like my shop bike, so I was obliged to buy a *John Bull* puncture outfit; fortunately my brother Norman was on hand to help me fix the oft punctured tyres that poor bike suffered. When I finally stopped delivering papers, Norman said the inner tube of my front bike wheel - it was the one that bore the brunt of the punctures -

had more *John Bull* patches than the original rubber.

In the summer of 1954, I decided to make a bit of extra cash by lending my paper round to another lad while I applied to work on one of the outlying farms, which paid much more than the newsagents. I managed to get a job along with a squad of kids hired by Sir Robert Hope, who farmed at Oxwellmains. Hired ostensibly for pea picking, the wages were exceptionally good - £2.18.0 [£2.90] - for a five-and-a-half day week from 8am to 5pm week-days and 8am to noon on Saturdays. My only apprehension about the job was the female workers. They were a formidable lot, especially the married ones; they were brave in a group and lethal when alone. Many a country hind has been booted in a tender part of his anatomy for following a lone fieldworker into the bushes to spy on a woman attending to a call of nature.

Most of the women wore men's clothes and *wellies* and the strange but serviceable rustic headgear known as an *ugly* which I have mentioned earlier; it consisted of a wire frame with a piece of coloured calico stretched over it which made a colourful bonnet that shielded the wearer's face and neck from the sun, rain and the ever-present winds. The *ugly* looked for all the world like a miniature version of the covered prairie wagons I'd seen in Westerns. Origi-nally worn by *bondagers* – the wives and daughters of farmhands who were expected to work in the fields along with their men folk - these women were little better than medieval serfs. Although the *bondager* had disappeared by the time I went to work in the fields, the *ugly* was worn well into the 1970s.

I dreaded the *Initiation*. Every new male worker - well, male teenager - was supposed to be subjected to this ritual at the hands of the women. I had heard from other kids that the women hounded their victims, chasing them until they were exhausted; then the women would grab the boy, undo his trou-sers and excite him. When he was ready, they'd push that part of his anatomy into a milk bottle filled with tractor grease and old engine oil, then leave him on the ground with his hands tied behind his back. I saw several tear-stricken lads untied by the sniggering hinds who, by way of consolation, would tell the victim that he was now a man and that if he didn't stop sniffling, they'd call him a *bloody jenny willocks* [East Lothian slang for the female *genitalia*]. I thought the whole business barbaric and said so within the hearing of a few of these harpies. From that day on, I was a marked man at every *lousin'* [literally 'loosening' or finishing time]. In those days, we were given *meenits* [minutes] - two fifteen minute breaks morning and afternoon; these were too short to permit any horseplay, so the dangerous time was noon *lousin'* or *denner* [din-ner] which lasted an hour. More of this comes later.

Although we were hired to gather peas - a contravention of the *Trades Description Act,* had it existed in those days, we never saw a peapod until about the last week of the seven or eight-week period of employment for the simple reason that the peas were never ready until late August. We were put to work in open fields around the farm or occasionally in the walled kitchen garden of Sir Bobby Hope's impressive house at Broxmouth Park. Once owned by Sir George Home, the last Earl of Dunbar, then by the Dukes of Roxburghe from 1638 until the early 1950s, the original house had been replaced by a modern version, although it was reckoned that the walled garden was original.

The first job we were given - on a rainy July morning - was singling leeks, a task which probably dates back to the Middle Ages as the humble leek was cultivated even then. I am sure it is mentioned in Chaucer's *Canterbury Tales.* A dozen or so older boys and men would start in a row with *grapes* [forks] to loosen the young leeks in the ground; the squad followed behind, bending down to grab a clump, shake off the excess soil, then separate the small leeks into bunches of 25 which were then tied together with a length of raffia string or straw. Each bundle was then laid into a wooden *trug* or wicker-work basket. I can't remember how many bundles went into each basket but I am fairly certain they held at least 500 leek plants. It was a fiddly, finger-numbing job I hated.

After the young leeks were taken away to be transplanted in the fields by women, we were given stints of weeding and thinning turnip seedlings; the soil around Oxwellmains was poor and stony and as you worked on your 'drill' or row, your hands got chapped and cut with stones, your fingernails were broken, your hands were stung by the small nettles that grew amongst the seedlings. These little feathery nettles stung just as badly as the adult ones. By the end of the first week of this, we were ready to give up -or at least I was. We did similar work in a beetroot field, then we moved to the more pleasant field at the *Deer Park* overlooking the East Links Golf Course and the sea. The field was sheltered to a certain extent by a red sandstone wall on the western side and a thick wood on the east; it was fairly pleasant work as carrots thrive best on sandy soil, so the work of weeding and thinning them was much easier than on the stonier soils reserved for turnips and beetroot. We had the trees for a natural toilet area, a vast improvement on the stunted thorn bushes which grew round the edges of the fields where we'd previously worked.

It was at *Deer Park* that I experienced my first lesson in human biology. Better known as SEX today, I still blush when I recall the incident. It isn't surprising that my interest in that particular sphere of human activity increased, for farms are veritable hotbeds of raw and plainly visible animal copulation. It's Nature after all; there is no sentiment or romanticism on a farm. Breeding is essential for the survival of the farm and its owners. I still shiver when I recall cows being taken to the bull for 'servicing' - a totally unemotional expression which while describing a necessary function, has nothing to do with the love and tenderness which human beings should aspire to in that most intimate of human acts. There was never any hint of embarrassment among the country folk when they talked about such things - in the context of animals at any rate; reproduction was all about keeping men and women in work. The same country folk could however be shy or rude - bawdy is perhaps a more apposite word - about human sexuality.

At Deer Park, the women and girls were allowed to visit the wood before the boys and men for their 'comfort' break. The boys were then led by the *gaffer* [foreman] to the same wood to relieve themselves. One hot August afternoon, we were trudging through the long grass at the side of the wood when we came across an unforgettable sight; there before our eyes was a naked man lying on top of an equally clothes-challenged lady. She looked up at my gawping, stupid face, smiled at me and said quite sweetly and innocently:

'Hello. It's a lovely day, isn't it?'

I stood there with a few others, open-mouthed, unsure of how to react. The man was resting on her and he never turned round to look at us, for no doubt he shared our embarrassment. A moment frozen in time was shattered when the *gaffer* came back to hurry us along. He saw the reason right away.

'C'mon, c'mon. Bobby Hope's no' payin' ye guid [good] money tae stand aboot gawpin' [looking] at a man an' wummin hae'in it aff.'

I was shocked by his coarse language and felt sorry for the young couple. I never cared for the *gaffer*, then or now, a man called Watson; even the bold female workers steered clear of him because he had the authority to hire and fire people. He could be quite brutal and unfeeling; his favourite ploy was to whack lagging boys on the buttocks with a stick. He warned the recalcitrant workers that three whacks in the same week meant they could 'collect their cairds' - meaning their National Insurance cards - for he would be sacking them. His treatment of young girls was even more unpleasant; he would stand behind a selected victim - usually a girl with a generous figure - and rub his stick between her legs and over her buttocks, whispering things none of us could hear. We knew it was dirty talk even if none of us had much idea of the meaning. One girl who broke down into tears told me this at the next break-time:

'He said ma jeans were too tight. But ma bum reminded him he'd to bring hame twa turnips for his wife. He said to keep away frae the bull in the hame field or else it'd think I was a coo. Ah'm no' wearin' onythin' red, so whit does he mean aboot the bull chasin' me?'

I tried to explain to her without embarrassing her. I said her tight jeans might make the bull think she was a cow ready for 'servicing'; I also told her that it was a myth that bulls attacked anyone wearing the colour red. Bulls suffer from colour blindness, or so I'm told. She wasn't interested in that little gem of fact. All she could think of was the 'servicing', which made her cry even more. I advised her to stick close to her friends and never be alone when the *gaffer* was around. He walks the streets of Dunbar today; he either doesn't recognise me or chooses not to acknowledge me. I prefer to keep it that way.

And then it was the boys' turn to be humiliated. I will never be able to prove whether the *gaffer* put the women up to an *Initiation Ceremony* but I think he'd overheard me giving advice to the generously proportioned girl.

# Papers, Peas, Potatoes and Pan Loaves

After the morning *meenits* break, the women announced that they would be on the hunt for a lad. They sat in the barn, drinking tea from their Thermos flasks and eating their *piece* [sandwich] while they cackled like twigs burning under a pot.

'Aye, we're gonnae get one of youse at denner time.'

They were looking at Jock the Wild Man - and more frighteningly - me.

'Oove [we've] had oor een [our eyes] on you pair for a while past. The day's the day.'

I don't think for a minute they knew anything about psychology but the way they went about their threatened treatment of Jock and I certainly had the desired effect. We were scared out of our wits. It was no use complaining to the *gaffer*, for he would have laughed in our faces.

I grew ever more apprehensive as dinnertime approached. The women turned every twist of the screw - if you will pardon that expression:

' We'll get ye. We ken a' the hidey holes. We'll get ye.'

Looking for some safe place to hide, Jock and I decided to split up, thinking that we'd have a better chance of escaping that way. He went off into the farm outbuildings. I ran to a large and deep corn kist [bin] that contained oats for the horses. And much else besides.

I lifted the lid of the chest slowly. To my surprise, three pairs of eyes met mine.

'Bugger off, Pugh-ey! We got here first.'

Recently, I saw the film *Schindler's List;* Oscar Schindler, a factory owner in Germany during the war saved some twelve hundred Jews from extermination in the Nazi concentration camps. One scene depicted a group of small Jewish boys seeking to find safe hiding places from the Nazis; one was a corn bin for horses. It brought back that particular memory of my childhood....

I left the three lads to their fate; behind me, I could hear the whoops and cackles of these women who were determined to wreak their vengeance on some male or other, possibly to relieve the animosity they harboured against their husbands. In those days, women were to a certain extent still regarded as second-class citizens, chattels, possessions; I have always hated that view of the other half of the human race. Where would we be without women?

I ran into a large barn, searching frantically for a corner where I might disappear. I could hear the women behind me, yelling and swearing. The barn was stacked almost to the roof with bales of straw. Almost. At the top, I could see a space about a foot wide. I knew that was where I had to be. I began to climb the bales as quietly as I could. When I got near the top, I heard a whimpering noise. Then a head stuck out from the straw. It was Jock the Wild Man.

'Jee-sus Kee-rist! I thocht it wis the wimmen! C'moan up! An' hurry!'

He hauled me up the last few feet and we lay on our stomachs, eating our pieces - well, chewing them, as fear prevented us from swallowing. We had small bottles of lemonade to wet our dry throats. We lay up there many dinnertimes; the women never found our secret place and we managed to escape their initiation rites all summer long.

At last, the *gaffer* announced that the peas were ready for picking, so we were taken by tractor-pulled trailers to the pea-field. At that time, the field straddled what would become the site of the *Blue Circle* Cement Company factory, now *Lafarge*. Even then, limestone was being extracted on a small scale and transported from the mine by means of a small single-gauge railway line. A small engine ran daily along the pea-field, driven by a man called Tommy Charters, who was curiously called the *Bum Boy*; I didn't know what a bum boy was then, so I assumed it was just a nickname.

When the bum boy drove past us at the pea picking, I joined in the ribald laughter. Later that summer, I discovered what it was a bum boy did. I was playing at the East or Coastguard Beach with David Barry, the coastguard's son. I was on the sands and this repulsive man - he reminded me of a Japanese actor I saw in the film *A Town Like Alice;* with his squint eyes, buckteeth and scrawny body, he came towards me on the beach. He started to run at David and I; David had more presence of mind than me and he went to his house, while I became the hunted quarry. I ran towards the sea, then I went back to the sands, realising my mistake. I wanted to get back to the esplanade, where I knew I'd be safe. I thought the man who chased me was doing so because I'd called him nasty names. He soon overtook me and began to pull down my short trousers. I was lying face down in the sand, scared out of my wits. Then I saw a little puff of sand explode at the side of my head. I turned round to look up at the Esplanade, where David Barrie's father was standing with an air gun. Mr Barrie called out to him:

'Let the lad go! If you don't, the next shot will be up your arse!'
He climbed off me and slunk away along the beach. David came to ask if I was OK. I said I was but I didn't know what the man had wanted. David's father put his arm round my shoulder.

'He's a bum boy, lad. A man who doesn't like women. You'll understand when you get older. He's a pervert.'
I wasn't versed in the intimacies of heterosexual love then. I asked Mr Barry why he'd called the man a bum boy.

'Because he's not normal, lad. He prefers men or boys to women. Keep out of his way in future.'

I most certainly did after that. I didn't call him names any more. Jock the Wild Man informed me that he was a *Bum Boy* or *Arse Bandit* - these expressions meant nothing to me.

'He sticks his thingy up ye.' Jock was serious. 'Always keep yir arse tae a hedge or a wall when he's aboot.'
At last, it was beginning to dawn on me. I thought it was disgusting that a man would want to do that sort of thing to another man.

At last, the pea-picking operation finally arrived. We'd looked forward to it all summer, simply because it meant that we'd be able to stand upright instead of crawling about on our hands and knees in fields open to the vagaries of the weather. I have to confess the pea-harvest was a bit of an anti-climax. It was yet another drudge task and the novelty of standing upright wore off after a couple of days. Sure, it was preferable to crawling about in the dirt; you stood upright, stripping the pea-haulms of their cargo of pods. The trick was to suspend the pea-haulm with one hand held at shoulder height so that the pods dangled, then you stripped them clean with your free hand. Another finger numbing exercise. The other dubious benefit - that of eating the peas - soon wore off and even today, I turn up my nose at more than two or three pods of raw peas. We threw the pods into large wicker or wire baskets collected by a carter with a Clydesdale horse pulling the cart. So that was the pea picking.

Looking back 50 or so years later, I suppose we were fortunate to have gainful employment in those impoverished days. The wage was good for the time but we earned every penny of it. My mother allowed me to keep 8 shillings [40p] of my earnings as pocket money, so contributing £2.10.0 [£2.50] each week meant that I was giving her nearly half of what my father sent home. That summer, I saved 5 shillings a week [25p] so that by the end of August, I had increased my National Savings stamps by the astonishing amount of £2.

Things were getting better all the time. *Wimpey* the builders who employed my Uncle Jimmy as a timekeeper began to expand the house-building business. The company needed skilled and unskilled labour for its Edinburgh sites and Jimmy offered to recruit Dunbar and other East Lothian men on condition that the company laid on transport to take the men to Edinburgh. Jimmy put an advert in the local Employment Exchange (presently occupied by *Lodge Dunbar Castle No 75*, beside the Bleachfield) for interested men to call at our house in Lammermuir Crescent. Within a week and after numerous knockings on the front door of No 75, Jimmy had cleared three hundred *dole* claimants off the unemployed register. He was so successful he was able to extend his recruitment to towns like Haddington and Tranent. Jimmy Cockburn it was who brought a fleet of yellow, *Wimpey* buses to this county; they plied between Dunbar and Edinburgh for many decades. I am pleased to say that many local men speak of him today with gratitude; he was a fine wee man, hard but fair in all his dealings with the labour force; he was also quietly proud of the men of Dunbar who took up work with *Wimpey*, whom he'd convinced were good workmen.

Despite my limited experience of the town women who worked in the local farms, I wasn't prejudiced against them in any way. However, the wives and daughters of men who lived and worked on the farms were a breed apart. They were ladies, as I would find out later when I worked in *Lipton's* grocery. The customers from the outlying farms and villages, mainly country women, were shy, polite, rarely pushing themselves forward or using the foul language I'd heard out of the mouths of the townie women workers at Oxwellmains. To my mind, the farm women were possessed of a quiet presence, a kind of natural aristocratic behaviour which comes from working and living on the land. They were heart-warmingly grateful for anything you did for them. They were the salt of the earth. Their lives were hard with few frills and they had few possessions or luxuries other than what the land had to offer. Although the *bondager* system had become history, farm workers' wives and daughters were still expected to lend a hand on the farms or in the farm kitchen, a watered-down version of the *bondager*'s lot. Perhaps that was slightly mitigated by better wages and perks. The women still felt they had to keep on the right side of the grieve or overseer so that their husbands remained in gainful employment. Living in tied cottages, a degree of deference was still expected, even if forelocks weren't actually tugged. The farm women's lives still consisted of drudgery, relieved by red letter days like harvest homes or *kirns,* as the barn dances and fetes were then known. There were flower and vegetable shows which usually ended in the warm conviviality of the *kirn,* where men and women danced, drank a bit and generally enjoyed themselves. As I grew older, I often cycled to villages like Stenton and Innerwick to enjoy the food and the fun until at last, I outgrew the *kirns.* Even so, I will never forget these evenings - usually occurring on a Friday or Saturday - when everyone had a good time, got a little tiddly and maybe a *bairn* was conceived when couples got home afterwards. Nobody tried to lord it over anybody else, not even the farmer and his family. They were convivial evenings when farmers, their families, their workers and their friends got together to enjoy themselves.

I have never lost my respect for these quiet, shy women who lived in often run-down cottages, keeping them spotlessly clean without *hoovers* and other modern aids; they pipe-clayed their doorsteps, they black-leaded their kitchen grates, their washing was snow-white and fresh from the east winds that dried them. They collected their milk in jugs from the cow byres, they kept hens that laid their breakfast eggs and tended little plots of ground given over to growing vegetables and flowers, relying on the weekly visits of van men or their Saturday jaunts to Dunbar for the shopping. When it rained, they dried their laundry on pulleys in the kitchen or hung it on clothes' horses before the fire, which was never allowed to go out. That wasn't unique to the farm women; most of the town dwellers - my mother among them - did the same. Often you would hear the ultimate accolade, the seal of approval when a woman said of another woman

'Aye, she hings oot [hangs out] a guid [good] washing.'

The farm women of my childhood are a dying breed. The little cottages where they once lived are bought by ex-city dwellers today - commonly referred to as 'white settlers' who give these residences ridiculous names like *The Howlet* or the even dafter *Mon Repos.* I love looking at the old sepia photographs of the country folk. They are timeless and eternal, like the Spanish peasants of a century ago, people who were once described as the true aristocrats of Spain. Many of these photographs show people in attitudes suggesting they are holding an invisible tool in their hands - a spade or rake or hoe, because these implements were extensions of themselves, dominating their lives and therefore affecting the way they stood. (They used to say that some men betrayed their occupation by the way they walked; the ploughman's tread was measured by the space between the furrows, the railway worker by that of the space between the sleepers). If you will allow me a brief, sentimental indulgence, I believe that the more man loses physical contact with the soil, the less feeling he has for it. Today's farm workers hardly touch the earth, rarely even walking over it; long gone are the gangs of men, women and children who worked together in the fields. The hand-held scythe which cut the corn in the days of my youth has been made redundant by modern machinery; even so, it is still used to level the grass by roadsides in out of the way places like Woodhall in the Lammermuir Hills, which brings me comfort.

While sentimental in mourning the passing of the old days, I am not blinded to the reality of them. Work on the farms was hard, tedious, backbreaking, especially in spring and autumn; an atmosphere of the medieval, feudal state still lingered, the farmer lording it over his workforce. What I regret is the passing of the care and patience of the farm folk working the land they loved; but such attributes have no economic value in the competitive, hard -headed world we live in today. However, if life is hard and not over-generous with its rewards, there isn't any justification for perpetuating it. The farm folk I knew were keepers of the land; they cared about and loved it. They loved the horses with which they came into daily contact. They didn't welcome modern mechanisation, for it made them obsolete, casualties of history. The pride they took in their work was quiet, not self-seeking or arrogant. Like the great, beautiful Clydesdale horses, a unique breed of people has passed from us.

But in 1955, I spent the summer at the pea picking and part of the autumn at the *tattie howkin'*. The local education authority allowed any school child a month's exemption from school to help with the potato harvest. I think this may have been a wartime arrangement that was allowed to continue. As I mentioned in Chapter 11, two of us in the class of 1955 - S2L - decided to apply, much to the annoyance of Frank Bonar, our English teacher that year.

In October 1955, I worked for two local farmers, Charles Spence at Pitcox and his father at Tynefield. I have to confess that I preferred father to son, the former being every city dweller's idea of a jolly farmer; the son was more remote and authoritarian. The father thought nothing of mixing with his workforce as the old-fashioned farmers used to. Spence senior was also very generous; he often came down to the potato field with baskets of windfall apples and enjoyed throwing them into the air and watching us scramble for them. He wasn't above providing us with hot cocoa and jam *pieces* [sandwiches] from a large urn on a tractor on cold autumn afternoons.

# Papers, Peas Potatoes and Pan Loaves

Dunbar was long famed for the quality of its potato crop; equally famous were the squads of *howkers* who came from near and far, some of them from Ireland. The Irish fieldworkers would move from farm to farm during the season, which lasted from late August to late October or early November. The potato harvest was a major event in the East Lothian agricultural calendar, providing work for hundreds of women and children for exceptionally good wages, for the time. I can't recall what women were paid but kids from Dunbar were paid £4:12:6 [£4.63] for a five and a half day week. This was precisely the amount of compulsory allotment deducted from my father's weekly army pay to support us. I was well pleased with my earnings during the four weeks I was at the *tattie howkin*.

Potato-lifting was done by hand in those days; it was hard, backbreaking work, even for youngsters. In autumn, the weather can be capricious and unpredictable; one day may be fine, with a diamond-clear sun, the next pouring with cold rain. Wet and exposed fields are the least convivial places to be in October but on chill, frosty days, the work was so intensive that after about half an hour, the heat from your sweating body soon inured you to the discomfort.

We started work at Pitcox one drizzly Monday morning, taken to the field in soft topped lorries. I will never forget the first day. The field was completely open apart from a low thorn hedge bounding the southern side, with a straggly belt of trees in the east. Unfortunately, the prevailing winds - and the rain - come from the northwest, so we had our fair share of wettings that first week. Mr Spence Jr. kept a watchful eye on us and he was right to do so. It was unwritten rule that all workers were allowed a *bilin'* [portion] of potatoes to take home in their *piece-bag* - usually a shopping bag which would hold about a half stone of spuds - every evening. Some of our number almost ended that arrangement because of their greed. The opportunists were removing half-sacks of spuds from the field, stashing them in the nearby hedge, then selling them off at ten shillings [50p] a half-hundredweight. Mr Spence detected their game simply by inspecting the hedgerows and trees after we had our *meenits* [tea-break] in the afternoon. He called us all together one afternoon, warning that the culprits would be instantly dismissed if they were caught. He then personally searched every worker's bag every evening before we were allowed on to the lorries. After a hard day's work picking spuds, all you can think of is to get home and have a hot bath; the constant searching held us up and the lorry never left on time for several days. Looking back, Mr Spence was entirely justified in his actions; getting a good wage with about a half-stone of free potatoes every day was certainly worth a good deal to our households. The greedy ones weren't interested in enriching their households, they were only after extra pocket money.

When we finished at Pitcox and watched the last potato clamp or pit being covered with straw and earth for winter storing, we were sent to Tynefield.

318

# Papers, Peas, Potatoes and Pan Loaves

The Pitcox lift had taken longer than expected, mainly due to a combination of wet weather and the heavy, clay soil, a feature of the farm. The soil clogged the tractor-drawn diggers and made the task of lifting the spuds more onerous, as you had to remove the soil before putting them in the wire baskets that stood to the side of your *stent* or allocated yardage of your patch. Tynefield was almost a joy to work; being close to the sea, the fields were of a light, loamy soil and there were belts of trees which offered us shelter. And of course, old Mr Spence was a cheery, generous man whom we all liked.

His grieve or overseer was a different man altogether. Known as a slave driver, he was nicknamed the *Black Bomber* and he lived up to his reputation that autumn, probably because of the limited time left of our school exemption. Years on, I don't bear him a grudge but in those days, I resented the man. (Now, he's a mild-mannered, gentle man; then, he was probably overworked and under the stress of harvest farming which was dependant on the weather. In those days, that was real stress). He allowed no time or energy for larking about. Being late in starting Tynefield, he decided to use double diggers - two ploughs working round the clock, one on either side of the field at all times. And then he added a third which harrowed the ploughed ground for potatoes buried either by accident or design.

Each worker had a measured *stent or stint;* the adult women had longer ones but stronger lads often found themselves working adult yardages. If any of us cheeked the grieve, he would simply turn away taciturnly and move the *stent* stick of the offender a bit further. Then he would tell the miscreant that he/she wouldn't have any breath to spare for impudence for a while. The period of the 'while' depended entirely on his whim and there was no right of appeal.

Double digging meant that you were no sooner finished with one lot of uncovered potatoes when the next digger was on you. As you stood by waiting for the plough to pass by, you were often asked to inspect the immediate ploughed area for buried spuds – the shirkers used to grind the spuds into the dirt with the heel of their boot. The potatoes were collected in *sculls* or round, wire baskets. The street-wise ones who were caught deliberately burying spuds had extra yards added to their *stents* by way of punishment. The carters who followed the ploughs to empty the wire baskets into their trailers would say nothing to the offender; they would simply nod to the grieve and point to the culprit. It was the grieve's custom to walk over the ploughed ground of the day before, scraping at the soil with his boot or a rake; if he found more buried spuds than considered average under natural conditions, the culprits were soon made aware of their negligence. After all, potatoes were a good cash crop and farmers couldn't afford to leave them for the seagulls who roamed over the fields all autumn. Also, after a heavy rainfall, the soil soon shows the results of deliberate burials, the potatoes shining white in the dirt, like small skulls surfacing in a graveyard.

# Papers, Peas Potatoes and Pan Loaves

When the diggers broke down occasionally, the event would be greeted with ragged cheers which were soon silenced by the grieve. He would walk up the line and detach every second worker and put them to the *harries* [gleaning]; these were paired off with a *scull* [wire potato basket] between them as they followed the harrow which uncovered the lost potatoes. At least it wasn't as backbreaking as the *stent*; usually, the less troublesome were afforded this privilege.

When a mechanised digger was out of action, the grieve would bring on a plough pulled by a horse pair. Being slower, the horses gave you a bit more time to 'clean your stent' as they used to describe the lifting of spuds. One incident with the horses sticks in my memory. The grieve was doing his usual patrolling; sometimes he relieved a ploughman and we swore he drove the tractor faster than anyone else. At any rate, on this occasion, he was driving a horse-drawn plough and noticed one lad had stopped gathering his quota of spuds.

'Whit's up, laddie? Are ye all right?'
Back came the immediate response.
'Horse stood on ma fit [foot], Mister.'
The grieve's face was expressionless, then he replied thus:
'Oh it did, did it? Weel, next time Ah come roond [round], jist you
staun' [stand] on his. Noo get back tae work afore Ah tak' ma boot tae
yir backside.'
He knew the lad was lying, as the horses were gentle, canny and sure-footed.

At last, we were nearing the end of the month's school exemption, something we regarded with mixed feelings, depending on the state of the weather. It was getting worse every day and in the last week of October, we had to shelter from the rain more frequently. Then the days turned frosty which made the soil difficult to work. The prospect of returning to the classroom was daunting but at least it was warm and not physical work. Then one day - I think it was a Thursday afternoon, the last of the month - the grieve came marching up with a notebook and stub of pencil.

'The Boss wants tae ken whae wid like tae work this Setterday efternoon.
The last field's no' feenished and yir a' gaen back tae schule on
Monday. The Boss sez he'll pay ye time-and-a hauf for Setterday
efternoon. Can Ah hae the names o' ony o' ye whae'll work the
full day?'
Several of the kids shook their heads but I wasn't one of them. I had to take every chance offered. There weren't enough of us, so the grieve came back after consulting Mr Spence. A few wavered, some said yes but still there weren't enough. After a further chat with the farmer, the grieve announced that we would all get sixteen shillings [80p]and a half-sack of spuds instead of the twelve or thirteen shillings already offered. The weaker vessels finally gave in. While not exactly collective bargaining - there was no effective union for

320

the farm workers then anyway - but the reluctance of a few had benefited the majority. I certainly couldn't afford to lose sixteen shillings and half-sack of potatoes worth about ten shillings [50p].

It was an extremely bitter Saturday; the sun came out and melted the frost, but by 3pm, you could feel the air frost on your cheeks. We sweated our guts out that day, earning every shilling. Old Mr Spence came out with his tractor laden with a cocoa urn and thick sandwiches cemented together with butter and home-made raspberry jam. Never was food and drink so welcome or demolished so quickly. Thus fortified, we set to for the last hour before the darkness came down. Of course, that was the reason for the cocoa and wads. As the last light faded behind Traprain Law, we were working on the few remaining drills of spuds.

We worked in the twilight, finishing the field at 5pm, the tractors chugging away with lights on full beam. Mr Spence came out on his tractor to thank us; then he endeared us all to him by announcing that he was upping the afternoon's work to a pound as he was so pleased with our efforts. He was a fair man and believed in a fair wage for good work done. So for that last week, my take-home pay was £5:12:6 [£5.63]. Our backs were sore and some of us had difficulty lugging our sacks of free spuds to the tractor that took us home. We were quietly proud of ourselves. I know my mother was proud of me, for she hugged me that Saturday night, a rare event. Then she handed me a whole pound for pocket money. The only problem was that I was too tired to go out and spend it.

So over that month, I had earned about £20 for the house and received nearly £3 in pocket money. I saved about £2, spending the other pound on sweets, chips and trips to the cinema. I was thankful that my mother promised me I wouldn't need to work for the rest of that year. I didn't argue with her.

In 1955-56, I managed to relieve the cash flow problem by securing a bursary of £40 from the East Lothian County Council Education Department, payable in three instalments of about £13 a quarter. These bursaries were awarded to deserving kids who'd shown merit and above average schoolwork but they had to be earned by performance every quarter, let alone every year. My bursary kept the wolf a little further from the door but when my marks dropped below the required level, the bursary stopped, so it was back to work again. The problem was, what would I do this time? I had long lost any enthusiasm for the early rise required for a paper round; besides, the wages were poor compared with what I had earned in the fields. I started taking an interest in shops and began to think of a job as message delivery boy.

My love of shops in Dunbar started when I was very young, especially at Christmas, when I window-shopped, thinking of the presents I would buy for my family and the ones I hoped to get - mainly Christmas annuals. However, when it came to employment, I lacked confidence; I agonised for months whether I would be accepted as a grocery delivery boy in *Cooper's, Lipton's* and the many family businesses. However, out of the blue came an opportunity I couldn't afford to ignore. My West Barns friend Tony Porteous decided he'd had enough of school when he reached age fifteen. He asked me if I'd like his job as *Lipton's* message boy and said he'd put in a good word in for me with the manager. I jumped at the chance that autumn of 1956. The pay was a pound a week, with 'tips' from generous customers. The job meant working two hours on Thursdays and Fridays and all day on Saturdays. The only thing that bothered me was the dreaded *Lipton* tricycle, more of which follows. Mr Ramsay was the manager of the shop in those days; he was a fine man and I was friendly with his daughter Ann, who is still a good friend. When Mr Ramsay retired or moved elsewhere, he was replaced by Michael O'Donnell, a dapper wee man with a moustache. His wife was a lovely lady and a great friend of my mother's; sadly, she died too soon. I spent two happy years with *Lipton's* and I am glad to say that I am still friendly with one or two of the staff to this day.

I started on a Thursday evening, Tony Porteous took me on his round to show me the ropes. The bulky, awkward tricycle or trike terrified me. He said not to worry, it was only used on Friday evenings and Saturday mornings, when orders were bulky in the former and used only in the latter for the delivery of pan loaves. I was still apprehensive.

'You'll soon get the hang of it' Tony said optimistically.

Little did he know of the extent of my ineptitude with all things mechanical, which persists to this day. Also, I am a reluctant convert to the computer, which allows me to write and change text with ease but which remains a closed book. I refuse to link up to the Internet, nor have I succumbed to an e-mail address. I am a dinosaur and am proud of the fact.

But let me return to that day in 1956, when I was hired by Mr Ramsay. The box-shaped trike was heavy and ponderous; it was painted in *Lipton's* distinctive green and was steered by means of a metal bar in front of you that you moved to the left or right as required. It tended to sway back and forth as you pedalled and it had what was called a fixed wheel. What on earth was that, I asked? Tony confidently said it was no problem. All it meant was that you couldn't back-pedal, as you could on an ordinary push bike. I supposed the mechanism was there for safety reasons since, if you attempted to back-pedal, you might jack-knife the contraption and cause an accident in the road. The brake was located under the steering bar and you needed - well I did - both hands to apply it. I hated the damned infernal thing and said so. Tony was unmoved.

'You'll be fine.'

If only he had known.

He accompanied me the first Friday evening and very quickly, I realised how heavy a load of groceries packed in cardboard boxes could be. The trike was loaded from the front and that evening, was stuffed to the gunwales. Tony kindly offered to ride it down the West Port, which isn't a steep decline, although it would prove to be my undoing. He was kind and said I would soon get the hang of it. Once on the level, he said it was plain sailing. Even on level ground, it was murder. I didn't feel I had the strength to propel the thing along the straight and level roads, let alone negotiate even the slightest incline. But I stuck to it and we weren't too late back from the round, when we were met by a slightly worried Mr Ramsay, a few minutes after 6pm, when the shop closed.

The Terrible Trike Tragedy occurred the very next morning. I loaded up the monster with dozens of pan loaves and shook in my sandshoes at the prospect of having to ride the damned thing down the West Port, even with Tony in support on a push bike. We set off slowly; I managed to negotiate the West Port corner without mishap, all of twenty yards from the shop. Then, as I pedalled painfully towards Friars Bank, the downhill part, I began to panic as the pedals began to whizz round out of my control. I heard Tony shouting out to me to remind me of the fixed wheel. I couldn't control the bloody machine and knew that I wasn't going to make it. In my panic, I forgot to apply the brake and stupidly tried to steer the trike onto the pavement. The next few seconds remain are a blur even today. All I can recall is lying in the middle of the road, the trike jack-knifed on its side, with dozens of pan loaves strewn across the road opposite *Castellau House*. Tony knelt beside me, asking if I was hurt. Then a policeman arrived on the scene from the nearby Police Station, followed by a second. While one examined me for injuries, the other gathered up the staff of life, an onerous task as many of the loaves had burst out of their reinforced wax paper wrappings . Cast your bread on the waters the Bible says. That morning, slices of bread carpeted the highway. I have often recalled the scene in slow motion, the way modern film directors do for dramatic effect. In my mind's eye, I can visualise the scene as the trike slewed out of control, shedding me and a hundred pan loaves across the road. I was more embarrassed than hurt that awful Saturday morning.

The only damage I sustained to my person was a grazed ankle and a cut hand which I had used to break my fall. Tony wheeled the trike back up the hill, with me walking the push bike. How my crest was fallen. An anxious Mr Ramsay listened to the tale of woe and decided that as Tony was still on the payroll, he and I would deliver the bread using ordinary shop bikes. A little while later, when Mike O'Donnell who had been a manager in the Berwick branch of *Lipton's* took over, one of his first concerns was to conduct a time and motion study. He asked the message lads about the time taken to deliver x number of loaves in one run using the trike and several trips to deliver the same amount of bread on ordinary bikes. Now *that* is what I call practical arithmetic! Mike thankfully came to the conclusion that the trike wasn't cost-effective, informed head office that it should be withdrawn and replaced by another pushbike. A hated relic of a bygone age was thus removed. I was happy.

# Papers, Peas Potatoes and Pan Loaves

After that, I positively loved my job with *Lipton's* at No 77 High Street. Before progressing further, perhaps it's appropriate to record a few words about its founder, Sir Thomas Lipton (1850-1931). He began life as a humble message boy, then a shop assistant and finally opened his chain of stores that made him a millionaire as well as a famous yachtsman who competed several times for the Americas Cup. Hailing from Ireland, he opened his first shop - the *Ham and Egg* shop in Stobcross, Glasgow in 1871. After that, he never looked back. In two decades, he had made millions. By 1898, he owned shops in virtually every city, town and reasonably sized community like Dunbar. His motto was *There is no fun like work.* I am sure he was a simple man of the people, who came from a humble background. A Victorian shopkeeper, he cared about quality, value for money, integrity and courtesy in his business dealings, expecting his staff to work to his high standards. His stores made a point of extolling the virtues of the personal touch, insisting that service was always given with a smile. His staff appear to have been happy and proud to work for him. Today's ubiquitous cliché 'Good day. How may I help you?' the stock in trade response by stores assistants to customers surely has its roots in Tommy Lipton's stores. His most famous commodity was tea, a blend of Indian and Ceylon. It was legendary and people drank it almost exclusively until coffee became the alternative beverage in the 1960s, when *espresso* coffee bars and cafes proliferated. Before that, coffee essence came in bottles, the most common being *Camp Coffee,* its consistency on a par with syrup of figs and tasting abominable. How many people recall the famous label on the bottle featuring an officer in the British Army being served his coffee by a turbaned Indian orderly?

It was many years later that I discovered that Tommy Lipton had sent free groceries to the people on St Kilda when they were staring starvation in the face in 1912. On another occasion, *Lipton's* was eulogised by the poet William McGonagall. A McGonagall poem celebrating the opening of the Newport Railway and Tay Bridge in 1878 included a reference to *Lipton's* Grocery Stores. Entitled *Railway Bridge of the Silv'ry Tay,* the doggerel publicises McGonagall's theory that the bridge would pay for itself by the sheer volume of passenger traffic:

*Because the thrifty housewives of Newport*
*To Dundee will often resort*
*Which will be to others' profit and sport*
*By buying cheap tea, bread and jam*
*And also some of Lipton's ham....*

Awful poetry it was, though the ham was excellent; McGonagall's prophecy wasn't realised, although he was probably right about *Lipton's* ham; the Tay Bridge collapsed with loss of life during a violent storm on 28th December 1879.

Today, *Ladbroke's* betting shop which occupies the site still bears the two brass plates under its windows, plates which message boys like myself were required to polish with *Dura-glit* every Saturday morning until we could see our faces in them. After that, we washed the two large shop windows, while Mike O'Donnell pasted the current advertising posters in the interior. Then we hauled down the canvas awning or sunblind to prevent the cooked meat in the window from curling in the sun. Then we had to unload the British Rail lorry which delivered the Saturday consignments of cheese, cereals, dried fruit, boxes of tinned food and tea chests. This was back-breaking work and we had to carry these bulky containers through the shop until Mike O'Donnell hit on the brilliant idea of opening the side windows at street level in Silver Street; these looked into the cellars, offering no more than a dim light. Mike had a wooden chute installed so that sacks of sugar, split peas, lentils etc - in hundredweight bags - could be slid down into the cellar. Great cheeses came in wooden crates in those days and they were rolled down the chute, much to the relief of lads like Derick Souness and myself. All we had to do after that was lift the bags/crates from the bench on to our backs and stagger a few yards to where they were deposited in the stone cellars and bays. The two lorry drivers, first the late Jimmy Fallon, then *King* Patterson, sadly also no longer with us, appreciated this innovation as it meant they could unload the lorries much quicker.

One delivery I shall never forget was a consignment of bananas by *Wood Omerod,* or *Wood O* as the wholesale fruiters were better known. Unpacking the fruit one morning, I was shocked to see a huge spider emerging from the wrapping; the lorry driver declared these were banana spiders and quite harmless. It gave us all a scare nonetheless, especially when it scuttled noisily under the large fridge in the back shop. We didn't waste any time enquiring whether it was venomous or not. I was told to flush it out by driving a broom handle under the fridge whereupon it was thoroughly despatched. Nowadays, perhaps the routine is to inform the RSPCA or the Department of Agriculture and Fisheries of rare species like the banana spider; in those days, we took no chances.

The female counter staff were lovely girls and while they teased us message lads unmercifully, it was all good, clean fun. The unofficial deputy manager was Ella Nichol, who 'walked out' with my brother Norman for a few years until they split over his fondness for the beer at weekends. (I have no idea where Ella is today but I do know she got married. Next in the pecking order was a slim, attractive lady called Margaret Hastie whom I remember wore quite high heeled shoes- but not on duty. Margaret is still around today; I have the impression that she moved to Port Seton, although maybe I am confusing her with Ella Nichol. My favourite however was Betty Leslie, a bonnie, buxom lass with lovely eyes and a beautiful smile. Betty hailed from Grantshouse and was gentler with me than the other girls. Needless to say, I had a crush on her, entertaining little fantasies about her the whole time I worked in the shop. She had an engaging laugh and her eyes always smiled when she laughed. Finally, there was Phyllis Smith, the youngest assistant who wasn't much older than me.

Memories. Some were interesting, others scary like the above while still more were funny. I now describe some of the tasks routinely performed by the manager Mike O'Donnell and some of the older members of staff.

Bacon joints - and I mean a large proportion of the pig - were boned and tied into a roll with strong twine. That and the various tinned cooked meats like corned beef, chopped pork, ham and the like were sliced on a vicious circular-saw cutter whose blade was activated by a large, black handle which was whirled round and round, thus propelling the part of machine holding the meat against the blade. Junior staff and message boys were strictly forbidden to use this machine for obvious reasons. I was fascinated by and feared it, especially when the hunk of meat had to be re-positioned as the meat was cut.

Cheeses came in large cylindrical wooden crates held together with wire; you had to snip the wire, then strip away the wooden slats and remove the cheese encased in a greasy muslin cheesecloth. Removing the cloth was a dirty, nasty job; the sticky goo got under your fingernails as you had to scrape the cloth to find its beginning and thus unroll the cheese. There was a knack in this; the job was solved by holding the free end of the cheesecloth in your hands and simply kicking the cheese free - rather like unrolling a bolt of cloth or a carpet. Simply? What I am saying? During the unravelling of the cheese-cloth, the cheese rind picked up bent nails, splinters of wood and any old rubbish lying on the floor. These unwelcome acquisitions had to be removed by hand from the rind. The cheese then was cut up into manageable wedge-shaped proportions using a fine wire with wooden pegs at either end for handles. The message boy assigned to this job lugged the wedge upstairs and set it on the marble counter in the front shop where it was cut up into standard pieces by Mike O'Donnell who used the upstairs shop cheese-cutter. It was a tedious job.

Butter also came in wooden crates, large blocks of it encased in silver paper and it too had to be sliced into quarter, half and pound blocks, then patted into oblongs with wooden pattens which bore the *Lipton* motif on them. These were weighed on a set of marble scales with various brass weights shaped like chess pieces. The standard weights ran from one to sixteen ounces. Being brass, these had to be polished regularly. And they had to be arranged in ascending order of weight; woe betide any member of staff who placed a weight in the wrong position.

Sugar came in large sacks and was scooped into reinforced blue paper bags that came in half-pound, one pound and two-pound sizes. Loose tea was similarly removed from the tea chests with a metal scoop and packed into quarter- and half-pound bags. The more expensive blends thankfully arrived pre-packed in stout cardboard boxes. Dried fruit was put on display in their wooden crates so that customers could choose what they wanted, attended by a member of staff who scooped the stuff into paper bags similar to the reinforced sugar bags.

Most grocers operated in this way in those days. The memory of the *bouquet* of smells that permanently permeated *Lipton's* many prandial delights makes my mouth water nearly fifty years on. The wooden floors behind the counters were sprinkled with sawdust to ensure the staff didn't slip on the greasy floorboards. The exotic smells came from the tea and unground coffee beans mixed with the delicious fruity *potpourri* emanating from the wooden crates containing dried apricots, apple rings, pears - they reminded me of lopped-off human ears - sultanas, currants, raisins, walnuts and almonds. Of the cooked meats, my favourite was chopped pork that came from Poland - was it called *Chorka*? - in six-pound cylindrical tins. I still eat the stuff occasionally but somehow it doesn't have the same taste and texture of the *Lipton* variety. I usually had a slice or two on a buttered roll every Saturday morning, before going out on my message runs. Mike O'Donnell used to joke that it was made from the frozen carcasses of cavalry horses killed in the Second World War, when Hitler conquered Poland in about three weeks. Jimmy Fallon, then *King* Patterson, our delivery men said that wasn't possible, as all the horses alive after the invasion of Poland in September 1939 had been eaten long before 1956, when the Poles were starving under the Communist regime.

It may be said with some justification that *Lipton's* not only kindled my interest in food but also in local history. I recall one really wet Wednesday in the summer of 1958, about a couple of hours before the shop shut for the usual half-day. In 1957 and 1958 I had been engaged as a counter assistant during the summer months, a job which paid three times the pay of a message lad. Because there were few customers that morning, Mike O'Donnell asked me to clear away the undergrowth and greenery which festooned the stone-flagged path to the cellars where we kept cardboard boxes for grocery deliveries. (Interestingly, the cellars to the rear of the shop have been converted into flats; today, a friend of mine, David 'Max' Field lives in No 3A Silver Street, where we stored the cardboard boxes and sometimes parked the delivery bikes). But to my tale. Mike O'Donnell put his hand on my shoulder that wet Wednesday morning.

> 'Right, lad. I have a job for you. The girls are getting wet every time they go for a cardboard box in the cellars. We need to clear all that growth away. OK?'

'We' meant me. So I set to with a small hand-axe. As I chopped and slashed the growth of *bunetrees* [elder bushes] rooted in the base of the wall, I looked up and saw a plaque carved on the stone wall, identifying what I had previously thought was just a flagstoned path. The plaque bore the name *St James Walk*. I called Mike who ventured to suggest that it might have been the name of a *vennel* [close] opposite another *vennel* which led from what was known as Monks' Walk which ran parallel to *Friarscroft*, which I would later learn was the site of the Trinitarian or Red Friars' religious house in the field on the other side of the boundary wall at the West Port. I was puzzled by Mike's suggestion.

'But how could it be?' I asked. ' R S McColl's sweetie shop is in the way.'

Mike thought for a minute, then said that the *vennel* would have disappeared when McColl's sweet shop was built. Today, looking back, I wonder if the monks had used the walkway to reach the sea to buy their dried or cured herrings. Does the plaque survive today? I think not, as the Silver Street outbuildings once owned by *Lipton's* were long ago converted into modern flats.

I thoroughly enjoyed my two summers working as a shop assistant. It not only meant more money, it was in many ways less onerous than lugging heavy grocery deliveries to the bikes, then cycling all over the new housing schemes as far as Belhaven. I think my weekly wage for both summers was £3:18:0 [£3.90] less a deduction of about seven shillings [35p] for a boy's Class I National Insurance stamp, something which I would learn of later when I joined the Ministry of Pensions and National Insurance in 1958.

I loved serving the public in my white uniform which consisted of a short pea jacket with detachable buttons - to allow it to be laundered - and long apron. I quickly got the hang of the money side, the prices of the various commodities and began to have my own customers who would ask to be served by the 'wee laddie'. Working behind the counter also brought an added bonus in the shape of Betty. I fell in love with her - well, maybe for one so young, that is an overstatement; I was certainly infatuated by and had a 'crush' on her. I suppose she was the first adult woman I was ever attracted to - barring the Cherry Lady in the painting that used to hang in my bedroom and which I have described earlier. In those days I was still painfully shy but not shy enough to ask her to come dancing with me in 1958. She smiled sweetly, indulgently and said she'd be taken up for cradle snatching. I think she was twenty; I was only seventeen. Nowadays, that would mean nothing but in 1958, the rules were different. However, I am glad to say that we are still friends to this day. When I was posted to Dundee in the Civil Service, I wrote to Betty regularly but our letters were of the kind written by pen pals. I often wonder how we might have turned out as a couple. To me, she is still the same as she was in those far off days, still gentle, still with the same winning smile, the same attractive figure....

As I said earlier, some of the ladies who were regular customers used to ask for me - not by name but often as the 'wee laddie' or 'the wee yin'. One elderly lady from Parsons' Pool insisted that I - and only I - should serve her. Mike O'Donnell used to try to attend to her, but she would shake her head.

'Na. Ah want the wee yin.'

He asked her why. She wasn't slow in answering.

## Papers, Peas, Potatoes and Pan Loaves

'Youse aye gie me the odd auld slice o' corned beef curled up wi' the sun. Ye hide it amang the guid slices.'

This was standard practice of course; too much waste would have brought down one of the inspectors from head office, always a traumatic time that happened at regular intervals. When the inspector called, everyone had to be on their toes.

Some of my customers were real characters. The old lady who complained about Mike's habit of slipping in stale corned beef slices also had a habit of asking for the same blend of tea every week. The first time I served her she asked for a brand I didn't recognise.

'Dividin' tea, son. Ah aye get dividin' tea. A quarter pund.'

Confused, I slunk away to ask Betty and Margaret what she meant. It was a standing joke among the staff. At first, they pretended not to know, then at last, Betty took pity on me.

'She means Dividend Tea, Roy. It's her favourite blend. She always asks for dividin' tea.'

Another of my odd customers was an elderly gentleman who with his wife ran a boarding house in the West End. His name was Connie - which I thought was a woman's name, later confirmed by D H Lawrence's novel *Lady Chatterley's Lover*. It was Connie's daily job to shop for the groceries. He suffered a little from malapropisms, always asking for *Black and Crosswell Soup* [Crosse and Blackwell]. Another regular request was for a pan-sliced [sliced-pan] loaf and a jar of *Gollywog Jam* - the gollywog being the trademark of *Robertson's* Jams - now no longer permitted on jam jars because of a non-sensical insistence on political correctness. I used to ask the old man what kind of jam he preferred; he always said the same:

'The usual. Gollywog Jam.'

I soon realised he meant *Robertson's* strawberry jam.

When I left *Lipton's* on Saturday, 17th August 1958 to enjoy a week's holiday before departing for my 'adult' job in the Civil Service in Dundee on 26th August, I went home with a really heavy heart. I had felt comfortable in that little world and loved the girls with whom I'd worked. What was worse, I thought I'd never see my beloved Betty again. Dundee might have been the moon....

Although *Lipton's* was clean and hygienic (well, relatively so), it wasn't without its rivals in Dunbar High Street - *Cooper's, A T Smith's, Purves* etc. Ronnie Purves was the last of his family to run a long-established business selling much the same fare as *Lipton's* but with a marked difference; the shop stocked a wide range of spices which gave a certain *piquancy* to the smells in that shop. It contained a long oak counter shiny with the grease of years of commerce. On the shelves behind the counter were numerous large glass jars containing things like cinnamon sticks. There was an area to the rear where were stored items like firelighters - they had a tarry, resinous smell - bundles of kindling, paraffin, *Brasso,* candles and black-leading for the old fashioned fire grates.

Earlier on, I referred to my mother's visits to a shop near the *Castle Hotel* which sold similar commodities and where she once asked for hairy toffee, because the cat always sat in the window on top of the tray. I think my Uncle Jimmy played the same trick. He had a thing about cats, did wee Jimmy. My Granny Cockburn's white Persian cat was called Pearl White after the film star in the silent screen days. One day, it devoured his pet canary when he let it out to fly in the kitchen in Castle Place. Granny Cockburn said it was his fault for not watching the bird - or more to the point, keeping an eye on the Persian. A few days later, when the family were having their evening meal, they heard a curious tap-tapping in the stone-flagged hall. Granny C. got up to investigate and found the cat with cockle shells glued to her feet. Jimmy looked at the cat, then Granny.

'It'll no' creep up on ony mair puir wee burdies' he said triumphantly.

On the subject of shops, another one I loved to visit was *Carmichael's Shoe Repair Shop* in the West Port because I loved the smell of beeswax and leather. And also to hopefully see Mr Carmichael's lovely daughter, Gwendoline. Gwen was about thirty when I was fifteen; she was married but that didn't stop me fantasising about her. Tall, with raven's wing black hair and cherry red lips, she made me think of the Snow Queen in the fairy tale, with her finger-nails painted a racy crimson. She had the most beautiful hands I had ever seen then. She was unattainable, like my Betty.

I still love grocers' shops, particularly the village kind. There are few left in Dunbar other than *The Crunchy Carrot.* Today's supermarkets lack the personal touch, the individual scents and smells of these little shops that made shopping an adventure. Shopping today is a pain in the neck. But fortunately for me, I have never lost the sights, smells and tastes of the fare sold in *Lipton's* and elsewhere. And the produce was international in those far-off days, long before anyone had envisaged a Common Market. Tea came from India and Ceylon, butter from New Zealand, cheese from Holland, coffee from Brazil, apples from Canada, bananas from Africa, corned beef from the Argentine and of course my beloved chopped pork from Poland. The whole world seemed to be feeding one small corner of it, the nucleus of a British Empire on which the sun was rapidly setting. There isn't much excitement in shopping any more, which is a great pity.

I mustn't forget the smaller businessman of that time, the mobile grocers and fruiterers. They were usually based in places like Innerwick, Cockburnspath and elsewhere. They were a godsend to isolated communities and farms. My Grandad Cockburn had been among them in his day, working as a horse-drawn van man with *A T Smith* at No 71 High Street. By all accounts, Grandad was a superb salesman, often following other van men and still outselling them by sheer force of persuasion. Perhaps selling groceries is something else besides gardening which I inherited from my grandparents. My grandfather died as a result of a van accident in 1922, aged 49. Partly his own fault - he'd imbibed a fair amount of whisky that Saturday night and fell between the cart shafts, cutting his cheek severely. The frost got into the wound and he died of cancer of the jaw a few months later.

One of the most famous and familiar sights was Jocky Patterson, the *Midnight Baker* from Innerwick. A lovely little character, he was called the *Midnight Baker* from his habit of delivering his wares - chiefly bread - in the Dunbar housing estates at about that time every Saturday night because no shops opened on Sundays in those days. Many a grateful but unsteady patron of the local pubs who'd found *Togneri's* chip shop closed to him feasted on Jocky's juicy midnight mince pies. Jocky Patterson went about his business quietly, walking miles in a night although he was badly lamed. He would stop off at a house and slip in a half loaf through the kitchen window left open for him. It was quite safe to do this in those days as well as leaving the key to your house on a string behind the front door. I recall at least one story about him. A few lads who'd had a drop too much stopped him for pies one night, thinking they could pull a fast one over him. While they were jostling him, it became clear to Jocky that they were trying to pinch a couple of pies. One of the local lads was explaining the reasons for Jocky's nickname and Jocky overheard him.

'But Ah ca' him the limpin' baker' he cackled.

By now, Jocky had twigged their game and he stood before them, barring any access to the back of his van.

'Na, ma wee mannie. A limpin MAN Ah micht [might] but Ah'm no' a limpin' baker.

Noo aff tae yir beds. Yir gettin'nae pies the nicht'

The numpties who disgrace today's streets would have probably mugged him, stolen the pies and the money from the leather bag he always wore round his shoulder, then kicked him senseless. But that night, the four or five of them went off as quiet as mice. How times have changed.

Today, shopping is a chore which most women hate. Like the steam railway engine, the road roller and the Clydesdale horses, the small rural family grocer is a thing of the past.

As I said earlier, I finally hung up my apron on 17th August 1958. Perhaps on reflection, the *Lipton* days were the happiest of my working life. I announced to Mike O'Donnell that like Derick, the other errand boy, I had been successful in the Civil Service Clerical Officer exam that spring. He offered to train me as a manager.

'You'll have your own shop in five years. You've got a feel for this kind of work. Soon it'll be supermarkets like they have in America and you'll have a grand salary, better than mine will ever be. There'll be great opportunities for commission on the produce you sell.'

# Papers, Peas Potatoes and Pan Loaves

I thanked him for thinking about my future career but refused his well-meant offer. I had made up my mind. He said mine was a wise choice, as the Civil Service job would offer a non-contributory pension at the end of my working life, at age 60. That last Saturday evening, I folded up my pea jacket and apron, stuffing it into the laundry basket, knowing that I would soon face a bigger, unknown world for which I knew I was woefully inadequately equipped. But go I must, leaving behind these carefree days and my sweet-eyed Betty, my love of those innocent, special days.

These days are gone forever, as is *Lipton's*. Its chain stores were swallowed in two major takeovers, one an amalgamation with *Presto,* itself a subsequent casualty of boardroom politics and finance. Character and individuality were early casualties; the new organisations had none of *Lipton's* style. I look back on these days with unashamed nostalgia. Like so many other concerns started by humble *entrepreneurs* in the nineteenth century, *Lipton's* is no more than a fading folk memory.

# 13

## The Seasons

Modern society has little time or inclination to observe the changing seasons simply because the majority of people no longer depend on the land for their livelihood. In the centuries when agriculture was vital to the survival and the economic prosperity of the country, people were more acutely aware of the seasons and the weather. The majority earned their living from the land; nowadays, the European Community rewards farmers who 'set aside' land - something unheard of even in my childhood except in the interests of crop rotation and 'resting' the land. The economics of modern agriculture are however lost on me; I fail to see why leaving good, productive land fallow can be of benefit to any community, be it European or not.

As a child of the 1950s, I loved every season in its own way, although I cared least of all for winter, an unproductive time. That may seem odd, what with Christmas and the prospect of snow, but there were long, dreary gaps when nothing happened and time lay heavy on our hands. There was no such thing as television to while away the long winter evenings and there wasn't much spare cash for trips to the local cinemas. All we had was the wireless or else we made our own entertainment but even that palled after a few weeks, as the weather limited our outdoor activities.

As children, we enjoyed every season, never treating them lightly for they all had something to offer. That may sound paradoxical; perhaps what I mean is that we never consciously thought about them, accepting them when they arrived. They came in their own time and we enjoyed what they each had to offer. Although my generation lived through the grey, gritty years after the Second World War, then the Cold War and the threat of atomic warfare, few if any of us really believed there was any real danger to the world. Children are remarkably resilient and can blot such things out of their minds for it's part of their nature to do so.

For me, the seasons were part of my education in a larger schoolroom. As well as developing the eyes and I suppose - I am sentimental - the heart which formal education failed to do, despite biology lessons and half-hearted attempts to teach us the science of observation. We had some art lessons and some poetry but I hated the poems we were made to learn in parrot fashion and chant in a dreary monotone. Besides, I had no aptitude for painting or drawing and the essay subjects we were given allowed little scope for the imagination. My love of good books would come later, influenced by my growing curiosity about the world and my response to its perplexities.

# The Seasons

No personal account of Dunbar would be complete without a passing comment on the seasons, so here follows four brief essays that hopefully will convey some of the impressions they printed on my immature heart. In these essays, Doon Hill, the modest eminence overhanging Dunbar, plays a part because it not only dominates Dunbar but also my childhood bedroom window. I had a clear view of some of it for several years. It figured largely as a symbol of comfort and peace; it predicted the weather and reflected the changing seasons, serving as both barometer and calendar. Sometimes a bluish shadow sloping eastwards, it indicated the onset of clement weather. When it was sharp with well-defined contours, it meant a storm was brewing. At times, it was hazy, a smoky smudge overhanging the town and so we knew rain wasn't far away. When it disappeared altogether, we knew it was raining. But it had other, subtly variable moods that came in late spring, most of summer and in early autumn. Often, it was soft and warm, showing its features and *flora* to best advantage, even when the sun didn't shine. Although Doon Hill lacks grandeur, it compensates for that with its quiet dignity, its solid, reassuring presence. It is the place to which I raised my eyes then and now for comfort and strength, just as it says in the Twenty-Third Psalm.

Let us suppose we were adults when we first set eyes on the earth and her seasons. I am prepared to bet that we would have thought we were entering a beautiful dream world. That was how I felt when I became conscious of Doon Hill for the first time. Even today, if on occasion, the seasons speak differently to me, memory has engraved an indelible series of images of a time that will always be special to me. As they say, what is remembered, lives on...

*Spring*

The months of March, April and May are generally regarded as spring, although some will argue that May month is the start of summer since what the calendars call Midsummer falls on 21st June. However, in the northern hemisphere, the astronomical spring commences when the sun influences the zodiacal sign of Aries, about the 21st of March; that period ends at the time of the Summer solstice on 21st June. For meteorological purposes and in common language, spring is regarded as consisting of the months of March, April and May. However, the popular conception of spring isn't that of the astronomer, so that in Britain, February, March and April are considered springtime. No doubt the arguments of my childhood friends on this point will persist. I suppose it all depends on what you consider spring in terms of weather. Having been born on 17th February 1941, when the snow was thick on the ground, I tend to consider my birth month as winter. However, enough of that.

These three months of what I consider spring were hectic, a time of ploughing and sowing and planting fields that had mostly lain dormant since October. Emerging from the long winter, Dunbar children would begin to take notice of their surroundings again. They didn't need a calendar to inform them that it was time to play out of doors and go for walks in the countryside; they didn't know then that they were re-connecting with or renewing the sense of wonder and mystery that stems from being close to the earth, the land. It was a time to look, listen and learn. At weekends, my brother Ken and I roamed the back roads; we knew where the plough was active long before we came to the field, for the seagulls massing in the sky were a dead giveaway; these hungry birds followed the age-old encroachment of the plough. We stood on the five-barred gates and watched the horse drawn ploughs bite into the soil, the bright steel blade turning over the earth's dark chocolate red, preparing its smooth, moist furrows for planting and sowing. It was timeless and ancient history; women walking the furrows with seed potatoes in their aprons and bending every now and then to plant the crop that would be harvested in six months' time. They were the salt of that rich earth, the descendants of the *bondager* women who still wore their *uglies*, or calico-covered bonnets, figures from a Thomas Hardy-esque landscape, had they known it. I had yet to discover the delights of Hardy's *Far From the Madding Crowd* and *The Return of the Native*.

March is invariably a blustery month in Dunbar, especially during the vernal equinox that occurs on the 21st day of that month, when day and night are of equal length. Severe equinoctial gales drove the sea against the harbour wall, shooting twenty-foot waves into the air. March always came in like a lion or a lamb, then went out the opposite way, as they used to say. It's an uncannily accurate folk tale. If it was quiet on the first day, the last was always wild. March can make a millpond or a maelstrom of the North Sea; when the seas run high and the few fishing boats are imprisoned in the Old Harbour for days. Many a March Saturday afternoon drew us down to the harbour to watch the great waves crash over the sea wall, sometimes dwarfing it. As March is noted for wind, we were forbidden to go to the harbour but we went anyway; we were also told that if we made faces and the wind changed, they would stay that way. We disobeyed the first and hoped the second was a fairy tale.

Recently, my friend Mark Beattie told me that he could never understand how the kittiwakes that nested on the castle walls always came back on the same day each year. I think he said it was on the sixteenth of March. (In 2005, he was proved right; they left on 20th August, a fact which amazed my friend Robin Murdoch. Mark once asked me this:

'How do they work it out when it's a leap year? They always come back on the same day in spring.'

I can't answer Mark's question. They came back on 16th March 2004, a leap year and again on 16th March 2006. Nature is indeed mysterious.

February and March bring lovely flowers. Daffodils and snowdrops were and still are my favourites. The first flowers to break through the hard earth are the tiny yellow aconites that quickly spread through the long grass,

# The Seasons

beside hedgerows. Next to arrive are the drifts of snowdrops, humble little flowers which are the true harbingers of spring. They say that the snowdrop came to this country during the thirteenth century, when some enterprising Crusader horticulturalist brought the bulbs from the Holy Land. If the tale is true, then it is the best reason I have ever heard in mitigation of the Crusades, a total waste of men and money expended in fruitless campaigns to contain the anti-Christ Muslims commanded by their brilliant leader, Saladin. The daffodil is a wild flower but it has been long-since been cultivated in domestic gardens. It's a flower of the woods, where it thrives best. We knew just such a wood for collecting bunches to take home to our mother. *Boorhoose* was a veritable carpet of yellow daffodils in spring. The estate manager was always on the prowl, looking out for daffodil thieves - not so much, I suspect for pinching the flowers but for destroying other more valuable plants and generally trashing the place. Having been a boy himself, he knew only too well the havoc a gang of kids can wreak on a wood even if they are only intent on picking a few flowers. He made it known that anyone caught in the act would be reported to the police. He once intercepted Ken and I on the road to Lochend with bunches hidden beneath our *burberries*; he let us off with a warning, possibly because we hadn't done any damage to the estate or taken more than a few blooms. But he said it would be the *polis* the next time. My mother knew perfectly well where the daffodils came from but always accepted them without censuring us; she would put them in a tall glass vase, the heady scent increasing in the heat of the living room fire.

All over Dunbar, gardens erupted with crocus flames, daffodils and then the yellow butter primroses. In the woods, clumps of primroses were hidden under drifts of leaves and it was hard to find them. Soon, the floor of the woods was a mass of shy little violets, then the dark inky bluebells with their intoxicating scent. Today, I have a good friend and former neighbour in Lammermuir Crescent in the 1950s, Violet, Betty Jeffrey's older sister; my mother told me she was called Violet after the woodland flower her mother picked when she was pregnant with her. The chinks of blue in the skies grew larger as March month came striding over the hills.

Spring was a time of great activity- and not only on the farms. I was put to work, clearing the garden of deadwood, the dry sticks of last year's flowering shrubs like the fuchsia bushes that stood sentinel on either side of the garden path at our front door. Suddenly, they came alive with greenery, their bare sticks transformed almost overnight. Then I set to in the vegetable patch, grubbing out the weeds and raking off the stones that poked through after the winter rains and snows. I never cut our grass before March, never planted any seeds until April, when the threat of snow was past. Yes, my Saturday afternoons were always busy in March and April, work I had to do on Sundays when I started working at *Lipton's* in 1956.

Washing lines billowed with bed linen and curtains during the annual madness of spring cleaning that gripped every household at that time of year. At night, we could hear the rooks cawing incessantly in Lochend Wood, noisily replenishing their untidy, straggling, lop-sided nests, their hoarse complaining and squabbling carried into my bedroom on the white air of March.

But the busiest places of all were the farms and smallholdings scattered around Dunbar. Veritable beehives of industry, the fields were alive with women planting, tractors sowing seed, shepherds lambing and cowmen calving. Soon, out of the way places were dotted with temporary *sheilings* - enclosures made from straw hurdles to give shelter to the new-born lambs and calves. Ken and I used to go to places like Little Spott to watch the new life coming into the world; we would look for the muddiest places and plunge into them in our *wellies..* It was great fun, splodging about in the *glaur* [mud] - usually a thick black or reddish treacle - until the inevitable happened. A *wellie* sunk too deep into the morass came off and you'd to hop about in one boot, looking for a dry place to put down your stocking foot while the entombed footwear was retrieved by a two-wellied companion. Ken hated hauling out my *wellie* because being heavier, it sank deeper into the mire. Even so, he'd pull it out, chortling at the farting/sucking noises it made, handing it back to me with some disdain and unimpressed by my attempts to humour him with impersonations of Long John Silver in *Treasure Island.* I can recall my repertoire even today:

> 'AAAAAAR AAAAAAR! Lost me wellie I has! Ah, Jim lad, be so good as to fetch me it! I'll gie ye doubloons, doubloons! Oor Wullie and da Bloons!'

Ken would sniff disapprovingly at my weak joke and my less than effective impersonation of Robert Newton in that famous role; in that respect, he hasn't changed his opinion of me in the intervening years....

The lambs and the calves staggered to their feet then as they do now and hopefully always will. They became more interesting on four legs, like all baby animals. The sight of them lying prostrate, bloody and streaked with slime did not appeal to me. But in a few days, the little lambs were transformed into clean, white fluffy bundles that made crazy, involuntary leaps into the air. They were so full of fun, curiosity and energy. I have always thought what a pity that a lamb grows into something as stupid - and ugly - as a sheep. Often, the little creatures would engage in races; one minute, a group would be standing around doing nothing except trying to nibble the grass, then one would suddenly race off and stop without warning, as if it were encouraging others to do the same. Off the little thing would dart again, this time followed by the rest. I have seen them race round the perimeter of a field in Spott for a few minutes, then they would stop abruptly, staring at us staring at them, four-legged animals curious about two-legged animals. Both were fascinated by each other.

Spring was the time for domestic cleaning in our homes, so the kids made themselves scarce to indulge themselves in bird-nesting. We did as little of the former and as much of the latter as we could. Ejected out of the house on a series of washdays, Ken and I would roam the woods and fields gladly. We loved to find the nests but we never took the eggs of wrens, sparrows, robins and blackbirds like some boys who stole them and blew them by pricking the shell with a pin. To us, eggs were life and life was precious. Ken and I were content to creep into a hedge and whisper to each other about the size and colour of the eggs we found. The robin's pale blue eggs are the best - a light fragile blue like a spring sky; the robin is my favourite bird because it's almost human - or at least it chooses human cast-offs like tins, flower pots and old kettles in which to build its nest and rear its young.

At the end of March, on the last Saturday night/Sunday morning, then as now, the clocks were put forward by one hour. Summer time began on that day. For us it meant nights were light longer and so we were able to play outside for an extra hour or so. Then suddenly, it was April, the first day of that month being special for *hunt- the-gowk*, or as we knew it, *huntygowk*. The game is as old as the hills - well, at least since the Middle Ages and possibly dating back to Roman times. It had undergone some considerable transformation by our time but its purpose hadn't changed; it made fun of people. Hunting the *gowk* or cuckoo is at least 500 years old in Scotland. The idea was to shout after someone, saying they'd something wrong with them. A sample of that humour follows:

'D'ye ken your shoelaces are undone?' (This said to someone reading a newspaper).

'There's a spider crawling up your neck!' (This said to some pigtailed girl).

'Your back-wheel's goin' roond the wrong way!' (This said to a passing cyclist).

There was another obscure ploy whereby younger boys were asked if they had been to the Brunt *Herber* [harbour], supposedly sited to the south of Doon Hill. Replying in the negative, they would be jeered for their ignorance and urged to cycle up there to find it. Of course it didn't exist - or did it? Someone recently suggested that the word *herber* might have been a corruption of *arbour*, meaning a bower or shady retreat with its sides and roof formed by trees, which is entirely possible. No matter, it was all good, clean fun, unlike much of what passes for humour today.

But April's main attraction was Easter which meant a trip to Oswald Dean or *Osie Dean* where the majority of Dunbar families traditionally had an all-day picnic on Easter Sunday and the annual ritual I describe in Chapter 7, the rolling of hard-boiled eggs. It is in some way a strange coincidence today but I am lucky to count as good friends Dot and Keith Knight who have renovated and extended the former Old Easter Broomhouse Mill at *Osie Dean* and now live there in splendid isolation. I envy them their home because that spot is one of my favourite childhood places.

# The Seasons

I always left the vegetable garden until Easter in case we had a late frost, then I'd buckle to. Into that good earth went seed potatoes - which must always be planted with the 'eyes' facing the surface. My brother Norman who once planted the vegetable plot was chided when no shaws appeared. I planted leeks, turnips, lettuces, beetroot and *syboes* [spring onions], onion sets and peas. The last were a bit of an excuse to forage for pea stakes - the discarded branches of fir trees - in Lochend Woods, traditionally known as *Wullie's Wud* after the gamekeeper Willie Gibson who lived there. Pea stakes were fallen dead fir tree branches whose needles had fallen off to leave a kipper-bone shaped branch. We always asked permission from Willie to enter the wood because we knew he was rearing young pheasants for the 12th August shoot. Because the female pheasant is easily scared, she will abandon her nest at the slightest provocation. Accordingly, we always went to Willie's cottage to ask permission to go into the wood near Lochend Cottage. Willie rarely refused us, knowing we wouldn't disturb his precious birds; he would come with us as he knew where the nesting sites were and so was able to direct us away from them. If the mother bird flew off, Willie had to hatch her eggs in an incubator and hand-rear the chicks until he could release them into the wild. It was a thankless job, though he didn't see it that way - unless he suspected that kids had deliberately scared the mother bird off the nest. His job was to provide sport for the landowner and his friends from August - when poor creatures like partridges and pheasants are slaughtered legally - until the February following. He did a good job.

At any rate, we were given an hour or so to gather our pea stakes, which we tied together in bundles, then strung them on our bikes. We waved goodbye to Willie, then made a detour to the other end of Lochend where we knew daffodils grew in profusion. There, we parked our bikes and ventured into the wetlands - Lochend is named for the Great Loch of Dunbar, a post-glacial loch drained during the Middle Ages - and yet in my day was still wet and boggy in places. I seem to recall one of the favourite places was known as *Sucker Island* on account of its treacherous mud. It was a veritable Mecca for small boys who could assuage their consciences and justify their pinched bunches of flowers by the dangers they'd undergone to get them. Many spring afternoons I heard wee lads warning each other of the danger:

'It's five fit [feet] deep! The mud at Lochend kin droon ye!'

They weren't exaggerating. The thick, black, evil-smelling mud was lethal; we used to avoid it by hopping from one grassy knoll to another, like island-hopping in a green slimy sea. Needless to say, *wellies* were required footwear for that operation.

After we tired of this game, we went back with our daffies to pick up the pea stakes, watching the chickens scratching in the woods near *Lochend Cottage* for grubs. Sometimes we found an occasional egg in the bracken but on breaking it, we usually found it was 'off'. The chickens belonged to the Lunam family; they lived their idyllic existence - well it was to me then - in a lovely stone-built cottage whose chimney exhaled the acrid but delicious smell of pine log smoke. As May and Norah Lunam's Grannie Herkes lived a couple of doors from us in Lammermuir Crescent, they were constant visitors to our back garden. As I have said earlier, the Lunams' cottage was near the site of a sawmill - or should I say the residue it left behind after it was dismantled, an ancient sawdust pile whose soft hill provided an ideal scenario for our games of Robin Hood. Many a time I have engaged the Sheriff of Nottingham in a duel of wooden swords on his sawdust castle at Lochend.. May, her brother Robert and sister Norah occasionally played in our backyard when they visited their grandmother Jenny, just as their cousins, the Fawcett boys and girls who lived with Jenny for a few years had once played with us there (Their brother David Lunam who lives a couple of doors away from me today wasn't born in those days).

Then suddenly it was the month of May and the weather grew increasingly hot so that we'd to complain about wearing too many clothes - vests, double-knit jerseys and liberty bodices (in the young). My mother was always afraid we'd catch spring colds, so she would chant this mantra:

'Ne'er cast a cloot [cloth] till May's oot [out]'.

She would wag an admonishing forefinger at us as she said the words. It was many years later that I discovered that the reference to May was not the calendar month but the May or blackthorn tree, whose white blossom emerges in early spring. So we could have divested ourselves of vests long before 31st May....

The hedges were the glory of that season, foaming with white blossom. The hawthorn of May gave way to the flickering lights that were the cabbage white butterflies, flitting in their crazy flights above the tops of the hedges. In the hedge roots, primroses softened the dark banks of turf that seemed greener at evening, when the last rays of the sun teased out their true colour.

My mother had every reason to be afraid of illness as she'd had her fair share of it in 1925 when she was aged 11. She was a victim of pleurisy, diphtheria and congestion of the lungs - all at the same time. They didn't think she would live but she did - for another 77 years. When I was a teenager, she was badly troubled by nerves and for two years, she slept propped upright in her bed by four large pillows. She said she had to have the pillows as she felt she was sinking into the floor when she lay flat. Then she developed boils in her ears - perhaps the result of deficiencies during the war years, when she gave us the nutritional food and starved herself as many mothers did. The local medical man Dr Anderson was kind and attentive but he could only prescribe *gentian violet* which was inserted into her ears on the end of a piece of cotton wool attached to a used matchstick. In those pre-NHS days, anything went. I shall never forget the relief she knew when just after the NHS came into being in July 1948, we had a new doctor whose skills were - to us- beyond belief, making of him some kind of god. Dr Alfred E Cordin cured my mother after about four weeks. He was a Clark Gable lookalike but also a damned fine physician. I have only a vague memory of the cure he administered over the several Sunday mornings he visited her. I recall him sitting her on a chair at the living room window, in the sunlight, pouring some warm oil, possibly something as simple as olive oil into her afflicted ears, then regularly changing the gauze dressings he used. For the first time in two years, she slept peacefully, without the need to lie propped-up in bed. Mum always said he was a true servant of the Lord, as well as a fine doctor. She was superstitious to a fault, bless her.

Our spring illnesses were the usual ones. Measles, chicken pox, scarlet fever, the 'flu or a bad cold. We suffered from mysterious seasonal aches and pains my mother called 'growing pains'. (No modern doctor I know nowadays ever describes these unexplained aches in young arms and legs in such a way). We were kept warm inside and out; we were treated to the rare luxury of a gas fire in our bedroom and a stone hot water bottle - called a *pig* - in our bed. It gave off so much heat that you couldn't put your feet on it without wearing two pairs of thick woollen socks. The hot water bottle and the gas fire sweated the fever out of you, then you were coddled for a week, fed with egg custards and other special foods and given your favourite comics to cheer you up. One of my best memories of one of the several minor illnesses I had was to wake up one morning in a room flooded with sunshine, tired but free from aches and pains. My mother came upstairs with a breakfast tray of boiled egg and toast, then she whisked me out of bed, wrapped me in a thick blanket and sat me on a chair where I ate the food while she changed the sheets and pillowcases. The sheer luxury of getting back into crumb-free sheets and cool pillows remains an indescribable luxury, one I have to do for myself today.

Spring was a busy time at school but it was also a time for the entertainment it brought. For me, spring was watching Doon Hill explode into green, the country roads smeared with the clods of red earth from horses' hooves and tractor wheels, the return of the kittiwakes every March where they nested on the ruined castle and the windows of the old granary at the harbour. The woods were carpeted with nervously shaking daffodils, fat, furry grey catkins, shy violets emerging beside a rotting log, grassy banks buttered with primroses with rabbits playing among them, frogspawn and tadpoles in Spott Burn, wind in the telegraph wires - a particularly memorable, poignant and lonely sound. Then came Easter in April, with promises of hard-boiled eggs rolled along the deep carpet of grass in Oswald Dean, playing *peevers* in the roads and *rounders* in the fields.

I loved - and still love - the full moons of that season. They seemed to sail serene among the clouds they illuminated, making them look like shoals of silver herring or the wavy lines left on Belhaven Beach by the receding tide. They bathed Doon Hill in an eerie, soft, lambent light that hinted of mystery and things of the past I could only sense in my childhood ignorance. I knew nothing of the two battles fought beneath it, one in 1296, the other in 1650. (Later in my life, I tried to evoke these childhood moons to a woman called Ina whom I loved; I described them as the wuthering lights that haunted me in those years – she forgave me for plagiarising that wild, strange and luridly magnificent novel by Emily Bronte because she said she knew exactly what I meant.

So that sums up what spring meant to me then and means to me now. Images from that unforgettable time are still vivid, still catch my breath, as does the beauty of the season.

*Summer*

Summer. The name has a magical sound. For young people, it meant freedom from school. Those long-ago summers of childhood belong to another world, one shrouded in partial shadow. Summers then seemed warmer and less wet than those we have come to expect in more recent years. Or is that another trick of memory? When you are a child, you never remember the dreary days of summer. The sun always shines when you're young - or so it seems at the time.

For me, summer began in June, usually a quiet, dependable and soft month, one filled with anticipation. We thought the school holidays would never come. Sometimes, in that month, we woke to a sea *haar* or *fret* that had slipped in from the sea, usually at the turn of the tide during the night. At that time of year, these *haars* were harbingers of heat rather than rain. By mid-morning, the sun would break through, burning up the grey gloom. In the morning, he schoolrooms at Woodbush were filled with a mild, incandescent light that matured into a soporific heat that made it difficult for us to concentrate on our lessons. In that final month of the summer term, the dust motes from the blackboard dusters our teachers banged on the board floated on the sun's rays in never ending showers of white light.

At night, the June moon hung fragile and pale in the sky, reminiscent of a Chinese lantern. It was a gentle, calm moon, not the strident yellow-orange harvest moons or the creased, worried moon face that hung over the winter rooftops. June nights were balmy, the smell of night-scented stock breathing in open bedroom windows and lulling us to sleep. I have never heard a nightingale in my life but owls there were in plenty, dusting the woods and fields with their wings as they searched for nocturnal creatures to feast upon. They hooted incessantly as they stood on sentry duty in the trees above the hedgerows, then they would swoop down on some unsuspecting little creature, shrieking triumphantly when they made a kill of some unfortunate wood mouse or vole. At weekends, Ken and I searched for owls sleeping during daytime but we never found one. They are shy birds that operate only in darkness. Wood pigeons called to each other in slumberous, monotones from the scented pines;

the ferns on the floor of the woods we went to exuded a hot, dusty, intoxicating bouquet. The long grass in the fields was dusted with the clover pollen that bumblebees disturbed in their forays for nectar. Butterflies executed their crazy, dizzy flight paths above the hedgerows and among the emerging flowers, dawdling in cabbage fields or weaving in and out of the tall white flowers of the hogweed that grew by the country roadsides.

And then at last, June was over and school came to an end. We were free, only to become slaves of childhood passions, greater and more insistent than schoolbooks and teachers. On that last day of the summer term, a bubble of children burst out of the school gates, scattering in different directions, whooping and whistling to announce their freedom. We whirled empty schoolbags and satchels round our heads or kicked them along the pavements, swaggering through the town streets so that everyone knew we were on holiday. Like released prisoners-of-war, we looked forward to weeks of fun. We had an excess of energy to burn. As soon as we got home, Ken and I took off our school clothes, consigning them to the chest of drawers until they were needed again in August. We wore the summer uniform of *Sloppy Joe* (the modern equivalent is the T-shirt or sweat shirt), canvas shorts secured with a snake-clasp elastic belt and sandals or sandshoes. We wore practically nothing else; socks, vests and underpants were packed away until school took up again. We looked forward to unfettered toes that attracted dirt or sand between them, arms and legs turning brown from a combination of sun, sea and wind. Sockless and pantless, we were ready for the summer and everything it had to offer. In chapter 5, I have described in detail what these summer pursuits were so it isn't necessary for me to revisit them here. But allow me to indulge myself a little.

July often came in with a day or two of sun-showers as my mother used to call them but the rain was warm and the sun soon came out again. I had my chores to do at home but as these were usually finished by lunchtime (dinnertime as we called it then) I had the whole afternoon and evening to do as I pleased. Conveniently, the rain often came in the morning but if I am honest, I remember more wet days in the month of July than in August; some days came in with a chill, mizzling rain from Doon Hill or a *smirr* of showers from the sea.

Often, I got through my chores quicker than usual but I still had to hang about in case my mother needed anything from the shops. On these mornings, Ken and I would play in the back garden, he with his *Dinky* toys, me with my beloved lead soldiers. We built roads in the dirt, flattening them with Ken's toy bulldozer. We fought pitched battles with my soldiers, fighting in a forest of potato shaws, lettuces and spring onions. We had snail races, the snails being liberated from their clusters at the bottom of the fuchsia bushes near the front door. But snails are exasperating creatures and rarely go where you want them to, a fact borne out by their erratic, crazy silver trails which prove they often double back, thus proving they are sightless creatures. Finally, scolded for our road-construction programmes by my mother ('Nothing'll grow there now!') we were ordered to restore the earth, replace the snails in their protective greenery, were chased from the garden and told to read our comics on the doorstep until dinnertime.

By July, the front garden was in full flower. The summer borders were a mass of nasturtiums or Golden Gleams, as my mother called them; great gouts of reds, yellows and oranges, their bright discs seemed to suck in the sun. There were antirrhinums or snapdragons whose blooms opened and closed like mouths when you pressed them between finger and thumb. The fuchsias were prolific, producing quantities of little ballerina-style flowers all summer long. I called them the dancing ladies with their scarlet skirts and purple legs. Granny Cockburn's roses were our pride and joy however. She planted them in 1933; when she died four years later, her lovely roses were well established. The bushes dwarfed Ken and I, the heads of the great blooms peered in the front window - great gouts of clotted cream, pale pink, deep scarlet, orange, red, gold and yellow which rarely ever adorned our living room in vases for my mother said it was a shame to cut them. They brightened our summer dinner table from outside, as my mother refused to put them in vases.

In June, the lengthening days unlocked the door to our summer world. We ran down long, endless corridors of sunlight and shade, mist and occasional rain. On July and August afternoons, we went to the East Beach as we couldn't afford the sixpence entrance fee for the outdoor swimming pool. Off we went with towels tucked under our arms like Swiss rolls minus the centre, it being the swimming costumes we wore under our scant clothes. After a quick swim and a stint of building sandcastles, we made little dams in the rocks, stemming the little rivulets or run-off water after high tide; we built makeshift houses out of small bits of wood and cork in front of the dam and I placed some of my lead soldiers among these miniature dwellings. Finally, we broke the dam and watched its waters engulf the soldiers and sweep away the little houses. Great fun.

We were always hopeful of finding the odd coin among the rocks or in the sand, a rare occurrence in summer. I occasionally raided the pewter jug where my mother kept pennies for the gas meter, stealing enough for a couple of frozen ice lollies which were sold from a small kiosk near the site of the former Amusement Arcade. I liked the blue spearmint variety that left their tell tale colour on your tongue and lips; others favoured the Orange Maid iced lollies that stained their tongues orange. We couldn't afford the price of a deckchair from the man who rented them out for an afternoon, so we parked our skinny bums on the sand, envying the children whose parents could afford chairs for the entire family.

These days by the seashore are readily conjured up by never-to-be-forgotten smells. The briny tang from the sea interspersed with the mouth-watering smell of hot dogs from the kiosk and the milky *bouquet* of the ice cream

# The Seasons

cones and *sliders* [ice cream wedged between wafers].  And of course, the natural playground formed by the rocks east of the rotting breakwater, its wooden slats encrusted with barnacles and other sea-creatures.  Even now, when I walk over these rocks, I recognise those to which we gave names according to their shape - *Vesuvius*, the *Castle*, the *Whale*, the *Cauldron* - made familiar by our fantasy games.  I can still identify those rock pools where we *guddled* [tickled] for the little brown minnow-like fish that darted among the fronds of seaweed; we also tormented the sea anemones with minute bits of gravel or crushed limpet shells which they sucked in and spat out.  We tapped the shells of the hermit crabs to frighten them and watched them withdraw into their borrowed shells.  I remember the bladder-wrack whose floating vesicles or bubbles we loved to pop, the *tangle* or oar-weed which festooned the beach until the next tide removed it. In August the oarweed lay for weeks and rotted, home to millions of maggots that wriggled among the dried black fronds that lay on the sand, the superscripture of a exceptionally high tide.

If summer was a time of myths and magic made flesh, that flesh could sometimes be disappointing, bringing broken-hearted joys.  Just when you'd made a new friend of a summer holiday boy or girl, they had to leave.  Although a fortnight isn't long, it seemed so then.  For the immature heart, it was a time of lightning flashes and thunderbolts that came and went as suddenly as the summer wildfire that zigzagged across the sea on oppressively warm nights.  Young loves - I should say young 'crushes' - can be terribly traumatic, although they had their lighter moments.  Of course, we knew nothing about sex and so our wooing of the girls of summer never got beyond holding hands and the occasional kiss.  We were puzzled by the white, deflated balloons that contained a cloudy liquid we found on the beach, trapped in the seaweed.  They seemed to increase during the summer months, whereas in the other seasons, they were hardly ever seen.  Jock the Wild Man enlightened us.

> 'Folk that dinnae [don't] want bairns [children] use them. The man pits it on his thingy so the wumman will no' get too excited. Ye see, if she gets too excited, she'd get a bairn.  They're tae stop the wumman gettin' excited.'

Well, I suppose he was on the right track, but for the wrong reason.....

Although our childhood summers were spent mainly by the sea, we didn't wholly abandon the countryside.  By the middle of August, the fields were prolific with mature wheat, oats and barley, swathes of grain that undulated like inland seas, animated by the wind.  I have this enduring image of a field of waving immature green wheat that to me looked like a woman's velvet dress.  Where does that come from?  Not Thomas Hardy, whose novels I read avidly in later years.  By August, the potato fields were maturing, having lost the white flowers that came in spring and the turnips were growing fat.  When we grew tired of a succession of days spent on sand and sea, I took Ken to Doon Hill, where the clouds cast vast fleeting shadows over the landscape; sometimes, it seemed to me that time itself had suddenly taken shape and was speeding away before our eyes, like in those documentaries we saw at the cinema which depicted the passing of the years in the same symbolic way. (Another crude cinematic ploy to denote the passage of time was to show pages of a calendar blown away by the wind). Little did we know then that time was indeed passing and with it, our youthful innocence.

In the brick-red hot breath of many August afternoons, Ken and I would walk to *Osie Dean*. We paddled in the wee burn, destroyed armies of thistles with our sticks which we imagined were swords; mine was called *Excalibur*, the fabled sword of King Arthur. Nettles were the sworn enemy; we cut huge swathes through their serried ranks, then pee'd on them for good measure. They stung our bare legs but we treated them with that well-known country antidote, the blessed *docken* leaf, which cooled the afflicted parts. It's a fact that wherever you find nettles, *dockens* aren't far away; I wonder if Nature arranged that? D*ocken* leaves applied to a stung part of the skin left a green, greasy mark there but they certainly took the heat out of the little white lumps that the stinging nettle raised, lumps that looked like the eggs of some insect.

Country smells at that time of the year are different but equally strident as those that come from the sea. Only a mile inland, our olfactory sense was assailed by the peppery dust that came from the roads and which got up your nose, making you sneeze. The all-pervading smell was a rich, heady mixture of crushed grass, leaves, wild flowers, the yeasty smell of wet corn - a particular favourite of mine then and now - and the clean, cool smell which rose from the fretting Spott burn that ran through *Osie Dean* as it bubbled over its peaty, rock-strewn bed on its way to the sea at Broxmouth. Forays into the countryside were often short because often, it was too hot for walking along the back roads, hot enough for shimmering, watery mirages that hovered over the tarred surfaces. Then, when the skies darkened with the threat of rain, we hurried past the water filter plant near Spott, forbidden to us because it was said that it was a whirlpool that could suck you into its depths. Needless to say, we couldn't resist investigating it; it was sinister, a deep pool of water, frothing and bubbling like a modern day *jacuzzi*. We didn't linger long there. (I have been back recently to look at the filter; it's empty now but I wasn't surprised to find it was a lethal 25 feet in depth). You can drown in a foot or less of water....

The first great spots of rain often overtook us at the crossroads at Spott road-end, at today's modern roundabout. Anxious, we looked back to Doon Hill to see if it were sheathed in mist or a *smirr* of rain. We knew we'd be fine if we could make Lochend Wood, where we could find shelter under the trees. Gaining the belt of trees opposite Hallhill Farm, we knew we would be fine; the great raindrops that kicked up the summer dust were immobilised under the spreading branches of the trees at *Lochend Cottage*. We stood under this natural umbrella, listening to the raindrops clicking on the leaves of broadleaf trees like sycamores, or plane trees as they are known in Scotland.

# The Seasons

At last, the rain went off and we could continue our way home, along the path once called *Lovers' Lane*, pausing to stop beside the *Wishing Tree*, an old blasted hawthorn which has fallen prey to the developers of the area now known as the *Hallhill Healthy Living Centre*. (The Centre's owner may congratulate himself on the choice of a politically correct title; Lochend and Hallhill were healthy living centres years long before the modern complex was built. We didn't need the running tracks, the sports fields and all that organised, narcissistic nonsense when we were kids; Dunbar and its environs was an unregulated and therefore natural healthy living centre. Try telling that to the man who thinks he has found the blueprint for healthy life). After our walk, we were given tea or as I suppose supper in today's parlance; we then sat out in the back garden at dusk - some child actually asked me recently what was dusk! It was a time of light blue skies marked by cloud patterns that resembled the ridges in the sand at low tide at Belhaven Beach. Some called them mackerel skies, after the patterns on that fish's skin  These skies turned golden in the westering sun; above Belhaven Church spire, the swallows began to gather, screaming in the still air until the darkness fell and night brought a loud silence. Then came a reflective hour or two of cool breezes or absolute calm, when the heavy scent of phlox or night-scented stock wafted to us from the garden. Doon Hill lay serene, sultry, the sun laying the last of its rays on its red earth and gorse, setting both alight. Or so it seemed to me. Sometimes on these quiet evenings, we would take a walk to Belhaven to watch the Bass Rock turn into the black sea snail I have always thought it was, framed in a salmon-pink haze and floating in a calm, blue sea.

Sometimes on August afternoons, we went along the East Links, home to Dunbar Golf Club, there to play in an area known as the *Vaults;* these were a group of four rocks near the shore which, as I said earlier we re-named the *Three Rocks* because we didn't rate the smallest of the four. Once, we made a raft of driftwood scattered along the shore, sailing it on the shallow *Fluke Dub,* a natural pond that was made by the rocks. At its edge was an old mine from the Second World War; we amused ourselves by throwing stones at the teats and when one of us scored a hit, he made the sound of an explosion. The golfers were nothing short of a bloody nuisance, interfering with our games of war and imagination. Occasionally, when the night was warm in the twilight, we stayed on to watch the light come on at Barns Ness Lighthouse, when the moon began to rise behind Doon Hill, casting her light on the fields and laying a silvery path across the sea to the May Island.

I recall so many soft, gold-tinted skies from that time. Often, I used to sit in our back bedroom, with the window open so that I could smell the sea at Belhaven as twilight fell. Then I'd go into the front room where the darkness was touching the street and the walls and the Doon with its subtle velvet, stealthily creeping up the crown of the hill to extinguish the last of the natural light. If our August mornings were ushered in by a strident sun doing its level best to penetrate our bedroom curtains, our August evenings were framed in windows whose curtains weren't drawn until the very last of the light faded, when we lay in bed unable to sleep because of the scent drifting up from the garden below and the intermittent flashing of Barns Ness Lighthouse.

August was a good time for food. New potatoes from the garden went into the pot washed but unpeeled so you could taste the earth on them. Other vegetables were pulled out of the earth as they were needed - a cabbage, late lettuces, the last of the *syboes* or spring onions and the final roots of beetroot which went into a salad made with ham or boiled eggs and garnished with the last of the parsley. But the potato was king.

In early summer, Togneri's fish and chip shop always put up the prices of chips because as was explained in a window poster, the chips were now being made with New Potatoes! Nobody minded. It was all part of the summer bounty; who could grudged an extra couple of pennies when the chips were so tasty? And believe me, they were; there was never a better feast in my childhood. I cannot forget that mouth-watering smell that emanated out of the West Port shop at the end of a tiring, adventurous day in the hills or by the sea. We salivated as we passed by and hoped our mother would send us back to get fish suppers. With empty pockets, we would avoid stepping on the cracks in the pavements - they brought bad luck - in the hope that Mum would scrape together enough cash to give us Togneri's chips for tea. It did happen, though not often enough for us, which was probably just as well, as so many families today rely on that unhealthy diet. On Saturday nights, I often hung about the shop door, hoping some drunk would take pity on me, thrusting his bag of unwanted chips into my eager hand. In those penniless days, I would have killed for a poke of Togneri's chips smothered in the inimitable brown sauce, which they concocted from the *HP* variety diluted with vinegar. Or so I am told.

If the summer days taught me lessons about Nature, the nights fed my young, impressionable mind. I began to feel that one day, I might be a poet because I loved being on my own, a necessary pre-condition of that sad state. I clasped my knees and rested my chin on them on quiet evenings, listening to the loud silence. Wasn't that what poets did to get inspiration? And I began to have quiet conversations with myself as the sky turned apple green, then dark vermilion, which showed the stars and the seagulls etched against the velvet sky. Just before dusk, the swallows congregated round Belhaven Church spire; when they gathered there or on telegraph wires, I didn't need a calendar to inform me that summer was almost over. Daily, they screamed and darted above the High Street tenements, so I knew they were preparing for their long flight to Africa, a sign that autumn was on the way.

It had to end, that lovely, soft time. It died slowly, giving out early warning signals of its departure. One day, the kittiwakes were roosting in the Castle Rock and the windows of the old granary; the next day, usually around

348

mid to late August, they were gone. (My friend Robin Murdoch and I walked along the harbour quay one Saturday evening in August 2005. He remarked how noisy the birds were that evening. The next morning, they were gone. He couldn't believe it. The harbour was silent again apart from a few disconsolate gulls that took possession of the rocky ramparts once more). I know this annual event was the first visible signs that summer was over; the second occurred at the East Beach. Seaweed dumped there by the tides was well rotted by the last week in August; it lay stinking at the high water mark, interspersed with the black frizzled line of dried bladder wrack. I knew that underneath this unsightly mess were millions of maggots, which spoke volumes to me; they were consuming summer before my eyes. In those days, I had no idea what symbolism meant. The beach was a hard surface we walked on the few days before school resumed; but if you stood long enough, you soon learned it was a mass of corruption and death. The stench was unbearably obnoxious; when we returned to the classroom, we could smell it at playtimes. We never went back to the East Beach again until the Burgh Council invited local farmers to cart away the putrid mess to spread on their fields. When we heard the tractors chugging away on the beach, we knew that summer was officially over.

*Autumn*

September found us incarcerated in school, the beginning of so many weeks that would stretch to Christmas which was a world away. The autumn term was the longest, which is why I did badly in exams. Academic failure apart, autumn was my favourite season and still is. In chapter 8, I have described a typical autumn Sunday in the 1950s. Every day in that time brought unique sights, sounds and smells. September was almost an extension of summer, with its quiet, soft, sunlit days. I always took a long time to settle down to schoolwork in that month, a fact reflected in my school report cards between 1953 and 1957. There was still enough light in these golden evenings for us to venture to the beaches and the fields before darkness fell.

In early autumn, we played in the Latch Park, the Curling Pond and the perimeter of Lochend Woods after school. September was the farmer's time. His word was law. We all knew that we mustn't interfere with his work, that everything was geared to the harvest - sacrificed isn't too strong a word - because we believed that the crops gathered in our local fields in those days after the war meant there would be food on our tables. We went to the fields after school to watch the garnering of the harvest, for we knew a good harvest meant we would survive. This was a legacy from the Second World War, when Britain relied on imported food from abroad. I recall kids going to nearby fields like the Sailors' Park at the back of our house, Newhouse Terrace (where Sholto Miller had prolific fields) and the Riggs opposite Gala Green, rented by the smallholder Nelson who once had a greengrocer's shop in Dunbar High Street.

# The Seasons

In those days, our favourite haunt was the field at the end of Lammermuir Crescent, where we went to look at the last square of corn being cut, its shrinking perimeter lined with farm workers and small boys wielding thick sticks, accompanied by dogs. They were there to kill the last frightened rabbits that ran out of the corn. I don't recall many 'kills' but it was fun to watch the chase led by excited boys and crazy dogs. In those days, corn was cut and sheaves were *stooked* [stacked] upright in tent-like formations so they could dry quicker. We used to hide in the *stooks*, especially when it rained. After the corn was winnowed in barns, the straw was built into haystacks, majestic works of art that dominated the shorn fields. Many a day I burrowed into a haystack to escape the sudden onslaught of an equinoctial storm. The haystacks were beautiful edifices, perpendicular, solid, rising to a point; now, the hay harvest offers us lines of gigantic hairy toilet rolls in the autumn fields. (Recently, my good friend Rosemary Bradbury, daughter of the pond master in the 1960s, informed me that my brother Ken kissed her in a haystack around that time!) The poetry of the earth, the haystacks and the farms are sadly gone forever.

I never cease to wonder at the variations in autumn colours, hues that can change overnight. The hedgerows of my childhood brimmed with honeysuckle and small dog roses; dry *stane* dykes were protected by the barbed wire of the prolific brambles that grew near *Boorhoose*. There we slaked our thirst and assuaged our hunger, eating *soor dooks* and the fat black brambles that stained our fingers purple. September was also the time of horse chestnuts and we went every weekend to *Boorhoose* to throw sticks into these great trees, hoping to gain the best nuts for our games of *chessies* in the school playground. I was always thrilled when my stick brought down a shower of the nuts; I eagerly broke open their prickly husks and marvelled at the shiny, brown fruits.

Autumn always reminds me of the Clydesdales at East Barns farm, where my aunt's prisoner -of -war husband, the Austrian Joseph Franc worked until he and Aunt Emily emigrated to Doncaster, where he worked in the coalmines. I loved the Clydesdales. They had large brown eyes like the chestnuts I gathered at *Boorhoose*. Joseph Franc let me ride on a Clydesdale horse in 1946; my legs were almost horizontal on that great beast's back; I think she was called Bess. I remember sitting on a stack of hay, watching Uncle Joseph - my mother always called him *Jofish* - brush the coats of the two Clydesdales he looked after. Joseph was as gentle as the horses themselves – how could he have been a soldier in the Wehrmacht? I recall these gentle, biddable beasts by their quiet compliance and their large, hairy soup-plate-sized feet they placed daintily on the earth, the plough behind making furrows they rarely looked back to see. When they did, I think they may have been seeking the assurance of the ploughman, that it was time to stop work. I loved those great beasts; they remain as warm blooded statues in my memory.

In autumn, avenues of trees are brushed as if by an inspired artist or set fire to by some deranged arsonist. Entire hedgerows are swept with yellow, gold, scarlet and red, a rich brocade of colour that still stops me in my tracks. As the season advanced, fields stripped bare gave a solidity to woods and hedges; in those days, I so wanted to talk to someone about the emotions which the Autumn colours stirred in me but there was no one. There never has been, although I still live in hope... surely I am not the only person who is moved by this beauty that unravels every year? Of course I'm not; other people see it - they are simply not moved enough to talk about it, in case people think they are odd. I find that sad....

Autumn in Dunbar was truly a season of mist and mellow fruitfulness. Moisture rose from the earth in late September and October, the freshly turned fields steaming in the morning as the sun drew the moisture from them. If the hills didn't bring the mist, it was the sea. Mist from the sea crept in at night, insinuating woods, copses, hedgerows. Walking to school, I loved the smell of rotting leaves, that rich, loamy smell; mixed with the sharp, bitter-sweet smell of wood smoke, I knew it most acutely when passing by *Lochend Cottage* whose gardens were stripped of everything save the Brussels sprouts, leeks and turnips, like the garden I worked at home.

In those days of awkward innocence, I was fascinated by a character called Johnny Appleseed whom I'd read about in some comic book. Johnny walked through the woods in his native America, his pockets filled with apple seeds which he scattered whenever he came to a clearing in the forest. If he in fact did exist, he would have been a favourite of our own home-grown version, John Muir, who left Dunbar in 1849 to live in Wisconsin, then went on to create the National Parks of America, notably Yosemite. To my shame - or perhaps to Scotland's - I never heard of Dunbar's famous son until the 1970s. But Appleseed I did know and taking my cue from him, I used to gather acorns and other seeds, scattering them in the woods I frequented as a boy. Maybe some have matured in the intervening years. I was a great student of trees then; I knew the different species and discovered that trees had their own specific diseases - yellow and red fungi, rot within the trunk etc. I knew this meant the tree was dying, so I scattered even more of the seed of these trees than others.

As I wrote earlier, September was usually a quiet, calm month, which the locals called an Indian summer - whatever that was. (Not many of our local people have lived in India). Soft autumn sunlight, no longer strident with the hot breath of summer imitated the colour of the yellowing ferns and bracken. Even if the sun was relatively warm during the day, it grew chilly at dusk and sometimes there would be a light frost although it never lay long in the mornings. September was a hectic time for nature as well as man; the hedges were brimming with berries and blackbirds that settled on the branches, stripping them bare or scuttling among the roots to retrieve fruit that had fallen as a result of our brambling forays. I also looked for the mushroom places we knew as fairy rings - dark green circles in the grass made by the decaying mushroom spores. I gathered my fair share of these mushrooms in a field near *Boorhoose*; one of the great horse mushrooms I gathered there could fill a frying pan, as I wrote earlier. That was my treat on Sunday mornings in the 1950s, when I'd sit on the back of my Uncle Jimmy's little scooter and he'd whisk me up the road to this field, sending me to forage while he smoked a *Woodbine*. Then one autumn, I discovered there were button mushrooms in the *Sailors' Park*, the field over the garden wall at Lammermuir Crescent. Dusk would find me with a little basket, wandering up and down the field which was fallow after many years of farming. I knew that horse manure was good for mushrooms; Mr Nelson, who rented the field from the Burgh Council had used horse-drawn ploughs. So it should have come as no surprise to find the little button mushrooms growing literally on our doorstep. They were small but appetising, white as the cheeks of babies; fried in butter with a bit of bacon, they were irresistible.

It was a good time for treats. There were apples for scrounging in gardens, beechnuts in the woods, brambles and blackcurrants in the hedgerows. Another treat for me was when my mother exchanged her butter ration for sugar with the Jeffrey family who had a cottage at the side of the railway near the former Spott Road, just beyond the bottom gate of the graveyard. Mrs Jeffrey used to give me a *piece* [sandwich] smothered in her homemade black-currant jam. Sadly, neither Mrs Jeffrey nor the cottage survive today.

The soft days seemed to slip by unhurried, unnoticed until near the end of that idyllic month, when the black smudges on the telegraph wires material-ised as swallows, massing for their long flight to Africa. When they gathered in large numbers, we knew that autumn was well into its stride and stride it did across both the land and the landscape of the mind.

As I mentioned earlier, in Sunday school in Belhaven Church, we were exhorted to go out collecting rose hips, from which rose hip syrup was made. The minister of the day, the Reverend J Ritchie, a kindly man who in my opin-ion has never been bettered by any other local minister before him or since, assured us that the syrup was sent to the improve the health of poor tribes in Africa under the Church's Overseas Mission - or whatever it called itself. I don't think he would have misled us. At any rate, we obeyed him and went out on Autumn Sunday afternoons with jam jars to collect the hips. A favourite place was just beyond the western entrance to Lochend, on the minor road to *Boorhoose* which then as now, dips and twists towards the A1 trunk road. I visited the spot in autumn 2005 and there they were, the thin straggly bushes which I reckon have grown there for over a century. It made me think of all those who are no longer with us, yet the rose hips still flourish. It's a rare sight, children gathering berries nowadays. In my childhood, we dutifully handed in our harvests to the Sunday school teachers.

October came in with hard frosts and bitter winds that moaned in the wires emptied of the schools of little swallows. The last fields of potatoes and turnips were harvested, the vegetables stored in clamps or pits and straw to protect them from the frost. There were few grey squirrels in those days but we saw them occasionally at Lochend, little grey squiggles snaking through the grass and gathering as many nuts as they could hold in their cheeks. Hedgehogs were rare but we saw one or two, stumbling about looking for dry winter quarters and rolling themselves in the thick piles of leaves for insulation against the cold and wet. Elsewhere, I have described the wonder of discovering a field mouse's nest/larder what is now Poplar Street, a sight I have never forgotten to this day.

October twilights and dusks seemed to generate a strange, eerie silence that wasn't quite soundless. How can I best describe that muted, breathing sound which hung over the landscape? It was like the distant rush of waves on the beach or traffic far away; perhaps it is best compared with the sound you hear when you hold a whelk shell to your ear, a sound they used to say was the echo of the sea. Yet there was nothing to be seen, nothing tangible. It was as if the sound came out of the earth, a whisper of silence, or the earth breathing.

When the sun faded earlier every day, my forays to places like Lochend and the Latch Park grew less. I loved the Latch Park, with its grey tree roots poking through the footpath, its grassy, wooded slope covered in bramble bushes and hawthorn, with their small red berries. It was a great place to play, swinging from a rope tied to a overhanging branch or lying listening to the wind, unseen by the occasional passer-by taking a short cut home. Sadly, Latch Park is but a memory; the wooded slope survives but the path has become overgrown with brambles and is a nondescript play area for today's Latch Park kids. Even the Curling Pond has lost its fascination; sadly neglected in the intervening years. We didn't linger long there on darkening October evenings because it was supposed to be haunted by the ghost of a man who'd committed suicide there, although I never knew anyone who said they'd seen the apparition. Was the story that of a shell-shocked soldier during the Great War who shot himself because he couldn't face going back to the trenches?

It was a lovely, velvety time, coming home from the woods, a last glimmer of light fading fast behind the spire of Belhaven Church. I was always glad to be home and to sit on the floor before the open fire, my knees drawn up to my chin as I watched the flames flicker in the grate.

It was many years later that I discovered D H Lawrence's moving poem *Ship of Death;* it seemed to sum up autumn for me, particularly the autumns of my childhood:

*Now it is autumn and the falling fruit*
*and the long journey to oblivion.*
*And it is time to go, to bid farewell*
*to one's own self and find an exit*
*from the fallen self.*

Some may find that morbid, yet there is a hint of renewal in the lines, a promise that a new self is waiting to be born, which is what I believe autumn is all about. It isn't a time of death; it is a time of sleep so that the earth may renew itself in spring.

So the season went on, the weather turning round, the sweet softness of September and the rough edges of October giving way to November with its rain and snow. The autumn equinox came thumping in from the sea on 22nd September and October was a month that brought high winds and pitiless seas. Street games ended sooner, night came down with a cold that permeated even the stoutest clothing so it was back to the fire and the gas-popping light. I recall mornings when the frost plastered the grass to the ground like stiff, white hair on a dead man's skull - not that I had ever seen one - I just had this vision of death being like that. One day, the trees were flamboyant with masses of colour, the next they were bare, a strong wind having sprung up during the night to scythe the leaves away. Bare trees are sad and when the leaves were gone, we knew that winter was near. And yet there were still sights to see; I recall with wonder the frost that even touched the spiders' webs in the hedges, the sun melting it and leaving the myriads of little webs glistening with small seed pearls of moisture.

Then came November, the dullest month of autumn's sisters, with her lank, wet hair. Farmers complained about the rain and the mist which turned the haystacks into piles of dirty white straw that hung sodden and haggard, like last spring's birds' nests. November was the first month of the porridge pot; every night, I would make enough for Ken's and my breakfast, a welcome addition to the morning rolls that were delivered to the house and left in a string bag that hung on the outside doorknob. Ken complained about the lumps in my porridge but I liked them.

November is a dreary month, a time of sea *haar* that thickens into a cold soup of rain and fog. In those days, we had a foghorn that sounded like a sick animal in pain. We paid fewer visits to the sea, as the Victoria Harbour was almost empty of boats, most of them moored in the inner or Old Harbour. This allowed fans of wind to blow uninterrupted over the greasy surface, creating dark ruffles and whorls of water. A *smirr* of rain was never far away, driving us home even before daylight had faded over the sea in the west. Some week-ends were clear, sunny days that allowed us to play in the maze of anti-tank blocks at Belhaven Beach, when a weak finger of sun lay on the Bass Rock. We watched that rock at frequent intervals, for when its lighthouse began to blink, we knew it was time to go home. By the time we reached Seafield Bridge and the Biel Burn, darkness was falling. The sun burned a smoky or-ange until it was snuffed out like a candle by North Berwick Law and night curled round the Bass like a black cat. The Bass kept up its conversation with the May Island light that passed its messages on to Barns Ness. We were always glad to get home on those chill November Saturdays, looking forward to the fire and our Saturday ration of sweets which we sucked as we listened to the wireless during the dank, wet nights that were November.

*Winter*

So, winter. It has few of the poetic qualities of autumn but when we were children, it had its attractions. How many children nowadays wake on a cold, frosty morning without central heating to look out of the bedroom window on the work of Jack Frost? Would they know who Jack Frost was? No. Well, perhaps. They would think of the diminutive police inspector played by David Jason in the TV series. . Our Jack Frost was a character we believed was responsible for the delicate, filigree silver necklaces and beautiful tracery etched on the windowpanes; we also believed in Santa Claus. Why? Because we wanted to. And why not? I realise now that believing in Johnny Appleseed, Jack Frost and Mr Claus is much the same as believing in Jesus Christ. But then I have always argued that the Christian Church has much to answer for, believing that only it has the answer to all mankind's woes. (However it must be said that it shares this trait with many other religions!)

How many children enjoy putting on clean pyjamas still warm from the smoothing iron heated over an open fire on bath nights? Sometime, when we were 'chesty', my mother rubbed *Vick* ointment over our thin upper bodies, wrapping us in a bit of old flannel to keep the salve off the sheets and our night clothes. A famous - and efficacious - cure for a winter sore throat was a heated sand-filled sock laid on the affected part. Our hot water bottles were none of the cissy, rubberised kind; the cylindrical stoneware *pig* was filled from the centre and made watertight by inserting a stopper with a rubber washer to stop it from leaking. Being stoneware, it kept in the heat for some considerable time so you couldn't put your feet on it unless it was masked by a thick, woolly sock or covering knitted for the purpose - and even then, we had to wear bed socks as well.

What sums up winter for me? Green tramlines emerging from noses too poor to own a handkerchief.... ....shivering kids on street corners.... ....frozen Brussels sprouts that had to be hacked from their stalks with a sharp knife.... ....small birds coming to the back door step seeking crumbs of bread and rice.... ....the occasional frozen blackbird or robin lying in the hedges.... ....the pig swill man calling for our kitchen waste with a promise of a free gift of a chicken and a hunk of pork at Christmas.... ....the small *Aladdin* paraffin oil heater lit in the bathroom to stave off frozen pipes, one of my mother's eternal winter nightmares which fortuitously gave us a heated room in which to dress on frosty mornings.... ....milk frozen in the bottles, the cream having to be dug out with a knife.... ....snow falling in the moonlight in January and February - rarely in December and certainly not on Christmas Eve.... ....the accumulations of un-trodden snow turning blue in the shadowy parts of the garden.... ....pale lemon moons whose strained, shocked faces stared into our bedroom when we drew back the thick curtains to look at Doon Hill before going to sleep.

My favourite winter month was of course December; it always brought the clear, cold weather that old folk said was healthy, as it killed off germs. As the days dragged themselves to the end of the year, we pestered the life out of my mother to hang up the paper chains and decorate a natural Christmas tree as described in greater detail in chapter 5. Then all of a sudden, the slow December days rushed headlong to the final week; we knew from school lessons that the 21st was the shortest day of the year, when darkness fell at 3pm and first light didn't arrive until 9am. By that day, the schools usually closed for the two-week Christmas break and we were free to pursue our winter pastimes and games. Many years later, I read the Elizabethan poet John Donne's ode *A Nocturnall upon S[aint] Lucie's Day, being the shortest day* or the twenty-second day of December under the New Style or Gregorian Calendar, the day of the Winter Solstice, when the sun enters the sign of Capricorn, the Goat. The first and last lines go thus:

*Tis the yeares midnight, and it is the dayes....*
*Both the yeares, and the dayes deep midnight is.*

So while daylight ebbed away to its furthest point, we were consoled by bright-berried Christmases that beckoned with tinsel-shimmering evenings, gifts, blazing fires. Sweet Christmastime, with the great orange, green and red paper bell which had pride of place in the centre of the ceiling of our living room. I swore to Ken I heard that paper bell tolling softly when the heat from the dying fire or the draft from the opened door made it turn from left to right, slowly but perceptibly. I told Ken that it rang at midnight on Christmas Eve and he believed me. I convinced him that the stars rang out in answer, that I could hear them tinkling in the frosty air, brushed aside by Santa Claus and his reindeer-powered sleigh. Maybe he was impressed by my knowledge of the names of Santa's reindeers -Dasher, Dancer, Vixen , Prancer, Comet, Cupid and Donner and Blitzen. (Rudolph was a later addition, the star of a popular song many years later). Ken often said he could hear Santa on the 'loof' of our house, bless him. When Christmas morning came, with our pillowcases at the foot of our bed stuffed with presents and sweets, I experienced a high I have never known since then. But it must be said that some adult Christmases have been indescribably sad for me; they are best left for another book, another story....

For that whole week of Christmas and New Year, we were happier than at any other time of year. I loved the decorations and the colour they brought into otherwise austere years, especially those after the Second World War; I loved the comforting fires, the treats of different food, the friendship between my young brother and I, a bond that gradually loosened by natural progression as the years went by. Christmas was our time. Then there was *Hogmanay* - not a time for children but still a good time, as we were allowed to stay up till midnight, to say goodbye to the Old Year and welcome in the New. It was a beloved time, even if my mother dreaded it and the drunk men she couldn't refuse to admit into the house, it being a Scottish custom. In those days, my mother didn't take alcohol but at *Hogmanay,* my Uncle Jimmy always ensured there was a bottle of sweet sherry for her. I loved that evening of the last day of the year. Hearts were more honest and open that night, people were warm and friendly to each other, their inhibitions loosened by drink.

After the evening meal, we kids were allowed to play with our Christmas gifts before the fire, listening to the wireless. There was usually a mystery play on the wireless, then long periods of Scottish dance music played by the massed fiddles and accordions of a man called Jimmy Shand. (I used to refer to him as Jimmy Shand and his Chandeliers). Although it was winter, my mother placed the dinner table at the window, its summer position, covering it with a pure white linen tablecloth. She spent the evening making sandwiches – egg and cress, tinned salmon, Spam and *Shipham's Paste.* There was always a plate of shortbread she bought in a tin with *Bonnie Prince Charlie* on the lid – I believe its name *petticoat tail* derives from the French *petit gateau* or *gatel.* Another plate contained thick slices of currant loaf she had baked herself - we never called it Black Bun in Dunbar. My Uncle Jimmy wouldn't allow any drink to be taken before the Bells at midnight. He ruled supreme in our house that night. When we heard the chimes of Big Ben in London on the wireless at midnight, we knew the New Year had arrived. We all raised glasses at the twelfth stroke, Mum with her sweet sherry, Jimmy with his whisky, Norman with his beer and Ken and I with ginger cordial. We then waited anxiously for the traditional First Foot who had to be dark-haired and bear a lump of coal in his pocket, along with a half bottle of the Wee Golden Wonder. (I have known my mother to refuse entry of a fair-haired man after midnight, telling him to come back after the proper First Foot had come!). Ken and I were allowed to stay up until 1am, then we were shoo'ed to bed, where we lay basking in the light of a paraffin lamp reading our Christmas books or listening to the adults making fools of themselves downstairs. On reflection, we were glad to escape from the adults, who, apart from my mother, seemed not to be their usual selves. Often, we would hear a lone piper playing along our street, the strains of his tunes fading as he made his way into the town. Then the house grew quiet as the early morning revelry died away into whispered wishes and hopes for the New Year that had come.

Then came January, a month which could delude you with uncharacteristic warmth in its first few days. On Twelfth Night, we dismantled the tree, put away the ornaments and the decorations, carefully folding them for next time. My mother would sigh as she swept away the last of the shed pine needles, muttering to herself that it would be the last year for that nonsense. (In later life, she loved Christmas with a real tree in my homes, probably because she didn't have to clean up the mess).

January excited the ubiquitous blackbirds to burst into song; they seemed to sense that the year had turned as they scuttered through the gardens and warbled loudly as dusk was settling; their song sounding sharper on the frost-laden air. There was brightness in the sunsets which belied the time of year but we weren't fooled by it, knowing the worst was yet to come. By the end of the month, the days and nights grew colder; the summer silver trails of snails were replaced by sparkling veins of frost. Numbness afflicted your fingers and toes and we got chillblains. It was a deadly dull month and often made me think of dreary November - unless there was a snowfall. Our garden was bleak, the vegetable patch containing the last of the Brussels sprouts, leeks and turnips; the front garden borders were empty, the rose bushes stripped down to bare, hard sticks that revealed their thorns. (I have always thought that a paradox – that the most beautiful of flowers should bear cruel barbs. Perhaps that's why the rose is the symbol of love, with its mixture of pleasure and pain).

The main respite of these post-Christmas/New Year weeks was playing indoors - in my case, with my lead soldiers, the number of which had usually increased after the gift day. I enacted my battles every night before the fire, then watched the flames form faces in the grate. The fireside had its Great War shell canister, polished to a high shine and containing the poker, the tongs for lifting coals which fell on the hearth and a rough-haired brush to sweep up the crumbs and ashes.

As far as I can remember, it rarely snowed in January. All we ever saw was a grey slurry or gruel around Hogmanay and on the first days back at school. The time for snow was February, as I was told; it was my birthday month and my mother told me that every year since 17th February 1941, when I was born, there had been snow or sleet or frost on my day. Ken and I were ever optimistic, dragging down our home made sledge from the rafters of the coal-shed, greasing the runners and repairing any broken bits. Our sledge was little more than the base of an old pram with sides but it served us well; we fixed wheels to it in late summer and autumn to collect the weekly bags of cinders from the Gas Works near Doon Avenue.

Despite it being a dreary month, January was a time for street games at evening. The worst winters on record for Dunbar and elsewhere in Scotland were 1947 and 1963; the former saw whole communities like Garvald cut off from the outside world. There, the Cistercian monks from Nunraw Abbey, which was being built in 1947, sledged into the village with their own baked bread and milk from their cows. In 1963, Dunbar was struck by a blizzard that left drifts of snow in the streets and country roads for a week. Snow was a capricious visitor but I can't recall a winter when none fell. When it did, our favourite sledging place was what then was the third green at Winterfield Golf Course, a decline we called *Death Valley*, opposite the modern day chalets. It was aptly named. The steep slope soon turned into iron-hard ice after many sledges tempered it; many an enterprising young lad with a home made sledge came a cropper on that slope. After a couple of hours of sledging, we were ready to go home. We were wet from spills, the dampness penetrated our winter clothes and even Jock the Wild Man surrendered to the all pervading cold. But he was always last to leave, trudging off into the darkness with his battered sledge. Many nights in that time, I lay awake with my feet on the hot water *pig,* hearing his distinctive cry of *Kreee-gah!* long after the rest of us were in bed.

Once, Betty Jeffrey and I made an igloo in our back garden, carving blocks of frozen snow out of the drifts against our garden wall with a bread knife. We got the idea from an episode of *Oor Wullie* in the *Sunday Post.* I invited Betty into the igloo but we made the mistake of taking candles inside. Betty and I were huddled in there for a while until the ice started to melt. Our igloo was soon reduced to a heap of dirty, dripping lumps.

On those winter nights, snow fell silently, stroking our windows with soft fingers. I used to look out of my bedroom window on such snowbound nights, wondering if I would ever see Doon Hill again. The next morning, I drew the bedroom curtains and was glad to see my lovely hill was still there.

February is noted for its treacherous weather. In England, it is a month known as *February-fill dyke* - which means that it fills the ditches with snow and icy water, so I believe. It's a month in which all kind of weather is thrown at us - rain, sleet, snow and wind. It invariably snows on my birthday, though in 2004, the weather was calm save for the high seas that threw up ferocious twenty-foot waves above the Victoria Harbour wall. The only consolation I had was that in my birth month, the woods and hedgerows brimmed with snowdrops, my favourite spring flower. When they pushed through the cold earth, I knew that spring was on the wing.

On Doon Hill, the snow lay long when it came. For days on end, it happed the hill in white ermine folds that turned blue at evening. Then, as the snow thawed, it brought black holes that started at the base and gradually crept up the slope. When the snow was nearly gone, I used to think that the lines of uncovered earth were like frowns or wrinkles on the brow of the hill..

Winters seemed longer in my childhood. They also brought more snow but this may be a combination of poor memory and too vivid a recollection of great snowfalls, particularly the dreadful one of 1947. It was a time for the fireside and ghost stories. The most famous and popular ghost story was centred on Bamburgh Close, reputedly haunted by the spirit of a piper who with his little dog, tried to find a supposed underground passage from No 25 High Street to Dunbar Castle. There may be some truth in this local legend but other towns in Scotland have such stories. For example, the same tale is told of a piper in Currie, Midlothian who tried to walk along a secret passage from Lennox Tower to Curriehill Castle, expiring on the way. On a late winter afternoon, the trick after school was to dare a school friend to enter the dark close and stay there for five minutes while the others made wailing, ghostly noises. Few stayed the course. In Dunbar, they say that the piper entered the ancient passage through a green door in the wall of No 25. Both survive, but as far as I am aware, no one has yet tried to negotiate the supposed tunnel. (My great-grandfather Cockburn lived in that close but if he had any theories about the story, he never passed them down). However, why let fact spoil a good winter yarn spun by the fireside?

The storms of winter lasted until early March, when brighter days brought back the kittiwakes to the harbour, thus completing the cycle of the seasons.

Looking back more than fifty years on, the four seasons were my most dependable friends. They brought experiences that few children today enjoy let alone understand. These experiences were rooted in the reality of that far-off time and they had their poetry. Hard facts were softened by the natural colours and light of Nature but they didn't mask the deadly seriousness of those times. Earth was indeed a playground but it was also a place on which many humble folk depended for a living, whether from field, furrow or fishes. I didn't inhabit an imaginary landscape. People of my generation lived through a world that is unrecognisable today. The academics and the historians think they know it all; however, they can only speculate or approximate the emotions and fears we experienced at the time. History is a reflection of life, best told by those who have experienced it; sadly, only the great and the good have left us memoirs. How I wish that the common people had been able to set down their stories....

# 14

## The Wider World

When I left Dunbar to begin my adult working life, I told friends and older work colleagues that I considered myself fortunate to have been spared from the dangers of the Second World War, Korea, Suez and all the other conflicts of the twentieth century. I have never regretted not having to do National Service which for me would have an utter waste of time - the Government's as well as my own. If, on the other hand, a spell in *khaki* had taken me to the Outer Hebrides to guard a remote lighthouse, I would have put that time to good use. I might have written a novel that could have changed the entire course of my life. But I disagree that National Service was a vital rite of passage that was necessary in the forming of character for every young man; for some it may have done, for me, I know that would never have been the case with me. National Service might have made me less vulnerable, les sensitive, more worldly wise, but I have no doubt in my mind that my character was formed during my Dunbar childhood.

The wider world. What did it promise all those years ago? Not a great deal. What's more, I worried about how would I survive in it? With growing apprehension, I realised that I would have to take a closer interest in things outside myself instead of always retreating into my own world. Life does not allow many of us that luxury. But although when I left school in 1958 and would meet people in my working life from all kinds of backgrounds, I never forgot those with whom I'd grown up or those kindly neighbours who lived in the small world of my street. I felt I should pay more attention to the grown-up neighbours, for in a way, they were a kind of extended family. So let me try to recall the memorable characters who lived in our street all those years ago.

I will start just before the intersection of Doon Avenue and Lammermuir Crescent, facing west. At No 29, lived Jimmy Brydon, a gentle man and gen-tleman who was known as the Blue Boy on account of a heart condition. Jimmy could have been mistaken for a coloured man. I never saw him dressed in anything other than his boiler suit or dungarees. He looked after his mother for many years until he died. I used to have long chats with Jimmy, a man I loved and respected. Now we skip across the intersection of Doon Avenue and Lammermuir Crescent. At No 31 lived Walter or Wattie Hutchison who worked at the gasworks and was the *leerie* or lamplighter when the streets were gaslit. In No 33 lived Mrs Barclay, a kindly soul whose son Ian Mouat was taken prisoner by the Japanese and horribly tortured after the fall of Singapore. Then at No 35 were Mr and Mrs Callow with their daughter Barbara and son Jim, - Jim still lives there today. Next door was Miss Mather, a tiny, neat, quiet wee soul, a character who could have been the artist Dudley D Watkins' prototype for Miss Meek, *Oor Wullie's* wee friend in the *Sunday Post*. Miss Mather kept her garden tidy, her cottage spotlessly clean. She was on the list of the Council's approved summer boarders. At No 39 lived John Mason and his wife with their sons Bobby and Gordon, great friends of mine. Then there was Jessie Dixon who looked after her brother Jim, a good friend of my brother Norman. Jim sadly suffered from a mental disorder and ended his days in the hospital at Herdmanflat, Haddington. Above them were the Dinnie brothers, known to me only through my work as a message lad with *Lipton's*. I thought they were eccentric, even mad, until I learnt recently that Jimmy Dinnie's (dinnae Jimmy, Jimmy dinnae as we kids would call up to his window on dark winter nights), brother T B Dinnie had been employed by the government as a rubber planter in Malaya and was caught by the Japanese when Singapore fell. T B Dinnie was another broken survivor of that awful war. Through the wall from the Dixons were the Robertsons, whose son Dave and I were friends. Further along lived the Paylors, after whom the cul-de-sac which housed the wartime air raid shelter was named. (I wonder if residents there today refer to it as *Paylors' Corner?*)

Further on lived Peter Marr and his wife Ina; Peter is still around, though sadly, Ina, a great friend of my mother's is gone. She frequently visited us when Peter was away on his deep-sea fishing trips. Nearby were the Pattersons, father and daughter Esther. Esther was a lovely young woman on whom I had a crush for a long time. She married David Smith, a local baker; sadly, she succumbed to cancer but not before appearing on *Songs of Praise* one Sunday evening to give thanks for her life. We were terribly proud of Esther and thought her very brave. At No 71 lived Mr and Mrs Melrose and their daughter Etta, a pretty woman and great family friend who died recently. Above the Melroses were the Marrs - Mr Marr and his daughter Isobel, with whom I remain friends to this day. We occupied No 75 until the 1980s, when my mother had to move to sheltered housing, being unable to look after the garden any longer. Next door were the Harkess family – Marion or Mairn as we knew her and her sons John and Tommy and daughter Anne. They were always known to us kids as Uncles and Aunt, while old Mairn was Grannie Harkess. Only Uncle John survives today, living in Beveridge Row at Belhaven.

In No 79 lived Jenny Herkes - another unofficial Grannie who lived with her husband, Tommy. Their son James, a Royal Marine, was drowned in the sinking of *HMS Repulse* in 1941. Old Jenny Craw, as she was known, was a real character who wore great gypsy-style earrings and would sit out in her front garden on warm days to eat crabs with a pin. (I recall her sitting on her garden seat even on chilly afternoons, happed in a great woollen shawl, enjoying her *poos* [crabs]. The Herkeses' lovely daughter Euphemia, always known as Effie or 'Fame was married to Sid Fawcett; they and their lively brood lived for a brief time at No 79, going to Yorkshire but returning periodically for holidays. As I wrote earlier, the Fawcetts and my brothers were great friends, as were their cousins the Lunams.

Above Gramma Herkes lived a quiet couple called Hume who as far as I can recall, didn't have any children. Mr Hume was a cabinet-maker, a sober, quiet gentleman who kept to himself. Mrs Hume was a shy but kindly soul who sadly became mentally ill after her beloved husband died. She had to be taken into care at Herdmanflat. We never saw her again. (Today, the Humes' flat is occupied by Dave and Alison Cockburn (nee Marr), two good friends).

In that four-in-a-block complex lived the Jeffreys, through the wall from Grannie Herkes. Mr and Mrs Jeffrey were the salt of the earth, great friends of my mother's. Their daughters Violet and Betty remain good friends to this day. Their father Morris hailed from Thorntonloch; after the war, he returned to his work at the West Barns Maltings. He was a tall, fine-looking man and Mrs Jeffrey was a pretty woman. I knew Betty better than Violet, who was ages with my brother Norman. I write of Betty in Chapter 9, when she tried to ruin my reputation while establishing her own!

Further along the street were the Smiths, another lively family with several sons and daughters, chief of whom I remember was William and Tommy. Tommy married Anna Bruce and they emigrated to Canada, though they make frequent visits to Dunbar to see Anna's mother. Nearby were the Punton sisters; Jenny worked in the fields and was still wearing her *ugly* or field headgear well into the 1970s. Then came a *cul-de-sac* next to which lived the Ballantynes; Hugh was an insurance agent and a very handsome man; he and his wife had only one son, Richard who became a policeman and married Ann Dann, with whom I worked in St Andrew's House, the aunt of my good friend Karen Cheetham (now Williams). Beyond the Ballantynes lived old Mrs Balloch and her son Willie, both quiet people who kept much to themselves.

At the very end of Lammermuir Crescent lived the Main family; I can't remember Mr and Mrs Main but I do vaguely remember their daughters. In my memory there were only three girls but fortunately, I was recently able to confirm that there were five – Helen, Kay, Margaret, Betty and Jane. Kay married George Murray after his first wife died; I was in love with George's daughter Alison from his first marriage but that belongs to another book. Betty Main and her husband moved to Haddington at some point; their daughter Dorothy (Dot) kindly put me right as to her mother and aunts. (Dot and her husband Keith live near Spott today and their daughter Susan married my cousin Moira Foggo's son Gary in 2004. I never cease to be amazed by such things which will be meat and drink to future genealogists). Above the Mains were wee Jeannie Gee and her two daughters Audrey and Jeanette. Jeannie Gee was in love with Freddy Craig, who lived a few doors away in the Crescent. Freddie was a bookie's runner in those days and looked the part as he slid along the crescent, his face half obscured by a greasy trilby. He was in trouble with the police and moved out of his flat in Lammermuir Crescent to live with Jeannie Gee, rarely venturing out until after dark. In those days, I didn't know about this little drama, but I was fascinated by the Gee family. I was in love with the younger daughter Audrey - from afar; I am sure my brother Norman took Jeanette dancing. Their mother -wee Jeannie, as she was always known- was a character, a snappy dresser like my mother which ensured their friendship.

Now we cross to the other side of the street, where hopefully my memory will serve me well as to the folk who lived there. The end house was a block of four; in one flat lived the Brading family; above them lived the Loughs –Tommy and Rena and their family. The Bradings' relative Christine married David Lunam and is a neighbour of mine today. Further on were the Gaffneys; Jimmy Gaffney played rugby with my brother Ken and his sister Jane works in the local private nursing home. Next to them was another family called Main who weren't related to the Mains at the end of the opposite side of Lammermuir Crescent. That Main family consisted only of mother and son. Mother Main was a bit of a character; she wore an imitation leopard skin coat and white ankle-socks. I shall never forget her starved face. Her son Jim was a bit of a bully at school. He once tried to blackmail some kids including myself to parting with their comics or else he'd belt them. He warned us not to tell our mothers. I alone did – and didn't have to pay his bribe. All he said to me was 'Ye shouldnae telt yir mither'. He was a shy bully - if you can understand that - and with hindsight, I have put that down to the fact that he didn't have a father to guide him. (I never had a father around during my formative years but that didn't make me a bully. I would argue my case against those feeble, wimpish social workers who today defend thugs who have turned out bad 'because their father deserted them'. My father was a soldier who was required to be somewhere else; he also deserted my family but that didn't drive me to delinquency. Modern day social workers are, to put it mildly, unrealistic dreamers. But let that pass).

At No 94 lived another Punton family, Isobel and her son *Pancho*. Further along at No 106 lived the Mellors family, consisting of Mrs Mellors, Terry and Robin; Robin was known as *Skinny*. He was a brilliant Latin scholar, as I recall. The next family I remember were the Macphersons who lived diagonally opposite our house. Mrs Macpherson was a frail, nervous lady whom we knew as 'Phersie and who worked in the High Street Cloakrooms now occupied by the Tourist Office and the *Tippecanoe Gallery*. 'Phersie had a son Colin and a daughter Chrissie. Colin was a great friend of my brother Norman; he emigrated to Canada, where he worked in service to the British Consul-General there, then to the writer Nicholas Monserrat who wrote the moving novel *The Cruel Sea* which was made into a classic, well-conceived semi-documentary film of a British warship starring Jack Hawkins and Donald

# The Wider World

Sinden. Colin's sister Chrissie joined the Auxiliary Territorial Service (ATS) and did her 'bit' during the war. I think she was happiest in uniform and her peaked kepi-style hat which I recall she wore at a jaunty angle when she came home on leave. In her old age, she lived next door to my mother in the *Bield* sheltered housing complex in Summerfield Road, where she died in the mid 1990s.

Above the Macphersons lived Alice and Jock Gillon; Jock did his best to provide for Alice. I wrote about her earlier in chapter 4, in the incident which I have called *The Face at the Window.* He died before Alice, who ended up in an East Lothian nursing home and died there in 2004. Poor Alice struggled hard to make ends meet; she was thin and worn out even in the 1950s so it is remarkable that she survived for nearly another half century. Next to the Macphersons/Gillons were the Watsons; the man of the house was known as *Spriggy,* a nickname given to him on account of his lean frame. His son Jimmy was the lighthouse keeper on the Bass Rock for many years. The Watsons' neighbour was the unforgettable and redoubtable Annie Lough, with her kids Sandy, Victor, Walter and Annette. Sandy, Victor and Annette are still around. Victor has been a county ranger for the past 30 years and is also an accomplished guitar-player. Annie had a heart of gold; when she died, I felt as if part of my childhood had been torn away.

After the Loughs came a road which led to Summerfield Road, conveniently placed for us in No 75, for as kids, we could see the tops of the fir trees at Lochend and part of Doon Hill. The first family after that were the Tait family. Old man Tait was proud of his garden; his son Adam was a great friend of my brother Norman, as they were both in the Boys' Brigade. Next door to them lived Ruby Johnson who was consumptive and a chain-smoker; a local GP told her that if she didn't give up smoking, she would never live to see her fiftieth birthday. She survived for many years after that and was a kind friend and neighbour to my mother in her own last years. Ruby was the salt of the earth; I loved her very much, for she was a familiar figure in my small landscape of that time. When she died recently, I felt that another great tree in the wood of my memory had fallen. (She makes me think of the man who once said that if he'd known he was going to live so long, he'd have given up his vices years ago).

Further down the street lived Mrs Huntly and her sons, Alec, George and the youngest who was known as *Snakeyhips*; George, the last of the family still lives in the family home. Next to them were the Ashtons, then the Johnstons - *Pelder* being the cognomen shared by father and son. Mr Johnston's daughter Margaret went into the Civil Service after she left school, largely on my recommendation. Underneath the Johnstons were Frank Butler and his wife, son Walter and a daughter whose name escapes me but whom I met in Dunbar in 2003. Then next to them were the Dores; old Liebe, the grandmother gutted herring at the harbour in the early part of the twentieth century. In her final years - I think she was over 90 when she died - she was a familiar figure, seated on a chair at the front door when the sun shone into the front garden late in the afternoon. Her granddaughter Evelyn (Evvy or Ebbie) is still a friend of mine today. Now my memory is beginning to falter, although I recall that at No 40 lived the Kearneys, Robert Kearney being our insurance agent, a familiar figure in the street and one of the few men in our street to own a motorcar in those days. Further along the street were the Grays whose house was opposite No 33, where Mrs Barclay once lived. Today, the house is occupied by Mark Beattie, who for many years was active in the *Dunbar and District History Society.* Beyond No 33, I knew only two families - the Andersons whose sons Robin, Sydney, Lexie were good friends, as was their sister Shirley, on whom I had a crush for a while. Shirley was an accomplished Highland dancer. Next to the Andersons were the Ballantynes – Chrissie and her husband Willie who cycled to his work and whistled the long day. Sadly, Chrissie sustained an injury which confined her to a wheelchair for much of her life. Her daughter Margaret is still around, doing sterling work in one of the local charity shops. Beyond their house, there were privately owned residences, mainly bungalows. One was occupied by the Currans; their grandfather (uncle?) John was known as John the Busman as he drove a funny van and ferried families returning from holiday and their luggage from the railway station to their homes. Last in the row was the neat bungalow owned by Hardi Douglas, yet another insurance agent; he lived there with his wife and two sons. Mrs Douglas was a lovely lady. I think the older son was called Ian who still lives in Dunbar and plays golf.

Although not a neighbour, one of my oldest friends who resides not far from the Douglas bungalow in one of her own is Betty Whitsun, who managed the emporium known as *Erinall's* in the High Street for many years. Betty and her widower father were great friends of my mother. I believe Mr Whitsun hoped that Betty and my brother Norman would marry one day. It wasn't to be; Betty made a bad first marriage but today is happily married to her kind, gentle and considerate second husband Hamish Murray. I count the Murrays among my few remaining loyal friends in Dunbar; Betty is always fulsome in her praise of me, though I can't think why.

Through my seasonal employment over the past four years with East Lothian Council's Museum Services, I have been fortunate enough to renew acquaintances of those faraway days, chief among them the Fawcett family. Through other activities, I am glad to say that I have met and cemented past friendships from school, notably with people like George Robertson and his wife Sheila, Karen Cheetham and her husband Peter and just recently William Jackson and his wife Ann, the Newcastle lady whose father, Mr Barnett, ran a fruit shop in the premises now occupied by *The Crunchy Carrot* – who says that history does not repeat itself? What goes round, comes round….There are many others too numerous to list here but without exception, all my renewed acquaintances so far have been happy and I feel sure will last as long as we are around.

In those days, apart from the fishermen, who were colourful characters with equally colourful names, there were others whose names I shall protect in the interests of litigation. *The Wee Chat* reputedly so-named for his propensity for gossip and his friend *The News of the World*; between them, they knew everything about everybody. There was *Mattie Bile,* the colourful - in more ways than one - chimney sweep, who appears in an anecdote in chapter 2. There are several stories told about *Mattie*, many recounted by himself. He once told my mother that one day, he was pushing his handcart laden with the brushes of his trade along a private lane in the West End, the upmarket part of Dunbar in those days. Passing one of the prestigious villas, the lady of the house called to him over the garden wall.

'I say there, my good man. This isn't the right road for you.'
*Mattie* stopped, wiped his hands on his boiler suit and looked her straight in the eye. He was afraid of nothing and nobody, small though he was.

'D'ye ken whaur Ah'm gaun, Mistress?'
Instantly, she snapped back, no doubt rattled by his (to her) impudent response:

'I have no earthly idea, my man. Now, would you please remove -'
She got no further.

'Weel, if ye dinnae ken whaur Ah.'m gaun, hoo the Hell d'ye ken Ah'm
no' on the richt road!'

A story my Uncle Jimmy loved to tell came from one of his favourite hostelries, *The Black Bull,* run by his old friend Ollie Potts, known for his pawky sense of humour. One Saturday night, at the height of summer, even Ollie's sense of humour deserted him in the face of a highly objectionable Midlands of England customer. Nothing pleased the man; the weather was rotten, the beer was rotten, the scenery was poor and his holiday accommodation and food were rubbish. Most of the customers were put off by his loud mouth or too polite to challenge him. Ollie was too busy to challenge him, so my Uncle did the honours. He turned round slowly on his high stool at the bar and said this:

'Ah take it ye dinnae care for Dunbar then?'
No, he didn't just dislike Dunbar, he didn't rate Scotland either. My uncle asked why he'd bothered to come on holiday and was told it was his wife's idea, she being Scottish. If he had had his way, he'd never have crossed the Border blah-blah-blah. He was surprised, he said, that so many of his countrymen took their holidays in the North. My uncle had had enough.

'Weel, noo, that's odd. There's a place no' very far from here where
quite a few o' your countrymen didnae just visit, they stayed for good.
Mind you, as I say, they were improved Englishman.'
Where on earth was he talking about and what did 'improved' mean?

'Oh, the place is near Stirling, a bonnie wee place called Bannockburn.

Aye, they liked it that much, they've been buried there since the year thirteen hunderd and fourteen. That's whit Ah call an improved English man.'

The pub erupted. The man's face turned a funny colour, something akin to that of beetroot.. He was quiet for the rest of the evening, so I am told.

Uncle Jimmy never understood my hankering to become a writer. He agreed with my brother Norman that Westerns and crime detective novels were all very well but in his view, most writers had brains filled with mush. Their taunts made me only more determined.

If anyone today were to ask me how I wish to be remembered, I wouldn't hesitate to reply. I am and always will be a Dunbar laddie for that is what and who I am. Many pennies went into the gas meter during my childhood; some were unable to cast a bright enough light on the darkness of those austere years. There is something of a moral there - or perhaps a symbolic truth. We spend money to gain the light because we are acutely aware of the darkness that is everywhere.

# Postscript

This book has been occasionally unforgiving; well it would be, as it is a personal account and therefore reflects my prejudices. I expect some people in Dunbar who read it will criticise me for all kinds of reasons, chiefly based on their own prejudices. During its writing, I was acutely aware that I was encroaching on the privacy of others, some of whom are no longer here to challenge my views; but many more still survive and may not agree with the views I express in this book. In mitigation, my path collided with the paths of others in the small, close-knit community of Dunbar, which made those encounters inevitable though it would be wrong of me to blame the community for the outcome of such encounters. Dunbar formed my character, made me who I am and what makes me tick. I am not ashamed of that, nor do I feel guilty about what I have written. But being me, I am nervous and apprehensive about the way this book will be received. I ask the forgiveness of those who are still around, especially if I have misrepresented them. I wasn't indulging in an ego trip, I was simply trying to remember....

Of course, the bulk of the writing comes from personal experience but if errors of fact have crept in, it's due to that unreliable vehicle, memory. I am lucky to be able to say that I have kept a good number of the friendships I made all those years ago - and made a few more along the way. Some send the obligatory Christmas Card 'to keep in touch'; they are, I am glad to say, in the minority. Many are no longer with us, while the best of those who survive keep cropping up like bad pennies, after long silences. I have friends I haven't seen or heard from for decades but when they turn up here, the friendship is still there, as fresh as it was so many years ago. Well the ones that were genuine remain so. My good friend David Ingram once said that it was difficult to make friends in Edinburgh, where he and I worked most of our lives and where he still lives. However, he also assured me that when you made a friend there, it's for always, no matter how long the separations, the silences. He is living proof of that. Friendship isn't a duty or a social grace; it is or should be spontaneous and sincere, despite what intervenes.

So many I knew in that far-off time are dead or scattered to the four winds. I suspect that like me, when they made it to adulthood, they found that justice is more sought after than mercy, prejudice takes precedence over understanding, superficiality before sincerity. It's only when we become adults, people with responsibilities whose life experience teaches them how important it is that we develop a sense of duty and loyalty. Then and only then, after personal tragedies and trials, do we realise the true meaning of friendship. The qualities of that unique and a-sexual relationship are sympathy, caring, kindness and ultimately, love. For we all have this great hunger to be accepted, for others to sympathise, care, be kind to and love us. To me, that is the purpose of human existence, the whole point of it. And of course being unconventional without being destructive. A former girl-friend of that time recently told me that unlike her, I haven't lived an ordinary life. I didn't deliberately set out to do so - or did I? Looking back, I guess I never wanted to follow the conventional pattern. I have regrets but these are the price you pay for not being 'normal' – whatever that may mean.

It's entirely appropriate that I should write the last few lines of this book on the seashore at Belhaven, not far from where I was born. I am sitting here among the sand dunes on a calm, quiet, sunny February afternoon with a notepad on my knees. Nothing much has changed here in the intervening years. Swans, gulls, eider ducks, curlews, oystercatchers, sandpipers, dunlins and terns haunt these beaches and waterways as they've always done. The wind that was blowing earlier had a cutting edge to it, tasting of salt as it sifted through the marram grass. It died down about half an hour ago and I am conscious of the loud silence typical of this place, interrupted only by the muted cries of children and a dog barking in the distance. These sounds remind me of the final lines from T S Eliot's poem *The Love Song of J Alfred Prufrock:*

*We have lingered in the chambers of the sea*
*By sea-girls wreathed with seaweed red and brown*
*Till human voices wake us, and we drown.*

Not far from where I am sitting, a flock of oystercatchers twitter on the shore, running about stiffly like wound-up clockwork toys looking for sea-creatures left stranded in the sand by the last wave; they poke about, then run in excitable bursts before the next wave sends them flying into the air with their distinctive 'kleep'kleep'. A few seagulls hover above, like scattered scraps of paper. A heavy sea is flowing, the tide is coming in fast; torn light flaps its rags over the Bass Rock, scraps of clouds hover over Doon Hill and there's a hint of rain in the air. The place is timeless, eternal, re-enacting scenes I have witnessed so many times before.

So what is there left of this place Dunbar, where my childhood years were spent? She's jaded, a pale shadow of her former self, even a little self-conscious of her decline. She has seen better, greater days, happier times. At least most of her landscapes and seascapes survive, having largely escaped the intrusions of industry save for the Lafarge cement factory, Torness Nuclear Power Station and currently, a growing number of private housing estates in and around Lochend which are sadly swallowing up the last of the places where I played as a boy. And yet there is hope for the future; I can sense a subtle change taking place, a hint of better things to come. Dunbar's loveliness may have been ravaged but no more than one would expect; word and canvas artists still have a worthy subject. And when all is said and done, in this obsessively computerised age, the blemishes can be airbrushed out.

It has been said that as children, we lead confused, divided, uncertain lives; if that is true, then I am a classic example. I now know that a deep, divisive line runs through our childhood years, a conflict created by our inner, private and outer, public lives. Were I religious, I might put this down to the struggle between what is perceived to be good and what is evil, but these are moralistic, over-dramatic words. I have always felt more comfortable with my inner world and I couldn't resist the temptation to retreat into it whenever I felt threatened or lonely. I still do. But it doesn't mean that I'm anti-social. I suppose it could be said that I never really grew up, but does anyone who is moved to write ever grow up? They inhabit a personal world, a necessary state for any writer worth his or her salt. The social side of me came late and still causes paradoxical feelings in me; I still find it difficult to sort out the sheep from the goats and vice-versa. That isn't a criticism of them, it's a comment on me.

There is more sunshine than rain when you're a child - and rain isn't always a nuisance. The colours it teases out of the landscape are vivid; the woods and fields grow greener and summers aren't monotonous weeks of wall-to-wall sunshine, which would have bored us. In those days, the air was cleaner and sweeter, the roads and pathways were more mysterious and not - emphatically NOT - a vast litter-bin. Our enjoyment of the world wasn't gained at the expense of the enjoyment of others, a fact which seems to escape many of the current generation of children and their parents who must bear the responsibility and the blame for their selfishness. One vital thing the children of my generation learned - unlike those of today - was that the world isn't and can't be a place for one long holiday; enjoyment and entertainment had to be earned and weren't an automatic right. I get the distinct impression that today, everything has to be fun before it can be learned. Education is a serious business, whether it is delivered in the schoolroom or in the fields. My generation didn't expect - far less demand - anything. We made use of what was there and when it wasn't, we made it ourselves. Anticipation - that most mouth-watering state of childhood - came before birthdays and Christmases and what little they brought was even more appreciated simply because it happened at all. I am not being unfair to today's children, who are under pressure from advertising and their peers; I feel sorry for them because when they become adults, they will learn the lesson that Diogenes, the Greek Cynic and philosopher taught - disappointment. (Diogenes is a particular favourite of mine; one day in Greece, he was observed kneeling with a beggar's bowl before some statue, asking for alms. When asked what he was about, he replied that he was practising disappointment. Perhaps he should be the patron saint of those who sell the *Big Isssue* or the growing number of homeless people). Recently, I informed a group of troublesome kids that they could join a support group that would help them with their problems. What group was that, they asked? Dickheads United was the response. For they are that and worse. I have watched kids set free from school sit on High Street seats meant for older people, mooching around the Town House Museum and coming back several times in the course of a single afternoon. It's clear to me that they are bored. How can they be, with a world of beauty around them? We have clean beaches, safe woods, lovely hills where they can wander to their hearts' content. I was never bored in my summer holidays and I and my contemporaries didn't want to encounter adults. These benighted kids seem to enjoy interfering with the lives of adults, making a nuisance of themselves. Do they hate their parents so much? Is it their way of getting their own back? They positively enjoy making a nuisance of themselves in the High Street. It seems to be their sole purpose in life. In what way have we failed them? Perhaps their parents have failed to instil a sense of fun in them, a fun that has to be tempered with consideration of other people's fun.

The past truly is another country. When I look back on my schooldays, which formed the bulk of my childhood, I have to admit to entertaining mixed feelings. Don't get me wrong; I was proud then and am proud today of Dunbar Grammar School - even if hardly any of the teachers can translate Jack Milne's Latin motto. The teaching methods in my time were different but different doesn't always mean better - and here I am arguing against my own philosophy which is that to be different is to be superior, not be a donkey led and hidebound by the convention. Our lessons were dinned into us, there was no attempt to make the getting of knowledge 'fun' and the proof of your worth was reflected in your passes - and the standards were more stringent then than today. That may be debatable but I can still calculate my bill at the supermarket checkout before the girl works it out on her electronic till. Many lessons were taught which were reinforced consciously or not, by what was expected of us at home. We were brought up to do as we were told, speak only when spoken to and never to answer back. Attention-seeking was something only badly-behaved and selfish children indulged in, remedied by a thick ear. We had to ask the permission of our parents to leave the table at mealtimes, were taught never to tell lies or cheat and among the boys, never to hit a girl or anyone smaller than ourselves. We also respected our parents and other adults even when they exasperated us or prevented us from doing something. These were good things and stood me in good stead in my adult life. But my main criticism of school was that we weren't encouraged to think for ourselves or question even unreasonably authoritarian teachers. (My wide reading reminds me of that terrible First World War, where a generation was 'lost' because few had the audacity to question the decisions of those in authority, those who demanded their right to be right was followed to the letter of the law they insisted was theirs alone).

From 1970 until I returned permanently to Dunbar in June 2000, I visited Dunbar as often as I could. I returned to it like a homing pigeon, a migrating swallow. I came back to renew myself when the world got too much for me, as it often did. I shall never forget the minute I stepped off the Edinburgh train at Dunbar station and sniffed that incomparable salt air, knowing that I was home again. If it is true that all departures diminish us and most arrivals make us glad, I have felt exiled from this little town for so many years. Exile is never more bitter when the heart wants to be elsewhere....

Memory is faulty and mine is no better than anyone else's. I have tried to record my experiences truthfully in this book. Many will find errors.

Ours is essentially a cynical age and there will be many who accuse me of being over sentimental. Let them. You don't escape your origins by assuming a smart disguise. Many seem to want to forget their pasts, their origins; by doing so, they deny who and what they essentially are or have become. As I said elsewhere, being someone doesn't have to mean being someone else.

I hope I have managed to forgive the hostile and jealous children I went to school with in that time. They were very real when I was at school but over the years, they have become inconsequential, silly little people. Some I would prefer not to meet again. Some were able to hurt me in ways that I would dismiss easily today. Maybe then, they were as confused as I was. To me they were pathetic. I was never part of a gang; when I tried to join one, I was accepted with reluctance and was often the butt of their silly jokes. They didn't want me, didn't want to have me in their little *cliques* and only accepted me so they could make a fool of me. Such people wouldn't know me - or want to know me - even if we met today on the High Street. Unlike them, I didn't feel I needed to prove myself by 'getting on' and going to London or wherever else they went to escape their humble roots. I recall their stupid nicknames – Eek, Deek and Louie. Well guys, if you are still out there, I forgive you, for none of you ever came near to knowing me as I was then and am now. Let's leave your mistakes in the dustbin they belong to.

I wonder what the new century will hold for Dunbar and if the children born in it will look back with the same joy on the childhood they spent here. In this post-industrial, post-Christian age, the prospects are not encouraging. Their world will be more regulated than mine was, in different ways of course. There will be more pollution. There will be more selfishness. There will be more materialism. Will the child of 2050 enjoy the things that we of a century before enjoyed? The answer is no. Their school playgrounds - if they still exist - will be sterilised, patrolled by wardens and anxious parents. It's happening now. The schools will be places they seldom visit for they will learn at home, from computers. They will be insular, less convivial and their games will be solitary, played in their own bedrooms.

This sounds like Orwell's depressing *1984*. I hope I will be proved wrong. I am the product of a 'mixed' marriage, having an English father and a Scottish mother. I don't think I have suffered because of that. From my mother, I learnt what it meant to be Scottish (emotional); from my father, I had the benefit of being 'literary' because I get my love of writing and the written word from him, even if he rarely spoke to me of such things. There is nothing in my childhood I could term' great' or 'heroic' - unless surviving it is qualified by those adjectives. I have few to measure myself against, certainly not those smug 'got ons' who migrated to London because that was the place to be in the 1950s. I met a 'got on' recently; he was a grade lower than me in the Civil Service but he was convinced that London made him. I slunk away without telling him my own lowly grade.

I take a certain perverse pride in the fact that some in Dunbar or those who once lived here will say of me that cynical phrase common in Scotland:

'Him write a book, Ah kent his faither.'

Few in this town knew my father, not even me. He was a distant, secretive figure in my emotional landscape and I preferred him that way. My role model was - is - Jimmy Cockburn, my uncle who has been dead for over forty years. There was a man, a hero, someone who was great. He was caring, kind, gentle and honest. So much so that he was black balled [refused membership] when he applied to join the local Freemasons'Lodge. I am certain it was his honesty that black balled him; he was better than any who belonged then and now to that organisation. He once told me that men in societies or clubs joined them because they needed the collective protection they offered.

'They cannae survive on their own. They have to have the numbers to bolster them up. For they all hae somethin' to hide. And the worst of them pretend to welcome ye, then stick the knife in.'

I am surprised that he even thought of joining the Lodge and often wonder at his reason. He was too honest, too straight - even if he had a back like that of Richard III.

The Scotland I knew is fast disappearing. Some aspects of its 'culture' I can well do without, the Scotland seen through the rheumy eyes of Walter Scott, who wrapped us in tartan and wrote dubious historical novels from which the country has suffered. Thankfully, new writers have come on the scene. The best of them was Lewis Grassic Gibbon, whose sensitivity and feelings for the Scottish landscape of his day has yet to be bettered. Another edifice which has lessened its influence on our thought and culture is the Church of Scotland and it's 'parcel o' rogues'. I for one am glad to see its decline, with its passion for burning so-called witches, its persecution of fine minds, its meddling, its cold, dreary charity.

The one regret I have today is that my mother never lived to see this book completed, although she was aware I was writing it and contributed a few anecdotes. In many ways, the book is her story as much as it is mine. Now the wind is rising and darkness falls on Belhaven. My notebook pages are spotted with rain. It's time for me to go. I think I will be able to reach Seafield Bridge 'The Bridge to Nowhere' before the tide cuts me off. This far in my life it never has done.